ASSESSING CONSTITUTIONAL PERFORMANCE

From London to Libya, from Istanbul to Iceland, there is great interest among comparative constitutional scholars and practitioners about when a proposed constitution is likely to succeed. But what does it mean for a constitution to succeed? Are there universal criteria of success that apply across the board? Or is the choice of criteria entirely idiosyncratic? This edited volume examines the idea of constitutional success and shows the manifold ways in which it can be understood. It collects essays from political scientists, empiricists, philosophers and legal scholars that approach the definition of constitutional success from many different angles. It also brings together case studies from Africa, Europe, Latin America, the Middle East and Asia. By exploring a varied array of constitutional histories, this book shows how complex ideas of "constitutional success" play out differently in different contexts and provides examples of how "success" can be differently defined under different circumstances.

TOM GINSBURG is Leo Spitz Professor of International Law at the University of Chicago, where he also holds an appointment in the Political Science Department. He currently co-directs the Comparative Constitutions Project, an NSF-funded data set cataloging the world's constitutions since 1789. His books include *Judicial Reputation: A Comparative Theory* (2015) (with Nuno Garoupa); *The Endurance of National Constitutions* (2009) (with Zachary Elkins and James Melton); and *Judicial Review in New Democracies* (2003). He is a member of the American Academy of Arts and Sciences.

AZIZ Z. HUQ is the Frank and Bernice J. Greenberg Professor of Law at the University of Chicago Law School. He was formerly director of the Liberty and National Security project at the Brennan Center for Justice and a senior consultant analyst for the International Crisis Group.

COMPARATIVE CONSTITUTIONAL LAW AND POLICY

Series editors
Tom Ginsburg, *University of Chicago*
Zachary Elkins, *University of Texas at Austin*
Ran Hirschl, *University of Toronto*

Comparative constitutional law is an intellectually vibrant field that encompasses an increasingly broad array of approaches and methodologies. This series collects analytically innovative and empirically grounded work from scholars of comparative constitutionalism across academic disciplines. Books in the series include theoretically informed studies of single constitutional jurisdictions, comparative studies of constitutional law and institutions and edited collections of original essays that respond to challenging theoretical and empirical questions in the field.

Books in the series

Assessing Constitutional Performance

Edited by

TOM GINSBURG
University of Chicago

AZIZ Z. HUQ
University of Chicago

CAMBRIDGE
UNIVERSITY PRESS

CAMBRIDGE
UNIVERSITY PRESS

One Liberty Plaza, 20th Floor, New York, NY 10006, USA

Cambridge University Press is part of the University of Cambridge.

It furthers the University's mission by disseminating knowledge in the pursuit of education, learning, and research at the highest international levels of excellence.

www.cambridge.org
Information on this title: www.cambridge.org/9781107154797

© Cambridge University Press 2016

This publication is in copyright. Subject to statutory exception and to the provisions of relevant collective licensing agreements, no reproduction of any part may take place without the written permission of Cambridge University Press.

First published 2016

Printed in the United Kingdom by Clays, St Ives plc

A catalogue record for this publication is available from the British Library.

Library of Congress Cataloging-in-Publication Data
Ginsburg, Tom, editor. | Huq, Aziz Z., editor.
Assessing constitutional performance / edited by Tom Ginsburg, Aziz Huq.
New York : Cambridge University Press, 2016. | Series: Comparative constitutional law and policy | Includes bibliographical references and index.
LCCN 2016020960 | ISBN 9781107154797 (hardback)
LCSH: Constitutions. | Constitutional history. | Comparative law. | Constitutional law. | BISAC: LAW / Constitutional.
LCC K3165 .A87 2016 | DDC 342–dc23
LC record available at https://lccn.loc.gov/2016020960

ISBN 978-1-107-15479-7 Hardback
ISBN 978-1-316-60835-7 Paperback

Cambridge University Press has no responsibility for the persistence or accuracy of URLs for external or third-party Internet Web sites referred to in this publication and does not guarantee that any content on such Web sites is, or will remain, accurate or appropriate.

Contents

viii Contents

Figures

Tables

Contributors

Zaid Al-Ali is a Law and Public Affairs Fellow at Princeton University, on leave from the International Institute for Democracy and Electoral Assistance.

Sumit Bisarya is Senior Project Manager, Constitution Building, International Institute for Democracy and Electoral Assistance.

Erin F. Delaney is Associate Professor at the Northwestern University Pritzker School of Law and Associate Professor of Political Science at Northwestern University.

Rosalind Dixon is Professor of Law, University of New South Wales.

Zachary Elkins is Associate Professor, University of Texas at Austin, Department of Government.

Roberto Gargarella is Associated Senior Researcher, Chr. Michelsen Institute and National Scientific and Technical Research Council, Argentina.

James Thuo Gathii is the Wing-Tat Lee Chair in International Law, Loyola University Chicago School of Law

Tom Ginsburg is Leo Spitz Professor of International Law, University of Chicago Law School; and Research Fellow at the American Bar Foundation.

Aziz Z. Huq is Frank and Bernice J. Greenberg Professor of Law, University of Chicago Law School.

David Landau is Mason Ladd Professor and Associate Dean for International Programs, Florida State University College of Law.

Hélène Landemore is Associate Professor of Political Science, Department of Political Science, Yale University.

Hanna Lerner is Associate Professor of Political Science, Tel Aviv University.

James Melton holds a PhD from the University of Illinois, Urbana Champaign.

Martha C. Nussbaum is Ernst Freund Distinguished Service Professor of Law and Ethics, Law School and Department of Philosophy, University of Chicago.

Martin Shapiro is James W. and Isabel Coffroth Professor of Law, University of California, Berkeley School of Law.

Ozan O. Varol is Associate Professor of Law, Lewis & Clark Law School.

Acknowledgments

We are grateful to Deans Michael Schill and Thomas Miles of the University of Chicago Law School for their support of our work, and to Leila Blatt for superb research assistance in preparing the volume. Ginsburg thanks the American Bar Foundation and its director, Ajay Mehrotra. We also thank the participants and commentators in the conference we held in April 2015 on *Assessing Constitutional Performance*, including Michael Albertus, Nathan Brown, Jose Cheibub, Adam Chilton, Javier Couso, Katalin Dobias, Justin Driver, Amanda Greene, William Hubbard, Alexandra Huneeus, Madhav Khosla, Alison LaCroix, Jennifer Nou, Michael Seidman, Nick Stephanopolous, Geoffrey Stone and Mila Versteeg. Finally, we are grateful to Claire Kim for help in the production process. Their contributions remind us that scholarship, like constitutional performance, is a collective enterprise.

INTRODUCTION

1

Assessing constitutional performance

Tom Ginsburg and Aziz Z. Huq

How should we evaluate constitutional performance? What should count as "success" in constitutional design? Is there a universal benchmark against which all constitutions, regardless of local circumstance, can be evaluated? Or is constitutional design as idiosyncratic as a person's choice in neckties? These questions, which are the focus of this volume, are necessarily raised by the emergent transnational practice of constitutional advice-giving and criticism. They are implicated every time a scholar, consultant, human-rights activist, or international organization expresses a position on a proposed constitution, whether in Somalia, Tunisia, Nepal, or the United Kingdom. They are thus necessarily questions for the governments and international organizations that fund such practices. And they are equally questions for the national publics engaged in the act of constitutional creation, who are often on the receiving end of international advice about what they should be doing. Finally, they ought to be puzzles for the growing coterie of scholars and jurists engaged in the comparative analysis and critique of new constitutions, a scholarly literature that often employs explicitly normative criteria in evaluating constitutional design. If we wanted to err on the side of grandiosity, we might even say they are questions implicated every time one decides that a constitution, as a going concern, merits our continued fidelity.

The contributors to this conference have been asked to respond, from a variety of perspectives, to the seemingly simple question of what counts as constitutional success (a term we will use interchangeably with constitutional performance here). By posing this concededly naïve question, we hope to draw attention to a normative terrain that has received surprisingly little attention from scholars and practitioners who assume, often implicitly, that there is a convergent consensus on what counts as "success" in constitutional design, and that therefore it is meaningful to praise or to blame a constitution for meeting or falling short of this desideratum. In so doing, we hope to provoke more careful debate among legal and political theorists about the plural possible meanings of constitutional success or quality. The chapters assembled in this book, we think, provide a series of important landmarks and provocations in that debate rather than a singular, definitive answer to our threshold question. We thus make no pretense of consensus. The contributors sharply disagree with each other (and us) about the meaning of the question, and the method suitable to its resolution. Their ensuing approaches range across normative criteria in ways that illuminate the plurality of potential criteria of constitutional success. Yet in their myriad approaches they also advance a collective agenda by focusing attention on the issue.

The normative pluralism evidenced in this volume does not mean that accounts of constitutional performance will simply collapse into first-order normative theorizing. We are cognizant that much work in political theory can be described as an effort to clarify the legitimate foundations and goals of political society, and thus to evaluate "small-c" constitutional success. In the classical world, Aristotle offered both taxonomy and evaluation of constitutional families, while Plato sketched an ideal-type set of political arrangements. Historians from Herodotus and Thucydides to Polybius, Livy, and beyond provided further data and evaluative criteria. Perhaps the most influential modern tradition has been the use of the social contract as a heuristic, first by Locke, Hobbes, and Rousseau, and most recently by Rawls, to identify normatively defensible terms of social cooperation. This political theory literature offers a rich array of potential normative frameworks for approaching very general questions about the functions and boundaries of the state as an institution. It does not, however, focus on the specific role of a written constitution in a way that yields straightforward normative criteria of *constitutional* success or performance. Moreover, to simply assume that any one account of political society or the necessary role of the state, whether drawn from Aristotle, Rousseau, or Rawls, resolves the question of constitutional success would hardly be a sufficient answer for most participants in contemporary constitution-making. These actors need to make decisions on real-world questions of constitutional design under less-than-ideal circumstances of time pressure and political constraint (Horowitz 2002).

Instead of trying to reason directly from first principles ourselves, we hope that by framing a relatively naïve question, and then eliciting views from a heterogeneous range of scholars immersed in distinct disciplines, as well as regional and country-level experts with specific experience of recent constitution-making, we can clarify the contemporary framing and analyzing of "constitutional success" in a systematic way. We hope, that is, to elicit a deeper understanding of how that concept – which is implicitly at stake in many practical and scholarly projects today – is in fact understood. Just as important, we hope to grapple with the open questions as to whether it even has a single referent when applied to constitution making contexts, whether it is more or less informed by certain normative commitments, and whether it is a coherent ambition at all.

In this Introduction, we begin at a high level of generality by giving an overview of several different perspectives that might be brought to bear in constitutional evaluation. We also identify as potentially useful one possible distinction of general application between internal and external criteria. This is the distinction between evaluative benchmarks that those within a constitution-making process bring to bear, as opposed to criteria that outsiders apply. Drawing attention to this distinction underscores the possibility that constitutional success is a relative matter: One's criteria depend on where one stands in relation to the relevant polity. We then go on to offer an answer of our own to the question of what counts as constitutional success. This comprises a set of four evaluative criteria that are intended to be applicable across a broad range of constitutional regimes and constitution-making circumstances (for an initial specification and discussion of this framework, see Ginsburg & Huq 2014). More specifically, we suggest that a plausible set of external criteria might include the following four goals: (1) the creation of public legitimacy; (2) the channeling of conflict into political venues rather than violence; (3) the reduction of the agency costs associated with government; and (4) the facilitation of public goods. We further suggest that these criteria are not by their terms limited to democratic systems. The observed set of constitutional regimes is broader than the set of democratic ones, and there is no reason to equate constitutionalism with democracy. Some authoritarian regimes seek to realize the very real benefits that can be obtained from constitutional governance (see Tushnet 2014; Ginsburg & Simpser 2014). In our view, there is no reason to define constitutional success in terms that arbitrarily foreclose the possibility of evaluation in nondemocratic contexts, even if some of our criteria (particularly the channeling of political conflict) are likely best realized in democratic rather than authoritarian contexts. After considering the general questions in this Introduction, we offer what we hope is a reasonably provocative analysis of the performance of a number of familiar and unfamiliar founding documents, including the 1787 American Constitution, the 2004 Afghan constitution, and the 1996 South African constitution, using our framework.

I METHODOLOGICAL CONSIDERATIONS

At a very minimum, any tractable method for evaluating constitutional success must be sufficiently sensitive to political, social, and geopolitical context. This means that one should assess the overall objectives of the drafting situation (which may have been several), and realistically evaluate progress toward them. One cannot impose fixed universal standards that are not plausibly achievable. Juba will not be Geneva anytime soon, and no constitutional scheme could make it so. Still, it is feasible to evaluate what *was* in fact within reach in South Sudan in 2011, given the goals of the drafters and the prevailing circumstances. This requires that we articulate with a reasonable level of specificity what major issues are to be resolved in constitutional drafting, and what that project set out to achieve in a particular case. It further involves taking seriously not only what constitutions can do but what they cannot do.

Stated in this fashion, the task of evaluating constitutional success still faces important theoretical and practical challenges. We highlight here what we believe to be the two main methodological difficulties hedging this task: the problem of determining what perspective to use, and the difficulty of conceptualizing and analyzing "gaps" between constitutional text and observed practice.

A   Internal v. external criteria

The evaluation of whether constitutions "work" or "succeed" is a surprisingly complex task (Pozas-Loyos 2012). Constitutions are (usually) written texts (although Erin Delaney's chapter (Chapter 14) analyzes the success of the United Kingdom's unwritten constitution) that were adopted in quite varied social, political, and geopolitical circumstances. A polity can reach for the instrument of a written constitution, indeed, with a wide range of purposes in view: Constitutions can be transformative, preservative, or even revolutionary. Some constitutions are designed to end civil wars. Others mark independence from a colonial power. Yet others make adjustments to ongoing institutions of governance, democratic or otherwise. These myriad purposes render the task of constitutional evaluation very complex, even pitched as a descriptive rather than a normative enterprise. In some cases, such as in South Africa in 1996, the purpose of a constitution may be relatively easy to describe (as we do later). But in other instances, for example Sweden's consolidation of its constitution in 1974, that description may be much more difficult. There is, moreover, no reason to suppose that all members of a polity will converge on the same aspirations for a constitution. To the contrary, endogenous disagreement and conflict over normative priors and ends may be endemic to the observed circumstances of constitution-making. As a result, there may not even be a shared "goal" or a single "intent" behind any particular piece of constitutional text (although this may also hold in respect to any legislated product of collective decision-making).

We can begin to discipline this complexity by observing that approaches to the task of constitutional assessment can roughly be divided by the perspective of the person engaged in evaluation, whether internal or external. First, on an *internal* view one asks whether the constitution has succeeded on the terms of the community to be regulated by that instrument. This species of stocktaking takes the objectives of the constitution as given, either by the document itself or by the relevant political community. It does not attempt to evaluate those goals from any independent vantage point. Instead, it relies upon self-declared or self-identified principles and goals, which might be defined in terms of institutional creation (e.g., has the constitution created a functioning election system? Has it led to the formation of a legislature or a government?), or in terms of desired policy goals (e.g., has the constitution allowed the unification of a geographic space, or fostered economic growth?).

Such an exercise at a minimum requires us to be able to discern relevant goals in the text of a constitution, derive such goals from the circumstances of its adoption, or deduce them from the writings of a specific constitutional framer. This is no simple task. It assumes that the relevant preferences of constitution-makers have been legibly expressed in constitutional text or can otherwise be inferred. When analyzing a joint product of multiple drafters, it assumes that their preferences can be cogently aggregated, notwithstanding the stability and coherence-related difficulties of collective choice mechanisms that have been identified by social choice theorists from Arrow onward (Arrow 1951; Huq Forthcoming 2016). Even in the absence of social choice problematics, it may not be possible to identify a coherent set of constitutional ambitions. Complicating matters yet further, constitution-making often unfolds against the backdrop of internal division and sharp, even violent, controversy within the relevant national polity. Under these conditions, it may well be doubted that stable internal criteria that are uniformly attractive to all contemporaneous participants in constitution-making are even available. What we take as such internal criteria after the fact may simply be the criteria most conducive to subsequent generations of political victors.

The identification and application of internal criteria, in short, raises a host of challenging normative and analytic questions. Several of the chapters that follow, including Martha Nussbaum's and Roberto Gargarella's, tackle these challenges head-on from the perspective of national or regional experiences. These chapters provide alternative, nationally inflected accounts of what it means to take seriously the internal perspective on constitutional success. In a similar vein, Ozan Varol shows that even if we focus on a specific constitutional task – the management of civilian-military relations – internal criteria can vary dramatically even in respect to a single constitution, while Hanna Lerner illuminates the plurality of potential benchmarks that might be salient in respect to the single task of managing religious diversity.

Alternatively, the exercise of constitutional evaluation can adopt an external vantage-point. This means considering the question of constitutional success not from the perspective of a constitution's designers, a founding generation, or some other participant within the relevant polity. Instead, it means assessing constitutional performance against a benchmark derived independently of local circumstances and contingent preferences within the relevant polity. It means asking, that is, not what renders *this* constitution a success but rather what makes a constitution *in general* a success. To frame the problem in this manner is to derive a definition of constitutional success from rather different materials from an internal perspective, but not necessarily to reach a different answer from internally oriented analyses. An external observer might converge on the same benchmark or standard as an internal observer, but he or she will likely do so for quite different reasons.

One set of external benchmarks proceeds from a normative account of desirable features or products of a constitutional order. For example, to many today, obvious and normatively attractive external benchmarks may include a constitution's success *vel non* in facilitating democratic rule, racial and gender equality, individual liberty (e.g., from torture or cruel, inhuman and degrading treatment), economic growth, or aggregate national welfare defined in other terms. Another might focus on the constitution as a device for generating an engaged and self-critical citizenry (Barber 2014). Among the chapters here, Rosalind Dixon and David Landau's contribution endorses democracy as a goal, while Aziz Huq advocates a minimalist benchmark of state stability. Their difference can be glossed, from one perspective, as reflecting the divergent accounts offered by Locke and Hobbes of the initial circumstances of social cooperation and contracting. While the Lockean perspective evaluates the quality of the social contract (at least for property holders), the minimalist Hobbesian view looks only at its (narrowly defined) efficacy.

External criteria can also be plural in character. Hélène Landemore's chapter on recent constitution-making efforts in Iceland in the wake of the financial crisis develops a rich, multicriterial account of constitutional success that usefully blends several strands of liberal democratic theory. Landemore weaves these strands into a mid-level account that offers traction in the assessment of specific constitutions. She incorporates both formal criteria such as clarity and coherence, as well as functional qualities such as whether a constitution helps resolve conflicts, expresses values, and protects rights. Hers is not the only such plural account available. Offering another set of external benchmarks that might provide traction in practice for evaluating constitutional drafts on the ground (so to speak), Yash Ghai (2014) has developed the following enumeration of benchmarks for a successful constitution: to ensure that power resides in state offices rather than individuals (i.e., the depersonalization of political authority); to create socially grounded structures through which the state can function; to separate the economy from the state so as to prevent corruption and monopolies; and to engender respect for human rights and the rule of law in the people.[1] The possibility of a pluralist external benchmark of the kind that both Landemore and Ghai have proposed raises interesting questions of how to aggregate and prioritize different goals, and in particular how to handle conflicts between a constitution's different aspirations.

Each of these two basic kinds of approach, internal and external, has its merits as well as its limitations. Each, we think, might play a role under appropriate conditions. On the one hand, an internal method takes serious account of the values, intentions, and aspirations of drafters and local political actors. As a consequence, it will often draw attention to matters directly within their control. For example, government officials can pass laws and hold elections more easily than they can in fact eliminate corruption and build democracy. Drafters may hence reasonably focus on the former rather than the latter. In addition, an internal approach may allow for more precise metrics tailored to the specific context and baseline condition of a polity at the time a constitution is adopted. At the same time, however, an internal perspective may fail to grapple with the *quality* of the constitution's contents in any meaningfully objective way. It is hardly worth celebrating the perfect implementation of a constitution when *all* those external to that project would condemn it as harmful and perverse. Nor is a constitution plainly commendable if its drafters intend it to have no colorable effect on the world. After all, it is not clear that

---

[1] From these general evaluative criteria, Ghai derives ten more specific mechanisms by which a constitution contributes to democracy and the rule of law: (a) affirming common values and identities without which there cannot be a political community; (b) prescribing rules to determine membership of that community; (c) promising physical and emotional security by state monopolization, for legitimate purposes, of the use of force; (d) agreeing on the ways in which and the institutions through which state power is to be exercised; (e) providing for the participation of citizens in affairs of the state, particularly through elections, and other forms of social action; (f) protecting rights (which empower citizens as well as limit state action); (g) establishing rules for peaceful changes in government; (h) ensuring predictability of state action and security of private transactions through the legal system; (i) establishing procedures for dispute settlement; and (j) providing clear and consensual procedures for change of these fundamental arrangements.

celebrating the enactment of laws to reduce corruption or promote democracy is sensible if those enactments have no impact on the ground.

An external perspective, on the other hand, might be able to bear a greater normative weight by appealing to more general normative criteria distinct from the parochial interests and limitations of a particular class of constitution-makers. It might also overweight contextual factors that cannot plausibly be within the control of constitutional actors. That is, external criteria are more likely to have serious identification problems that preclude their serious application in explaining outcomes. This may well be especially the case with welfarist criteria, a point that Huq's chapter develops. External criteria also necessarily assume that certain goals are categorically more important than others without regard to drafters' or a polity's aspirations. They thus embed at their inception an assumption that the distinctive ambitions and aspirations of a given polity are irrelevant. This might seem in some instances anti-democratic, and perhaps even redolent of the colonial past of many nations now engaged in constitution-making. More theoretically, the invocation of external criteria might be taken as inconsistent with the national-identity-shaping purposes of a new constitution.

The chapters that follow, as we have noted, alternatively take internal and external perspectives on the problem of assessing constitutional success. We think that this mixed approach represented by the volume as a whole points toward a basic fact about criteria of constitutional performance: Those benchmarks are perspectival insofar as they are necessarily embedded in specific attitudes and positions in regard to a given polity. Rather than reducing to a singular understanding, in short, constitutional success may be inevitably plural in character.

B   Measuring the "gap" between text and performance

Whether an external or an internal perspective is adapted, an additional level of complication must be considered. This arises from the necessary multiplicity of analytic levels and purposes in play within any constitutional regime.

It is easy to assume that the assessment of constitutional performance would simply involve a comparison between written provisions with observed political practice at a given point in time. If constitutions are effective, the gap between textual aspiration and performance will be small; if the gap is large, the constitution should be deemed ineffectual.[2] But this simple evaluative strategy runs directly into a problem engendered by the multiplicity of

---

[2]   Or a "sham" constitution, to quote Walter Murphy's phrase recently revived by Law and Versteeg (Law & Versteeg 2013).

provisions contained in most constitutions. Let us say that it is possible to aggregate the complex intentions (short and long term) of all relevant participants in constitution making to formulate a singular "intent." Even then, not all provisions of constitution may be amenable to the same strategies of implementation. To begin with, different provisions require different time periods to effectuate. On the one hand, Bisarya's chapter identifies "transitional" constitutional provisions that are designed to mediate the transition between old and new constitutional dispensations within defined time periods. On the other hand, Lerner's chapter on religious liberty explores how durable constitutional arrangements can influence the formation of religious social life, reinforcing some identities while undermining others, over a long time frame.

Constitutional provisions might also interact in complex ways with the trajectory of other state institutions or exogenous shocks in ways that make simple analysis of the gap between text and performance misleading. This is most plainly the case, as the chapter by Tom Ginsburg, Zachary Elkins, and James Melton explores at length, with the rights provisions of constitutions. As they demonstrate, simply measuring the degree of rights protection (to take one example) is clearly inadequate. Some rights (e.g., a criminal procedure right such as the right to counsel or a right to health) may be beyond reach without major transformations of state bureaucracies; others (e.g., a right to form political associations) may be easy to implement without delay through simple changes in statutory text.

Yet a further complication arises when a constitution simply codifies already existing behavior, and so presents no "gap" between text and practice. On the one hand, the fact that it successfully describes extant political realities does not mean that the constitution itself has does any work. Perhaps it promotes the continued existence of those political conditions, but ideally, we want to know that the constitution has made a *difference* in political life (for example, by parrying some process of secular decline). On the other hand, when is it safe to assume that the function of a constitution is transformative as opposed to preservative? Positive theories of constitutional creation (Hirschl 2004) have underscored their "hegemonic preservation" function. That is, the reason some constitutions may be adopted in the first place is that they preserve and entrench the authority of existing power holders sufficiently to mute their resistance to change. It may well be that a specific provision of a constitution "succeeds" (at least from an internal perspective) if it operates as an effective friction on social or political changes. The elements of the 1787 US Constitution that preserved slavery and that undercut the ability of national institutions to confront head-on the moral iniquity of the "peculiar institution" provide a useful reminder that such preservative elements of a constitutional text can play important roles in practice.

Because of this complexity, the most intuitive approach to evaluating constitutional performance – that is, taking snapshots at a given point in time – is likely to be inadequate, or even in some instances misleading. Rather, one needs to consider issues of trajectories of different institutions over time, and the difficulty of changing deep-rooted patterns of political and social behavior, when evaluating a constitution. Moreover, even a piecemeal evaluation of given provisions demands a theoretical framework to identify the ex ante desired direction of social, political, or institutional change.

C   Summary

The evaluation of constitutional success cannot proceed without making certain theoretical choices. To begin with, it is necessary to choose between an external and an internal perspective. Criteria generated endogenously to a constitution-making polity may overlap with those developed for general, transnational, and trans-temporal application, but they will have different origins and different justifications. Having established a perspective from which to view constitutional performance, the person engaged in evaluation must then decide how to analyze the "gaps" between text and observed performance. With those problems under control, we proceed to set forth some threshold considerations about how to think about internal criteria, and then identify an exemplary set of external criteria. In both cases, our immediate ambition is relatively modest: To show that an approach based on either internal or external criteria is at least plausible, and thereby to demonstrate that the task of thinking hard about what counts as constitutional success is not without its rewards.

II   THE DOMAIN OF PLAUSIBLE INTERNAL CRITERIA

Necessarily, the world of internal criteria will be large and heterogeneous. But is there anything at the threshold to say about how we can identify plausible internal criteria against which to assess implementation? At the most concrete level, they comprise the specific steps or policy goals articulated by the explicit terms of a constitution. Varol's chapter on transitions from military rule provides useful examples of specific steps related to a quite particular, discrete goal. Rather more abstractly, Zaid Al-Ali uses the construct of "the people" as mobilized in specific contexts, as a source of internal criteria, in his chapter on constitutionalism during the Arab Spring. More concretely, we might instead focus on the aspirations of the individuals who drafted or ratified the original constitution. Nussbaum's analysis of the Indian Constitution from the perspective of Ambedkar is a useful example here. More broadly, many American judges purport to be "originalists," in the sense of reading the US Constitution in light of either the original public meaning of its terms (i.e., the way its ratifiers would have understood it) or in terms of the original intentions of its drafters. This position is hardly uncontroversial or unproblematic when it comes to constitutional interpretation (see, e.g., Berman 2004). But is not obviously untenable, at least as a political posture.

In some instances, a threshold bundle of steps is explicitly set forth in a constitution's transitional provisions. In Somalia's 2012 constitution for example, the steps identified in transitional provisions as necessary predicates to stable governance were themselves not fulfilled. As Bisarya's chapter eloquently explains, the first deadlines specified by the document were violated within a matter of weeks. Although the drafters had expected the deadlines to operate as a spur to institutional entrenchment, instead, their rapid violation, seemingly without consequences, rendered the whole constitutional scheme more or less stillborn. By contrast, in other cases, such as neighboring Kenya, a Constitutional Implementation Commission (CIC) created under the 2010 constitution worked as a kind of self-assessment device to measure progress on all the concrete steps required for transition and beyond. As Gathii explains in his chapter analyzing the Kenyan case closely, the Kenyan Constitution has indeed made considerable progress, in part due to the CIC, but also in part due to the good fortune of having a transformative chief justice. His account seems to be ambivalent about the probability that the view will be quite as sanguine in 2020 or 2025.

Once a constitution has navigated its threshold translation from the page to political practice, it will often stipulate yet further steps in respect to further institutional development. These can include the following: holding elections on a given timeline; passing implementing legislation or organic statutes required by the constitution (e.g., to create voter rolls, or facilitate the creation of political parties); establishing and funding new state institutions (e.g., courts, ombudsmen commissions, administrative agencies, electoral commissions); and making appointments to offices stipulated in the constitution and in newly legislated institutions. When a constitution directs these kinds of institutional start-ups, a simple evaluation of whether these steps have been pursued will reveal, at least in part, how much progress in constitutional implementation has been made, as well as potentially casting light on the location of constitutional blockages. That simple exercise, as a result, can generate useful recommendations for improvement or textual amendment on a going forward basis.

At a higher level of abstraction, constitutional texts will often articulate broader, explicitly normative principles and goals such as dignity (in the case of the German Constitution), liberty and the "general welfare" (the American Constitution), equality and fraternity (the Indian Constitution), racial justice and reconciliation (the South African Constitution), economic growth and poverty reduction, democratic government, and the accountability under law of former leaders. In each case, a general high-level ambition specified in the preamble or subsequent constitutional text can serve as an internal touchstone of constitutional ambition – a point developed by Gargarella using the concept of a constitutional "drama." Since these ambitions tend to be abstract in nature, and hence necessarily dependent on a diverse range of social currents and institutional dynamics, the specific contributions of a constitution to their achievement may well be difficult to measure. For example, Nussbaum's chapter explores the legacies of the Indian Constitution in respect to the caste system, and offers a nuanced consideration of why the drafters' ambition of eradicating caste fell short.

Despite the difficulties implicit in any evaluative effort, any internally oriented assessment of a constitution's implementation ought to at least catalog and consider these self-declared principles because these will often (albeit not always) reflect hopes and aspirations shared by many ordinary citizens. To define constitutional success in purely technocratic terms, focusing myopically upon institutional creation and operation, would be to ignore the politically constitutive function of organic documents, as well as (in appropriate cases) their democratic aspirations. At the same time, many of these self-declared principles will overlap with the external criteria we describe later.

III   AN EXAMPLE OF MID-RANGE EXTERNAL CRITERIA

The range of potential external criteria against which constitutional implementation might be evaluated is as varied as the range of scholars, jurists, and philosophers proposing them. As we observed earlier, one way of reading much historically canonical work in political theory is as an extended, if sharply contentious, inquiry into what renders a constitutional legitimate, binding, or otherwise acceptable constitution. Our goal is not to canvass that enormous field here, or to adjudicate among its competing positions. Rather, we set aside here the standard set of ambitious abstract values articulated in many constitutional texts (e.g., liberty, dignity, equality, the general welfare) – values that are both controversial and susceptible to diverse interpretations. Instead, we postulate that mid-range metrics of performance will provide more analytic traction. By "mid-range," we mean to capture a set of concerns related to the successful ongoing operation of a political order over some extended period of time that includes not just the immediate translation of textual provisions into real-world institutions but also their operation for a period of some years or even decades.

In the balance of this Introduction, we develop and then apply one set of mid-range criteria of constitutional success. In so doing, we do not claim to have identified the only possible array of mid-range benchmarks, or to have described standards that are immune from criticisms – indeed, several of the chapters that follow, including Landemore's, Delaney's, and Nussbaum's, offer pointed critiques of some elements of the mid-range quartet of benchmarks developed in this Introduction. We nevertheless believe that these metrics capture those aspects of institutional performance most likely to be salient to the successful operation of most written constitutions (although we cannot rule out the possibility of a constitution to which none applies).

Moreover, we develop these criteria with an eye to those values and norms that are most likely to be shared by external advisors to constitution-making processes today, as well as the local political elites and interest-groups that serve as their interlocutors on the ground. In particular, we think these goals can claim a tolerably broad reach, and capture most of what is generally thought to be desirable in a written constitutional scheme under the particular circumstances in which constitutions today tend to be crafted (e.g., after prolonged civil or international crisis; after violent domestic political disturbances; or at the end of long-standing military or authoritarian rule). Of particular note, all of these desiderata are capable of being secured even in nondemocratic regimes. In this sense our framework is not a conceptual replication of democracy but rather comprises a sketch of the functional metes and bounds of constitutionalism. As a result, we hope that our quartet of mid-range benchmarks possess some evaluative traction in a broad range of practical, real-world cases, and therefore have some claim to both utility and to general applicability.

The four generally applicable mid-range criteria for evaluating successful implementation of a constitution that we advance here can be summarized briefly: (1) *sociological legitimacy* in the eyes of the public; (2) the *channeling of potentially violent political conflict* into constitutional institutions and nonviolent forms; (3) the *control of the agency costs* associated with the institutionalization of government; and (4) the *creation of appropriate public goods*. To emphasize, this quartet of ambitions is not the only imaginable set of mid-range external criteria. To the contrary, different analysts are likely to come up with different lists, and, as we have noted, in Landemore's and Ghai's cases, have indeed done so. Moreover, our benchmarks are also not exclusive of other potential ambitions, whether external or internal. They provide, in other words, a useful corner of common ground, rather than filling the field.

A   *Legitimacy*

Successful states require some measure of legitimacy among the general public – i.e., a shared normative belief held by a substantial number of the public that the constitution warrants respect and fidelity. In the short term, popular disaffection for the state is likely to render policy initiatives difficult to carry out as a consequence of frictional resistance. In the long term, moreover, illegitimate states are much more likely to rely on expensive and destabilizing techniques of repression to sustain power. Constitutions are a potent source of popular legitimacy, diffusing the need for violence or repression, even if the need for state coercion is never entirely dissipated (Schauer 2014). The constitutional text can also serve as a focal point for emotional investment and attachment among the people, and therefore help forge a common identity among diverse people by reflecting or creating some quantum of shared normative sentiments (cf. McAdams 2014). At a very minimum, it can accrue symbolic value that can be exploited to engender popular loyalty to the state. Finally, in democratic contexts, it can also help facilitate participatory politics. Fidelity to the constitution provides a normative justification for democratic participation, as well as a framework for the quotidian operation of such politics.

Popular legitimacy, however, is not an inexorable by-product of constitution-making. Especially in highly diverse societies, a constitution may be legitimate among some populations and not among others. In 2015, for example, Nepal adopted a new constitution that sparked violent protests among the southern Madhesi communities that dominate the southern Terai plain below the Himalayas. Madhesis viewed the new constitution as unfairly tilting political power toward upland groups and, at least at the time of this writing, had succeeded in catalyzing a constitutional amendment that offered partial redress. A key question from an evaluative perspective, one closely related to the problem of sociological legitimacy, is whether the constitution successfully defines a set of overarching values and identities that can in fact create a sufficiently integrated political community. In particular, we might ask whether, especially under conditions of ethnic or religious diversity, a constitution provides a working solution to the problem of common governance without suppressing the causes of disagreement through illegitimate means (e.g., by installing persecution and political disempowerment, or engendering ethnic cleansing). A constitution might fail to offer a core of common values or institutions. Alternatively, it might founder by proposing values that turn out to be divisive in practice. For example, a constitution can either define citizenship in an effective and nondiscriminatory way, or it can craft the bounds of citizenship in ways that deepen fissures in the polity. The degree of identification with the constitution, and the state it creates, therefore is one measure of legitimacy.

In addition, a sound constitution will produce a political system that is viewed by citizens as successful at an aggregate or institutional level, even if the citizens disagree with transient government policies or specific office-holders. In this sense, one good test of constitutional legitimacy might be the difference between citizens' views of their constitution as a whole and their perspective upon a given government or class of officeholders. If a constitution remains respected and legitimate regardless of fluctuating evaluations of transient officeholders, this may count in favor of it being ranked a success. But if, as Ghai fears, citizens do not generally distinguish between officers and their occupants, then the constitution has not succeeded. Worse, as Huq suggests in his chapter, it may be that the failure to depersonalize political power entails a failure to create a state. To be sure, data about citizens' normative views of the constitution, as opposed to specific officeholders, may be very hard to obtain in any particular context. Indeed, in societies recovering from large-scale social or geopolitical conflict, or where a single political grouping possesses a supermajority share of political power, citizens might have difficulty distinguishing between legitimacy of the constitution and the government it produces, at least in the short term. It may well be that systematic acquisition of such legitimacy-related data is needful and important for evaluating how constitutions are faring as going concerns, and therefore should be gathered in the future.

At least as a conceptual matter, then, it is plausible to think that we can assess constitutions by evaluating their ability to induce a belief among the diffuse public in the legitimacy of durable constitutional institutions (as distinct from temporary officeholders), and then to assess constitutional implementation by seeking evidence of such legitimacy. This evidence may take the form of survey evidence or analyses of popular protests and other forms of popular mobilization for or against the state. Such evidence may not exist now, but at least theoretically can be collected. That evidence may be hard to secure in some instances does not detract from the more basic point that it is at least a conceptually plausible benchmark for evaluating success in most instances.

B   Channeling political conflict

All societies confront internal political disagreements of varying intensities. The question is how such disagreements are articulated and whether standing mechanisms exist for their resolution. Successful constitutions channel conflict through formal political institutions, as opposed to forcing antagonists to take disagreements to the street or the *maquis*. Constitutional institutions for channeling conflict are especially important in societies recovering from violent conflict. If political violence persists in the form of civil war, terrorism, or generalized riots, or if popular protests imperil a post-conflict government, then the flow of political conflict has not been effectively managed. To be sure, civil society (i.e., intermediating institutions such as parties, unions, religious organizations) can play a role in mediating conflict, as the recent bestowal of a Nobel Peace Prize on the Tunisian National Dialogue Quartet reminds us. Quite apart from the value of state mediation of potentially violent social conflict when civil society is weak, it seems unlikely that informal institutions can play a mediating role consistently and stably across time.

Again, there is no necessary linkage in practice between constitutional creation and the mitigation of serious political conflict. Episodes of constitution-making can sometimes exacerbate social cleavages, especially if some forces are excluded from the constitution-making process. Quite apart from the results of constitution-making, which generated discord in the Nepali case, the form of constitution-making *process* also matters. For example, Landau (2013) has developed an important and penetrating analysis of how constituent assemblies in Latin America have been recently exploited, for example, by the Chavez government to consolidate power in Venezuela in a way that engendered sharp division. In the same work, he also identifies a similar dynamic in the Bolivian context. Constitution-making in Egypt in 2012 and 2013 similarly revealed, confirmed, and perhaps even deepened sharp social divisions between the Muslim Brotherhood, the even more hardline Nour party, a fragile liberal and secular urban class, and the entrenched bureaucratic-military state. The constitution produced through that process did not reflect a substantive consensus across these sharply polarized groups. Nor did it involve an inclusive process in which differences were recognized, prioritized, and managed. Instead, it is plausible to think that the erratic and opaque constitution-making process deepened internal political conflict and accelerated a violent breakdown in civil-military relations. In contrast to that dismaying trajectory, it will often be the case that a "big-tent" approach to constitution-making can help lead even bitter enemies to agree on the fundamental rules, and thus channel their disagreements through formal political institutions.

The particulars of constitutional design matter here. Ghai has usefully emphasized the idea that a constitution must both facilitate the agreed-upon institutions through which state power is exercised, and also provide for the participation of citizens in affairs of the state, particularly through elections, and other forms of social action, including legitimate protest. He also argues that the document must also allow for modification of these fundamental arrangements when it is revealed that they are not working – a theme taken up by Delaney's consideration of the unstable and unpredictable pathways for constitutional change under the unwritten British constitution. We agree with Ghai and Delaney that some channels to enable the expression of public sentiment are probably necessary. We resist, however, the further conclusion – implicit in Delaney, explicit in Ghai, and defended in this volume by Dixon and Landau – that these must be democratic in character. Recent Chinese history can at least arguably be read as evidence that popular responsiveness can be secured with only weak democratic paraphernalia. Observed forms of responsiveness under Communist rule in China might not be as normatively desirable as the parallel mechanisms observed in European and American democracies, but it may well be that they provide sufficient stability and predictability in nonpolitical cases to count as "successful."

Assuming that a constitution takes a democratic path, moreover, it is likely not the case that merely establishing political fora that can operate as alternatives to open conflict suffices. The aspiration toward democracy can conflict with other ideals. Poorly designed parliamentary bodies or electoral rules may provide new forms of representation, but they can simultaneously deepen existing lines of ethnic or racial division, accelerating what would otherwise have been latent or dormant conflicts. Poorly drafted, ambiguous, or merely incomplete constitutional texts may instead generate new, alternative flashpoints for conflict. The task of the constitutional designer, in short, is not simply to install democracy. It is to fashion rules for institutionalizing extant conflict without exacerbating it.

A central cluster of institutions in this regard are those that resolve disputes about the basic rules of the political game. Constitutional courts have emerged as central players in many systems, not only in their paradigmatic role of protecting rights but also in coordinating and resolving conflicts between different government bodies (Ginsburg 2003). But many other such institutions can fulfill the same function of resolving disputes among power holders. These include independent commissions (such as those often tasked with resolving electoral disputes, allegations of human rights violation, or corruption charges), appointed presidents, and even hereditary monarchs (which, for example, in the Spanish transition from military rule during the 1970s, played a very important role).

The basic need, though, is that some kind of institution must likely be available to step up, resolve disputes between powerful factions within or around government, and thereby avoid the acceleration of political conflicts or a collapse into political paralysis. The particular form of this institution is secondary in importance.

One final strategy for containing and managing political conflict is worth flagging: Constitutions can lower the stakes of electoral defeat (or, in nondemocratic contexts, defeat within intra-elite political contests). One important mechanism that serves to minimize the costs of political defeat, and therefore to lower the stakes of governmental turnover, is the establishment and protection of constitutional rights. If a constitution permits some stakeholders – be they political factions, members of an ethnic group, or even a single dictator – to dominate through violence other groups after assuming office, those out of power lose the incentive to stay within the bounds of constitutional competition. If the costs of losing in politics are too high, incumbents will respond by entrenching their political power or otherwise refusing to vacate their offices. Examples of such entrenchment can be observed, as of this writing, in locales as diverse as Turkey, Hungary, and Malaysia – previously three tolerably well-functioning democracies. Such self-dealing is, among other thing, well understood as a form of agency cost – a more general topic to which we turn next.

C *Limiting agency costs*

A major ambition of constitutionalism is typically understood to be the promotion of government action on behalf of the citizens rather than of itself or transient officeholders. This aspiration fails, the result is termed "agency slack." The ensuing agency costs, to use the economic terminology, come in many forms, but often arise when a government official exerts effort solely on his own behalf (e.g., by collecting bribes rather than taxes), violates citizens' basic rights (e.g., by acts of predation or physical violence), or fails to do any work at all. A related risk is political entrenchment in which an officeholder or party seeks to remain in power beyond his or her legitimate term. Obviously, the larger the private rents from political office are, the more incentive officials have to hang on past their appropriate departure dates. And, as Kurlantzick (2013) has documented in respect to new democracies such as Indonesia, both governmental lethargy and corruption run the risk of engendering public dissatisfaction with a political order and a constitution. The net result can be a rush toward authoritarianism. In response to this risk, there are many constitutional institutions and design fixes, ranging from some sort of separation of powers to presidential term limits to counter-corruption commissions.

It is plausible to evaluate a constitution, therefore, on the basis of whether the mechanisms that it adopts are successful in practice.

How can agency costs be evaluated? A minimal indicia of high agency costs in democratic regimes, as Ghai has noted, is the absence of government turnover after poor performance. When a particular government performs poorly under some relevant metric, he plausibly argues, it *should* be removed from office. Turnover can be entrenched with term limits (although these tend to focus on individuals, rather than parties or factions, which can be sources of agency costs). When term limits provide that political figures must leave office, we can observe whether they do in fact leave (Ginsburg, Elkins, & Melton 2011). To be sure, sometimes term limits can be amended, and this is hardly a sign of constitutional failure, so long as the result is not the permanent entrenchment of the relevant officeholder. Their artful circumvention, as with Russian president Putin's brief sojourn in the prime minister's office earlier this century, is yet another signal of high agency costs.

Another warning sign for evaluating agency costs – and one available whether a regime is democratic or authoritarian – is the level of observed corruption, say, measured by the volume of dollars in private rents diverted from the public fisc. To be sure, in some contexts, petty corruption might be beyond the ability of any constitutional scheme to eliminate. But constitutional design might exacerbate the degree of corruption. Kurlantzick (2013), for example, has suggested that political decentralization of the kind associated with constitutional federalism can exacerbate the size of private rents by diffusing the number of choke points at which an official can seek bribes: In effect, corruption becomes a kind of antic-ommons problem. Corruption also may or may not prove tolerable in the long term depending upon whether it engenders massive public dissatisfaction of the kind that catalyzed the 2011 popular uprising in Tunisia and, more broadly, the Arab Spring. In contrast, it is reasonably clear that large-scale corruption by high-level political figures and government officials is something that an effective constitution should be able to deter or minimize. Thus, we can expect improvement on corruption measures in successful constitutional schemes, while poor constitutional schemes might exacerbate such measures. One might also examine specific efforts to reduce agency costs. Parliamentary investigations, judicial inquiries, and the successful use of mechanisms to remove from office corrupt or law-breaking officials are all indicia of success in this regard.

D Creating public goods

The flip side of agency costs is what economists call public goods. These are non-rivalrous and non-excludable goods such as national security, the infrastructural predicates of economic development, environmental protection, and the like. Such goods are likely to be systematically undersupplied through purely private mechanisms because private producers will not be able to capture all of the profits that reflect their social gains. On some accounts, it is the very purpose of the state to produce such goods (although the linkage between state-making and the provision of public goods is sometimes stressed to the exclusion of other plausible and important factors, see Huq 2014). To achieve this goal, it is likely crucial to have an effective regulatory environment and a public security system (e.g., police, intelligence services, and a military) that is non-predatory. While the precise mix of public goods in any particular context should, ideally, depend on the preferences of the citizens and so should be responsive to changes over time, it is nonetheless plausible to think that some rough evaluation of the extent to which constitutionally created institutions meet public demand for such goods is a measure of the underlying constitution's success.

We do not mean to suggest, however, that all constitutions be judged against the same benchmark of public good production. As we have already noted, many constitutions are written in conditions of profound inequality and under pressure from deeply felt and broadly held socioeconomic aspirations. Constitutional rights in such countries do more than limit government predation. They also provide for affirmative duties and blueprints for government to move toward in the provision of health, education, and welfare. It would not be plausible to evaluate these regimes' success in producing public goods using the same benchmark used to assess a developed, stable country undergoing constitutional change. (Constitutions in the former type of nations may be less successful in absolute terms, but it is plausible to think that they are able to quicken accelerations in the production of certain public goods relative to those of the latter nations.) Rather, the appropriate metric of a constitution's success in producing public goods will take a realistic account of the baseline conditions at the time of constitutional adoption, along with the possibility of rapid gains, and only then consider how (if at all) the constitution has enabled an advance from a starting position. At the same time, it must be recognized that many of the outcomes relevant to an analysis of public goods (e.g., levels of law and order, the environment for doing business, and metrics of social and economic performance) have only a tangential relationship with particular constitutional choices. Exogenous shocks (whether positive or negative) can have a much larger causal effect on their variables. That being said, however, a careful and counterfactual inquiry might be able to establish some plausible relationships between the constitutional text and the observed level of public-good production.

To summarize, we have suggested a quartet of mid-level benchmarks of constitutional success that are analytically distinct, but surely related. In particular, we think that the four measures identified here are likely to be mutually reinforcing in practice. When government agents are unable to exploit the state for their own ends, more public goods may be produced, which in turn may enhance regime legitimacy. Greater sociological legitimacy can allow the state to produce public goods at a lower cost, and perhaps can dampen political conflict. When political conflict is channeled through legitimate institutions, people will be more willing to invest in these institutions, which may ultimately support the state (i.e., increasing sociological legitimacy), which in turn will prevent capture by one faction and thus diminish agency costs. The categories thus represent a set of external criteria that accord with intuitions about what constitutional government can and should do.

IV　THREE CASE STUDIES: EVALUATING THE US, AFGHAN, AND SOUTH AFRICAN CONSTITUTIONS

We conclude by offering a sketch of how our four external criteria might be applied to three constitutions. Two are relatively familiar constitutions, at least to us, and, we suspect, to many of our readers: The US Constitution of 1787 and the South African Constitution of 1996. The third is relatively novel, we suspect, to many: the Afghan Constitution of 2004. By applying our quartet of values to such disparate and different circumstances, we hope to demonstrate how application of our four-factor mid-range framework can illuminate different elements of constitutional functioning, allowing for a more nuanced and careful evaluation of what counts as "success" in constitutional design.

A　*United States*

Although often viewed as a success merely because of its extraordinary endurance, the US constitution of 1787 can plausibly be ranked as a success with appropriate qualifications on at least three of four of the grounds that we have identified. To anticipate our main objection up front, it is with regard to the task of channeling political conflict that we think that the US Constitution cannot be ranked a clear success – as the Civil War of the early 1860s was to show.

The success of the US Constitution in terms of eliciting popular legitimacy can be gauged in many ways. Most obviously, public polling by the Pew Charitable Trusts and other research organizations consistently finds high levels of identification with the United States and its constitution. Outside of a handful of lonely voices within the ivory tower, there is no popular movement to rethink the Constitution. To the contrary, popular movements, to be sure, routinely mobilize to make claims *under* the Constitution, no matter how far removed their interests are from those of the Framers of the 1780s. Consider, for example, for the individual right to bear firearms (once labeled a fraud by Chief Justice Warren Burger), the right to be free of a federal healthcare mandate, and the right to marry a person of the same sex. Even if these are mobilizations aimed, at bottom, toward altering the constitutional order (in two of three cases, successfully), they were nonetheless framed and articulated as claims *under* the Constitution. In a more historical vein, one might further note that social movements and their leaders from Frederick Douglass to Rand Paul have articulated their claims for sweeping change in terms of fidelity to the Constitution. Perhaps because it is highly inflexible and difficult to change, that is, the Constitution may have engendered a distinct form of claim-making, somewhat loosely within the four corners of the constitutional text. This has the effect of ratifying the normative legitimacy of that text even while seeking to wreak effective change to its contents. The Constitution, in short, provides the grammar of national popular mobilization for social change in the United States. Perhaps ironically, the fact that the Constitution exercises a virtual monopoly on the vocabulary for radical claim-making is testimony not only to the deep plasticity of the American constitutional order but also to the tenacity of its grip, and hence its deep-rooted sociological legitimacy.

Similarly, the US Constitution should be ranked as a success both in terms of its ability to tamp down agency costs and also its catalytic role in the creation of national public goods, most importantly a common economic market across the several states and a military capable of resisting European depredations in the antebellum era, and then, after World War II, establishing the terms of Pax Americana globally. At the Republic's beginning, corruption was almost a "national fixation" and a serious threat to the sort of civil virtue republican theorists had lauded (Teachout 2013). Hence, when King Louis XVI gave Benjamin Franklin, then ambassador to France, a diamond-studded snuffbox, it was the object of much controversy. From the corrupt Yazoo land deal of the 1790 to the Crédit Mobilier scandal of 1872 to the Teapot Dome scandal of the 1920s and more recent imbroglios such as Abscam, there is no shortage of evidence that individual politicians have abused their offices to obtain private rents. Yet while some contemporary American commentators bemoan the asymmetrical access and influence of the wealthy on congressional decision-making, there is little reason to think that corruption and rent-seeking have fundamentally compromised the operation of ordinary American political institutions, at least for a majority of citizens. Indeed, it is quite possible to argue that those scandals of underprovision and neglect that most afflict, say, many urban underclasses are perhaps better chalked up to the *success* of democracy rather than to the failure of a Constitution that was partly prompted by fears of redistributive politics.

The case for applauding the US Constitution is only strengthened by considering its long-term effect on the production of public goods such as a national free market and a robust military apparatus. As ongoing historical work by Alison LaCroix on the antebellum period of 1800–1860 richly illustrates (2013, 2015), the second and third generations of American politicians labored under much uncertainty as to whether the Constitution allowed such measures as a national bank and interstate roads and canals. In time, and perhaps under the pressures of exigency, the Constitution was read to contain the necessary resources to build both a financial and a physical infrastructure of the sort needed for effectual operation of a unified national market. The long twentieth century has similarly witnessed no shortage of federal expenditures designed to keep this market working, even if Americans have widely disagreed on their necessity of wisdom. From the Interstate Commerce Commission of the 1880s to the New Deal administrative agencies of the 1930s and the Great Society social welfare programs of the 1960s right through to the massive federal liquidity injections deployed to stave off the 2008 financial crisis, the Constitution has proved a near-inexhaustible source of legal authority for public goods arguably needful to the national polity. The same can be said on the foreign affairs side. The rise of American military power, of course, needs no proof today; rather, what may warrant more careful consideration is the arguable excess of national resources assigned to military ends not in response to immediate threats but rather as a function of the political dynamics fostered by the Constitution's division of war powers and the power of local-constituency preferences in the House (Thorpe 2014).

On the final metric of channeling political conflict, however, it is plausible to think that the US Constitution of 1787 should not be ranked a success. The issue, of course, is the sectional divide over slavery, which was left (at best) unresolved by the 1787 document, and in practice was staved off with legislative gag-rules and ad hoc sectional compromises through the first half of the nineteenth century. As Mittal and Weingast (2013) have cogently argued, while the issue of slavery threatened to unravel the constitutional order several times over that period, it was not until the Civil War of the 1860s that the issue was finally eliminated as a source of potential national dissolution (which is quite different, we emphasize, from a just resolution of the moral claims of former slaves, or a solution for enduring welfare effects of slavery and race prejudice). On this accounting, the Constitution simply failed to supply a solution to the key sectional division. That it required war, not legal or constitutional arguments, to mend that seam is some reason to think that on precisely the most neuralgic point of national division, the Constitution failed.

Of course, it may have been a much better constitution that emerged after the post-Civil War amendments, one not merely designed to keep the peace but to transform the polity in a major region of the country. For the roughly one hundred years it required to begin to implement the vision of social and political equality, the Constitution did serve as a vehicle for channeling political conflict among elites, but at the cost of repressing minorities and outsiders. Constitutional protections did not prevent the maintenance and growth of a racially restrictive order sustained by both state power and extra-state violence. Constitutional institutions facilitated political cartels, such as the coalition of Southern Democrats and Northern Republicans that dominated national politics for nearly a century. But it is also the case that the Constitution provided language and law that led to inclusive transformation, through the courts and eventually through Congress. While the relative role of law is a hotly debated issue (Rosenberg 1992; Klarman 2005), it does seem that the Constitution has done a better job of channeling conflict than in the decades preceding the Civil War.

B South Africa

The South African Constitution of December 10, 1996, is unusual in that what Gargarella calls the central drama – the need to transform a society scarred by racial inequality in every sphere – was clear to all concerned, and was clearly demarcated in the preamble to the Constitution.[3] As the Constitution turns twenty, there is much debate about the extent to which it has achieved those goals. The dominant narrative at the time of this writing is one of dashed hopes, in which unrealistic expectations met the hard realities of governance and the difficulties of reversing entrenched historical injustice.

---

[3] The entire constitution lays out its own purposes quite explicitly in the preamble. The constitution, it notes, is adopted so as to "Heal the divisions of the past and establish a society based on democratic values, social justice and fundamental human rights; Lay the foundations for a democratic and open society in which government is based on the will of the people and every citizen is equally protected by law; Improve the quality of life of all citizens and free the potential of each person; and Build a united and democratic South Africa able to take its rightful place as a sovereign state in the family of nations." Constitution of South Africa 1996, preamble.

Our own framework helps to provide an external perspective on this debate. To begin with, the 1996 constitution seems to score decently on metrics of legitimacy. Political institutions enjoy moderate rates of legitimacy (Gibson 2014) with scores of both confidence and legitimacy improving over time. Mattes (2007) argues that public attitudes of African respondents are in fact quite complex, and did not conform to either the "unrealistic expectations" or "dashed hopes" of the conventional wisdom.

The 1996 constitution has also been reasonably effective in channeling conflict, perhaps better than could have been expected. Potential spoilers, be they recalcitrant Afrikaner fringe of the Nationalist Party or Chief Mangosuthu Buthelezi, the Zulu leader of the Inkatha Freedom Party, have all been brought into the fold. There has been little political violence, even if criminal violence remains at epidemic levels, as we will discuss at greater length momentarily. Territorial cleavages apparent at the outset of the constitutional negotiations of the 1990s have, by and large, dissipated through a combination of special accommodations at the outset of the constitutional order and also by virtue of the existence of a single dominant political party (the African National Congress, or ANC) that integrated and channeled diverse interests.

When it comes to control of agency costs, on the other hand, the very presence of a single dominant party confronting a weak and delegitimized political opposition has led to predictably disappointing outcomes. Corruption of both the petty and grand types is apparent from the troughs to the peaks of political life. But at least as of now South Africa ranks only in the middle of the pack in Transparency International's annual corruption survey. Under President Jacob Zuma, moreover, public attention has turned to excesses of the ANC and of Zuma himself. And the fact that some corrupt schemes do result in trials – forty members of parliament, for example, were charged with fraud for misuse of official travel vouchers in 2005 – suggests the presence of some impartiality in the judicial system. Still, the overall assessment here depends very much on the baseline chosen. If one compares South Africa with Zimbabwe, it looks quite good, but it does not approach the levels one would expect in the ranks of the rich industrial democracies to which the country aspires.

Finally, the question whether the Constitution effectively enables the production of public goods such as security from crime, health care, and education has been central in the debates that have emerged around the twentieth anniversary. Across all measures, the social gaps between black and white remain severe, and progress is slow. For example, policing resources are woefully inadequate, with the wealthy (white and black) finding private substitutes while the poor remain highly vulnerable. Recent empirical studies suggest that the perceived failure to remedy the deep physical insecurity of the Apartheid era has undermined trust and confidence in the state more generally across all social classes (Bradford et al. 2014). It is hence arguable that from the perspective of many South Africans on the ground, this element of the Constitution's basic function has not been fulfilled.

It is beyond our mandate to explain how this pattern of successes and failures arose. Nevertheless, it is worth noting that in the eyes of many South Africans, the original sin of the 1996 constitution was to make peace with international capital and to provide for continued protection of (highly inequitably distributed) property rights. At the same time, by including many social and economic rights in the organic document's text, the drafters invited an ongoing dialogue between political branches, as well as among the people at large, on the state provision of these kinds of public goods. Many of the most famous decisions emanating from the nation's Constitutional Court – such as *Grootboom* on housing, *Mazibuko* on water, *Treatment Action Campaign* on health – have articulated a promising approach to adjudicating social and economic rights. Whether these judicial decisions have made a difference on the ground, however, is a difficult question, but some scholars suggest that they have been effective in calling attention to these issues and in mobilizing civil society (Langford et al. 2015). If the constitution has failed to supply public goods, therefore, it may well nonetheless have provided some tools for the people to demand them themselves.

C Afghanistan

After the Taliban collapsed in 2001, an international coalition led by the United States converged on Afghanistan to install a regime more closely aligned to its geopolitical and security interests. The resulting provisional administration, led by President Hamid Karzai, was responsible for installing a new constitution and managing new elections and a transition to a democratically selected government. The initial document, the December 2001 Bonn Agreement, was produced after a thin process of public consultation, and reflected a process of internecine bargaining between international players and different Afghan warlord factions that had been previously brought into government through appointments and regional spending. The Karzai administration midwived a new constitution in 2004, which led to a reinstallation of many familiar figures, including Karzai himself, in power (for more detailed accounts of this history, see Ginsburg & Huq 2014; Huq 2009).

Against this rather inauspicious beginning, Afghanistan scores surprisingly well in terms of sociological legitimacy – although recent military gains by the Taliban may cast this welcome news into doubt. The Asia Foundation's annual surveys of the Afghan people, for example, show a population that believes the country is generally moving in the right direction, notwithstanding staggeringly high levels of corruption and state violence. Strikingly, in 2013 more Afghans registered a belief that their country was heading in the right direction than Americans when asked the same question. The data suggest that the Afghan people understand the myriad challenges their government faces (perhaps unlike Americans?), and also appreciate the current measure of political stability in the teeth of observed insecurity, violence, and corruption. As Robert Crews has recently argued (2015), Afghans well understand that they stand within a vortex of international forces well beyond their control. Moreover, notwithstanding the long tenure of President Karzai in office, Afghans can point to several successful exercises in democratic governance, ranging from the 2004 constitutional Loya Jirga (which was widely viewed as a success despite the machinations of Karzai and his foreign backers), to vigorously contested parliamentary elections in 2005 and 2010 under the 2004 dispensation.

Second, in its early years, Afghanistan's constitution has provided a plausible framework for cabining and constraining the nation's turbulent and fractious ethno-political factions. It is important to recognize that this project of crafting and managing a workable framework for governance and political negotiation has had to occur against the backdrop of a resurgent Taliban, which has benefited from Pakistan's provision of strategic sanctuary (Guistozzi 2009). To begin with, cooption through offers of cabinet positions or gubernatorial appointments mitigated outright conflict, largely ending the horrific destruction of the 1990s civil wars. Some former warlords, such as Guldbudin Hekmatyar, remained militarily active outside the national government. In contrast, many others, including Abdul Dostum, Ismail Khan, and Mohamed Fahim, were folded into the new dispensation. Paradoxically, peace was bought by tainting the very government that it enabled, as warlords decided they could make more money in the system than outside it. Worse, the constitution contains flashpoints that might generate future conflict. For example, confusion abounds about institutional roles because of some shoddy constitutional drafting. President and parliament thus have fought over elections and who gets to interpret the Constitution. At one point the parliament set up an alternative institution to interpret the document, snatching the job away from the Supreme Court. The result was a debilitating impasse.

Paradoxically, the Constitution's success in drawing in potential spoilers has simultaneously raised agency costs denominated in terms of rights violations and financial corruption, both venial and venal. On the one hand, human rights abuses by government actors and allied powerful third parties (e.g., local militias; tribal leaders) remain grave and pervasive. Of particular important here is the serious failure to vindicate the gender equality commitments of the 2004 Constitution. That document's guarantees of equality for women have been woefully unfulfilled, despite impressive strides in education, leaving many women highly vulnerable to the overlapping threats of family, village, and state. On the corruption front, moreover, the government's response to endemic deceit, bribe-taking and outright theft in the new national administration has been at best anemic, in part because President Karzai intervened repeatedly in cases involving close associates. The result is poor performance on the third measure of our quartet.

Finally, the fourth metric of public-good production generates another disappointing assessment. Consider two key public goods: the national economy and human security. On the one hand, Afghanistan's official economy is overshadowed by illegal economies – most importantly the opiates trade, but also trafficking in women (for prostitution), and a transit trade in goods purchased duty-free in the Gulf and smuggled into India and Pakistan. On the other hand, both the police and the army remain exceedingly weak, despite large infusions of international aid. The recent defeats of the Afghan national army in the north of the country suggest that the state's apparatus for maintaining its integrity, as well as preserving public order, remains quite weak – in part because of the endemic corruption that the 2004 Constitution failed to stanch.

In sum, the 2004 Constitution is a genuinely mixed picture – scoring high for legitimacy and for channeling political conflict but faring poorly because it created new loci of internecine discord while failing to generate public goods.

V   CONCLUSION AND OVERVIEW OF THE BOOK

We have aimed to demonstrate in this Introduction that constitutions can be evaluated either in terms of internal or external criteria. Neither is wholly satisfactory, and in all likelihood some mix of both should be brought to bear in most cases. We have further offered some examples of plausible internal and external criteria. Our ambition in so doing, however, has not been to demonstrate that these criteria are necessarily the wisest or the most normatively desirable exemplars of the genre. Much more modestly, we hope to have demonstrated that there is some value to thinking systematically and carefully about the task of evaluating constitutional success.

We close with a brief overview of the structure of the volume. The first part of the book comprises four efforts to answer the question of how to evaluate constitutional performance by identifying, at a high level of generality, a generally applicable answer to that question. The contributors to this part, however, diverge as to whether the relevant criteria should be internal or external. They also explore different objects of inquiry, ranging from the effect of constitution-making on state structure, state stability, or democracy, to the quality of the text itself. To begin with, Aziz Huq draws on a strand of political theory going back to Machiavelli and Hobbes to identify state maintenance as a central function of constitutional design. This leads to a very narrow definition of plausible general criteria for constitution-making. Taking a very different approach, Hélène Landemore uses the availability of plural constitutional drafts from the Icelandic debates of 2008–2009, each of which emerged from a different sort of drafting process, to investigate what renders a constitution "good." Rejecting the narrow normative grounds espoused by Huq, she offers a robust and comprehensive account of qualities that render a draft, at least ex ante, successful. These papers offer *external* criteria. In contrast, Roberto Gargarella urges an internal benchmark. Drawing on the work of famed Argentinian jurist Juan Bautista Alberdi, he proposes an approach that is primarily attentive to the threshold "dramas," or problems, confronted by constitution-makers. He then illustrates this method with examples drawn widely in time and space within the Americas. Finally, Martin Shapiro offers a challenge to the measurement and assessment of success by raising the issue of political parties, which are both produced by but also interact with formal institutions to provide the lifeblood of constitutional action.

The next part of the book takes Gargarella's observation that sometimes a constitution is designed to resolve a very particular policy problem as a starting point, and asks whether there is a general criterion that might be applied to evaluate success when different constitutions seek to resolve the same problem. Drawing on his extensive work on Turkish constitutionalism, Ozan Varol develops a general taxonomy for analyzing the role of constitutions in managing transitions from authoritarian, military rule and civilian, democratic regimes. Deeply informed by the Turkish context, Varol's approach also provides a perspective from which to analyze the relative success (or failure) of other such transitions, for example in Pakistan, Indonesia, and South Korea. Next, Hanna Lerner considers how constitutions engage with the problem of managing religious conflicts and tensions. She entangles the role of constitutions in both protecting individuals' right *to* religious freedom and also their right to be free *from* religious dispensation. She then applies her analysis to a range of mid-twentieth-century constitutions that had to grapple with the problem of how to integrate (or not) religious preferences and divisions into the structure of the new state. Sumit Bisarya examines the general phenomenon of transitional provisions, which often serve as the bridge between an old constitutional order and new one. While relatively clear in terms of evaluation, they also present challenges and can often serve as points of crises. Drawing on close case studies of Tunisia and Somalia, he suggests a lens for evaluating these critical parts of written constitutional schemes. Zachary Elkins, Tom Ginsburg, and James Melton look at the challenge of implementing constitutional rights, and focus especially on the importance of time. They challenge, on theoretical and empirical grounds, approaches that simply compare constitutional text with performance on some human rights indicator at a single point in time. And Rosalind Dixon and David Landau defend and explore the possibility of a democratic criterion for constitutional endurance in democracies. They investigate the qualities a constitution must include to be effective as a democratic matter, using the concept of a constitution's "basic structure" as a tool to explore how to evaluate both initial design and subsequent change.

The final part of the book turns to a series of case studies. The aim here is not to be comprehensive (an ambition that would, in any case, be infeasible) but rather to provide a rich counterpoint to some of the earlier chapters. In each case, the author explores the implementation of a given constitution (or in the case of Zaid Al-Ali, set of constitutions) and provides their own view about the perspective to be deployed in examining our core question. The four examples are different in timing and in the nature of the relevant bundle of founding aspirations. In each of these chapters, the author navigates between praising successes, and, perhaps inevitably, cataloging failures, in a highly contextual fashion that illuminates the limitations of generalizing analyses.

To begin with, Martha Nussbaum explores the 1950 Indian Constitution from the perspective of one of its key drafters, Bhimrao Ramji Ambedkar. Picking up on themes explored in Part II of the book, Nussbaum uses Ambedkar's concern with the mitigation of caste-based discrimination as a platform to examine whether, and how, the Indian Constitution could promote the well-being of some of the most disadvantaged members of Indian society. A close observer of the drafting of the 2010 Kenyan Constitution, James Gathii explores the ambitions of that document. Considering the effects of five years' institutional progress (rather than the half century in which the Indian Constitution has been in effect), Gathii identifies key personnel decisions and legislative choices that will have an effect going forward on how the ambitions of the constitution for ethnic peace and accountable government will be achieved. Zaid Al-Ali takes a larger historical and geographic sweep by considering the effects of constitution-making in the Arab world after the Arab Spring. Al-Ali is skeptical about the availability of external criteria of the kind we set out here, but instead focuses his keen and close eye on two waves of Arab constitutions. Finally, Erin Delaney examines the recent period of change to the venerable and idiosyncratic British Constitution. She shows how a variety of forces have contributed to a rapid shift of the basic mechanics and pace of constitutional change, suggesting that constitutional success is elusive and that significant risks are emerging in seeking a balance between stability and flexibility. Her chapter furnishes a useful juxtaposition to, and perhaps confirmation of, the argument laid out in Dixon and Landau's chapter, although the latter focuses more on consolidated written constitutions.

To conclude, it is apparent that the contributors to this book disagree, sometimes sharply, on the validity or either external or internal criteria either in general or in particular cases. Rather than settling this debate, the chapters in this book provide perhaps a collective analysis of myriad potential approaches to the task of evaluating constitutional success – an analysis that, we hope and expect, will be of interest and value to both academic experts on constitutional design, and also those engaged in the practical task of facilitating the creation of sound constitutional documents. It is up to the reader to assess our own collective performance in this regard.

REFERENCES

Arrow, Kenneth. 1951. *Social Choice and Individual Values*. New York: J. Wiley.

Barber, Sotirios A. 2014. *Constitutional Failure*. Lawrence: University of Kansas Press.

Berman, Mitchel. 2004. "Originalism is Bunk." *NYU Law Review* 84: 1–96.

Bradford, Ben, Aziz Z. Huq, Jonathan P. Jackson, & Benjamin Roberts. 2014. "What Price Fairness when Security Is at Stake? Police Legitimacy in South Africa." *Regulation and Governance* 8: 246.

Crews, Robert. 2015. *Afghan Modern: The History of a Global Nation*. Cambridge: Harvard University Press.

Ghai, Yash. 2014. *Chimera of Constitutionalism: State, Economy, and Society in Africa*, available at http://web.up.ac.za/sitefiles/file/47/15338/Chimera_of_constitutionalism_yg1.pdf

Gibson, James L. 2014. "Reassessing the Institutional Legitimacy of the South African Constitutional Court: New Evidence, Revised Theory" available at www.nylslawreview.com/wp-content/uploads/sites/16/2014/11/Gibson .pdf

Ginsburg, Tom. 2003. *Judicial Review in New Democracies*. New York: Cambridge University Press.

Ginsburg, Tom, Zachary Elkins, & James Melton. 2011. "On the Evasion of Executive Term Limits." *William and Mary Law Review* 52: 1807–1872.

Ginsburg, Tom & Alberto Simpser. 2014. "Introduction." In *Constitutions in Authoritarian Regimes*, edited by Tom Ginsburg & Alberto Simpser. New York: Cambridge University Press.

Ginsburg, Tom & Aziz Huq. 2014. "What Can Constitutions Do? The Afghan Case." *Journal of Democracy* 24: 116–130.

Guistozzi, Antonio. 2009. *Koran, Kalashnikov, and Laptop: The Neo-Taliban Insurgency in Afghanistan 2002–2007*. New York: Columbia University Press.

Hirschl, Ran. 2004. *Towards Juristocracy?* Cambridge: Harvard University Press.

Horowitz, Donald. 2002. "Constitutional Design: Proposals versus Processes." In *The Architecture of Democracy*, edited by Andrew Reynolds. New York: Oxford University Press.

Huq, Aziz. 2009. "The Story of Hamid Karzai: The Paradoxes of State-Building and Human Rights." In *Human Rights Advocacy Stories*. New York: Foundation Press, pp. 514–515.

2014. "Does the Logic of Collective Action Explain Federalism Doctrine?" *Stanford Law Review* 66: 217–302.

Forthcoming 2016. "The Constitutional Law of Agenda Control." *California Law Review*. 104: ___.

Klarman, Michael. 2005. "Brown and Lawrence (and Goodridge)." *Michigan Law Review* 104: 431–489.

Kurlantzick, Joshua. 2013. *Democracy in Retreat: The Revolt of the Middle Class and the Worldwide Decline of Representative Government*. New Haven: Yale University Press.

LaCroix, Alison. 2013. "The Constitution of the Second Generation." *University of Illinois Law Review* 2013: 1775–1786.

2015. "The Interbellum Constitution: Federalism in the Long Founding Moment." *Stanford Law Review* 67: 397–445.

Landau, David. 2013. "Constitution-Making Gone Wrong." *Alabama Law Review* 64: 923–980.

Langford, Malcolm, Ben Cousins, Jackie Dugard, & Tshepo Madlingo, eds. 2015. *Socio-Economic Rights in South Africa: Symbols or Substance?* New York: Cambridge University Press.

Law, David & Mila Versteeg. 2013. "Sham Constitutions." *California Law Review* 101: 863–952.

Mattes, Robert. 2007. "Building Popular Legitimacy for the Democratic, 'New South Africa': A Partial Success Story?" available at www.yale .edu/macmillan/apartheid/mattesp2.pdf

McAdams, Richard. 2014. *The Expressive Power of Law*. Cambridge: Harvard University Press.

Mittal, Sonia and Barry R. Weingast. 2013. "Self-Enforcing Constitutions: With an Application to Democratic Stability in America's First Century." *Journal of Law, Economics and Organization* 29: 278–302.

Pozas-Loyos, Andrea. 2012. *Constitutional Efficacy*. PhD Dissertation, Department of Politics, New York University.

Rosenberg, Gerald. 1992. *The Hollow Hope*. Chicago: University of Chicago Press.

Schauer, Frederick. 2014. *The Force of Law*. Cambridge: Harvard University Press.

Teachout, Zephyr. 2013. *Corruption in America*. Cambridge: Harvard University Press.

Thorpe, Rebecca. 2014. *The American Warfare State: The Domestic Politics of Military Spending*. Chicago: University of Chicago Press.

Tushnet, Mark. 2014. "Authoritarian Constitutionalism." In *Constitutions in Authoritarian Regimes*, edited by Tom Ginsburg & Alberto Simpser. New York: Cambridge University Press.

PART I

DEFINING CONSTITUTIONAL
PERFORMANCE

2

Hippocratic constitutional design

Aziz Z. Huq

I INTRODUCTION

Is there a criterion that can be used to evaluate constitutions written in Pretoria in 1996, Philadelphia in 1787, and Baghdad in 2005? Can the organic documents produced by democrats, oligarchs, tyrants, and theocracies all be judged by the same metric? This chapter, in taking up these questions, develops a benchmark for constitutional success with a general, albeit not universal, scope. That benchmark is independent of local criteria or prejudices, and relies instead on an analysis of the minimal conditions for constitutional success. Focusing my inquiry in that fashion, I contend that the most plausible touchstone of constitutional success is the avoidance of self-defeating constitutional design. It is a constitution purged of elements that conduce, perhaps unintentionally, to the breakdown or collapse of the state that the constitution endeavors to underwrite.

To situate this inquiry, it is useful to recall the dichotomy that Tom Ginsburg and I posit between metrics for evaluation of constitutional "success" that are internal and ones that are external in character. An internal criterion is one applied by a member of the polity engaged in constitutional creation or evaluation. An external criterion, by contrast, is one employed by an outsider such as a comparative constitutional scholar or a foreign advisor to constitutional drafters. So defined, the internal/external distinction turns on *who* applies the standard, not what the standard is. Human rights norms, for example, might be invoked both by participants to a drafting process as an internal criteria, or instead by transnational advocacy groups as a generally applicable external standard. Moreover, there is often leakage between internal and external criteria. Evaluative criteria deployed by participants in

Thanks to Josh Chafetz, Mike Dorf, Tom Ginsburg, Amanda Greene, Eric Posner, Aziz Rana, Dana Remus, and Mike Seidman for helpful comments on this chapter.

a constitution-making process are not autochthonic. They can leach their content and orientation from global intellectual currents (Ginsburg et al. 2008). Nor are external criteria necessarily loosed entirely from the gravitational force of the local circumstances of their intellectual production. Political rationality, in my view, lacks any transhistorical, acontextual form. Nevertheless, the distinction is useful insofar as it draws attention to the fact that criteria of constitutional success play different roles in different circumstances. And different standards might fit those distinct circumstances better than a single norm.

This chapter focuses on the availability of an external benchmark capable of being applied by an outsider to a political community at the moment in time when a constitution is being proposed or debated. That standard should not be tailored to specific social, cultural and geopolitical contexts. It must instead be capable of application across a very broad range of quite heterogeneous cases. To frame the inquiry in this way is to take men and women as irreducibly different, and irredeemably committed to beliefs most generously described as eccentric or idiosyncratic. It is to embrace the observed global "diversity of irreducibly different regimes, liberal and nonliberal" (Gray 1994: 730), and then to seek a definition of constitutional success that has broad traction despite that diversity.[1]

If we select randomly from the pool of historical exemplars, the probability that participants in two distinct instances of constitutional creation happened to possess and apply wholly convergent internal criteria is vanishingly small. To the contrary, it is likely that even the different participants in the same enactment process tend to hold conflictive, perhaps incompatible, criteria. The absence of overlap between these criteria will sometimes undermine the possibility of "incompletely theorized agreement" (Sunstein 1995). The potential for inferring constitutional benchmarks of general applicability from local norms, therefore, is rather limited. Further, while it is always possible to say that a constitution fails to conform to a certain normative benchmark – a substantive theory of justice, certain "core" rights, or a comprehensive moral or political doctrine – such complaints must not be confused or conflated with a judgment of *constitutional* success or quality. Unless having a constitution is identified with fidelity to a particular normative theory, moral doctrine, or account of legitimacy, that is, the complaint lacks generality.

[1] The framework offered here diverges both in method and ambition from the metrics Tom Ginsburg and I offer in the Introduction. Whereas those metrics are crafted for practical use given a large amount of agreement on the basic functions of a state, this analysis works from the ground up to generate a minimalist theoretical account of constitutional purpose.

Despite the difficulty of this enterprise, we routinely observe scholars and jurists offering advice to constitutional drafters, or scholarly comparisons of different constitutions, seemingly without reliance upon local norms. Ex ante advice and evaluation turns implicitly on context-independent benchmarks. General advice is offered notwithstanding the existence of sharp normative divergences between national cultures, and despite deep normative conflicts within constitution-making contexts. Such advice even may be thought most valuable when local antagonisms are most unreasonable and categorical. External criteria also implicitly aver their compatibility with all or most internal criteria.

To be clear, the criteria identified through such an inquiry need not be valid *sub specie aeternitatis*. They should provide *to the greatest extent feasible* an external benchmark for constitutional designers and comparative scholars seeking to evaluate a constitution qua constitution. To seek such a goal is not to repudiate the relevance of internal criteria. To the contrary, a central aim of my argument here is to limn an external criterion that is maximally compatible with such internal criteria, as well as free-standing normative principles of justice, rights, or the like. Further, although I focus here on *written* constitutions, I am fully cognizant of the long-recognized fact that constitutions need not be memorialized to be efficacious (Bagehot 2009), and also of Oakeshott's (1991) critique of planned, as opposed to organic, political orders. The analytic framework offered here can extend without much complication to unwritten, organic constitutions.

In the course of this inquiry, I advance two complementary theses, the first negative and the second affirmative. First, I resist a cluster of frequently deployed welfarist criteria of constitutional success. The class of welfarist criteria I reject are both *maximizing* and *aggregative* in character. It is common in both the empirical and the theoretical literature to employ proxies for maximum aggregate social welfare such as gross domestic product (GDP), per capita income, or other monetized metrics. Implicit in their deployment is a goal of maximal aggregate welfare, a goal that falls firmly within the mainstream of consequentialist and utilitarian methods (Williams 1973). I readily concede that maximum net welfare may be a perfectly sensible measure for some purposes. Mine is not a critique of the empirical study of national-level welfare measures per se. What I contest here is rather its feasibility for a constitutional designer as an ex ante measure of her success. To lean upon such criteria *at the moment of constitutional creation*, I suggest, may be incoherent, impractical, and self-defeating.

Second, I derive a chastened account of external criteria from a minimal account of a constitution's operation. Historicizing accounts of the term "constitution" expose its recent, somewhat hybridized, vintage that blends ideas from classical thought, ecclesiastical practice, and early modern political theory (Maddox 1989; Stourzh 1998). Stripping away the resulting excrescences that now dominate thinking about constitutionalism (Castiglione 1996), I offer a parsimonious account of a constitution likely to be accepted notwithstanding differences in internal criteria: A *constitution is a legally authoritative written account of at least some of the institutions necessary for the operation of a state over a given geographic space for some extended period of time.* Given my definition, I suggest that disparate constitutional creators can converge on a single external criterion notwithstanding their different internal criteria: A *constitution succeeds qua constitution so long as, and to the extent that, its design does not contain elements that are likely to conduce unintentionally to the breakdown or dissolution of effective state functioning that it aims to enable.* Although still consequentialist in spirit, this criterion is less epistemically and cognitively demanding than a strict focus on welfare maximization. It counsels the architects of a new written constitution very simply to avoid designs that will come down around their ears. In that sense, it is akin to a maximin decision rule (Peterson 2009). Although it bears some resemblance to the heavily criticized precautionary principle (Sunstein 2009), it rests on independent epistemic and normative grounds, and does not exhibit the flaws identified in that rule. Rather, it boils down to a Hippocratic approach: first, avoid doing harm.

My recommended lodestar of avoiding self-defeating constitutional design may seem exiguous given the quanta of ink spilt on the subject. But the rate of constitutional failure – the average lifespan of a constitution now not exceeding two decades (Elkins et al. 2009) – suggests that the task of avoiding self-defeating constitutional design is more demanding than commonly believed. Reflection on the causes of constitutional failure, moreover, suggests that it is harder than might first seem to diagnose pathological provisions. However easy it is to evade even obvious errors in the cold light of academic debate, sidestepping design pitfalls presents particularly hard challenges in the heat and passion of constitutional creation (Elster 1995). Even modest external criteria, therefore, may in practice be too demanding for real political actors.

A chastened approach is not without respectable precedent. In his unpublished 1772 tract, "Considerations on the Government of Poland and its Proposed Reformation," Rousseau cautioned that sound "institutions for Poland can only be the work of Poles," such that a "foreigner can hardly do more than offer some general observations for the enlightenment, but not for the guidance, of the law-reformer" (Rousseau 1997: 177). Of course, Rousseau then goes on to offer what can only with the greatest of euphemistic elasticity be labeled "general observations." But the force of his cautionary note remains: The role of external criteria of *constitutional success* – as distinct from other normative benchmarks – may well be chastened, and therefore consistent with a wide array of other moral, normative, and political theories of constitutional quality.

II AGGREGATIVE WELFARIST METRICS OF CONSTITUTIONAL QUALITY

There are innumerable imaginable criteria for evaluating the success of constitutions that *purport* to universal domain. Constitutions might be ranked, for example, in terms of their success in fostering some group of human rights (Ginsburg et al. 2008; see also Hafner-Burton and Tsutsui 2005 and 2007), a defined set of essential human capabilities (Nussbaum 2007), democratic rule (Foweraker and Landman 2002; Stanger 2004), or even conformity with a transcendental normative framework supplied by a holy text, such the Koran in the case of Muslim societies (Arjomand 2007). Such accounts of constitutional success are disqualified from my analysis by dint of their controversial normative foundations. As a purely predictive matter, it seems certain that the demesne of these supposed universalistic benchmarks is likely to remain contested for the foreseeable future.

Nevertheless, at this moment in our historical and intellectual development, there is one external criterion of constitutional success that does purport to universal applicability and that claims to stand above normative disagreements. I label this criterion "maximal aggregative welfarism," or MAW, a term intended to encompass a range of observed benchmarks. A MAW metric has three elements. First, it ranks the goodness of the states of affairs in terms of the characteristics of those states. Second, it picks out for evaluative purposes the concept of utility, which is "taken to stand for a person's conception of his own well-being" as the salient characteristic of consequentialist analysis. Finally, it ranks states of affairs by the sum total of individual utilities, and assigns priority to the state with the largest sum (Sen 1979: 463–64; see also Williams 1973). Translated into a command for constitution makers, a MAW metric directs that a constitution may be elected if and only if the ensuing sum-total of individual utilities is at least as large as under alternative dispensations (Sen 1979: 464). Lacking direct access to welfare or utility information, it may be necessary to deploy a proxy for the latter. The most commonly used proxy is GDP per capita. My focus here, though, is not on the adequacy of any one proxy. It is rather on the potential of MAW generally to serve as an external criterion as earlier defined.

This potential is assumed more often than examined. Indeed, the assumption that an aggregated social welfare is an appropriate measure of constitutional success is prevalent, albeit in an undertheorized fashion, across both the theoretical and the empirical literatures on constitutional design. Hence, in the empirical literature, Alesina and Spolaore (2003: 156–73) use GDP and per capita income to evaluate constitutional regimes. In their explicit evaluation of constitutional performance, Persson and Tabellini (2005) examine a wider array of economic performance metrics, including government spending as a percentage of GDP, rent-seeking, and size of government. In a more theoretical vein, Vermeule (2013: 23) calls for constitutional rulemaking to be conducted in "a spirit of welfare-maximization," criticizing design decisions that focus on one species of political risk without accounting for countervailing risks engendered by precautionary measures. McGinnis and Rappaport (2013), in contrast, argue that the US Constitution of 1789, glossed in an originalist light, will tend to maximize aggregate social welfare because of the supermajority character of its origin.

To be clear, these authors do not explicitly set forth aggregative welfarist metrics as benchmarks for constitution-making. Empiricists such as Alesina, Spolaore, Persson, and Tabellini use country-level observations and ask what is learned about certain institutional design choices via econometric analysis where the dependent variable is GDP. In contrast, McGinnis and Rappaport reason backward from a belief in the success of the US Constitution. Rather than supplying general recommendations, they mine a nostalgic vein, striving to vindicate as neutral and ahistorical an interpretive strategy (originalism) that in fact emerged out of a particular historical and partisan-political matrix (Greene 2009). Vermeule is vague as to whether his analysis speaks to constitution makers or implementers. Yet he can plausibly be read as endorsing an aggregative welfarist benchmark of global ambition. Indeed, I believe that a fair reading of all of these otherwise divergent analyses uncovers a widely held belief that measures of aggregative welfare are well fitted to the enterprise of constitutional evaluation. That distinctive benchmark of constitutional success, which is taken often as uncontroversial and hence in no need of defending, invites further analysis.

It is not feasible or wise to rely exclusively on MAW criteria to evaluate constitutional design, especially as a contemporaneous matter – or so I shall argue here. This claim against a singular reliance on such criteria has three elements, each of which have independent force and all of which apply without regard to the particular concerns that a given proxy (e.g., GDP or per capita income) might implicate.

First, except in unusual circumstances, defining and applying MAW measures raises hard questions of scope. That is, it is not clear whose welfare counts, or how it should be counted. Second, reliance on such grounds may be infeasible as a practical matter. Impediments to a constitution's adoption, as well as capacity constraints upon relevant actors, limit the extent to which aggregative welfarist goals can be pursued. Once such limitations are accounted for, straightforward prescriptions about how to maximize aggregate welfare may also be difficult to formulate. Finally, there is a potent conflict between the instrumental character of MAW and the public psychology of constitutionalism. Drawing on criticisms developed against certain forms of utilitarianism (Williams 1973), I suggest that a constitutional design explicitly justified on aggregative welfarist grounds is in sharp tension with both the circumstances and the necessary ambitions of constitution-making. Let me explain each of these points in turn.

Whose welfare?

A metric that aggregates and maximizes welfare across a population dispersed in time and space requires some baseline assumption about the identity of the salient population. In ordinary cost-benefit analysis, the identification of the relevant population is often a simple matter. But more complex questions can arise in situations of substantial expected demographic change (Broome 2000). In the constitution-making context, however, the boundaries of the relevant population whose welfare is at stake are often not determined prior to the constitution's coming into force. Although theorists have sometimes assumed that the population covered by a constitution is organically formed and therefore self-evident (e.g., Rousseau 1997: 172–73), matters are rarely that clear-cut. Even without accepting the Hobbesian dictum that a political community can by definition come into existence only in the instant of constitutional contracting, there are ample practical reasons for doubting the existence of an a priori political community in all or even most cases of constitution-making. Geographic boundaries, for example, may be up for grabs because of secessionist movements (Weinstock 2001). Even when some territory is clearly covered, domestic irredentism directed at neighboring lands may raise questions about the relevance of other populations. Further, even when a polity's geographic contours are beyond doubt, who precisely within that area counts as a member in good standing for aggregative welfarist purposes may be uncertain.

The American experience provides instances of all these kinds of ambiguity. Initially, it was not clear whether all thirteen former colonies would ratify the

1789 Constitution. As a result, the drafters and ratifiers of that document were uncertain of the precise geographic and demographic scope of the new political regime (Maier 2011). Moreover, even once the threshold geographic bounds of the new dispensation were settled on May 20, 1789, with Rhode Island's ratification of the Constitution, uncertainty still persisted about precisely who counted as a member of the polity. The status of free African-Americans was not settled even provisionally until the 1857 decision of *Dred Scott v. Sandford,* which held that blacks, both free and enslaved, failed to count as citizens and correlatively fell outside the legal shelter of the 1789 Constitution. Moreover, it was not until 1924 that Congress by statute extended citizenship to all members of American-Indian tribes. This shows that constitutions do not always settle elementary questions of membership or geographical bounds of a polity. For decades, even centuries, it may thus be unclear whose welfare is to be maximized by a constitutional text.

If the identity of the relevant population is uncertain, then a constitutional designer may want for any clear benchmark of *whose* welfare to aggregate when setting pen to paper. Under those conditions, it seems incoherent or question-begging to appeal to estimates of future aggregate welfare when the identity of the relevant population being aggregated remains up for grabs. The American case, moreover, suggests that the decision to include or exclude a given subpopulation (say, native Americans) might significantly alter the welfare consequences of given constitutional designs. Equally, expanding or contracting the geographic and demographic scope of a polity might recalibrate the desirability of design features such as decentralization, proportionality in electoral rules, or entrenched minority rights. An added complication is that even once borders are set, the net welfare effects of constitutional creation can be ambiguous because of externalities on neighboring populations (if such externalities are even thought to count in the balance). The history of Native American relations with the federal government is again evidence of this. In all, the decision about whose welfare counts is not easily settled by looking to future estimates of welfare.

In addition, there is a related puzzle as to how the welfare of different generations subject to a new constitution should be compared and aggregated. Standard economic theory supplies powerful arguments in favor of intergenerational discounting of goods and commodities (Samida and Weisbach 2007; but compare Kysar 2007). In contrast, so-called pure discounting of well-being is sharply contested by some (Broome 1994: 131), but stoutly defended by others (Weisbach and Sunstein 2009). Whatever its technical form, the logic of discounting has unsettling implications for constitutional design. If both well-being and goods are to be discounted, constitution makers should concern themselves with immediate consequences while maintaining a relative indifference to the distant future. If intergenerational welfare aggregation requires a steep discounting of the value of future public goods, it might even be that constitutional design should simply ignore future generations and minimally invest in long-term institutions with a public good character. This in turn may imply that a minimalist constitutional architecture is almost always preferable. These conclusions are in some tension with the common idea that the very purpose of a constitution is to create the institutional preconditions of durable economic growth (see, e.g., North and Weingast 1989) and to entrench the preferences of an enacting generation, and in particular to create patterns of institutional development that ensure their reproduction across subsequent generations. The application of intertemporal discounting to constitutional design thus raises difficult normative questions about why a current generation should invest time and effort into institutional creation that benefits primarily distant future generations – a "dead hand" problem, but in reverse.

Incentive incompatibility and time inconsistency

The second cluster of concerns about a MAW metric is more general in character. They apply even if a constitution is installed with clear and uncontentious demographic and geographic boundaries. The concerns have an empirical predicate and a theoretical armature. The empirical predicate is that "the task of constitution-making generally emerges in conditions that are likely to work against good constitution-making" (Elster 1995: 394). The theoretical predicate is that constitutional design must sharply trade-off between the goal of overcoming barriers to constitutional creation and the goal of maximizing long-term aggregate welfare. As a result of these constraints, constitutional designers cannot simply strive to maximize welfare without accounting for parochial and highly idiosyncratic local concerns. Generalizing design lessons from past experience, moreover, is highly epistemically demanding in light of the need to account for the divergent local constraints attendant on different instances of constitutional creation. As a result, maximizing welfare may be beyond the reach of most constitutional designers.

Consider first the practical problem. Constitutional design almost never proceeds unencumbered by parochial politics, by scarcities of time and knowledge, or by the burdens of the past. Perhaps most importantly, the task never occurs on a social and political tabula rasa. It rather unrolls against a backdrop of competition amongst extant political elites, as well as other interest groups.

Influential political factions are unlikely to relinquish power voluntarily merely because a new constitution is in the works. As a result, it is almost always the case that such factions exercise formal or informal vetoes over constitutional design. They may demand certain structures of political representation to ensure their continued influence. Constitutions, rather than revolutionizing, may calcify. Consider the role of the several states in the US context: The Delaware delegates to the Philadelphia Convention came to the Convention with instructions to insist on the equality of voting power for all states (Elster 1995: 374), guaranteeing a bias in favor of historical distributions of political power. Alternatively, elites might engage in "hegemonic preservation" by installing mechanisms to protect against redistributive measures and so maintain economic and political status (Ginsburg 2003; Hirschl 2007; Miller 2000). Even when elite bargaining does not lead to specific design choices, it might preclude other choices from being adopted. Institutions may be intentionally shrouded in a "veil of vagueness" within the constitutional text, deferring conflict by clouding the downstream effects of constitutional choice (Olsen 1997: 221). This limits the degree of textual specification feasible in a constitutional draft.

Complicating matters yet further, there are almost always nontrivial epistemic and cognitive constraints on constitutional designers. Constitution makers usually act within severe "environmentally constrained boundaries" (March and Olsen 1975: 154). This is partially a result of the temporal and political constraints on most constitutional-making processes, which are often played out in the shadow or wake of war, crisis, or national deliquescence. It is also a consequence of the fact that information about the incentives and preferences of potential counterparties or geopolitical influences may simply be unavailable. Participants are also likely to have well-developed, deeply internalized, and highly imperfect frameworks for obtaining and assimilating new knowledge (March and Olsen 1975; Olsen 1997). Hence, they may be incapable of updating effectively in response to new information about counterparties and changed circumstances.

Finally, drafters rarely "inherit a blank slate that they can remake at will," but instead "find that the dead weight of previous institutional choices seriously limits their room to maneuver" (Pierson 2000: 493). Commenting on the post-1989 eastern European constitution-making processes, Claus Offe observed that new institutions were designed "through the replication of old or spatially distant" exemplars, with participants alternatively offering a "model of the past or their own society" or an "imaginary transplantation of institutions across time and space" as benchmarks (Offe 1996). The rationality of constitutional designers, in short, is bounded in idiosyncratic and potent ways. To the extent that one views a course of action as unavailable to an agent if "historical, cultural, or psychological" circumstances mean it could not possibly come to mind (Williams 1973: 86), constitutional designers may in practice lack the conceptual and cognitive instruments to pursue aggregative welfarist goals to their logical conclusion in the first instance.

Beyond these practical difficulties, there are theoretical reasons to think MAW criteria will founder. The most intractable is a problem of time inconsistency. Constraints on constitutional design that emerge from existing distributions of political and social power, as well as epistemic and cognitive distortions, bite hardest at the moment of constitutional creation. But in subsequent periods, participants in a constitutional dispensation confront a distinct and different set of problems related to preserving a constitution and fostering economic growth or political stability. This means that the optimal design at the moment of a constitution's creation may be substantially different and distinct from the optimal design in later periods. Something of this dilemma is captured in Rousseau's contrast between the prince and the lawgiver: "The latter is the mechanic who invents the machine, the former is merely the workman who puts it together and makes it work" (2012: 191). By distinguishing these tasks and assigning them to different actors, Rousseau implicitly recognized that constitutional desiderata are likely to change in the wake of enactment.

Again, the American context supplies ready examples. The 1789 Constitution entrenches state governments' role in shaping the federal election and selecting federal lawmakers by vesting states with authority to define the electorate, delegating electoral regulation in the first instance to the states, and embedding state institutions into the process for selecting both the Senate and the Electoral College. The large role of state institutions in federal political processes is not plausibly understood as an efficient design choice aimed at maximizing social welfare. Rather, it was a necessary compromise in light of the abiding strength, circa 1787, of state institutions as vessels for political mobilization and nodes of political power. It is quite plausible to think that nationalizing the channels of national electoral choice would have lowered the social costs of governance while accelerating the integration of the national polity. Any efficiencies available from such nationalization, though, did not count from the perspective of 1787: The prince's problems crowded out entirely the lawgiver's. Without accounting precisely for the former, it is inapposite to criticize the latter's failures to maximize welfare.

Another example is the distinctive forms of constitutional protection elicited by economically powerful elites in the 1787 Constitution. Such elites, when confronting political reform movements, often fear confiscatory policies enabled by new institutional structures (Przeworski and Limongi 1993). To induce these elites into a constitutional bargain, it may be necessary to embed rights against redistributive policies into a constitution. The US Constitution's Contract Clause, Taking Clause, and diverse protections for slave property (including limits on congressional authority over the slave trade and the infamous three-fifth rule for congressional apportionment) are probably best understood as precisely this sort of compromise (Elster 1995: 217; see also Waldstreicher 2010). The constitutional compromises necessary to induce slave-holding factions' entrance into the 1787 constitutional deal had what might, at best, be called an ambiguous welfare effect. (Note again that the magnitude of this effect from the perspective of constitutional drafters varies depending on whether African-Americans' welfare "counts" – and note further that the fact that it obviously does for us does not settle the question.) Setting aside the (obvious and decisive) normative objections to slavery, the narrow point here is that there is a difficult trade-off between the threshold demands of elite constitution-making and the long-term ambition of maximizing a population's aggregate welfare.

The prince's perspective may have dominated in another way during the American constitution's creation. A threshold element of new nationhood in the late eighteenth-century American context was the creation of new non-governmental institutions, such as national political parties, with the attendant social infrastructure of allegiances and activists, national networks of financial institutions, and national markets. Each of these required reciprocal investments by regional political and social elites. Yet each regional elite might plausibly have withheld their cooperation for fear that others would either free-ride or would exploit sunk investments by changing the rules of the political game in later periods. One important function played by the new constitution was to alleviate such barriers to cooperation. In the US context, one means of its doing so was through the adoption of a rigid text that could not be amended by one faction as a way of exploiting others' sunk costs. Yet after the initial constitutional deal had congealed, and distinctively national institutions and patterns of interest-group politics began to emerge, a less rigid constitutional text may well have been desirable, even necessary, for the nation's survival and prosperity (Huq 2013a). Short of a two-speed constitutional amendment regime that differentiated explicitly between different periods of constitutional development, both goals would be hard to achieve. In consequence, constitutional drafters faced a perilous trade-off in the American context, with different species of constitutional design being appropriate at different moments of time.

A related problem is the downstream effect of constitutional rights. Imagine that one condition of a new constitution's adoption is the entrenching of certain minority rights, say, to religious freedom or cultural autonomy. These rights will be a friction on welfare maximization. There is a well-known impossibility result in welfare economics, developed first by Amartya Sen, called the paradox of a Paretian liberal (Sen 1970; see also Gibbard 1974). Sen demonstrated that it is not possible to be committed to both a parsimonious definition of liberty and also to the achievement of Pareto efficiency, which is a relatively undemanding welfarist criterion. Although there are ways to avoid the paradox, Sen's result implies yet another trade-off between the prince's and the lawgiver's ambitions: Any welfare maximizing constitutional design must be tailored to the distinct circumstances and trade-offs in rights allocation necessary for a constitution's creation.

Time inconsistencies of this kind suggest that constitutional designers cannot merely ask what maximizes aggregate welfare in the abstract. They must instead employ a hierarchy of criteria in which lexical priority is assigned to the first-period problem of managing the delicate process of constitutional adoption, and in which the subsequent-period task of maximizing aggregate welfare takes a back seat. The existence of several constraints on the domain of institutional design choices, in other words, has destabilizing effects on the confidence of prescriptions that rely on formal models of constitutional development. The task of constitutional design may instead be infected with the problem of the second-best (Lipsay and Lancaster 1956). This theoretical result, familiar from welfare economics, holds that when one optimality condition cannot be satisfied, a next-best solution may involve changing other parameters away from the values that would otherwise be optimal. The theory of the second best implies that even if there were a set of institutional design prescriptions thought to maximize welfare, it would not be possible to unbundle those recommendations, and to press for some when others are off the table due to the threshold conditions of constitution-making. It is a prescription for uncertainty: a pyre for any map toward sound constitutional design.

These difficulties are not merely hypothetical. Consider the by-now well-trodden debate about the comparative merits of presidentialist as opposed to parliamentary systems of government. As things now stand, the canonical criticism of presidentialism offered by Juan Linz (1990) has recently come under sustained and powerful criticism for failing to account for selection effects (Cheibub 2006). So let us assume that concerns about the stability of presidential system are indeed overwrought. Does that further suggest that the choice of a presidential system can be justified in long-term aggregative welfarist terms? The answer may depend on the particular set of economic challenges facing a polity. As Elster (1995: 209) notes, "some institutions may be feasible or effective only at specific level of economic development," such that the welfare effects of selecting between presidentialism and parliamentary forms of govern-ment turns on factors that vary wilxsdly between different contexts. The varying economic effects of presidential as opposed to parliamentary government is illuminated by a pair of recent studies focused on distinct elements of national economic performance. On the one hand, Persson and Tabellini (2005: 162) find that "under assumptions of conditional independence and linearity, the negative constitutional effect of presidential regimes on governmental size is large (between −5% and −8% of GDP) and robust to specification." On the other hand, Kohlscheen (2010: 63) finds that presidential regimes are much more likely to default on sovereign debt due to the different "micro-political games" fostered by the presence of a "compensation instrument directly tied to the survival of the executive" in parliamentary systems, i.e., the no-confidence vote, but not in presidential systems. Depending on whether fiscal discipline or credibility in the international bond market matters more (and also whether they conflict), these studies point in different directions in choices over pre-sidential and parliamentary systems. Complicating matters further, a decision can in practice be rendered even more intractable by uncertainty over the downstream effects of many important constitutional design choices given the state of social science evidence. Przeworski and Limongi (1993), for instance, emphasize the fragility of tractable inferences about the economic effects of democracy. Although research has advanced since they wrote, it remains the case that there are many dimensions of constitutional design choice that have not been subject to systematic study.

In sum, constitutional makers face considerable practical and theoretical obstacles to maximizing aggregative welfare. Of course, the mere prospect of such obstacles might not be preclusive. In the context of ordinary regulation, cost-benefit analysis is thought feasible notwithstanding deep epistemic and political difficulties. But whereas regulators can create institutions to concen-trate expertise and eliminate political biases – striving for optimal conditions for MAW analysis – constitutional designers do their work frontally exposed to the most destructive gales of historical change, and confront theoretical difficulties that regulators need not overcome. Their difficulties, in short, are plausibly understood to be of a different order of magnitude.

General objections to welfarism

To this point, I have implicitly assumed that MAW is a benchmark for evaluating constitutional design that implicates no controversial normative question. But evaluative criteria that focus on individual welfare, and that do so through some form of sum ranking, are themselves instantiations of substantive normative positions. As such they are hardly beyond controversy, and indeed have been exposed to considerable critiques within philosophy. As a benchmark for constitutional success, MAW metrics do not evade all of the concerns raised within philosophy literature. Three objections, developed most forcefully by Bernard Williams (1973), spill over to this context.

First, aggregative measures famously ignore distributive effects, and permit intra-population trade-offs that intuitively seem inconsistent with the project of constitution-making, and that instead arguably fail to "take seriously the distinction between persons" (Rawls 1972: 27). Hence, Williams (1973: 105) observes that a utilitarian calculus can, given a certain distribution of pre-judicial preferences targeting a certain racial minority in a jurisdiction, favor the "removal" of that minority. The same result can be reached (perhaps even compelled) if welfare is evaluated through a proxy such as per capita GDP: If the relevant minority is defined as outside the relevant polity, as African-Americans were in 1857, exploitation or "removal" of the relevant minority is especially easy to justify within the bounds of constitutional (if not moral) logic. Without relying upon what Harsanyi (in Sen and Williams 1982: 55) calls a "distinction between rational wants and irrational wants," it is hard to see how such conclusions can be avoided, notwithstanding their intuitive repugnance. To the extent participants in a constitution-making process disfavor a logic that would permit, or worse require, these results, aggregative welfarism might not appeal to them.

Second, Williams (1973: 116–17) developed a critique of utilitarianism based on the notion of commitments, understood as plans or projects that are central to a person's identity that cannot be abandoned in favor of the maximization of an impersonal aggregate of individual well-beings. When a person has plans or projects to which he or she is deeply committed, and that in some sense constitute "what his life is all about," Williams argued, it is "absurd to demand of such a man, when the sums come in from the utility network … that he should just step aside from his own projects."

Williams's argument from integrity applies, mutatis mutandi, to the project of constitution-making. On the one hand, Rousseau (2014: 227) is partly correct when he defines the "end" of political association as simply "the preservation and prosperity of its members." On the other hand, it is rarely the case that those who craft a political association care solely for the survival of that entity, and have no views about its substantive content or its direction and development over time. Indeed, to ask those who craft a society's foundational text to focus solely on aggregate welfare defined in the abstract is to ask them to exhibit a near superhuman degree of altruistic alienation from their own historical and social commitments. It is to ask them to set aside their own perceptions of the most hazardous political pathologies, and their own deeply felt and hard-won moral commitments. And most damningly, it is to ask them to set aside the very reasons that almost certainly impelled them in the first instance to set aside private profit and enter public life to engage in constitution-making. As with many of the recommendations proffered by the rational choice theorist, it is starkly incentive-incompatible. It is also sharply at odds with observed experience. As a historical matter, we simply do not see such inhuman detachment. The US Constitution, for example, may claim to merely "secure the Blessings of Liberty to ourselves and our Posterity." But in fact it is striated by the interests of state governments, slave-holders, and sectional interests.[2] In effect, demanding that constitutional drafters forego the very commitments that drove them to the barricades in the first instance is to ask for the psychologically inconceivable in circumstances in which the merely feasible may already be a tall order.

My final criticism of MAW benchmarks for constitutional design begins from the simple observation that it is highly unlikely that the members of a polity in which a constitution is being made themselves treat aggregative welfare as the sole bellwether of social choice. Few leaders hoist the banner of national GDP – as opposed to dignity, honor, or the common weal – when marching to war.[3] As Rousseau keenly noted, a constitution is unlikely to secure popular legitimacy and credibility unless "the law reigns over the hearts of the citizens" (Rousseau 1997: 178). But a constitution explicitly founded on MAW principles is unlikely to rouse hearts or kindle patriotic affiliations. Rather, the constitution must be modified away the welfarist optimum to cultivate appropriate public sentiments. In a rather marvelous turn of phrase, Rousseau intimated that this may be done via "children's games; through institutions which seem idle and frivolous to superficial men, but which form cherished habits and invincible attachments." Consistent with his insight, we see a proliferation of constitutional language concerning national flags, languages, and other expressive accouterments – none of which can be justified on direct welfarist grounds. Welfarist criteria, instead, might be taken to require a "division between a utilitarian elite and a non-utilitarian mass" that may, in practice, be rather practically untenable (Williams 1973: 139–40). Even if plausible, this sort of

---

[2] This is related to a familiar criticism of third-party enforcement solutions to collective action problems in the rational choice literature, i.e., the difficulty of imagining incentives for that enforcer not to shade rationally on her obligations.

[3] The current Chinese leadership may be an exception, but even they seem to perceive a need for some shared normative commitments too.

"government house constitutionalism" (Sen and Williams 1982: 16), seems unattractive as a starting point, at least for any constitutional order that has pretensions to democratic self-rule.

This last concern is related to the worry nicely captured in Bruno Frey's observation that a constitution "for knaves crowds out civic virtue." On Frey's persuasive account, the explicit provision of rewards and sanctions for socially desirable and reprehensible conduct respectively can lead individuals to perceive those concerns as extrinsic limits, and to abandon intrinsic motivations (1997: 1044–45). Echoing Rousseau, Frey can be read to suggest that a central purpose of constitutions is to "mold aspirations," to "shape expectations" and generally to serve to "rationalize actions," (Preuss 1991: 119), and that reliance on explicitly consequentialist instruments will generate dispositions and beliefs that are themselves irreconcilable with efficient government. Echoing the worry about government house constitutionalism, Frey's arguments provide yet another reason to think that aggregative welfarist criteria cannot easily be pressed into the service of the constitutional designer.

Reevaluating the role of maximum aggregate welfare considerations in constitutional design

No instrument that ranks constitutions by calculating the sum of individual well-being produced by a document can stand as a universally acceptable metric for constitutional success. Such an instrument must navigate normatively freighted questions of how to define the relevant population; account for first-period bargaining dynamics, epistemic constraints and later-period changes; and answer psychological objections commonly lodged against utilitarianism that have particular force in the constitutional context. Concededly, these overlapping objections are miscellaneous in character. Some are theoretic; others are empirical in their thrust, and so plainly apply only when certain conditions are met. Yet others, including the arguments about government house constitutionalism and vice crowding out virtue, dispute the psychological plausibility of welfarist targets at the cusp of a new constitution's operation. An advantage of this heterogeneity is that readers may be unmoved by some arguments, but still persuaded by others. Their conjoined effect, nevertheless, is in my view to undermine the plausibility and general applicability of an aggregative welfarist perspective on constitutional design that now dominates both theoretical and empirical debate.

To be clear, my claim is *not* that MAW has no relevance as a general matter, or that it should be a categorically impermissible consideration at the constitutional design stage. Rather, the considerations arrayed here suggest that any effort to *reduce* the evaluation of constitutional success to this one metric is unlikely to work. Aggregative welfarism does not stand outside the zone of expected normative disagreement embodied in the very diversity of internal criteria for constitutional quality. It cannot be operationalized without making controversial normative judgments. Its promise as a parsimonious measure against which different constitutional designs can be laid should therefore not be overstated.

III   HIPPOCRATIC CONSTITUTIONALISM: A MINIMALIST ACCOUNT OF CONSTITUTIONAL SUCCESS

Through the balance of this chapter, I sketch an alternative external metric of constitutional success that is more modest in its aspirations than aggregative welfarism, a metric that avoids the latter's limitations as a measure of constitutional success. This alternative benchmarks warrants the adjective "Hippocratic" because, parallel to the Hippocratic oath, it rests on the obligation to "take care that ... no hurt or damage" is inflicted via constitutional design (Copland 1825: 258).[4] Rather than a maximand, it counsels for attention to a floor for constitutional performance. The Hippocratic criterion for constitutional quality or success that I propose can be defined as follows: *A constitution succeeds qua constitution so long as, and to the extent that, its design does not contain elements that are likely to conduce unintentionally to the breakdown or dissolution of effective state functioning that it aims to enable.* In contrast, a constitution that unintentionally creates the conditions for, or a substantial risk of, the failure of the state that it is intended to establish should be adjudged a failure.

My claim is that this Hippocratic criterion is the most plausible external standard for evaluating constitutional success ex ante with broad applicability. I do not claim that the Hippocratic criterion is exclusive. To the contrary, it can operate alongside a wide range of internal criteria. To be sure, in some instances, there is conflict between the Hippocratic goal and internal criteria. It is instead, in that sense, pluralist in the sense developed by Isaiah Berlin.

In what follows, I begin by briefly outlining the origins of the term "constitution" and its modern usage. I then unpack the definition of Hippocratic constitutional quality, offering examples of its usage and anticipating some criticisms based on its similarity (but not identity) with contested concepts such as the maximin criterion for social choice and the precautionary principle.

---

[4]   As an aside, I am quite aware that the Hippocratic oath is more extensive in its regulative coverage: I use it here in its colloquial if incomplete sense as a heuristic device.

A short history of the term "constitution"

The term "constitution" emerged from a confluence of conflictive and inconsistent intellectual streams. It did not accrue its familiar contemporary implication of a written basic law until the sixteenth or seventeenth century. Previous usages entangled the term with distinct and different referents. In one of its earliest invocations,[5] Cicero used the term "constitutio" as a descriptive term for a political community "as it actually is," even though at the same time he possessed and deployed a concept of higher law that regulated and limited the latter (Maddox 1989: 51–55). Medieval ecclesiastical law deployed the term to pick out certain kinds of decrees (Hulsebosch 1998) Later thinkers such as the English political theorist Bolingbroke, invoking analogies between bodies political and natural, used the term to pick out the complex nest of institutions, practices, and customs that possessed effective legal force in England during the late seventeenth century (Stourzh 1998: 43). By the eighteenth century, the term had come to be aligned with written statutes and charters of rights as a consequence of the polemics of Thomas Paine and others. From its association with Paine and like-minded thinkers, a substantive gloss also accreted to the term, concerning then nascent aspirations of de-personalized limited government. It was only in this period of Enlightenment thinking that the idea of a written constitution came to be linked to the goal of a rule of law supervening and straitening the rule of man (Castiglione 1996). It was in that perfectionist spirit that Article 16 of the French 1789 Declaration of the Rights of Man and of the Citizen announced solemnly that "any society in which rights are not guaranteed, or in which the separation of powers is not defined, has no constitution." In short, the modern idea of a constitution has, by dint of the circumstances in which it assumed general currency, became aligned with, and entangled in, a liberal aspiration for limited, constrained government. At least today, the constitution without constraining rights is a rara avis.

But there is reason to think that these historicist glosses can be scraped away to reveal a minimalist account of what a constitution is and does. There is in particular no reason apart from blind fidelity to historical etiology to assume an affiliation between constitutionalism and the liberal aspiration of limited government. To the contrary, a constitution's distinctive function is more simply to provide a framework for the stable and predictable exercise of state power. That state may be liberal and minimalist or expansive and antiliberal. At whatever end of the liberal spectrum it falls, a state may benefit from a constitution. But a constitution without a state to organize is

---

[5] Aristotle's famous taxonomy, of course, used the term "politeia," not constitution (Pitkin 1987).

a categorically different beast from those exemplars generally grouped under that term.

Stated more forcefully, a constitution may do far more to enable the leviathan of the state than to tie it down. It typically assigns and clarifies roles amongst different state actors in a way that resolves coordination problems, induces stability, and generally facilitates the more effective use of state force. There is no particular reason to think this will produce liberal, let alone liberty-related, goods as outputs. At the same time, by solving the state's difficulty in making credible commitments in international financial markets, a constitution that divides and checks governmental powers can facilitate the state's fiscal expansion (North and Weingast 1989). Along this important, yet often ignored, margin, a written constitutional can literally engorge the state. Again, the necessarily liberal tilt of this dynamic is hard to discern. In sum, constitutions are intimately linked to the fostering and enabling of *states*, entities that over the eighteenth and nineteenth centuries transformed into "the most efficient engine of expansion and governance that the world had seen for centuries" (Maier 2014). A constitution's goal, then, is not *self*-preservation but *state* preservation.

On this account, the enterprise of constitution-making is implicitly committed to the Hobbesian dictum that there is nothing, or almost nothing, worse than the absence of a state. Just as Hobbes's skeptical view of the state of nature was animated by his experience of civil war, a contemporary constitutional analyst might consider the recent histories of Syria, Libya, or Somalia as a tutorial in the horrors of statelessness. Correlatively, there is no necessary nexus between constitutionalism and the recognition of basic rights, which are contingent, not necessary, features of constitutional design. It would be passing strange, for example, to reject the self-appellation of the 1789 American Constitution on the ground that it lacked any enumerated rights. Further, defining constitutionalism in terms of rights would raise insuperable questions about how to prioritize, define, and measure given rights. No less than liberal liberty, rights are no necessary corollary to a written constitution.

A minimal account of constitutions

Stripping away liberal accoutrements from the term "constitution" reveals a more useful, if more minimal, understanding of the core function of a constitution that can serve as a plausible universal criteria of constitutional performance. Given its close entanglement with the project of building states – liberal, communist, tyrannical, or democratic – it seems to me plausible to posit that "constitution" should be understood, at least for present minimalist purposes, to include a legally authoritative written account of at least some of the institutions necessary for the operation of the state over a given geographic space for some extended period of time. So long as official behavior is effectively coordinated, we can profitably speak of a constitution regardless of the normative quality of that behavior (Hardin 2015). On this view, a constitution's function is most intimately tied to the project of creating or maintaining a state through the textual articulation of formal institutions designed to extend in space and time.

States are necessarily territorial in nature (Copp 2005: 4). And they are intended to be temporally durable. A constitution articulates protocols and fashions official institutions such as a legislature, an executive or a judiciary as solutions to the coordination, collective action, commitment, and agency problems implicit in such an enterprise. The nature of the ensuing states – be it secular or sectarian, democratic or tyrannical, extractive or inclusive (Acemoglu and Robinson 2013) – is only weakly determined by the fact of having a constitution (e.g., it rules out constitutional design that changes dramatically every six months). Moreover, while it is hard to imagine a constitution that creates or ratifies no official institutions tasked with state management, it is equally unnecessary to identify any one specific institution that is necessary for the label of "state" to be affixed. Rather, to be a constitution maker, it is enough to accept a version of Hobbes's belief that to lack a state is to be in a condition far darker, far more dangerous than (almost) any sort of state at all.

In my view, this definition captures a core, irreducible function of constitutions in relation to the project of state-maintenance without committing to any further normative or positive aspirations. In this fashion, the definition is intended to be as consistent as feasible with as large a set of internal criteria as can be imagined. Whatever preferences and beliefs the participants in constitution-making processes bring to bear, therefore, the account offered here should prove compatible. Moreover, this definition is consistent in the mine run of cases with a wide array of purportedly universal normative criteria, including human rights, capabilities, maximum welfare, and other theories of justice.

This understanding also sidesteps several misleading implications, while providing a useful spur to thinking about constitutional success. Hence, it does not imply that written documents are necessary for a constitution, or that a written constitution where one exists is exhaustive. Instead, it acknowledges that some nations lack written constitutions, and that even where a written constitution obtains, it produces policy effects largely through diverse, unpredictable interactions between design features on the one hand and informal social norms, longstanding political practices, and an array of nonstate institutions such as political parties, market structures, and financial institutions on the other. My definition nevertheless assumes that a constitution is oriented toward the creation of state institutions, that the state is territorial in scope, and that one of the basic functions of the state of some stripe, facilitated by the constitution, is to exercise some measure of coercive control, or jurisdiction, over persons within its territory. It assumes, that is, that anarchists don't write constitutions.

Hippocratic constitutionalism as a minimal account of constitutional success

Starting with this minimal understanding of what a constitution does, it is possible to develop a related minimal account of constitutional quality or success. The idea that success turns on the absence of elements likely to conduce unintentionally to the breakdown or dissolution of effective state functioning that the document aims to enable, in essence, points to a kind of Hippocratic threshold for constitution makers. Their first, and central, tenet should be to do no harm. Elements that produce a breakdown of state functioning, either by endogenous interactions or through particularized interactions with local circumstances, are to be strongly disfavored. This definition, however, sets to one side cases of transitional constitutions, where the regime's terminus is anticipated and welcomed as the gateway to a more permanent regime (Rosenn 1990).

The definition presumes that the central ambition of a written constitution is the creation of a temporally durable and reasonably effective set of state institutions. Whatever else divides them, it posits, all constitution makers see the need for a state. Hence, to focus on the state-enabling role of constitutions is to drill down to a common functional core that comprises a minimal condition of welfare enhancement under almost all circumstances. In this fashion, the Hippocratic criterion is generally welfarist in orientation. That said, it is not maximizing in ambition. It is rather easy to imagine circumstances in which a constitution succeeds in the sense of fostering successful state institutions, which in turn cultivate merely a tolerable misery, or trap peoples in a local utility maximum. Such instruments might "work" as constitutions, but fail comprehensively on other terms.

What, though, does state failure mean exactly? Precise quantification of the latter term is feasible, as King and Zeng (2001) demonstrate. For my purposes, though, it suffices to have merely an intuitive sense of the term (cf. Rotberg 2002). It is enough to say that the concept of state failure implies an ongoing, comprehensive inability of otherwise duly constituted institutions to fulfill their anticipated governance responsibilities in a stable fashion. The failure of the American Articles of Confederation is one famous example. More recently, we might look to examples such as Somalia or pre-1971 Pakistan, which failed for different reasons. Also, the failure of the Weimar Constitution, although not accompanied by state breakdown in strict terms, might also fall within the class of aversive counterexamples: The regime that ensued is that rara avis that was worse than the absence of any state at all. No doubt, there are many pathways to state failure, many close cases, and many instances in which some, but not all institutional behavior will fit the bill. As a correlative, there are many forms of statehood, and beyond a weak form of legality and regularity, they may be quite diverse.[6] These ambiguities at the margin, no less than the causal pluralism of state failure, are not terribly relevant here: It is enough for my purposes that the core idea of state failure is clear enough to focus our attention as constitutional designers.[7]

Also, it bears reiteration once more that a Hippocratic benchmark for constitutional design focused on state failure is not intended to be exclusive. To the contrary, it can operate alongside a wide variety of internal criteria and normatively committed external criteria (e.g., Rawls's or the capabilities approach; socialism; or even racial apartheid). Rather than purporting to be exhaustive, the Hippocratic benchmark is valuable precisely because it provides a single narrow evaluative criterion closely linked to the necessary ambitions implicit in writing down a constitution. Applied ex ante to a proposed constitutional design, moreover, the Hippocratic benchmark does not compel a binary response. Rather, it asks an analyst to identify risks of state failure that emerge causally from constitutional design. Its application nevertheless requires attention to both purely endogenous design risk – when a given constitutional design feature is likely to conduce to breakdown regardless of circumstantial variation – and dynamic risks – produced by the interaction of a constitution's design and the particular circumstances in which a constitution is adopted. In focusing upon the diverse sources of catastrophic system failure, my approach echoes Charles Perrow's (2011) account of how to handle catastrophic risk in infrastructure design via "target reduction." In both

---

[6] A worry here is that reliance on the idea of state maintenance implicitly smuggles in other normative considerations. My aim is to minimize the normative connotations of state maintenance by maintaining as capacious and catholic a conception of the state as possible. Hence, I am not committed to any specific institutional forms of statehood. I am committed, though, to the idea of a state comprising temporally durable institutions of some sort that work to promote the state as a going concern.

[7] Alternatively, the analysis here might be refined by recognizing a close relation between the constitution and the state, and by suggesting that the definition of a successful constitution is at its core parasitic on the definition of a successful state.

contexts, the analyst's goal is to isolate the most important concentrations of design-induced catastrophic risk, and then to consider whether those risks can be plausibly mitigated or diluted. A central task for scholars and jurists engaged in evaluative comparatives of new written constitutions should similarly comprise an exhaustive identification of all the potential downward institutional spirals immanent in a constitution's design.

Constitutions can engender self-destructive outcomes in several ways, and an application of the Hippocratic benchmark needs to start with some sense of when a design feature conduces to state failure, rather than some abstract theory. We gain this sense largely through an examination of past constitutional histories. At the same time, a priori analysis is not irrelevant. For instance, it is important to remain cognizant of Vermeule's (2013) caution that institution design risks can be bilateral, such that both the inclusion and the exclusion of a certain design feature can have adverse effects. Nevertheless, the complexity of risk analysis renders comparative and historical analysis of constitutional dynamics especially important. Realistically, it is only through the examination of historical experience that we obtain some perspective on whether a particular design feature conduces to the risk of state failure, and then secure some estimate of the risk's magnitude. Even then, it is quite plausible that analysts will disagree about what counts as a self-defeating constitutional design decision. Although I identify some examples below, I readily concede that others may think my examples are more manageable than I make out, whereas other flaws are more painfully disabling. Such disagreement, though, is to be welcomed rather than shunned. It is the sort of analysis that Hippocratic constitutional design ought to foster.

It is not my aim here to chart comprehensively the full spectrum of endogenous design risks, or to predict how future academic work (empirical or qualitative) might go about mapping that terrain. Rather, I will highlight some examples of serious risks, one pertaining to the institution of judicial review, and the other related to emergency powers. The first is purely endogenous, and the second emerges from the interaction of constitutional design with local political circumstances. The first concerns the 2004 Afghan constitution, which created a risk of state failure by creating two seemingly final forums for the resolution of contested constitutional questions. That constitution envisaged both a Supreme Court with a power of constitutional review in Article 121 and a "Commission for Supervision of the Implementation of the Constitution" in Article 157. In 2007, the executive and legislature lined behind each of these two bodies, creating a sharp conflict among national political institutions as to how constitutional conflicts would be resolved (Ginsburg and Huq 2014). That conflict created a substantial (and ex ante predictable) risk of state failure that could have precluded resolution of all contested constitutional question, while driving a wedge into the functioning of ordinary government. It did so without any offsetting gain. By 2015, though, Afghan political institutions had largely overcome that risk by reaching a working compromise over the different functions of the Court and the Commission. Although Afghan institutions were able to navigate the crisis, their experience nonetheless has a simple lesson for constitution makers that when the power of constitutional review is being assigned, only one body should receive it.

Second, emergency powers provide an important example of bilateral design risk. On the one hand, as early as Rousseau (2012), it has been clear that the absence of any emergency powers can engender a fatal inflexibility in constitutional dispensations. On the other hand, it is also familiar that an overly permissive emergency powers clause can accelerate the collapse of a democratic constitutional regime. The canonical example is Article 48 of the Weimar Constitution, which authorized the Republic's president to use military force when in his opinion law and order were seriously threatened. Between 1919 and 1932, Article 48 was invoked more than 250 times, and became the primary source of law-making authority. The Reichtag was side-lined, and eventually dissolved using Article 48 (Gross and Aoláin 2006: 83–84). The failure-related risks of emergency powers, in short, are bilateral: An analyst must reach a judgment about which risk is more salient based on her assessment of the circumstances in which a given constitution is adopted.

All this may seem uncontroversial enough. But more ambitious inferences can also be drawn by Hippocratic methods. For instance, it may well be that my minimalist benchmark for constitutional design counsels for resistance to democratic or rights-related goals under quite specific (albeit likely narrow) circumstances. The goal of state creation or preservation, that is, can conflict with other deeply held normative ambitions. Hence, it seems to be quite plausible to think that installation of certain forms of democracy under conditions of sharp ethnic or religious division would conduce to state failure. Equally, it is quite possible that violations of free associational or religious expression rights (e.g., forms of lustration or bans on fascist parties) might be justified in certain circumstances as necessary to the survival of the state. Such normative conflicts, as Berlin most famously argued, are inevitable (unless one is very lucky) and extremely hard to resolve. It is by no means clear that state preservation will always be prioritized, and it is quite plausible to think constitutional designers will sometime pursue internal desiderata at the risk of state failure. Moreover, that arguments based on the risk of state failure are vulnerable to strategic misuse seems clear – but also no justification for their categorical rejection. Such hard choices, though, are perhaps the normative kernel of constitutional design's difficulties.

The criterion offered here has a certain kinship with the maximin criterion for social choice and the precautionary principle. Like those decision protocols, it focuses asymmetrically on potential bads, and ignores potential goods. The modesty of the Hippocratic criterion's expected scope of operation, however, means that it is not subject to the serious criticisms offered of both maximum and the precautionary principle. For example, Harsanyi (1975) has used numerical examples to show that maximin generates implausible results when the probability of the worst outcome is very small. My formulation of the Hippocratic benchmark, though, isolates likely sources of catastrophic risk and excludes instances in which the likelihood of catastrophe is exiguously small. In addition, my use of a maximin-like criterion can be justified by the observation that our knowledge and confidence about potential goods and potential bads in the constitution-making context is asymmetric. It is straightforward to catalogue a pool of self-defeating design margins, and we know that all constitution makers will seek to avoid state failure. By contrast, variation in internal criteria means we can say less about what qualifies as a constitutional triumph, and claims to that effect will generally be contestable. Hence, there is in fact a rather basic asymmetry between "goods" and "bads" in the constitutional creation context. A maximin-type measure is well suited to such cases of asymmetrical information (Rawls 1974).

While consequentialist in general orientation, the Hippocratic benchmark is less vulnerable than MAW to the feasibility and motivational critiques developed previously. Simply put, it demands less cognitively of constitutional architects merely to refrain from self-defeating design feature, especially if the enumeration of such features is relatively brief. Because it is largely negative in character, the Hippocratic benchmark also implicates to a much lesser degree concerns about time-consistency, distributive justice, and integrity.

Finally, the criticisms of the precautionary principle that have been refined by Vermeule (2013) and Sunstein (2009), among others, are not forceful in this context. Both Vermeule and Sunstein caution against cognitive bias in the perception of different risks, and stress the need to attend to both the magnitude and probability of all risks. Both points are well taken, but they do not impinge on the modest and justified asymmetry embedded in the Hippocratic benchmark. As noted already, the latter is not intended to be exclusive – but rather a threshold test that accounts for risks that would prevent a constitution from creating a stream of future benefits in the first instance. The Hippocratic benchmark also purport to account solely for one set of threshold risks common to all (or almost all) instances of constitution-making, risks that if realized would mean that no other benefit could accrue from constitution-making. In operation, moreover, the Hippocratic oath can and should be attentive to bilateral risks, i.e., ones that emerge if too little or too much of a design feature is included, as the example of emergency powers illustrates.

At best, therefore, the Hippocratic benchmark would operate with lexical priority in relation to other internal and external criteria of constitutional success, and not crowd out other potential evaluative tools. It would, to be sure, install a bias against heady aspirations at the inception of any constitutional analysis. But this asymmetry would, I suspect, operate as a moderating antidote to the utopian projects and distant fancies that ordinarily attend constitution-making.

IV   CONCLUSION

The Hippocratic benchmark does not at first encounter sound very demanding, even as a threshold evaluative instrument that can coexist with other internal and external criteria. But it is worth recalling again that, nostalgic deification of the American Framers aside, written constitutions are almost never drawn up in ideal circumstances (Elster 1995). Instead, these documents tend to be the fruit of violent conflict, social or economic upheaval, or tectonic shifts in geopolitical alignments. Participants in constitution-making processes usually operate under tremendous immediate circumstantial stresses. They are at eminent risk of error, and perhaps court disaster if they delay. Partly as a result, they often reach first for off-the-rack exemplars from the past or from superficially salient examples in the international domain. Further, recall that constitution makers operate under tremendous political constraints. Past institutions usually do not vanish into air, while whatever elites exist at the moment of constitution-making are hardly likely to stand by while their power is dissipated. A constitution can only be as good as the elites let it be, and this will often be not very good at all.

The alternative I offer here takes full account of these circumstantial limitations. It is also appropriately chastened by the difficulty of accommodating the full spectrum of internal criteria imaginable. Heeding first Rousseau's advice, it skirts what Oakeshott (1991: 27) described as "the politics of the felt need ... not qualified by a genuine, concrete knowledge of the permanent interests and direction of movement of a society," a fallacy into which aggregative welfarism can easily fall. Heeding next Machiavelli's advice, it takes the ambition of "*mantenere lo stato*" seriously, perhaps even at the cost of abrogating other attractive normative aspirations. To offer a Hippocratic account of constitutional success, therefore, may well be to articulate a metric that plausibly can be applied and satisfied in many instances in the teeth of both circumstantial constraints and deep normative disagreement. For better or worse, it is a rule for practical men and women, rather than a noble aspiration that eludes realistic human grasp.

REFERENCES

Acemoglu, Daron, and James Robinson. 2013. *Why Nations Fail: The Origins of Power, Prosperity, and Poverty*. Reprint edition. New York: Crown Business.

Alesina, Alberto, and Enrico Spolaore. 2005. *The Size of Nations*. The MIT Press.

Arjomand, Saïd Amir. 2007. "Islamic Constitutionalism." *Annual Review of Law and Social Science* 3 (1): 115–40. doi:10.1146/annurev.lawsocsci .3.081806.112753.

Bagehot, Walter. 2009. *The English Constitution*. Edited by Miles Taylor. Reissue edition. Oxford: Oxford University Press.

Blume, Lorenz, Jens Müller, Stefan Voigt, and Carsten Wolf. 2008. "The Economic Effects of Constitutions: Replicating – and Extending – Persson and Tabellini." *Public Choice* 139 (1–2): 197–225. doi:10.1007/s11127-008-9389-4.

Broome, John. 1994. "Discounting the Future." *Philosophy & Public Affairs* 23 (2): 128–56.

——— 2000. "Cost Benefit Analysis and Population." *Journal of Legal Studies* 29 (S2): 953–70. doi:10.1086/468101.

Castiglione, Dario. 1996. "The Political Theory of the Constitution." *Political Studies* 44 (3): 417–35. doi:10.1111/j.1467-9248.1996.tb00592.x.

Cheibub, Jose Antonio. 2006. *Presidentialism, Parliamentarism, and Democracy*. New York: Cambridge University Press.

Copland, James. 1825. *The London Medical Repository*.

Copp, David. 1999. "The Idea of a Legitimate State." *Philosophy & Public Affairs* 28 (1): 3–45. doi:10.1111/j.1088-4963.1999.00003.x.

Elkins, Zachary, Tom Ginsburg, and James Melton. 2009. *The Endurance of National Constitutions*. Cambridge, UK; New York: Cambridge University Press.

Elster, Jon. 1995. "Forces and Mechanisms in the Constitution-Making Process." *Duke Law Journal* 45 (2): 364–96. doi:10.2307/1372906.

Foweraker, J., and T. Landman. 2002. "Constitutional Design and Democratic Performance." *Democratization* 9 (2): 43–66. doi:10.1080/ 714000250.

Frey, Bruno. 1997. "A Constitution for Knaves Crowds Out Civic Virtues." *The Economic Journal* 107 (443): 1043–53. doi:10.1111/j.1468-0297.1997 .tb00006.x.

Gibbard, Allan. 1974. "A Pareto-Consistent Libertarian Claim." *Journal of Economic Theory* 7 (4): 388–410. doi:10.1016/0022-0531(74)90111-2.

Ginsburg, Tom. 2003. *Judicial Review in New Democracies. Constitutional Courts in Asian Cases*. First edition used edition. Cambridge, UK; New York: Cambridge University Press.

Ginsburg, Tom, Svitlana Chernykh, and Zachary Elkins. 2008. "Commitment and Diffusion: How and Why National Constitutions Incorporate International Law." *University of Illinois Law Review* 2008: 201.

Ginsburg, Tom, and Aziz Huq. 2014. "What Can Constitutions Do? The Afghan Case." *Journal of Democracy* 25 (1): 116–30. doi:10.1353/jod.2014.0005.

Goodin, Robert E., ed. 1998. *The Theory of Institutional Design*. Cambridge, UK; New York: Cambridge University Press.

Gray, John. 1994. "After the New Liberalism." *Social Research* 61 (3): 719–35.

Greene, Jamal. 2009. "On the Origins of Originalism." *Texas Law Review* 88: 1.

Gross, Oren, and Fionnuala Ní Aoláin. 2006. *Law in Times of Crisis: Emergency Powers in Theory and Practice*. Cambridge, UK: Cambridge University Press.

Hafner-Burton, Emilie M., and Kiyoteru Tsutsui. 2005. "Human Rights in a Globalizing World: The Paradox of Empty Promises." *American Journal of Sociology* 110 (5): 1373–411. doi:10.1086/428442.

2007. "Justice Lost! The Failure of International Human Rights Law to Matter Where Needed Most." *Journal of Peace Research* 44 (4): 407–25. doi:10.1177/0022343307078942.

Hardin, Russell. 2015. "Why a Constitution?" In *Social and Political Foundations of Constitutions*. Edited by Mila Versteeg, and Dennis Gilligan. Cambridge, UK; New York: Cambridge University Press.

Harsanyi, John C. 1975. "Can the Maximin Principle Serve as a Basis for Morality? A Critique of John Rawls's Theory." *American Political Science Review* 69 (02): 594–606. doi:10.2307/1959090.

Hirschl, Ran. 2007. *Towards Juristocracy: The Origins and Consequences of the New Constitutionalism*. Cambridge, MA; London: Harvard University Press.

Hulsebosch, Daniel J. 1998. "The Constitution in the Glass Case and Constitutions in Action." *Law and History Review* 16 (02): 397–401. doi:10.2307/744108.

Huq, Aziz Z. 2013a. "The Function of Article V." *University of Pennsylvania Law Review* 162: 1165.

2013b. "Libertarian Separation of Powers." *New York University Journal of Law and Liberty* 8: 1006.

King, Gary and Langche Zeng. 2001. "Improving Forecasts of State Failure." *World Politics* 53 (04): 623–58. doi:10.1353/wp.2001.0018.

Kohlscheen, Emanuel. 2010. "Sovereign Risk: Constitutions Rule." *Oxford Economic Papers* 62 (1): 62–85. doi:10.1093/oep/gpp005.

Kysar, Douglas A. 2007. "Discounting . . . on Stilts." *University of Chicago Law Review* 74: 119.

Linz, Juan J. 1990. "The Perils of Presidentialism." *Journal of Democracy* 1 (1): 51–69.

Lipsey, R. G., and Kelvin Lancaster. 1956. "The General Theory of Second Best." *The Review of Economic Studies* 24 (1): 11–32. doi:10.2307/2296233.

Maddox, G., 1989. "Constitution." In *Political Innovation and Conceptual Change*. Edited by Terence Ball, James Farr, and Russell L. Hanson, 50–65. Cambridge, UK; New York: Cambridge University Press.

Maier, Charles S. 2014. *Leviathan 2.0: Inventing Modern Statehood*. Cambridge, MA: Belknap Press.

Maier, Pauline. 2011. *Ratification: The People Debate the Constitution, 1787–1788*. 5.8.2011 edition. Simon & Schuster.

March, James G., and Johan P. Olsen. 1975. "The Uncertainty of the Past: Organizational Learning under Ambiguity." *European Journal of Political Research* 3 (2): 147–71. doi:10.1111/j.1475-6765.1975.tb00521.x.

McGinnis, John O., and Michael B. Rappaport. 2013. *Originalism and the Good Constitution*. Cambridge, MA: Harvard University Press.

Miller, Gary. 2000. "Rational Choice and Dysfunctional Institutions." *Governance* 13 (4): 535–47. doi:10.1111/0952-1895.00145.

North, Douglass C., and Barry R. Weingast. 1989. "Constitutions and Commitment: The Evolution of Institutions Governing Public Choice in Seventeenth-Century England." *The Journal of Economic History* 49 (04): 803–32. doi:10.1017/S0022050700009451.

Nussbaum, Martha C. 2007. "Constitutions and Capabilities: Perception against Lofty Formalism." *Harvard Law Review* 121: 4.

Oakeshott, Michael. 1991. *Rationalism in Politics and Other Essays*. Expanded edition. Indianapolis: Liberty Fund.

Offe, Claus. 1996. "Designing Institutions in Eastern European Transitions." In *The Theory of Institutional Design*. Edited by Robert E. Goodin. Cambridge, UK; New York: Cambridge University Press.

Olsen, Johan P. 1997. "Institutional Design in Democratic Contexts." *Journal of Political Philosophy* 5 (3): 203–29. doi:10.1111/1467-9760.00032.

Perrow, Charles. 2011. *The Next Catastrophe: Reducing Our Vulnerabilities to Natural, Industrial, and Terrorist Disasters*. With a new preface by the author edition. Princeton: Princeton University Press.

Persson, Torsten, and Guido Tabellini. 2005. *The Economic Effects of Constitutions*. The MIT Press.

Peterson, Martin. 2009. *An Introduction to Decision Theory*. First edition. New York: Cambridge University Press.

Pierson, Paul. 2000. "The Limits of Design. Explaining Institutional Origins and Change." *Governance* 13 (4): 475–99. doi:10.1111/0952-1895.00142.

Pitkin, Hanna Fenichel. 1987. "The Idea of a Constitution." *Journal of Legal Education* 37 (2): 167–69.

Preuss, Ulrich K. 1991. "The Politics of Constitution Making: Transforming Politics into Constitutions." *Law & Policy* 13 (2): 107–23. doi:10.1111/j.1467-9930.1991.tb00061.x.

Przeworski, Adam, and Fernando Limongi. 1993. "Political Regimes and Economic Growth." *The Journal of Economic Perspectives* 7 (3): 51–69.

Rawls, John. 1972. *A Theory of Justice*. Cambridge, MA: Belknap Press.

——— 1974. "Some Reasons for the Maximin Criterion." *The American Economic Review* 64 (2): 141–46.

Rosenn, Keith S. 1990. "Brazil's New Constitution: An Exercise in Transient Constitutionalism for a Transitional Society." *The American Journal of Comparative Law* 38 (4): 773–802. doi:10.2307/840612.

Rotberg, Robert I. 2002. "The New Nature of Nation-State Failure." *The Washington Quarterly* 25 (3): 83–96. doi:10.1162/01636600260046253.

Rousseau, Jean-Jacques. 1997. *Rousseau: "The Social Contract" and Other Later Political Writings*. Edited by Victor Gourevitch. Cambridge, UK; New York: Cambridge University Press.

——— 2012. *The Major Political Writings of Jean-Jacques Rousseau: The Two "Discourses" and the "Social Contract."* Edited by John T. Scott. Reprint edition. University of Chicago Press.

Samida, Dexter, and David A. Weisbach. 2007. "Paretian Intergenerational Discounting." *University of Chicago Law Review* 74: 145.

Sen, Amartya. 1970. "The Impossibility of a Paretian Liberal." *Journal of Political Economy* 78 (1): 152–57.

——— 1979a. "Personal Utilities and Public Judgements: Or What's Wrong with Welfare Economics." *The Economic Journal* 89 (355). 537–58. doi:10.2307/2231867.

——— 1979b. "Utilitarianism and Welfarism." *The Journal of Philosophy* 76 (9): 463–89. doi:10.2307/2025934.

Sen, Amartya, and Bernard Williams, eds. 1982. *Utilitarianism and Beyond*. First printing edition. Cambridge; New York: Cambridge University Press.

Stanger, Allison. 2004. "How Important Are New Constitutions for Democratic Consolidation? Lessons from the Post-Communist States." *Democratization* 11 (3), 1–26. doi:10.1080/1351034042000238149.

Stourzh, G. 1998. "Constitution: Changing Meanings of the Term from the Early Seventeenth to the Late Eighteenth Century." In *Conceptual Change and the Constitution*. Edited by Terence Ball and J. G. A. Pocock, 35–54. Lawrence, KS: University Press of Kansas.

Sunstein, Cass R. 1991. "Constitutionalism and Secession." *The University of Chicago Law Review* 58 (2): 633–70. doi:10.2307/1599969.

——— 1995. "Incompletely Theorized Agreements." *Harvard Law Review* 108 (7): 1733–72. doi:10.2307/1341816.

——— 2009. *Worst-Case Scenarios*. Cambridge, MA: Harvard University Press.

Vermeule, Adrian. 2013. *The Constitution of Risk*. New York: Cambridge University Press.

Waldstreicher, David. 2010. *Slavery's Constitution: From Revolution to Ratification*. First edition. New York; Godalming: Hill and Wang.

Weinstock, Daniel. 2001. "Constitutionalizing the Right to Secede." *Journal of Political Philosophy* 9 (2): 182–203. doi:10.1111/1467-9760.00124.

Weisbach, David, and Cass R. Sunstein. 2009. "Climate Change and Discounting the Future: A Guide for the Perplexed." *Yale Law & Policy Review* 27 (2): 433–57.

Williams, B. 1973. "A Critique of Utilitarianism." In *Utilitarianism: For and Against*. Edited by J. J. C. Smart and Bernard Williams, 77–150. Cambridge, UK: Cambridge University Press.

3

What is a good constitution? Assessing the constitutional proposal in the Icelandic experiment

Hélène Landemore

Between 2010 and 2013 Iceland engaged in an unprecedented experiment in peacetime constitutional redrafting. The process included innovative participatory methods, including a National Forum, an elected Constitutional Assembly of non-professional politicians, and the well-known use of online crowdsourcing for twelve successive drafts of the constitutional proposal (which earned the latter its international, and perhaps overhyped, reputation as the "crowdsourced constitution"). Begun in the aftermath of a cataclysmic banking and financial crisis, which was estimated to have destroyed assets equivalent at the time to seven times the country's annual GDP, and spurred on by the new political personnel that came to power after the "Pots-and-Pans" revolution of 2008, the constitutional process ultimately led to a proposal that was approved by a two-third majority of the voters in the fall of 2012. After further amendments by legal experts, the proposal was offered to the Althingi (the Icelandic Parliament) as a bill to be discussed and voted on in the spring of 2013. To many commentators' surprise, however, the bill was shelved at the eleventh hour for reasons that seem more political than substantive (Gylfason 2013b). The crowdsourced constitutional proposal is now considered dead by its opponents and "on ice" by its advocates (2014). It is unclear at this point whether it still stands a chance to be adopted as such in the near future.

The question that interests us here, however, is whether the crowdsourced proposal meant to replace the 1944 constitution was a *good* constitution – not merely in the sense of having been produced by the right kind of process but in

I would like to acknowledge and thank the Yale McMillan Center for funding the translation of the expert-written constitutional proposals used in this chapter. I thank Dr. Jón Skaptason for the translation and former Supreme Court judge Hjörtur Torfason for checking it. I also thank various audiences for useful feedback on the chapter, including participants in the conference "How Do Constitutions Succeed?" organized by Tom Ginsburg and Aziz Huq at the University of Chicago Law School on April 24–25, 2015. Special thanks also to Joshua Braver and the editors of this volume for insightful comments on various drafts.

a thicker, more substantive sense, which is entirely independent of the process that led to it. Previous work on the Icelandic experiment has focused on procedural aspects of the constitutional process. For example, in past work I argued that the Icelandic constitutional process aimed to be inclusive of the full diversity of the Icelandic people's views and to the extent that it succeeded, could be expected to have produced a substantively sound constitution, that is, a constitution tracking relevant facts and values of the Icelandic people in the twenty-first century and channeling its collective wisdom (Landemore 2015). The constitutional proposal could be expected to be good, in other words, in the sense of meeting objective (though not necessarily universal) standards of quality. Such work, however, said nothing about the actual substance of the constitutional document itself, focusing instead on the properties of the procedure. What interests us here is the possibility of testing the claim that the Icelandic constitutional proposal was a *good* constitution, not just the result of a good procedure (since even good processes, after all, sometimes produce poor results).

A difficulty in performing this substantive assessment is that a constitutional proposal that has not become law does not lend itself to empirical validation or testing. It is thus impossible to say whether this constitutional proposal would have succeeded in its implementation and in terms of the governance outcomes it would have generated on the short, mid, and long term (although one can probably speculate about plausible outcomes). By the kind of external standard recommended by Ginsburg and Huq (Chapter 1), in which a first condition of success is existence, it is simply the case that the old 1944 constitution has proved more "successful" than the crowdsourced one, which was supposed to replace it.

My question here shall thus be a different one, and one that is to some extent orthogonal to the other contributions to this volume. It is not: Was the crowdsourced constitution successful? But: As a constitutional text, is it any good? In other words, does the crowdsourced constitution have properties that make it deserving of being implemented – to become an actual constitution – including perhaps because it is likely to be successful? Another question is comparative: Is it "better" in any meaningful sense than the existing constitution? Is it better than rival constitutional drafts that were written at roughly the same time?

A reason to focus on this particular constitutional proposal in this particular country, as opposed to any other constitutional proposal in any other country, is partly access (I happen to have sources there that I do not have in any other country) and partly the fact that the Icelandic situation offers several advantages, including crucially the fact that several quasi simultaneous, fully developed, and non-rushed draft proposals are available for comparison.[1]

Two of those drafts were written by experts roughly at the same time as the crowdsourced constitution and were meant to serve as the original blueprints for the latter. This convenient fact renders the assessment of the crowdsourced constitution more feasible, in that it sets a realistic benchmark of what was feasible at the time, as opposed to the too low bar of the now undeniably dated 1944 constitution and the too high bar of a "perfect" constitution with no detectable flaws whatsoever.

Was the crowdsourced constitution substantially any good? The fact that the crowdsourced proposal was approved in a 2012 referendum would seem to speak to its strengths. Conversely, the fact that the Icelandic Parliament ultimately shelved it would seem to speak to its weaknesses.[2] In order to answer the question with some rigor, we need to determine the standards by which a constitution could be said to be "good." Section 1 turns to this normative task. Section 2 then introduces the various candidates for assessment in the Icelandic case. As it turns out there were there are at least five texts available – the original constitution, two proposals written by experts, the crowdsourced proposal submitted to the 2012 referendum, and a later version of the crowdsourced proposal edited by legal experts and submitted as a bill to Parliament. Section 3 takes a first stab at assessing these various texts in the absolute, in comparison with each other, and in light of two of the normative criteria delineated in Section 1 (rights-heaviness and democraticity). I conclude that the Icelandic constitutional proposal was in general a good proposal and an undeniable improvement over the 1944 constitution and the expert drafts along several important dimensions. It also had a bonus feature that marks a great constitution, namely, to be inspiring, as it has the best preamble of all the competing drafts.

1   WHAT IS A GOOD CONSTITUTION?

There are several answers one could try to give to such a daunting question, all of which refer to distinct standards of evaluation. Carey (2009) argues that three features characterize a high-quality constitutional document according

---

[1]   Other examples of constitutional drafts that it would be interesting to compare in similar fashion are the Girondin proposal drawn up by the marquis de Condorcet as an alternative to the Jacobin one of 1793 and Siéyès's proposal for 1799 that Napoléon radically altered and then adopted. Thanks to Joshua Braver for this point.

[2]   Unless Gylfason (2013b and 2014) is right and the failure of the constitution is simply a coup of the politicians, which is highly plausible from his account. But I want to bracket this possibility for now.

to the relevant academic literature: (1) "democracy"; (2) temperance; and (3) durability. Democracy refers to a property of the institutions defined by the constitutional context. Temperance refers to qualities within a constitution that establish limits on the power of officeholders, lowers the stakes of politics, and encourages moderation and measured deliberation.[3] Durability, finally, refers to constitutional stability and resilience over time.

In the following I propose to embrace these criteria, while refining them and adding a few. But let me first point out that I take for granted that in order to be considered a *good* constitution, a proposal must first minimally qualify as a constitution, even a bad one. A constitution is, arguably, a body of fundamental principles or established precedents recognized as legitimately governing, or meant to be recognized as legitimately governing, a state or other organization.[4] This body of principles or precedents stipulates the powers and limits of the government and guarantees certain rights to the members of the organization. Two important functions of a constitution are thus to serve as a second-order procedure determining how a polity is, on the one hand, to go about its first-order decisions and, on the other, to protect certain fundamental individual rights. Notice that nothing in this definition suggests that a constitution needs to be written.

Assuming a given considered text or set of precedents qualifies as a constitution as just defined, what are now the criteria for a "good" constitution? The first criterion I propose to introduce has to do with the formal qualities of the constitution itself. Of all the criteria offered later this one is probably the least favorable to unwritten constitutions. Formal qualities include concision, clarity, and logical coherence. For a written constitution, these qualities can be assessed in terms of how well the text is written, how clear it is in structure and organization, and whether the parts add up to a logically coherent whole.

Concision may seem like an odd and perhaps unnecessary requirement. Yet long-windedness can eventually get in the way of clarity, as it did in the case of the 300-page European constitutional proposal that was ultimately rejected in various referendums. The US Constitution, which sets the benchmark for brevity, has been praised for this feature, which some credit as an explanation of the extraordinary longevity of the text. There is, further some reasonable empirical evidence that long constitutions are "worse" – in terms of governance outcomes – than shorter ones (Tsebelis and Nardi 2016).

---

[3] With these latter criteria, we are presumably entering the domain of "just" constitutions. Does a "good" constitution need also to be "just"? I assume that the answer is yes, at least partly.

[4] Freely adapted from the online Oxford dictionary definition: www.oxforddictionaries.com/us/definition/american_english/constitution

Clarity and logical coherence, on the face of it, need no justification. They seem essential in determining what others have called "interpretability" or "the ability to produce inter-subjective agreement about the meaning of a text" (Melton, Elkins, Ginsburg, and Leetaru 2013: 400). One could nonetheless argue that too much clarity and coherence are in fact liabilities in a context of deep disagreement and partisan divide. Ambiguity and lack of clarity, by contrast, may help parties achieve "incompletely theorized agreements" (Sunstein 1995) on a common, ambiguous text that lends itself to a multiplicity of interpretations. To the extent that a constitution is a social contract, however, clarity and coherence remain, as in most contracts, preferable to obscurity and contradiction. The fact that societies occasionally benefit from deferring to judges or national legislatures the task of interpreting the meaning of ambiguous and conflicting clauses should not turn strategic lack of clarity and coherence into a normative ideal, when it simply reflects the constraints under which constitution-makers are sometimes forced to operate.

Independently of the formal qualities, other important standards of quality would seem to be how well a constitution is likely to do what a constitution as defined earlier is supposed to do, namely, first, serve as a second-order procedure for the resolution of first-order political disagreements and, second, protect individual rights. The first of these two criteria would presumably have to be measured in part in terms of how coherent and plausible the proposed distribution of powers, rights, and duties is and how likely it is, in light of the most up-to-date legal and social scientific knowledge on the topic, to disentangle the Gordian Knots of politics by planning for ways to channel conflicting claims into formal political institutions and procedures. A good constitution would thus ensure that all reasonably foreseeable conflicts among political actors are given clear procedural solutions, including by determining which authority has the final say on an issue and how (e.g., a Supreme Court, using simply majority rule). I propose to call this criterion "conflict resolution propensity" or, more colorfully, Gordian Knot factor. The higher the factor, the more propensity the constitution would have to diffuse conflicts.[5]

The second function – rights protection – can be crudely approximated by a third criterion, which I propose to call "rights-heaviness." By heaviness here, I refer both to the number and quality of rights entrenched in the constitution. A minimal threshold for a good constitution would be entrenchment of basic human rights. Going up the ladder of goodness, better constitutions would thus entrench second- (socioeconomic) and third-generation (collective)

---

[5] This Gordian Knot factor is the ex ante version of what Ginsburg and Huq (this introduction) propose to measure ex post, in an empirical fashion, namely, how good a constitution is at actually channeling political conflict once it is implemented.

rights. One would presumably need to weigh different types of rights and different rights within each type differently.

There are certainly practical problems with such a criterion, in that stuffing a constitution with a long list of pie-in-the-sky rights should not suffice to make it "good." However, it seems intuitively plausible to argue that how much a constitution details and entrenches individual rights, while not a guarantee that the future regime will respect them in any way, should probably factor in our evaluation of its goodness. This criterion is also one for which economic levels of development may need to be taken into account. One cannot expect the same level of rights-heaviness in the constitution of an emerging country as in the case of a highly developed one like Iceland. Context-sensitivity should thus somehow factor in our weighing of the rights introduced in a constitution.

Returning now to the substantive standards previously laid out by the academic literature on constitution-making, I propose to rephrase the standard of "democracy" listed by Carey as a less elegant but more accurate criterion of "democraticity." That democraticity is a desirable substantive criterion by which to assess the ex ante goodness of a constitution is largely taken for granted by normative theorists and empirical political scientists alike. As Carey puts it, "democracy may be the most prominent among constitutional ideals" (Carey 2009: 156). By democracy Carey himself refers both to the kind of ideal expected to be found in the text of constitutions themselves and the kind of inclusive and participatory principles that govern constitutional processes.

"Democraticity," as I propose to use the term, is meant to capture how far along on the continuum from less to more democratic a constitution is. Contrary to Carey, I propose not to include consideration for rights, including human rights, under the democracy criterion but file consideration for rights under a separate, previously mentioned category: rights-heaviness. It is, after all, possible for a liberal but undemocratic constitution to respect a number of rights, while violating political equality.

Turning now to the criterion of temperance, Carey describes it as consisting in "limiting the power of office-holders, lowering the stakes of politics, and encouraging moderation and measured deliberation" (Carey 2009: 157, citing Przeworski 1991; Weingast 1997; Rasch and Congleton 2006). From an institutional point of view, temperance essentially translates, into "division of power, such that no political actor can unilaterally make decisions and enforce them" (Carey 2009: 157, citing Madison 1788). Measuring temperance could be done by considering whether the proposed constitution establishes a system of checks and balances, counting how many veto points there are in the system (i.e., how many institutional actors must agree to a policy change for it to happen) or alternatively looking at what voting thresholds are in place. All these measures have been argued to, among other things, slow down the pace of changes, force those that are adopted toward the center of the policy space, and generally help prevent government abuse of individual rights (Tsebelis 1995, 1999; Tsebelis and Money 1997; Riker 1982, all cited in Carey 2009: 157–158).

I propose to break down this essential criterion of temperance into two: temperance per se, which captures the constraints on political actors as just described, and, in my view distinct, the ability to promote deliberation. The latter criterion could be phrased as "deliberative capacity," using John Dryzek's term to characterize "the extent to which a political system possesses structures to host deliberation that is authentic, inclusive, and consequential" (Dryzek 2009: 1382). Though the focus on inclusiveness in Dryzek's formula suggests that deliberative capacity is connected to democraticity, the two, I believe, should be analyzed as independent characteristics. Deliberation is a value that is emphasized by deliberative democrats but needs to be separated from democraticity per se. It also needs to be distinguished from temperance because its virtues are not merely to foster consensus and moderation. Properly conducted deliberation, under the right conditions, has also the distinct property of producing epistemically superior solutions (as argued in, e.g., Landemore 2013). Containing a deliberative capacity would thus seem like an important quality for a set of institutions meant to resolve conflicting claims.

A seventh criterion worth considering is whether the document expresses values and principles that citizens can be expected to recognize as legitimate – in other words to what degree it captures the spirit of a given people. I propose to call this quality "value fitness" (or "value representativeness"). This criterion, it should immediately be said, should be subject to constraints of justice and human rights. It wouldn't seem right for a constitution to accommodate, for example, racist prejudices and thus it is perfectly reasonable to expect other criteria to trump value fitness, as was the case in the institution of the German and Japanese constitutions after World War II or in South Africa after the end of Apartheid. Nonetheless, subject to what could be defined as the satisfaction of lexically prior criteria (such as rights-heaviness), value fitness seems a prima facie reasonable and desirable benchmark of constitutional goodness. The new South African Constitution, though breaking radically from racial prejudices still widely shared in the population, was attuned to the specific history and, among other distinct features, linguistic diversity of the South African people. Good constitutions, in other words, are not one-size-fits-all. Like fine jackets, they should be custom-tailored to their people.

One way to measure value fitness is to compare, prior to implementation, the proposed text with the results of a deliberative poll or equivalent (e.g., the National Forum in the case of Iceland). The more key concepts, principles, and provisions found in the constitution match those expressed by the larger population or a representative sample of it, the higher value fitness or representativeness one can consider the constitution to have. Another, more imperfect way to test whether the text properly captures the spirit of the people is the degree of actual, post-hoc legitimacy that a constitution enjoys once implemented. Post-hoc legitimacy, however, is far from a foolproof benchmark, as circumstances may dictate a rejection by the people, even as the substance of the text genuinely reflects the spirit of the people.[6] In other words, the criterion of value fitness is distinct from sociological legitimacy, whether expected or actual. Another way to say this is that value fitness is more of a substantive, normative criterion, rather than a procedural, descriptive one. That said, value fitness is likely to increase post hoc legitimacy and thus durability. It is thus valuable instrumentally as well as in and of itself.

Because value fitness is important, another criterion needs to be introduced: adaptability, or the ability of a constitution to adapt to changing mores and social needs and understandings, that is the ability to grow and evolve, like a living organism. This quality could be measured by considering the number and scope of amendment procedures included in the proposed constitution and whether they apply to what is sometimes seen as the untouchable core of a constitution or its more superficial layers.

Finally, because in particular the latter adaptability criterion may introduce the danger of great instability (the possibility of constitutional replacement in the guise of amendment), all of what comes before would have to be compatible with a ninth criterion of expected minimal durability. This criterion has more to do with the "likelihood" of success of a constitution than its a priori goodness per se, but without it a constitution could troublingly be said to be "good" even as it has absolutely no chance of lasting long enough to make any difference in the world. This criterion is equivalent to Carey's "durability" – which I propose to rephrase as "expected durability," to emphasize that it is the ex ante value that matters, and which I would additionally make a threshold criterion. In other words, the criterion of durability matters only up to a point.

---

[6] For example, in 1999 Venezuela and 2004 Bolivia the Congress and historical political parties were so unpopular and the demand for a constituent assembly so intense that any proposal coming from Congress would have lacked post-hoc sociological legitimacy. Alternatively a constitution may capture the spirit of the people but lack in so many other qualities that it ultimately proves unpopular and illegitimate in practice. Thanks to Joshua Braver for these examples and helping me clarify this point.

Where to place the threshold is a thorny issue, but one could argue that two generations would seem like a minimum duration for constitutional stability. Thomas Jefferson suggested that constitutions should be written for the living and should be revisited every generation or so. But that does not mean that the expected longevity of a constitution should only be one generation. Ideally each generation would be free to revisit their constitution, but if they decided not to do so they should have the luxury of not having to change it for some time. Given that the current length of a generation is generally to be twenty-five years (whereas the actual average life-expectancy of constitutions around the world is only around nineteen years (Elkins, Ginsburg, and Melton 2009)), two generations would take us close to an expected longevity of fifty years.

All these nine criteria together – formal qualities, Gordian Knot factor, rights-heaviness, democraticity, temperance, deliberative capacity, value fitness, adaptability, and minimal expected durability – should be combined in some context-sensitive fashion, which would need to be specified further, adding for example lexical priority considerations or a different weighing of the various criteria, in order to assess the ex ante quality of a constitution, that is its quality as assessed prior to its implementation. In other words, a good constitution would score minimally high on all (or at least most) of these criteria, which together would form the highest possible bar. A good constitution would thus (1) be a clear, concise, logically coherent document; (2) offer reasonable procedural solutions to foreseeable political conflicts; (3) protect and entrench rights of various kinds, first and foremost human rights, as well as (4) entrench democratic principles – centrally political equality and majority rule. It would further delineate (5) a temperate political system, characterized by (6) deliberative capacity. It would contain (7) values and principles that are representative of citizens' preferences while allowing for (8) the possibility of change over time and yet retaining (9) a decent (sufficient) life expectancy.

For additional points – for a "great" as opposed to just "good" constitution – I propose finally to add a tenth requirement of (10) "inspiration." A great constitution would thus be one that is beautifully written and likely to generate emotions such as love and admiration among its own people and beyond, among current and future generations. Such a text would be conducive, in the best case scenario, to the "constitutional patriotism" theorized by Habermas and observed in the case of some historic constitutions – the American one to begin with.

The following goes some way toward assessing the goodness of the Icelandic constitutional proposal in light of two of these criteria: rights-heaviness and democraticity. My main question is: Was the proposed constitution a good constitution by at least those two standards? How did it compare in those respects with the existing constitution? How did it compare with the two expert-written drafts that were written and circulated at the same time as examples of what a new constitution might look like?

2 ASSESSING THE CROWDSOURCED CONSTITUTION

In order to assess the value of the crowdsourced constitutional proposal – hereafter constitutional proposal C, which is both for "crowdsourced" (though the term is slightly exaggerated) and for Constitutional Council – I utilize the original constitution from 1944 (hereafter O) and two other draft proposals written by experts in the Constitutional Committee as preparatory material and templates for the Constitutional Council – entitled in the Icelandic "Example A" and "Example B" (hereafter A and B) – for comparison. In my view this comparative element is essential to measure the intrinsic "goodness" of a constitution if one is not to judge the proposal by the too low standard set by the previous constitution (which was written in a different time under different circumstances for a different people) and the unrealistically high standards of ideal theory only (the perfectly "just" constitution, if there is such a thing). In other words, my aim here is to assess whether the Icelandic constitutional proposal was a good constitution, not a perfect constitution. In Amartya Sen's terms, I am seeking to identify a high local optimum, as opposed to the global one (Sen 2009). Let me now introduce each constitutional text in turn.

The 1944 constitution (O)

The original constitution that forms the first point of comparison dates from June 17, 1944. This constitution is a slightly altered version of the one granted by Danish rulers in 1874, the so-called constitution on the Special Affairs of Iceland, itself inspired by the Danish Constitution of 1849 and the Belgian Constitution of 1831 (Torfason 2009, cited in Bergsson and Blokker Forthcoming: 154). In 1944, when Iceland unilaterally declared her independence from then Nazi-occupied Denmark, the Althing agreed on a new document, while also proclaiming a referendum on the old and new constitution. In May 1944 an election was organized. Almost 98% of the population turned out and among them 97% of the voters voted to break off the current relationship law with Denmark and 95% approved a constitutional republic.

The 1944 constitution, however, which was hastily put together by replacing "King" with "Elected President" in the original document and making minimal changes to the latter, was not all that "new" and was in fact always intended as a temporary document (Árnason 2011: 345; Jóhannesson 2011: 63–68, cited in Bergsson and Blokker Forthcoming). As a result, it has been described as a "mended garment" (cited in Gylfason 2014: 2) with the flavor of an "imposed constitution" (Levinson 2005, cited in Bergsson and Blokker Forthcoming). Politicians promised to revisit it at some later point to give Iceland a true custom-tailored document but they came and went over the years without ever delivering on this promise (Gylfason 2014). One of the reasons for this failure to update or change the document is the relative rigidity of the text (the amendment procedure is complex and demanding). Since 1944, the Icelandic Constitution has nonetheless been amended seven times so far, mostly due to changes in Icelandic constituencies and the conditions of voting eligibility. Additionally, in 1991 the organization of the Icelandic Parliament changed so that it now worked in one house rather than two as before. Extensive modifications were also made in 1995 when the human rights sections of the constitution were reviewed.

The expert drafts (A and B)

These expert drafts were part of a two-volume report that was formally submitted by the Constitutional Committee to the Constitutional Council at its first meeting on April 6, 2011. They were meant to serve as templates for what a new constitution might look like. I refer to each of them as Example A and B (their actual titles in the report).

The Constitutional Committee was a seven-member committee appointed by parliament and "consisting mainly of academic experts from a range of fields (law, literature, natural science, and social science)" (Gylfason 2014: 7). Its job had been to organize a National Forum upstream of the constitutional process; prepare a nationwide election of twenty-five representatives to a Constitutional Assembly tasked with writing a new constitution; and also prepare the ground for the Constitutional Assembly by offering an analysis of the 1944 constitution and gathering information on foreign constitutions and other relevant material. Specifically, the Committee's mandate included "suggestions to the Constitutional Council (CC) regarding potential changes to the existing constitution."

Although the Constitutional Committee offered the expert drafts in good spirit and, according to one of its members "constantly kept in mind that we were NOT the body elected to revise the constitution, but rather a committee entrusted to provide relevant information and facilitate the work of the Constitutional Council," one of the seven members of the Constitutional

Committee signed the report with the reservation that he believed that the committee was exceeding its mandate by proposing these texts to the constitutional assembly (Gylfason personal communication, March 2015, emphasis in the original). The intention was that the twenty-five members of the Constitutional Council would use these examples as templates for what a new constitution might look like. The proposals were meant to be complete in the sense of covering all relevant aspects of a constitution. In theory, each proposal was self-sustaining.

Sources differ in the account of how the expert drafts were written. Insiders say that the Committee worked as a group on both proposals and wrote them in parallel, one chapter at a time. "Many paragraphs were left unchanged [from the original constitution] but [the committee] took care to maintain inner consistency in each draft" (Pétursdóttir personal communication, April 2015). They also justify the offer of two proposals as a deliberate way to avoid "'dictating' any changes to the Constitutional Council" and to provide them with more than one option so as to "open [the options] for discussion without promoting one particular solution" (Pétursdóttir personal communication, April 2015).

Outsiders offer a slightly different story, arguing that the two drafts resulted from serious disagreements between two particularly vocal members of the constitutional committee, who decided to write two different versions reflecting their disagreement (Gylfason personal communication, March 2015). Others claim that Example A was written by a single person (Björg Thorarensen) during a previous period (2005–2007) of discussion about the revision of the existing constitution (Olafsson personal communication, March 2015).[7]

C: The crowdsourced constitution

The crowdsourced constitutional proposal, finally, was written by the twenty-five Constitutional Council members. They wrote it over a four-month-period (from April 6 to July 6, 2011). Over that period they crowdsourced twelve successive drafts online (by posting them on their own special page and on

[7] It is perhaps worth mentioning that yet another expert draft was circulated after the crowdsourced bill stalled in Parliament. It was written by two members of the Constitutional Committee, who became vocally opposed to the popularly approved constitution shortly after it stalled in Parliament. The interesting fact about this late proposal, which was otherwise never seriously discussed, was that it left out national ownership of natural resources and equal voting rights across the country, two principles specifically endorsed by the majority in the referendum (Gylfason personal communication, March 2015). I leave this late coming expert-written draft outside the comparison.

Facebook among other places). The crowdsourced constitution integrated the Icelandic values identified by a National Forum, which had taken place in the summer 2010. The details of the remarkable process that led to this output have been extensively covered elsewhere (e.g., Gylfason 2014; Landemore 2015) and so I leave the account out of this chapter. The proposal is well known because it was translated in English early on and made widely available on the Internet.

The crowdsourced constitution exists in at least two versions: the proposal that was submitted for referendum and the version amended by legal experts just after the referendum and submitted as a bill to parliament. The latter one, which I will call the "professional" version of the crowdsourced constitution (P), is a supposedly improved version of the proposal after it was given to the Parliamentary Committee for careful legal editing. In theory, the Parliamentary Committee respected the letter of the referendum-approved proposal and simply attempted to make sure the text was in line with the outcomes of the nationwide referendum as well as respected Iceland's commitments to previously adopted international treaties. In light of the referendum results, one radical change was thus to reintroduce the mention of the Evangelical Lutheran Church as the national church of Iceland (as in article 62 of the 1944 constitution, which had been eliminated from the new proposal).[8] This reversal was seemingly, though somewhat controversially, justified in light of the referendum results, in which 57% of the voters expressed a desire to retain a constitutional provision on the state church.

While this change was at least justifiable, legal experts more problematically altered other aspects of the original spirit of the proposal.[9] Among the more egregious changes, the experts suggested a redrafting of the natural resource provision – article 34 – in a direction that favored the vessel owners (the

---

[8] The original version of the proposal only contained in its article 19 a reference to a state church whose status the Parliament was made free to maintain or amend, conditional on any change to the status quo being approved by referendum.

[9] For example, the group of experts decided to compile the content relative to the limits of various rights and liberties covered in different articles (articles 9–18) into one single article (article 9.2). The legal experts presumably thought that this amounted to a minor technical change. As it turns out, however, the Council of Europe's Venice Commission, a group of European legal experts who were asked to give their opinion about the final version of the constitutional draft, identified a problem with that very article by pointing out that grouping all restrictions to human rights irrespective of the differences between rights (e.g., between socio-economic rights and group or so called "third generation" rights) was a source of confusion and substantive problems. The Commission worried, specifically, about "the risk that, under these circumstances, the general restriction formula be too open and inconclusive from the perspective of such rights." See the final report of the Venice Commission, adopted on March 8–9, 2013, specifically p. 8. The report is available at: www.venice.coe.int/webforms/documents/? pdf=CDL-AD(2013)010-e.

"oligarchs" of Iceland) by making the occasional use of natural resources for profit much cheaper than the Constitutional Council intended (Gylfason 2014: 17).

As a result of these substantive problems with the professional bill (P), as well as some procedural issues (it is not clear that the Parliament had any legitimate mandate to rewrite the constitutional proposal in the first place) and partly because I am also more interested in testing the epistemic properties of a text written by non-experts than an hybrid output, I focus here primarily on the referendum-approved version of the "crowdsourced" constitutional proposal (C). While the referendum-approved version could have used some light legal editing and – more questionably so – the reintroduction of the state church clause in the text, it seems that the Parliamentary Commission went too far in the rewriting process.

Let me add a word about the meaningfulness of comparing those drafts. It is certainly methodologically problematic to compare a constitution written in 1944 and a constitution written in 2011. For one, the standards for assessment have changed over time. We now generally value more democratic and open systems. We have also considerably expanded the list of rights we consider necessary to entrench in constitutions. By all those standards O is bound to fare worse than any of the more recent proposals (even thought it was amended in 1995 to introduce a list of human rights absent from the original version). That said, it is interesting to see in what ways a contemporary proposal is able to improve on an old text. Indeed all three recent proposals (A, B, and C) objectively improve on the existing constitution.

Comparing A, B, C (and P to some extent) allows us to compare apples to apples – since all drafts were written at least within a few years of each other – although we do have to take into account the fact that A and B came first and were used as templates for C. An improvement in C over O should only be considered an indication of the greater wisdom of a popular constitutional assembly if it was not also included in A or B (the experts that could also have rewritten the original constitution). The great similarities between A, B, and C, as we will see, indicate that the popular constitutional assembly was only marginally wiser than the expert committee that way. Nevertheless the marginal improvements turn out to be quite crucial. It is also worth keeping in mind that the expert drafts were themselves written on the basis of – or at least with the knowledge of – a fair amount of popular input (the input gathered during the National Forum 2010 and summarized in a report handed to the drafters). In that sense the work of the committee was not a pure product of insulated expert reflection.

3 ASSESSMENT

In the following I first offer a brief synthetic and overall assessment of the main and most striking characteristics of each constitutional benchmark. I then turn to the constitutional council's proposal (the "crowdsourced" one) and assess it more specifically in light of two of the normative criteria listed in Section 1: rights-heaviness and democraticity.

Holistic assessment

The original 1944 constitution possesses little of the distinct and personal character of future proposals. There is no preamble, the seven chapters do not have titles, and the list of institutions and rights have nothing particularly Icelandic to them. It introduces the country as a "republic" (the word democracy is nowhere to be found). The constitution is all about the president and the Althingi, whose functions are the object of respectively Chapters 2 and 3 (which count twenty-eight articles each). Citizens and citizens' rights and freedoms come last (Chapters 6 and 7), with eighteen articles (three for the religious freedoms, listed first, and fifteen for all the other rights). The list of human rights was in fact added by amendment in 1995. There is little to no consideration of children's rights, the environment, or animal protection. Some articles are downright dated, such as the article making it mandatory for people who do not pay fees to a religious association to pay it to the University of Iceland instead.[10] There is also no clear separation of power – the president jointly exercises legislative power with the Althingi and exercises executive power with the Cabinet and ministers, an issue that had long seemed problematic to many Icelandic commentators.

Most problematically, though, the 1944 constitution is not based on the democratic principle of one person, one vote. While it is compatible with strict political equality, it does not entrench it, and thus fails to protect it. In practice the 1944 constitution allows for the current voting system, which gives more weight to the votes of people living in certain districts. For example, after the 2013 Parliamentary elections the Southwest district received thirteen representatives against eight for the Northwest district, even though the Southwest district has three times more people than the Northwest district.[11] The apportionment of seats (which is determined by the electoral law) is clearly not proportional but the constitution does not say it has to be.

---

[10] In fairness, this article also specifies that the latter provision can be amended by law, an amendment which was finally passed in 2005.

[11] Source: www.kosning.is/althingiskosningar/tolfraedi/skipting-kjosenda-eftir-kjordaemum/.

The constitution only makes sure that the disproportion does not exceed a ratio of 1:2. The fifth paragraph thus states:

> If the number of voters on the voting register represented by each parliamentary seat, allocated or distributed, becomes in one electoral district one half of the number represented by each parliamentary seat in another electoral district, the National Election board shall revise the number of seats representing each electoral district with the aim of reducing this difference.

At the limit, this allows the Northwest district to have 2,600 voters per seat against 5,100 voters per seat for the Southwest district. The vote of citizens in the Northwest thus counts for almost twice the vote of citizens in the Southwest. This situation, which results in the underpopulated countryside having a disproportionate voice in Parliament, has been a subject of debate and discontent among Icelanders for quite some time. One of the conclusions of the brainstorming that occurred during the 2010 National Forum upstream of the drafting process was the idea of a more equal voting system.

A and B

A and B are important to compare because they reflect respectively what appear to be a progressive and a conservative version of the same expert-written draft. They are very much alike in structure and content (respectively nine and ten clearly titled chapters, with almost identical titles), except for some crucial divergences in terms of the authority of the president, the separation of powers, and the presence or absence of a state church clause. As a result, it looks as if A was written first and then B was copied and pasted from it but tweaked so as to reflect a different, on my reading slightly more conservative, set of values.[12] Only B has a preamble though both proposals try to capture something about the Icelandic people, while proclaiming respect for the dignity of man, the environment, and a commitment to peace with other nations. Noteworthy is the fact that A uses "Iceland" as the subject. B uses "We, the People." Only B says something about the "intention" of the polity, namely, to work "with other nations and promote peace." Example A lists three "cornerstones" of Iceland, namely, "democracy," "the rule of law," and "respect for human rights." B lists three slightly different ones:

[12] Gylfason also reports that of the four lawyers on the Constitutional Committee, two appointees of the then opposition parties now back together in government "were quite determined, and quarreled a lot as polar opposites, giving the other committee members the impression that they thought that they alone knew what to write" (personal communication, March 2015). In his view it is possible that Examples A and B were proposed to the council as alternatives they were supposed to choose between (Gylfason personal communication, March 2015).

"democracy," "human rights," and "integrity." A describes Iceland as a "free and sovereign republic." B describes it as a "Republic with a parliamentary government."

As per the recommendations that came out of the National Forum in 2010, both proposals further place the chapter on human rights at the front of the constitution (Chapter 2 in both cases, after the chapter on "Foundations"). The "progressive" proposal A puts the Althingi before the president (Chapter 3 versus 4). B does the opposite. They both include a controversial article on collective ownership of natural resources. They both contain an article on the status of the Evangelical Lutheran Church. Draft A, however, skirts the issue by deferring the question of the status of the Evangelical Lutheran Church to a referendum. By contrast, B maintains it as the official Church of Iceland, while at the same time emphasizing that the state shall support and protect all lawful religious associations. Both A and B pay attention to new forms of discrimination the constitution should protect individuals from. A, the more exhaustive in that respect, thus lists discrimination on the basis of disability, sexual orientation, age and domicile, in addition to the original gender, religion, opinion, race, and color. B commits to the principle of equal votes (articles 50). A does not and simply follows the precedent set by O on that front.

The crowdsourced constitution (C)

The crowdsourced constitution includes nine titled chapters and is closest in structure to A. Additionally, it has a more extensive, richer, and more inspiring preamble than either A or B, starting with "We, the People, who inhabit Iceland" – clearly a combination of A's reference to the country and B's reference to the nation. It lists four core principles of the country: freedom, equality, democracy, and human rights (a list that is more logical and complete than the list of three principles in either A or B). It states, amongst other things, that the purpose of the Icelandic people is to create a just society as well as promote the welfare of the country's inhabitants. It emphasizes the necessity to encourage the Icelandic culture and respect the diversity of the life of the people, the country, and its biosphere as well as promote harmony, security, and happiness amongst the Icelandic citizens and coming generations. Happiness, in particular, makes an entry in only this proposal. It is a direct and explicit borrowing from the American constitution.[13] Finally, the

---

[13] The word was insisted on by Pastor Örn Jónsson, who justified his choice to me this way: "I pressed for including 'happiness' like in the American constitution. I can take the credit for

preamble commits to work toward peace with other nations and respect for the earth and mankind. The poetic quality of its language, which transpires even in translation, comes from the fact that an actual poet – Hannes Pétursson[14] – was consulted by the two people who, for the most part, wrote the preamble. It should be acknowledged that the inclusion of a preamble in the proposal was a controversial issue within the Constitutional Council as some members saw the very idea of a preamble as "un-Icelandic" or "un-Scandinavian" (most Scandinavian constitutions don't have one), while others felt rushed into endorsing the proposal, as the Council was running out of time at that point.

Unlike A and B, C characterizes Iceland as a "parliamentary democracy." The term "democracy" or "democratic" occurs four times in the text. Iceland is in fact a semi-presidential regime, with both a directly elected president with non-trivial powers and a prime minister. Like A and B, C places "human rights" and rights relative to nature early in the document (Chapter 2, which is titled "Human Rights and Nature" – as opposed to "Human Rights" only in A and B) in a section that includes thirty-one articles. Like A and B, C includes an article on natural resources as collective property (article 34). It places the Althingi (Chapter 3) before the president (Chapter 4) and the ministers and the Cabinet (Chapter 5). There is a clear sense that the colorful articles and aspirations are put at the front of the constitution, and the final chapters are devoted to more technical, less inspiring sections (for example the chapter about foreign affairs and final provisions).

Like A, C favors a much clearer separation of power between the president and the Althingi (article 2). Like B, it maintains the default status of the Evangelical Lutheran Church as the national state-supported church, but introduces the need to put any change to the status quo to a referendum (perhaps borrowing from B).

How rights-heavy and democratic is C?

In the following I propose to assess C by two of the normative standards from Section 1, namely, rights-heaviness and democraticity, while simultaneously comparing it to the competing proposals. I will not spend any time analyzing the standard of formal quality, though it seems to me that the proposal is strikingly clear, concise, and coherent. C is also much clearer than O according to native speakers, due to the archaic formulas that are to be

that. Life should be good. I preach the Gospel, which means good news" (Skype interview, July 17, 2015).

[14] One of the most famous, celebrated, and widely translated of living Icelandic poets.

found in the 1944 constitution. But in its formal qualities the crowdsourced proposal is not strikingly better than either A or B, which are equally clear, concise, and seemingly coherent.

I also leave outside of this analysis the ability of the proposal to channel and resolve conflict (the Gordian Knot factor) and the criteria of temperance, as they are hard to assess by a non-expert in constitutional matters and political systems, though I note that when it comes to temperance, C includes a separation of power already remarked upon and notoriously absent from O.

One can make quick work of the value fitness criterion since the work of the Constitutional Council was explicitly based on the findings of the National Forum of 2010, which places C at a considerable advantage with respect to O. C is also almost surely marginally superior to A and B in that respect as well, even though the Constitutional Committee wrote both examples on the basis of the results of the National Forum, if only because C was crowdsourced to the larger public during the drafting stage and morally validated by a (non-binding) referendum. The only sticky point in terms of value fitness, perhaps, is the "state church clause" (article 19) since, as already mentioned, the results of the referendum were largely interpreted to indicate that the Icelandic people wanted to maintain a mention of the Evangelical Lutheran church as the national church in the text of the constitution (by 57% of the vote).

The adaptability criterion is also more successfully met in C than any other rival texts. Article 79 of O requires that for any amendment voted by Parliament, Parliament has to be immediately dissolved and new elections organized. The new Parliament in power has then to pass the resolution unchanged, which is then confirmed by the president of Iceland. In other words any amendment has to be voted upon twice, once by a Parliament that more or less commits suicide by approving the amendment, and another time by a new Parliament that may come to power with other preferences. Note also that there is no referendum planned about amendment proposals, except for one question, the status of the Church under article 62. In other words, the people are not to be directly consulted about any constitutional amendment proposal, except on the Church status.

O's very high bar for change is partly what explains the failure of the 2010–2013 constitutional process in Iceland. By contrast, C, which was meant to replace O, would have made constitutional change much easier. According to its article 113, once Parliament has passed a bill to amend the constitution, the only required additional step is the organization, within a time frame of three months, of a referendum of all eligible voters for approval or rejection of the bill. In cases where Parliament is nearly unanimous about the proposed amendment ("if five-sixths of the members of the Althingi has passed the bill"), the referendum can be canceled by Parliament and the bill turned into law nonetheless.

A and B are similar to C in that respect, except that A demands that in the popular referendum the valid votes represent at least 30% of all registered votes and B sets a supermajoritarian threshold for the vote in Parliament (2/3 of the Althingi votes must be cast in favor of the amendment). Neither A nor B allows Parliament to pass an amendment without a popular referendum.

C would thus have been a much more adaptable constitution – perhaps too much so in fact. From that point of view, P (the version of C revised by legal experts) offers a compromise between O and C in that its article 113 follows C for the most part but crucially reintroduces O's double parliamentary approval for bills aiming to amend the provisions of Chapter II of the constitution, namely, the chapter on Human Rights and Nature. This cautious move reflects the belief (apparently increasingly shared in the legal community) that not all parts of constitutions are equal and that some should be more difficult to amend than others. Indeed, in recent years there has been some scholarly attention to the idea that some provisions ought to be harder to amend than others, or even unamendable (Jacobsohn 2006; Ginsburg and Melton 2015; Dixon and Landau, Chapter 10). What this suggests is that there are trade-offs between too much rigidity and too much flexibility and that some nuanced solution like the one offered in P should probably be considered.

Finally, regarding the expected durability criterion, Elkins, Ginsburg, and Melton plausibly credit the crowdsourced proposal with a life expectancy of sixty years (Elkins, Ginsburg, and Melton 2012). This hits the minimal bar of fifty years proposed earlier. Comparatively one may note that O has de facto survived more than seventy-one years, although it is of course possible that this performance is entirely accidental, especially considering that this original constitution was always meant to be replaced early on.

Let me now focus on rights-heaviness and democraticity, namely, the degree to which the proposal expresses a commitment to a variety of rights and democratic values and principles. Those are two important criteria that can be assessed by a close reading of the text without mobilizing technical knowledge of the likely effects of political systems. Discussing them will also allow me to touch in passing on the "deliberative quality" of the political scheme set up by the proposal. Unsurprisingly perhaps, I conclude that C scores higher on those two criteria than O, A, or B.

"Rights-heaviness"

As already said, the proposal counts a total of thirty-one articles related to "human rights and nature." According to external observers, Iceland's proposal is "moderately rights-heavy" (where the measure is of the percentage of rights included in the constitution across seventy or so distinct rights that have been specified in constitutions since 1789) (Elkins, Ginsburg, and Melton 2012). The Venice Commission praises the proposal for "new provisions [. . .] aiming both to extend the scope of protection and to better reflect the international human rights obligation" (Venice Commission Remark 27). It singles out in particular article 112 as of "great importance" in that it stresses the obligations of Iceland under international agreements and requires that all holders of governmental powers respect rules on human rights (Remark 26). The Venice Commission also remarks that "the scope of protection has especially been widened by adding new socio-economic rights (article 22–25), as well as more or less 'collective rights' (article 32–36), called by the explanatory bill 'third-generation rights'" (Venice Commission Remark 28).

C is definitely more rights-heavy than the existing constitution, which does not include for example the rights of children, right to a healthy environment, freedom of the press, right of petition, right to fair compensation, state duty to protect culture, right to life, right to health care, right to safe work environment, right to a reasonable standard of living, and the freedom to view government information that one finds in the new proposal. It is also substantially rights-heavier than A and B, since it includes a much more extensive list of rights relative to the environment, as in article 33, which states that "All shall by law be accorded the right to a healthy environment, fresh water, unpolluted air and unspoiled nature." It includes rights that are not listed in either O, A or B, such as the right to the internet (15) and various socioeconomic and collective rights that may even seem excessively generous and difficult to uphold (as pointed out by the Venice commission, Remarks 32–33). It mentions explicitly "sexual violence" as a type of violence the state should protect individuals from. Unlike O, A, or B, it also devotes a separate and extensive article to the rights of children. It mentions still more sources of discrimination than A, including genetic character, ancestry, and political affiliation. Finally, it offers a more "open and comprehensive approach to the right of freedom of religion" in that it extends the scope of this freedom to what C calls "view of life" and "personal conviction" and P rephrases as "philosophy" and "conviction." According to the Venice Commission, this extension as well as the inclusion of the right to change religion or faith form "a substantial improvement compared to the current Constitution" (Remark 55).

The reason why C is more rights-heavy than the other texts can arguably be traced to the crowdsourcing moment. According to internal reports, the Council had originally set out to be as inclusive as possible on matters of human rights and specifically on matters of sexuality. Yet it took the influence of outsiders for them to write the text they ultimately wrote. Pastor Örn Jónsson thus reports that article 6, in particular, was influenced by emails, letters, and online posts from the transgender community, which made them realize that the first draft they had put on the Internet was not inclusive enough (personal communication, July 17, 2015).

The proposal came close to being even more inclusive and rights-heavy on one particular dimension, that of religious rights. Article 18 in particular was initially set out to include the following sentence: "All registered religious communities and life-views communities shall be protected by the State." The intention was to transfer the protection ensured by article sixty-two in the current constitution to all registered religious and life-views communities. The sentence was cut out at the last minute because the group couldn't come to an agreement on this issue and had to take a vote. The majority came down against keeping the clause, on the argument that it could be used to protect all sort of "life-views," including that of neo-Nazis (Pastor Arnfridur personal communication, July 17, 2015).

While the superior rights-heaviness of C on all competing constitutions is undeniable, it has its weakness: excessive vagueness, resulting in a lack of clarity. The Venice Commission thus points out that it is "regrettable" that "most of the provisions concerned are worded in general terms, not providing sufficient clarity on whether and which concrete rights and obligations can be derived from them" (Venice Commission report, Remark 32). While the Venice Commission is mostly concerned about the risks of disappointing the public, which is a valid concern, from our perspective the worry should be also that the constitution will not be "good" in the sense of having the kind of formal quality that ensures proper interpretability and thus usefulness.

"Democraticity"

One striking feature of C is that it put citizens' rights at the forefront of the constitution. This is in keeping with the recommendations that emanated from the National Forum 2010, and were also followed by the expert drafts.

Putting the Icelandic people and their rights first seems, symbolically at least, like a democratic improvement over the past emphasis over state institutions.

Arguably, though, the main democratic superiority of the crowdsourced proposal over O, which it shares with B but not A, is its explicit commitment to the principle of "one person, one vote." Article 39 thus states explicitly: "The ballots of voters everywhere in the country shall have equal weight." Similarly B states in article 50: "The weight of votes in nationwide elections and elections in each electoral district shall be equal." By contrast Article 31 of the old constitution is compatible with the principle of equal representation but does not entrench it (see above). Since A's article 22 is a strict copy-paste of that original article, it suffers from the same problem.

Additionally, C describes Iceland as a "parliamentary *democracy*" (article 1, my emphasis), not merely a "republic" like O or B. A also describes Iceland as a democracy but since it is not constitutionally committed to the principle "one person, one vote" (the way B is), because it strictly follows O on the voting system, it clearly loses out to C on this dimension. Finally, an explicit reference to democracy is made four times in the crowdsourced constitution (in the preamble, as one of the four "cornerstones" of Iceland, as well as in articles 1, 18, and 24), against no reference at all in the original constitution, two references in A (preamble and article 14), and three in B (preamble, articles 14 and 15).

Another striking democratic superiority of C over all competitors is the degree to which it creates institutional avenues for popular participation (see also Elkins, Ginsburg, and Melton 2012). Important elements of direct democracy are thus introduced in the crowdsourced constitution, allowing the public a role in the determination of the status of the Evangelical Lutheran Church as national church (any change to the status quo introduced by Parliament must be approved by referendum) and the approval of certain treaties (such as a treaty to enter the European Union). C also includes a "right of referral," by which 10% of voters may demand a referendum on any bill within three months of its passage (article 65), subject to some exception (such as the budget). Additionally, and most innovatively, the draft introduces what is elsewhere sometimes called a Citizens' Initiative (article 66). This participatory mechanism allows 2% of the population to present an issue to the Althingi, which the Althingi is free to ignore, and 10% to present a bill to the Althingi, which the Althingi can either accept or make a counter-proposal to. In the latter case, if the bill of the voters has not been withdrawn as a response, the Althingi must present both the popular bill and the Althingi's counter-proposal to a referendum. C also allows the public to approve removal of the president by Parliament (article 84) as well as constitutional amendments (article 113). Finally, candidates for president must have the prior endorsement of 1% of voters (78).

These elements of direct participation are very distinctive of the crowd-sourced constitution and have been internationally celebrated, including by the Venice Commission.[15] By contrast, the 1944 constitution contains only a provision to allow the public to vote on bills that have been returned to Parliament by the president. A and B are notably more participatory, but not to the same extent as C. A, for example, also has a Citizens' Initiative article (article 46), which allows 15% of the population to trigger a referendum on a bill (subject to some exceptions like the budget). B's article 94 in the chapter on national referenda specifies that 15% of the population can force the president to refuse to confirm an act of law or resolution of the Althingi and refer the matter to a national vote. Again, these participatory provisions are not nearly as expansive as those found in C.

These elements of direct democracy arguably bleed into the criterion I earlier called "deliberative capacity," to the extent that they put "the public in conversation with their elected representatives" (Elkins, Ginsburg and Melton 2012: 2). They render more porous and thus more effective the communication channels that are supposed to exist between the formal and the informal deliberative tracks of a properly functioning democracy (Habermas 1996). C – more so still than either A or B – thus meets the "democraticity" criterion along specifically deliberative lines.[16]

Last but not least, another characteristic one may easily associate with "democraticity" – transparency – is a central theme in C, to an extent unmatched by A and B, let alone O. The word transparency is used three times in C. Article 15 on the right to information states that

> Public administration shall be transparent [. . .] Information and documents held by public authorities shall be available without exception and the access of the public to all documents collected or paid for by public authorities shall be assured by law. A list of all cases and documents held by public authorities, their origin and content shall be open to all.

---

[15] Article 128 of the report states: "The Venice Commission welcomes the clear intention that underlines the above-mentioned provisions, namely, to enhance citizens' opportunities to influence legislation and more generally the decision-making on issues of key interest of the public. It finds this aim entirely legitimate and understandable in the specific socio-economic and political context of Iceland, and recalls that, this is also a part of a certain tradition of direct participation that exists in Iceland."

[16] Beyond the deliberation between government and citizens, the draft promotes intergovernmental deliberation, with for example article 108, which makes it a duty of the national government to consult local government for issues related to them.

Article 16 requires "transparency of ownership" in the media. Article 51 finally aims to make contributions to candidates and their associations fully public. The goal is "to keep costs moderate, ensure transparency, and limit advertising in an election campaign." At least two other articles explicitly aim for transparency, even if they do not contain the word. For example, article 29 prohibits members of the Althingi from participating in deliberation on parliamentary business that concerns their special interests, or those of persons with close ties to them. Article 50 on disclosure of conflicts of interest for Althingi members and their duty to provide information on their financial interests similarly aim at transparency, without the word. A similar article, article 88, exists for ministers, who are under a "duty to disclose information on their financial interests."

CONCLUSION

Confronted with the task of assessing whether the crowdsourced Icelandic constitutional proposal of 2012 would have made for a "good" constitution, but deprived of any empirical measures of the success of a proposal that was never implemented to begin with, this chapter followed the distinct strategy of trying to offer some plausible ex ante criteria susceptible to guide the assessment of constitutional proposals in general and then applying some of those to the particular case of the Icelandic proposal. I offered a total of nine such criteria – formal quality, conflict resolution propensity (Gordian Knot factor), rights-heaviness, democraticity, temperance, deliberative capacity, value fitness, adaptability, and durability. I also added a tenth bonus feature of "inspiration." Further research would need to deepen the justification of the normative criteria proposed, including by arguing why constitutional "goodness" must include (as it does in my account) considerations of justice. Further research would also need to flesh out the way in which all these criteria inter-relate. Doing so would require distinguishing between the different types of criteria invoked, from the more universal (conflict resolution, temperance) to the more particular (democraticity, deliberative capacity). It would also require specifying the ways in which the combination of these criteria should or should not be made context-sensitive so as to take into account, for example, the history or level of economic development of the considered country (or organization). All in all, what these tasks require is the development of a proper philosophical framework for what a good constitution is.

Applying some of these criteria to the specific case of Iceland proved challenging and interesting in various ways. I suggested that the crowdsourced draft scored high on criteria such as formal quality, temperance, deliberative capacity, value fitness, and adaptability. I documented through a more thorough analysis that the text scored highest than competitors on "rights-heaviness," and "democraticity." I thus conclude that the Icelandic proposal was in many respects an improvement over the 1944 constitution and was also comparatively better in important ways than the rival expert drafts. By most of the criteria proposed here the crowdsourced constitutional proposal was overall a *good* constitution, which would have been made better if the constitutional council had been given more time to sort out some remaining issues. Whether it would have a *successful* one, once implemented, is of course a matter of further speculation.

REFERENCES

Árnason, Ágúst ThóR. 2011. "A Review of the Icelandic Constitution – Popular Sovereignty or Political Confusion." *Tidjschrift voor Constitutioneel Recht* 3: 342–351.

Bergsson, Baldvin Thor, and Paul Blokker. Forthcoming. "The Constitutional Experiment in Iceland." In E. Bos and K. Pocza (eds), *Verfassunggebun in konsolidierten Demokratien: Neubeginn oder Verfall eines Systems?* Nomos Verlag: 154–174.

Burton, Michael, Richard Gunther, and John Higley. 1992. "Introduction: Elite Transformations and Democratic Regimes." In Richard Gunther and John Higley (eds), *Elites and Democratic Consolidation in Latin America and Southern Europe*. New York: Cambridge University Press.

Carey, John M. 2009. "Does It Matter How a Constitution Is Created?" In Z. Barany and R. G. Moser (eds), *Is Democracy Exportable?* New York: Cambridge University.

Dryzek, John. 2009. "Democratization as Deliberative Capacity Building." *Comparative Political Studies* 42 (11): 1379–1402.

Eistenstadt, Todd. A., A. Carl LeVan, and Tofigh Maboudi. Forthcoming. "When Talk Trumps Text: The Democratizing Effects of Deliberation during Constitution-Making, 1974–2011." *American Political Science Review* 109 (3).

Elkins, Zachary, Tom Ginsburg, and James Melton. 2009. *The Endurance of Constitutions*. Cambridge: Cambridge University Press.

2012. "A Review of Iceland's Draft Constitution." Available at http://compara tiveconstitutionsproject.org/wp-content/uploads/CCP-Iceland-Report.pdf.

Ginsburg, Tom and Zachary Elkins. 2014. "Stjórnarskrárgerð á tímum gagnsæis: Ísland í samanburði (Drafting Constitutions in an Era of Transparency: Iceland in Comparative Perspective)." In J. Ólafsson (ed.), *Experiments in Democracy – Iceland in Crisis and Recovery*. Reykjavík: University of Iceland Press & Bifröst University: REF.

Ginsburg, Tom and James Melton. 2015. "Does the Constitutional Amendment Rule Matter at All? Amendment Cultures and the Challenges of Measuring Amendment Difficulty." *International Journal of Constitutional Law* 13(3): 686–713.

Gylfason, Thorvaldur. 2013a. "Democracy on Ice: A Post-Mortem of the Icelandic Constitution." *Open Democracy*, June 19. Available at www .opendemocracy.net/can-europe-make-it/thorvaldur-gylfason/democ racy-on-ice-post-mortem-of-icelandic-constitution.

2013b. "Putsch: Iceland's Crowdsourced Constitution Killed by Parliament." *Blogpost*, March 30. Available at www.verfassungsblog.de/ de/putschicelands-crowd-sourced-constitution-killed-by-parliament/.

2014. "Constitution on Ice." Available at https://notendur.hi.is/gylfason/ Constitution%20on%20Ice%207.pdf.

Habermas, Jürgen. 1996. *Between Facts and Norms*. Cambridge, MA: MIT Press.

Jacobsohn, Gary Jeffrey. 2006. "An Unconstitutional Constitutional Amendment? A Comparative Perspective." *International Journal of Constitutional Law* 4 (3): 460–487. doi:10.1093/icon/mol016

Jóhannesson, Guðni T. H. 2011. "Tjaldað til einnar nætur: Uppruni bráðabirgðarstjórnarskrárinnar (Preparing for the Short-Term: The Origin of the Interim Constitution)." *Icelandic Review of Politics and Administration* 7 (1): 61–72.

Landemore, Hélène. 2013. *Democratic Reason: Politics, Collective Intelligence, and the Rule of the Many*. Princeton: Princeton University Press.

2015. "Inclusive Constitution-Making: The Icelandic Experiment." *Journal of Political Philosophy* 23 (3): 166–191.

Levinson, Sanford. 2005. "Imposed Constitutionalism: Some Reflections." *Connecticut Law Review* 37: 921–932.

Madison, James, Alexander Hamilton, and John Jay. [1788] 1961. *The Federalist Papers*. New York: Mentors.

Melton, James, Zachary Elkins, Tom Ginsburg, and Kalev Leetaru. 2013. "On the Interpretability of Law: Lessons from the Decoding of National Constitutions." *British Journal of Political Science* 43 (2): 399–423.

Przeworski, Adam. 1991. *Democracy and the Market*. Cambridge: Cambridge University

Rasch, Bjørn Erik and Robert D. Congleton. 2006. "Amendment Procedures and Constitutional Stability." In R. D. Congleton and B. Swedenborg (eds), *Democratic Constitutional Design and Public Policy*. Cambridge, MA: MIT Press.

Riker, William. 1982. *Liberalism against Populism*. Prospect Heights, IL: Waveland Press.

Sen, Amartya. 2009. *The Idea of Justice*. Cambridge: Belknap Press.

Sunstein, Cass R. 1995. "Incompletely Theorized Agreement." *Harvard Law Review* 108: 1733–1772.

Torfason, Hjörtur 2009. Influential Constitutional Justice: Some Icelandic Perspectives, World Conference on Constitutional Justice, Cape Town, January 23–24, 2009.

Tsebelis, George. 1995. "Decision-Making in Political Systems: Veto Players in Presidentialism, Parliamentarism, Multicameralism and Multipartyism." *British Journal of Political Science* 25: 289–325.

   1999. "Veto Players and Law Production in Parliamentary Democracies: An Empirical Analysis." *American Political Science Review* 93: 591–608.

Tsebelis, George and Jeanette Money. 1997. *Bicameralism*. New York: Cambridge University Press.

Tsebelis, George and Dominic J. Nardi. 2016 "A Long Constitution Is a (Positively) Bad Constitution: Evidence from OECD Countries." *British Journal of Political Science* 46 (2): 457–478.

Weingast, Barry. 1997. "The Political Foundations of Democracy and the Rule of Law." *American Political Science Review* 91: 245–263.

4

When is a constitution doing well? The Alberdian test in the Americas

Roberto Gargarella

INTRODUCTION

It is my impression that the notion of "constitutional performance" refers to an evaluative rather than to a statistical process. But, of course, everything depends on how we define the terms we want to use. In my view, in order to determine whether a Constitution is performing "well" we need to initiate a complex theoretical reasoning, which I shall begin to explore. Alternatively, however, we may stipulate that (say) the idea of "constitutional success" means something like (say) constitutional *stability* – this being a historically important candidate for playing this role, as I shall suggest. In this way, we gain the possibility of measuring the concept but – this is my opinion – at the risk of undermining the attractiveness, complexity and richness of the notion of "constitutional performance." Of course, it is absolutely important to compare Constitutions according to (say) the stability they achieved, and to measure such things. But it is not clear to me that, in this way, we will be measuring "constitutional performance."[1] In association with the notion of "constitution," the idea of "performance" appeals to a complex process, which – it is my impression – should not be simply reduced to a statistical analysis.

In what follows – and based on previous studies about constitutionalism in the Americas – (Gargarella 2010, 2013), I will explore this discussion with some more detail, and propose an approach to "constitutional performance" that is both contextually and normative sensitive, and which is based on the teachings of nineteenth-century constitutional scholars. I will illustrate the potential of this alternative understanding through four examples related to early constitutional history in the Americas.

[1] In a similar vein, Jon Elster states: "it is not clear … what to understand by a 'flawed constitution'" (see Jon Elster. 2014. *The Political Psychology of Constitution-Making*. Princeton: Unpublished paper in file with the author, 36).

WHEN IS A CONSTITUTION DOING WELL? THE EXAMPLE
OF THE CHILEAN CONSTITUTION OF 1833

After the independence years – around 1810 in Latin America– most countries in the region began to explore ways to (re)organize their institutional structure, usually with the help of a new Constitution. The conditions within which these new Constitutions grew were extremely difficult for a variety of reasons, including the fact that the new societies were socially divided and character-ized by profound inequalities; the presence of strong *caudillos* who repre-sented, in many occasions, a serious "internal" threat to the new projects; and also the existence of the "external" threat posed by foreign countries (most typically Spain, trying to re-built its lost Empire). Under these conditions, almost every legal initiative was condemned to failure. For instance, the vastly influential *Libertador* Simón Bolívar was personally and intensively involved in this process of constitutional creation but none of his many initiatives, of a rather authoritarian character, prospered.

However, in the midst of these difficulties, the Chilean Constitution of 1833 emerged and very soon attracted the attention of political activists and legal experts in the region: It was an example of a well-written Constitution that – contrary to what was the dramatic rule of the time – remained in place and finally became the most stable Latin American Constitution in the nineteenth century. The Constitution was in force during more than ninety years, only receiving a few modifications in the late nineteenth century. Two of its main features, related to the two main parts of every Constitution, namely, the organization of rights and the organization of powers, are worth mentioning. On the one hand, the Constitution organized its system of rights according to the needs and demands of the Catholic Church: Only the Roman Catholic religion was recognized and accepted, and all other civil rights were made dependent on that initial premise. On the other hand, the Constitution made all the different institutional powers dependent on the will of a hyper-powerful president.

For many, such a design had helped Chile to find the formulae for stability – a stability that most other Constitutions in the region had enormous difficul-ties to ensure. Not surprisingly, then, the 1833 Constitution became, for numerous political leaders, the nineteenth-century legal model to be followed by all those interested in re-organizing the new nations – in the same way that the US Constitution remained, for similar reasons, as a decisive example, coming from the eighteenth century.[2] For instance, salient Peruvian and

---

[2] The US Constitution, like the Chilean one, also emerged within a political context character-ized by disorder, disunion and instability. This is why it soon became – like the Chilean Constitution would later become – a symbol of order and stability.

Argentinean public figures – many of them in exile in Chile – were fascinated by the Chilean example, which promised to ensure the kind of order that their countries lacked. It is clear – and it was clear then – that the Chilean document was not the only or main reason of Chile's exceptional political stability (details follow), but it seemed also apparent that the "success" of the Chilean experiment was also somehow related to the nature of the Constitution. In Argentina, Juan Bautista Alberdi – one of the most influential legal scholars of the time – dismissed an idea that was popular among his colleagues, according to which the country had to fully embrace the US constitutional example. For Alberdi, the US example was only partially useful. In what concerned the organization of the Executive Power – he maintained – it was necessary to adopt the "happy" and "sensible" Chilean example, which had managed to successfully combine the required virtues of a republican government with the guarantees that monarchies offered for ensuring "order and peace" (Alberdi 1981: 75). He then quoted Bolívar, stating that Spanish America required "kings with the name of presidents" and praised Juan and Mariano Egaña – two of the main legal minds behind the Chilean text – for the ability they had demonstrated in "mixing the best features of the old colonial regime with the best elements [included in Latin America's first Constitutions]" (Alberdi 1981: 75). Similarly, Gabriel García Moreno, who would soon become the president of Ecuador, learned about the 1833 document while developing an official mission in Chile. A few years later, as the president of his country, García Moreno promoted a Constitution (the 1869 Constitution), which was very similar in character to the Chilean one, both in its strong presidentialist political structure; and in the way it fused the State with religion.

In sum, this imitative process of constitutional creation moved many Latin Americans to look back, either toward the Chilean nineteenth-century example, or to the US eighteenth-century one, in the search of inspiring examples. Considering these antecedents, one could say that the association between "good performance" and "stability" or "order" was reasonable, at least at that time. However, I think that those associations (say, between "stability" and "good performance") are still relevant today, among contemporary scholars looking for examples of good constitutional performance. For this reason, in what follows, I will try to challenge these common understandings by offering a different approach to what a "good constitutional performance" is. This alternative approach, I hope, will also find good grounding on American Constitutional history. My presentation should provide normative reasons to demonstrate why the choice of an example like that of Chile 1833 does not represent a model to be followed by those interested in constitutional design.

More generally, I shall claim that stability should not be taken as a good metric for "constitutional success."

THE (QUALIFIED) ALBERDIAN TEST FOR CONSTITUTIONAL PERFORMANCE

In this section, I shall present an alternative approach to "constitutional performance," which is in part based on Juan Bautista Alberdi's ideas, and for that reason I will refer to this alternative approach as the "Alberdian test for constitutional performance." The test consists of two parts, one that is more "contextual" and the other that is more "theoretical." In other words, the test is neither a pure "contextual/comparative" test, which denigrates theory or wants to present itself as being neutral or indifferent to theory, nor a purely abstract test, this is to say independent from or indifferent to its surrounding reality.

Alberdi, I believe, suggested this approach in his well-known book *Bases y puntos de partida para la organización política de la República Argentina* – an exceptional and very early work on comparative constitutionalism. According to him, a good Constitution was that which was able to identify and address the *main dramas* of its time, and at the same time provide *proper legal means* for tackling those problems. His "two-steps test", as I understand it, required the help of normative theory (i.e., in order to identify the "best" available means) and also a comparative exercise, highly sensitive to the needs and difficulties of the time.

When Alberdi presented his view, he was probably interested in challenging what seemed to be a shared view at his time, among legal scholars. Most scholars, in fact, appeared to be skeptical about the virtues of Latin America's early constitutional law. Alberdi, by contrast, praised those early legal proposals, in general, because he believed that they properly addressed the main problem affecting the region during those years, namely, the problem of independence. He stated: "Independence and external freedom were the vital interests that concerned the legislators of the time. They were right: they understood the needs of their time, and they knew what to do" (Alberdi 1981: 26). In other words, for Alberdi, early constitutional scholars, in Latin America, had properly recognized the need of using the constitutional energies in the direction of ensuring external independence. (Perhaps, then, the creation of powerful Executive powers, and systems of concentrated authority had to be seen as attractive legal responses, in the face of that initial drama.)

By the mid-nineteenth century, notwithstanding, Alberdi considered that there existed new fundamental problems, which required new constitutional answers, different from the ones that had prevailed in the early years. "At that time" – he claimed – "what was required was to consolidate independence through the use of arms; and today we need to ensure that independence through the material and moral enhancement of our peoples. The main goals of that time were political goals: today we need to concern ourselves with the economic goals" (Alberdi 1981: 123). Accordingly, in his draft for what would then become the Argentinean 1853 Constitution, he proposed adopting a legal organization that provided robust guarantees to what he called "economic liberties"; a strong presidentialist system; and limited "political liberties" (which he assumed would be developed in a third constitutional period).[3]

So, here we have a different and more sophisticated understanding of what a proper Constitution is, and – as a result – what could be considered, after some time, a Constitution that worked well. A proper Constitution is the one that recognizes what the *main* (political, or social, or economic) needs or *dramas* (my terms) of the time are; and then selects *adequate* means for overcoming those dramas or achieving those goals. A proper Constitution helps society to solve those fundamental problems or achieve those desired goals. Of course, I do not want to propose a very strict understanding of the idea of *dramas*. It seems clear that, at any point in history, any society faces different and relevant dramatic situations (i.e., poverty, inequality, slavery, massive violation of human rights, situations of discrimination against large groups of disadvantaged people, etc.). In addition, it seems also reasonable to think that societies lack the energy or chance to address all those dramatic situations at the same time. So, I will not claim that a particular society misused its political and legal energies, if it did not address all or (what one assumes to be) the most important "drama" that it faces. I do not want to subscribe such a demanding view. For the purposes of this chapter, I will consider that a society made a proper use of the instruments that are under its control (typically, its Constitution and other legal tools), first, if it properly dedicated them to address at least one of the significant social dramas that it faces.[4]

---

3   So, in his view, some crucial problems ("dramas") could fade away quite soon and/or on a quite precise date of time (i.e., consolidating independence was a problem of utmost importance at one point, but after a few years and some serious efforts, most countries could assume that it was not a serious problem anymore: they had finally become free States). Accordingly, the arrival of a new political era (i.e., the coming of the post-independence period); or the emergence of new fundamental problems (i.e., a profound economic crisis) could provide good reasons for promoting new constitutional reforms. In this respect – it seems clear – Alberdi did not favor the idea of enacting a Constitution once and for ever: Good political leaders had to be alert and sensitive to the "needs of the time."

4   I think that Alberdi would agree with me in this point: We should not become absurdly demanding concerning the implications of this test, and thus try to determine exactly what

Having introduced the "contextual" aspect of the Alberdian test, let me now move to its more "evaluative" or "normative" aspects, which are crucial for defining what the "main" dramas are, or how "adequate means" could look like. It seems obvious that, in order to assess whether the *goals* and the *means* recognized or adopted by a specific Constitution are reasonable, we need the help of a normative theory. The task of providing this theory is unavoidable, even though many *natural law* thinkers of Alberdi's time (and even more clearly during the US Founding Period) frequently assumed that such a task was simply unnecessary (following John Locke, many legal scholars simply referred to the "self-evident truths" of politics). Alberdi, for example, based his opinions on a solid and robust normative theory, which was mainly supported by *classical liberal* ideas (Alberdi 1954). Together with many of the most influential liberal thinkers of his time, Alberdi considered a powerful State as the main threat to individual liberties. The Colombian intellectual José María Samper canonically synthesized these ideas in his famous "*Ensayo sobre las revoluciones políticas y la condición social de las repúblicas colombianas,*" making reference to the *individualist, anti-collectivist and anti-state* position that many of the members of his generation took for granted (Jaramillo Uribe 1964: 50). This theoretical perspective of a liberal kind was obviously behind the types of solutions that Alberdi suggested for the mid-1850s crisis (economic freedoms; strong protections to contracts and property rights); and also behind all the friendly but not complacent analysis that he presented about the first Latin American Constitutions (Alberdi 1981).

In the following pages, I will employ this "Alberdian test" in order to evaluate the performance of different constitutional projects. This exercise will require me to examine specific Constitutions according to the way they understood the "needs of their time" and provided "proper" answers to them. I will consider that a solution is "proper" when it is both contextually sensitive and at the same time adequate to (previously defined) fundamental normative values. In other words, I will not consider a solution "proper" as a result of its simply being "rational" for the achievement of a certain end (i.e., "political repression is a rational means for achieving order in the short run").

The test has potential for examining a Constitution both ex ante and ex post its promulgation. *Ex ante* – and through the help of both our theoretical understandings and past experiences – we can assess the main aspects of particular constitutional projects. We may determine, for instance, whether

the main tragedy of the time and what *the best* legal remedies are. In order to talk about a successful Constitution – I would suggest, trying to interpret Alberdi – it should suffice with finding Constitutions that manage to address *some* of the most relevant problems of the time, through *reasonably adequate* remedies.

(in principle) a specific constitution is well prepared to achieve certain goals or confront certain evils, or by contrast it just promises to radicalize the existing problems. Ex post, the constitutional practice, in combination with certain normative assumptions, helps us evaluate the specific performance of a specific Constitution.

Now, the test that I will use in the following pages will differ from Alberdi's test in at least one crucial aspect, related to the substance of the normative theory that I will employ. Let me briefly explain my proposed view in the following section.

AN EGALITARIAN NORMATIVE FRAMEWORK

In the analysis that follows I will be accompanying my contextual approach with a particular normative theory, which I will name "egalitarian." As I said, I do not want to appear too demanding in what concerns my theoretical assumptions. In part for that reason, I shall ground my normative assumptions on two fundamental values that I consider to be intimately related to the America's legal history, from its very beginning. I do not need to demonstrate the presence of those historical links, in order to affirm my normative view, but in any case I want to provide some evidence in favor of my historical claim.

The two normative values I will be thinking about are those of *individual autonomy* and *collective self-government*. They refer to two fundamental values that occupied – and, I believe, still occupy – a significant place in American political discussions. Of course, the main military combats that emerged in the region since the independence were not fought with idea of "autonomy" written in the flags of the contenders. However, they did write in their banners expressions such as "religion or death," which in the end referred to the place occupied by the notion of individual autonomy in the new nations. That particular dispute – related to the place of the Church in the organization of the new societies – was decisive in American public life, during decades (and perhaps until today), and became manifest in multiple debates about the influence of the Church on civilian disputes; the scope of the State's authority; education; and, more generally, the interpretation of constitutional rights (i.e., does the right of freedom of expression or the right to tolerance include the right to maintain blasphemous beliefs or advance blasphemous ideas?).[5]

---

[5] Of course, this crucial dispute about religion and the State-Church relationship only represented a portion of a larger dispute related to the authority of the State vis-à-vis issues of personal morality (including, for instance, the criminalization of gambling; drinking; homosexuality; etc.).

In similar terms, it is not difficult to recognize the enormous influence exercised by the ideal of collective self-government in the Americas. It should be enough to state, for example, that the same independence revolutions were crucially based in the republican vindication of the right of the Americans to govern themselves. Those revolutions were directly based on a claim for self-government, which was at the same time a claim against the domination of foreign countries – England, in the case of the United States; Spain, in the case of most Latin American countries; Portugal, in the case of Brazil. From the early motto *no taxation without representation*, presented by early American colonists against England, the demand for self-government always occupied a privileged place in the early disputes that took place in the new societies. Perhaps more interestingly, that claim continued playing a central role in the new nations *after* independence, although in a very peculiar way. Very commonly, in effect, those groups who had been convoked to the war of independence, took part in it, and offered their lives in it, made the ideal of self-government their own. Those individuals – as the historian Gordon Wood always emphasized in his study of the American Revolution – began to use the doctrines that were inculcated to them, against the leaders of the revolution (Wood 1969). They demanded a more definite role for the people at large in the decision-making process; they asked for more space and opportunities for political participation; they disputed the restricted political organization that emerged the independence.

Now, my previous claims should not be read as stating that the ideals of individual autonomy and collective self-government commanded or guided all the relevant social and political disputes in the region, since independence. By contrast, I believe that the different political conceptions that began to gain influence in the region since the independence years, dishonored, in one or another way, in more or less dramatic forms, those two ideals. In my view, *conservative* conceptions tended to dishonor both ideals, as a result of its political elitism and moral perfectionism; more *radical* conceptions, and as a consequence of their political majoritarianism, tended to affirm the value of self-government, but were at the same time ready to sacrifice individual autonomy for the sake of the former; while *liberal* conceptions tended to do the opposite of radicals, this is to say, they were open to sacrifice the value of self-government in the name of protecting individual autonomy. Then, and in contrast with these three views, I call *egalitarian* those conceptions that struggled for both ideals at the same time.[6]

---

[6]   Even though I have proposed my own definitions about these terms (see Gargarella 2010, 2013), I do not need to press with those definitions here. It should suffice to appeal to concepts similar to those that prevailed during the Founding Period. A good start in that search could be

The egalitarian perspective seems to refer to an "empty box" in the history of constitutionalism in the Americas. In any case, in what follows, I will use that conception as a regulative ideal that will help us to assess the performance of actual institutional arrangements and also the actual choices made by political leaders and legal doctrinaires. In order to evaluate the "success" of a particular Constitution, then, the questions we will have in mind will be like the following ones: What was the social/national "drama" that this particular Constitution came to confront? Was this a problem or ideal that was worth addressing/pursuing in those particular circumstances? And, more significantly, were the means chosen for those purposes appropriate? The egalitarian framework would help us to give content to the "normative" aspects included in those questions. Expectedly, we will find Constitutions that come closer to the defined standpoint, and Constitutions that remain far from it.

In the following pages I will illustrate this view through four examples, related to different constitutional models: the first, a conservative model, as the one proposed by Simón Bolívar; a second one promoted by the Egaña's in Chile, and Gabriel García Moreno in Ecuador (which I take to be conservative in a stricter way); third, a radical model (mainly through the example of the work of some US antifederalists and some progressive Latin Americans); and fourth, a liberal model, as the one advanced by James Madison in the United States.

Summarily speaking, I will claim that

(i) Simón Bolívar's Constitutions – Constitutions of conservative character – properly recognized one of the main tragedies of the time, namely, the existing difficulties for *consolidating independence*; but failed concerning

Bartolomé Mitre's work *Conservative ideas of the good type*, published the July 24, 1857, where the Argentine politician (which would become president of the country) Mitre lucidly examined the political landscape in Argentina and in the region. Mitre then referred to the three main political factions that dominated the region – namely, liberals, conservatives and radicals. In his words: "Among us, and also in all the other American countries, there have been three main parties that represented the main tendencies of society, and came to rule the country at one point. The three parties are the conservative party; the liberal party; and the radical party" (Donghi 1980: 183). Mitre characterized these parties in the following way: The conservative party, he said, "has been first monarchist, then favorable to the landowners, immediately then favorable to the proprietors, and in the end it became reduced to men of influence and good sense, who oscillated between progress and resistance." Then he described liberalism as a "reformist" party; responsible of enacting "memorable laws"; defender of "ideas an progress"; and the one that "always rejected the influence of caudillism." Finally, he presented the radical party claiming that it "has been represented, among us, by the Barbarians. Artigas, Ramírez, Aldao, Rosas, those were the apostles of the radical party, the party that advocated for an exaggerated democracy and equality, that downgraded the intelligence to the level of barbarism, instead of trying to raise the masses to the level of intelligence" (Donghi 1980).

the main solutions that it proposed, namely, the *concentration of power* and the centralization of the territory.

(ii) The Egaña's (1823/1833) and García Moreno's (1869) conservative Constitutions failed both in assuming that the main tragedy of the time was the *lack of religious sentiments* among large sections of the population; and in considering that the dire use of the *coercive powers* of the State was an appropriate response in the face of that situation.

(iii) Many of the most radical constitutional proposals of the eighteenth and nineteenth centuries, in the Americas, properly recognized the value of *collective self-government* as one of utmost constitutional relevance; but tended to choose at least partially unacceptable means for promoting that goal (namely, means that implied severe curtailments to the ideal of individual autonomy).

(iv) The Federalists' 1787 liberal Constitution properly recognized that the problem of *factions* represented a significant threat to the political order of the time; but partially failed with regard of the means it chose for confronting that evil (this, by choosing means that implied severe curtailment to the ideal of collective self-government).

Simón Bolívar's constitutional project

Facts. A Latin American hero in the fight for independence, Bolívar, was deeply implicated in the drafting of constitutions in the region. Not surprisingly, then, his numerous constitutional speeches, proposals and drafts were profoundly marked by his previous involvement in the independence battles. There are two elements, in particular, which I would highlight from Bolívar's involvement in that period. First of all, I would mention his fears about the future of the independence revolution: Bolívar was extremely worried about Spain's military attempts to recover its former colonies in America. Second, I would underline his conviction about the need of concentrating political and military authority in the hands of the Executive, so as to ensure a successful end to the independence fight. These two elements, it should be noted, directly refer to Bolívar's main constitutional creed: They tell us what was, for him, the *main drama* affecting the region – the drama of independence – and also what was the *main means* he suggested, in order to overcome that drama, namely, a strong authority, embodied with full military and political powers.

One interesting illustration of this interplay between the drama that he envisioned and the particular institutional solution that he had in mind appears in his harsh analysis of Venezuela's 1811 Constitution, which, among other things, provided for a tripartite executive. Bolívar was furious about this constitutional proposal that was elaborated in his country, because it contradicted all his suggestions about institutional design for times of crisis – the Venezuelan document dispersed rather than concentrated authority. This is why in his "Memorial to the Citizens of New Granada by a Citizen of Caracas," written in 1813, he maintained that "among the causes that brought about Venezuela's downfall the nature of its constitution ranks first, which, I repeat, was as contrary to Venezuela's interests as it was favorable to those of her adversaries" (Bolívar 1951: 22).[7] Notably, Bolívar faulted the seemingly radical constitution of 1811, which actually survived only a few days, for making the consolidation of independence impossible. Similarly, in his famous "Discourse from Angostura," of 1819 (a discourse that was pronounced at the time he was inaugurating the second national congress of Venezuela), he urged his fellow citizens to "put aside the triumvirate which holds the executive power and center it in a president. We must grant him sufficient authority to enable him to continue the struggle against the obstacles inherent in our recent situation, our present state of war, and every variety of foe, foreign and domestic, whom we must battle for some time to come" (Bolívar 1951: 190). To state it more clearly: Bolívar was convinced both about the importance of drafting a Constitution for this time of (independence) crisis and also about the need of concentrating powers in order to overcome that crisis.

Bolívar maintained these basic constitutional ideas during most of his life: from an initial period, when he was fascinated by the British (monarchical) model, to his more mature years, when he was more clearly influenced by the French, Napoleonic legal model. One can recognize the impact of the British example, for instance, in his influential "Letters from Jamaica" of 1815 and also in his famous "Discourse from Angostura" of 1819. In those documents Bolívar praised the English example, and particularly its adoption of a powerful

---

[7] He also stated "[the] most grievous error committed by Venezuela in making her start on the political stage was, as none can deny, her fatal adoption of the system of tolerance, a system long condemned as weak and inadequate by every man of common sense, yet tenaciously maintained with an unparalleled blindness to the very end" (Donghi 1980: 18). A few years later, in the speech he delivered at the inauguration of the second national Congress of Venezuela, in Angostura, he went back to his criticisms of the original Venezuelan constitution, now in order to object to its federalist character. He stated that "no matter how tempting this magnificent federative system might have appeared, and regardless of its possible effect, the Venezuelans were not prepared to enjoy it immediately upon casting off their chains. We were not prepared for such good, for good, like evil, results in death when it is sudden and excessive. Our moral fiber did not then possess the stability necessary to derive benefits from a wholly representative power; a power so sublime, in fact, that it might more nearly befit a republic of saints" (Bolívar 1951: 181).

Executive and a conservative Senate. He stated: "No matter how closely we study the composition of the English executive power we can find nothing to prevent its being judged as the most perfect model for a kingdom, for an aristocracy, or for a democracy. Give Venezuela such an executive power in the person of a president chosen by the people or their representatives, and you will have taken a great step toward national happiness" (Bolívar 1951: 187–188). Bolívar also argued that the hereditary senate could become the "soul" of the republic, an institution capable of resisting all institutional catastrophes.[8]

Later on, however, Bolívar abandoned this initial (British) source of inspiration and began to follow the example of the Napoleonic Constitutions, although he never admitted it. This latter influence was reflected, for example, in the constitutional document which he wrote for Bolivia in 1826: This created a life president with the power to designate his vice-president and his successor; interrupted the standing tradition of a tripartite structure of power; and strictly reduced the power of the municipalities. In a message to the Congress of Bolivia, in 1826, he presented one of his strongest and clearest defenses of a proposal he had supported throughout his life, that of a life-term, non-accountable president. He said:

> The President of the Republic, in our Constitution, becomes the sun which, fixed in its orbit, imparts life to the universe. This supreme authority must be perpetual, for in non-hierarchical systems, more than in others, a fixed point is needed about which leaders and citizens, men and affairs can revolve. "Give me a point where I may stand," said an ancient sage, "and I will move the earth." For Bolivia this point is the life-term President. (Bolívar 1951: 598)

His constitutional ideas also became highly influential in the public life of other Latin American countries. For instance, General Andrés Santa Cruz proposed a Constitution of this type for the confederation that he presided over between Peru and Bolivia; while General Flores in Ecuador and the Mexican conservatives in 1836 also favored this kind of institutional model (Ayala 1995; Safford 1985: 366).

---

[8] Bolívar's concerns with stabilizing institutions and "neutral" powers seemed to derive from the influence of Constant, who was at the time closely read by both liberals and conservatives. For Frank Safford, "Constant conceived of the constitutional monarch as a neutral balance wheel, moderating conflicts among the executive, the representative and the judicial powers. Bolívar followed this scheme both in distinguishing the president (constitutional monarch) and the actions of his ministers and in placing moderating power in the hands of the censors [the 'Moral Power']. This Constantian conception of a moderating power was also found in the Mexican centralist constitution of 1836, known as the Seven Laws" (Safford 1985: 367).

Values. If we were to evaluate the Bolivarian approach to constitutionalism according to the proposed Alberdian test, we could suggest a double conclusion, partly positive and partly negative. The positive side would be related to Bolívar's identification of the main political problem or tragedy of the time, to be confronted through the use of law, namely, the independence problem. We may disagree or not about the relative importance of that difficulty, but it is clear that it represented a huge and crucial political issue: The new Constitutions of the new nations would have been unwise if they did not provide a due consideration of it. More specifically, if we took into account the two main normative values here defended, this is to say the values of collective self-government and individual autonomy, Bolívar's choice seemed reasonable. In fact, the problem of independence undoubtedly represented the first and more pressing concern for anyone interested in the promotion of any notion of collective self-government. In addition (and even though the first reason would have been already sufficient for our purposes) it is clear that for those interested in promoting the value of individual autonomy, the kinds of threats posed by a brutal Imperial force represented an evil of utmost relevance. In sum, even though many of us could have mentioned other priorities, it is clear that Bolívar chose to work with problems of absolute legal relevance.

The conclusion, however, should be different regarding Bolívar's suggested proposals, and particularly concerning the concentration of territorial, political and military authority, which I think we should consider unacceptable from a normative standpoint. I understand that my point in this respect is not absolutely obvious, but let me put it in this way, so as to clarify what I mean by it: One cannot at the same time value collective self-government *and* the concentration of authority, which represents the denial of the former claim. Collective self-government requires the people's deciding and/or controlling (in one or another not insignificant way) all or most issues of public relevance.[9] The alternative of delegating all those decisions to an enlightened and non-controlled savior may be considered more efficient or acceptable for different reasons, but those will not be reasons based on the value of self-government.

These foreseeable problems were then confirmed or aggravated through the actual political practice. In fact, during the Latin American Framing Period,

---

[9] Recall, for example, how Thomas Jefferson defined the ideal of a "republican government" – *his* ideal of government: "[A] government by its citizens in mass, acting directly and personally, according to rules established by the majority." And he added: "[E]very other government is more or less republican ... in proportion as it has in its composition more or less of this ingredient of the direct action of the citizens" (Jefferson 1999: 207). "In general," he added, "I believe that the decisions of the people, in a body, will be more honest and disinterested than those of the wealthy men." He presented this view in a letter to John Taylor, from May 28, 1816 (see Jefferson 1984: 1392).

most political activists and doctrinaires interested in the value of self-government clearly recognized the existence of a tension between their most cherished value, and Bolívar tendency to concentrate political authority in his own hands. For instance, the first liberal Peruvian Constitution was written in 1823, this is to say more than a decade after the first experiments of Bolivarian constitutionalism. With the Bolivarian experience in mind, Peruvian liberals proposed an institutional system that in many ways reacted to it. Their creation resembled, in many ways, that of Venezuela 1811, which had infuriated Bolívar: It included, for instance, a plural Executive composed of three persons, which Bolívar had deemed the main cause of Venezuela's downfall. During the Peruvian constitutional debates, the influential deputy Sánchez Carrión stringently condemned the Bolivarian alternative of designing a hyper-strong Executive.[10] In his opinion, "three people will not get together to oppress the rest of us." He declared: "[A] government by one is efficient if what we want is to treat human beings as beasts . . . but what I want to defend is freedom, this is also what the people want. Without freedom I do not want anything: the idea of having only one person in charge of the government brings me back the image of the king . . . of the tyranny" (see Basadre 1949: 12). In Colombia, this anti-Boliviarian trend reached its extreme, with some liberal and radical activists, like Ezequiel Rojas, openly defending the virtues of tyrannicide.[11]

---

[10] In the letters he signed as the *Solitario de Sayán*, Sanchéz Carrión ferociously attacked the monarchist alternative, defended by important military leaders such as the Argentinean general San Martín. Given the character of Peruvian people, he stated, "[if we accepted a constitutional monarchy] we would become excellent vassals and never again citizens: we would have servile attitudes, we would find pleasure in kissing the hand of the Majesty" (Portacarrero 1987: 92).

[11] Another common radical strategy for combating the powerful executive was to limit the term of its mandate. During the famous "Río Negro Convention," in Colombia, the representatives of the so-called *Radical Olimpo* proposed, among other things, restricting each presidential mandate to only two years. The so-called radicals justified this remarkable decision-making reference to their fears of tyrannical governments. They had come to power with the help of the authoritarian General Mosquera and they seriously distrusted his intentions and ambitions. The exceptional adoption of a two-year term of mandate represented, then, a good example of what most radicals were ready to do in order to reduce the powers of executive. Similarly, the early constitutional proposal of 1813 in the *Banda Oriental* not only restricted the military and legislative powers of the executive but also reduced its mandate to a one-year term. In Chile, too, the fight against the "excessive" powers of the executive constituted one of the main political goals of the populist groups throughout the century. This fight became particularly intense after 1848, when groups such as the *Sociedad de la Igualdad* and the *Asamblea Constituyente* began to press for the adoption of immediate political reforms, and obtained its initial fruits by the end of the century, through the work of Manuel Antonio Matta and his Radical Party.

In other words, an ex post study of Bolivarian constitutionalism would tend to ratify our ex ante fears about its main features. More specifically, those who stressed the values of individual liberties and collective self-government found good reasons to resist Bolívar's constitutional projects, particularly after they realized how hyper-powerful Executives, like the same Bolívar, tended to exercise their political powers.

In sum, we have good motives for objecting to an institutional model based on the concentration of authority, as the one that Bolívar presented after the independence. Early constitutional history in the Americas clearly supports this point.

Constitutional conservatism: Egaña's constitutionalism/García Moreno's 1869 Constitution

Facts. Herein I will examine the strongest version of conservative constitutionalism that appeared in the Americas, during the Founding Period. The Constitutions that I will here explore are strictly conservative both in what concerns the way in which they organized powers and the way in which they conceived of the bill of rights: They are deeply marked by their moral perfectionism and their political elitism.

Chile's 1833 Constitution and Ecuador's 1869 Constitution represent two of the most extreme and "pure" examples of conservative constitutionalism, thorough the Americas. The Chilean 1833 document – which was drafted, among others, by Mariano Egaña – was a more sophisticated and less moralistic version of the 1823 Constitution, which had been written by Mariano's father, the enormously influential Juan Egaña (who in this opportunity played a shadow role, as his son's advisor). The 1823 Constitution was an extreme version of moral perfectionism: The State appeared then committed to directly supervise the moral behavior of each single inhabitant of the country. In fact, the Constitution was accompanied by a monumental "Moral Code," which regulated almost every aspect of the public and private life, from the national dances, to the national music, gambling, vices and a long etcetera. At that time, Juan Egaña made clear that all constitutional rights would be interpreted according to the requirements of Catholicism. In this respect he asserted, for example, that "It is a mistake to allow every type of insult and calumny, to allow attacks upon the most sacred and inviolable principles of morality and religion, with the expectation of punishing its authors later ... *The sum of the evils produced by a free press on religion, morality, the mutual concordance among individuals and even the exterior credit of the nation is much greater than the goods it produces*" (Egaña 1969: 84–85, emphasis added).[12] "Speech and writing," for him, were open to regulation: "[T]hey belong to political jurisdiction," he argued, "since they can so greatly influence the domestic and social order" (Egaña 1969: 84–85).[13]

Although clearly based on this 1823 antecedent, the 1833 Chilean Constitution showed less extreme and less moralistic features. In any case, concerning the organization of rights, the Chilean document was exceptionally committed to Catholicism: The "Catholic, Apostolic and Roman religion" was established as the country's only religion "with the exclusion of the public exercise of any other" (article 5). Concerning the organization of powers, the 1833 Constitution established severe limitations to political participation or active citizenship (age, wealth, and literacy, according to article 8); created a weak Congress (which was opened only for three months every year, according to article 52); and also a hyper-powerful Executive, which among other things was allowed to declare de estate of siege (article 82, inc. 20) and thus limit the already limited rights of the people at large.

For many, this (conservative) combination of moralism and authoritarianism began to represent the best existing formulae for having a durable Constitution. As mentioned earlier, the Ecuadorian García Moreno, who learned about this Constitution in Chile, tried to reproduce this model in Ecuador, in 1869, after assuming the presidency of the country. At that time, the elected president made one of the clearest and more telling conservative speeches in the history of Americas' conservative constitutionalism. For our purposes, his speech seems particularly telling: García Moreno exposed the main aims of his project (what he was going to be fighting for) and also the constitutional means that he was going to use, for reaching those goals. In one of the main passages of this speech he stated: *"[T]he first [goal of my power] will be that of harmonizing our political institutions with our religious beliefs; and the second will be that of investing our public authorities with the forces required to resist the assaults of anarchy"* (Romero and Romero 1978: 115).

In this, as well as in other speeches, García Moreno made clear that the main problem that he wanted to address by using the country's constitutional

---

[12] "In my own republic," he added, "I would only allow liberty of the press for those older than forty; but young people's works would always be subject to revision . . . In all nations we find age requirements for becoming a senator, and advisor, a director of morality, religion, or education: why, then, should we allow the most corrupt and thoughtless to ... teach and address themselves to the whole nation . . .?" (Egaña 1969: 84–85).

[13] These public expressions, he insisted, should not offend the "mysteries, dogmas, religious discipline, and the morality generally approved by the Catholic Church" (Donoso 1967: 136–137). All written material, then, was to be subject to the preliminary "advice of good men," who would inform the writer of all the censurable elements which appeared in his work (Donoso 1967: 228–229). In addition, Egaña's Constitution declared the Catholic religion to be the official religion of the country, and seriously restricted the public practice of other beliefs.

energies was the Catholic Church's insufficient influence upon the nation's political life (and, more generally, the nation's dramatic situation, which he described as one of moral decay). In addition, García Moreno made clear that his proposed legal solutions were going to be fundamentally based on the dire use of the State's coercive powers.

On the one hand, the entire section of rights became organized around the needs and demands of the Catholic Church. In fact, in a decision that was going to be absolutely exceptional in the entire history of conservative constitutional though, García Moreno made the very condition of citizenship dependent on one's religion. More precisely, only Roman Catholics would be able to become citizens of Ecuador. In addition, article 9 of the Constitution established that the Catholic, Apostolic and Roman religion was going to be the only religion of the country, with the total exclusion of all others, and that the political power were obliged to protect and ensure due respect to it. All other rights were then put into question and subordinated to the (alleged) needs of Catholicism. For example, article 102 of the Constitution proclaimed that "the expression of thoughts" would be totally free from preliminary censorship as long as these expressions respected "religion, morality, and decency" (see Reyes 1942; Borja and Borja 1951). García Moreno justified the restrictions on a free press included in the new Constitution, asserting that "the demagogic press, unbridled as never before, insults our religion and our chastity, calls for revolutionary passions and favors anarchy" (Reyes 1942: 113). The Church played a fundamental role in this structure, given that, in accordance with a decree of December 1871, a group of its members had to check the morality of all materials before they were printed, including privately owned material which offended the church's morality. All questionable writings were then burned in a public ceremony. In a similar way, the Constitution recognized the people's right to association as long as they "respected religion, morality, and public order" (article 109). Moreover, the document explicitly established that these associations would be "under the authorities' surveillance."[14]

On the other hand, the organization of powers of the 1869 Constitution also followed the Chilean 1833 example. Article 59, for example put the president in charge of the "internal order and external security of the Nation," giving the

---

[14] In fact, what followed after the approval of the Constitution made clear the actual implications of the president's words and constitutional proposals. García Moreno organized a secret police; persecuted dissenters; and imprisoned those whom he considered enemies of the country. As one of his main political enemies, Juan Montalvo, maintained: "García Moreno divided Ecuador in three equal parts: one was sentenced to death, the other was sent to exile; and the final one condemned to slavery" (Bossano 1959: 70).

president ample discretionary powers. Meanwhile, article 60 conceded him all the traditional extraordinary faculties that conservative Constitutions delegated to the president (i.e., the possibility to declare the *state of siege*), but also adding a few untraditional powers, such as the "supreme inspection" in everything related to "police," "education" and "beneficence" (article 60, inc. 9). It goes without saying that, during his government, García Moreno exercised those powers with shameful meticulousness.

Values. If one had to assess (this strong branch of) conservative constitutionalism from the proposed Alberdian schema, the evaluation would be fundamentally and seriously negative (although the final evaluation will also include some nuances). This claim, it must be noted, directly contradicts alternative approaches, which for instance see the Chilean 1833 Constitution as actually the best Latin American example of a "successful" Constitution.

In my view, conservative constitutionalism fails at both levels, this is to say both in what regards the identification of the main drama or set of problems of the time, and in the legal remedies it proposed for curing those problems. In what concerns the first question (the national drama), conservative constitutionalism had a poor diagnosis of what the main evils affecting the newly independent societies were. For conservatives, the new societies were mainly characterized by their moral decay and the political ignorance of the masses, evils that in part explained and in part followed the anarchical impulses of the independence revolutions.[15] As the Colombian Sergio Arboleda stated, "all the incidents of our revolution originated in one and the same principle and were aimed at achieving one and the same goal: its principle, the anti-Catholic French revolution; its goal, the destruction of the moral feelings of the masses" (Albarracín et al. 1988: 278).[16] These assumptions were, empirically speaking, fundamentally wrong (details follow): It was far from obvious that the new

---

[15] The Peruvian Bartolomé Herrera espoused one of the most extreme versions of this view, asserting that "the people, that is, the sum of individuals of all ages and conditions, have neither the capacity nor the right to create laws. Laws are eternal principles originating in the nature of all things, principles that cannot be clearly perceived except by those who are accustomed to the difficulties of this mental effort and exercised in the arts of scientific investigation." Most significant political leaders, however, adopted a somewhat different position (Basadre 1949: 60)..

[16] Similarly, Mariano Ospina Rodríguez made reference to the "wild anti-Christian movement" that originated at the time of independence. In Peru, the influential cleric Bartolomé Herrera (probably the best example of Peruvian conservative constitutionalism) denounced that "the people have become the slaves of what is called the will of the people ... slaves of the will of demagogues." Bartolomé Herrera pronounced this sermon in the Te Deum celebrated at the anniversary of Peruvian independence in the College of San Carlos (1846) (see Romero and Romero 1977: 136, 138). Peru, he continued, has become "the prey of the ... malevolent and anti-social mistakes publicized by the French Revolution" (Romero and Romero 1977).

societies were above all suffering from situations of moral decay, as it was far from obvious that their problems originated in or were intimately related to the absence of religious fervor. The conservatives' analysis resulted even more implausible in normative terms. From the perspective that it is here defended, at least, the conservative approach appears in direct and serious tension with both the ideals of individual autonomy and collective self-government.

Not surprisingly, this initially wrong understanding of society's evils was then translated into bad recipes destined to cure those evils. The conservative model, in fact, mainly suggested the use of the State's coercive powers with a dual purpose (as García Moreno had made clear in his inaugural speech): imposing the official religious creed, and avoiding social disruptions of any kind (disruptions that would suggest the fatal deterioration of the moral building of society, and reveal the political ignorance of the masses). Again, from the normative perspective that we are here maintaining, this remedial recipe could not be less attractive. On the one hand, the morally perfectionist view in which it is based constitutes simply the antonym of individual autonomy. On the other hand, the politically elitist view in which it is supported directly contradicts the ideal of collective self-government.

Having said this, let me pause for a while and explore a slightly different approach to this extreme conservative model, which could help understand the attention that this model gained during the time it was in force. The idea would be that, behind their aggressive, traditionalist rhetoric, conservatives fought for the establishment of *order* – mainly understood as a synonym of political stability – which was a highly prized within these new independent societies. Arguably, the value of order could or should also be appreciated by those who are mainly concerned by other, say, more noble values, such as autonomy or self-government. Order or political stability – someone could claim – is the precondition of everything else: Without order we can neither live a safe personal life, nor enjoy a valuable communal life. There is obviously some important truth in these sayings, but nevertheless those conclusions should be resisted for a variety of theoretical reasons. Let me mention a few of them:

First, political stability should not be confused or wrongly associated with constitutional authoritarianism: The terms are not synonyms, and political stability does not necessarily require authoritarian Constitutions, as most nineteenth-century Latin American conservatives seemed to assume. Second, empirically speaking, nineteenth-century conservatives tended to be too quick in both attributing the achievement of political stability to the adoption of certain conservative Constitutions (i.e., the adoption of the Chilean 1833 Constitution, details follow), and in associating political breakdown with the adoption of alternative, republican Constitutions (i.e., as Simón Bolívar did, concerning the Venezuelan 1811 Constitution). Third, the valuable search of order does not need to come together with the kinds of political medicines actually offered by conservatism (i.e., political repression; moral repression). Fourth, the conservatives' search for order has normally been based on disputable assumptions about democracy and the working of modern societies (such as "personal dissidences and political pluralism undermine democracy"; or "the people acting together tend to be guided by passions, rather than reason"). Fifth, the conservatives' model of order has usually been based on obnoxious normative assumptions about individual autonomy and personal capacities (such as "what is good for individuals is independent from what they believe or want for themselves").

As a final note, let me just illustrate how the actual practice of conservative constitutionalism helped to enrich and ratify concerns that liberals or radicals could have presented ex ante. The examples that I have in mind refer to the Chilean Constitution of 1833, which – it must be remembered – represented the (seemingly) best (and more "successful," in the narrow sense) example of conservative constitutionalism. Critics of the Chilean document, like the noted liberal intellectual José Victorino Lastarria, objected to that Constitution for a variety of reasons, but mainly because it did not contribute to what its defenders always said it had mainly been contributed, namely, to the achievement of social peace. In Lastarria's words,

> Is it the case that this politics obtained what it wanted, that it guaranteed order and tranquility forever, putting an end to revolutions and turmoil, and making national freedom possible? ... For us ... clear adversaries of this way of doing politics ... the answer to that question is negative, and we ground our judgments in facts. (Recall) all the conspiracies and tumults ... the revolutions and battles of 1837, 1850 and 1851; and (all the years in which) our republic has been under state of siege and extraordinary powers ... which have demonstrated that neither the revolutions nor the disorders have come to an end (in the long period in which the Constitution has been in place). By contrast, what is clear is that it has been necessary to rule without it, by sacrificing the national liberty in order to perpetuate such an erroneous politics ... the dominant restrictive or absolutist politics has been incapable to maintain order, because that politics itself is a threat to justice ... the only possible base to tranquility and progress in human societies! Is it possible to think, however, that without those measures and those extraordinary faculties we would have had more disturbances and a more terrible anarchy? Surely no, because ... liberal politics and the rule

of law are the best means for achieving order and the more solid guarantees for security and tranquility. (Lastarria 1906: 215–216)[17]

This is to say, for Lastarria, the actual practice of the 1833 Constitution provided him with good reasons for objecting to precisely the Constitution's most cherished virtues. Another noted liberal, namely, Justo Arteaga Alemparte reached exactly the same conclusion than his colleague Lastarria. For Arteaga, it was clear that "all the troubles" that affected Chile during the years of the 1833 Constitution, were "a consequence of that same Constitution" For him, the causes of Chile's stability resided, instead, "in the character and necessities of its inhabitants, and the conditions of its soil, rather than in the 1833 Constitution." Without that Constitution – he concluded – "we would have had less troubles and more progress" (Alemparte 1870: 28–29). And also: "[T]he Constitution has understood how to provoke turmoil; but it has not been able to prevent or overcome it. To make it responsible for the success of the country is … absolutely unjust" (Alemparte 1870: 31).[18]

Radical constitutionalism: from the antifederalist's case to the case of Latin American radicals

Facts. The period that preceded the enactment of the US Constitution (1776–1787) has sometimes been described as a period of radical constitutionalism (Wood 1969). Although, in fact, during this period there were written different Constitutions, of different kind, it is actually true that some of these

---

[17] For Lastarria, it was clear that the 1833 Constitution had failed in its main purposes, which became apparent given the "amount of conspiracies, revolutions and disturbances that have shocked the country since 1837." This is why he began to look for an alternative, which he found in the ideal of "ensuring respect to political institutions and protections to the individuals, through justice and the law" (Donoso 1967: 448).

[18] For Alemparte, all the "tumults and commotion" that affected Chile, "occurred under the imperium of the 1833 Constitution" (Alemparte 1870: 28–29). If the Constitution undermined rather than favored the country's peace and political tranquility, then it was necessary to look for the causes of Chile's exceptional political stability somewhere else. For Arteaga Alemparte, those causes resided in extra-constitutional factors, such as the "character" and the peculiar "needs" of Chileans; or the "conditions of the soil" (Alemparte 1870: 20, 30). The Constitution's answer, instead, tended to be always the same: the state of siege. Like Lastarria, Arteaga Alemparte maintained that all authoritarian responses had dramatically failed. In his words, "we have had authoritarianism, strong constitutions, brutal governments in all the South American countries." That history illustrated the hopelessness of the authoritarian solutions. "Repression" – he claimed – was not the solution (Alemparte 1870: 33). For that reason, it was necessary to equilibrate powers, ensure a proper balance between liberty and authority and defend a proper representative system (Alemparte 1870: 37).

document appeared to put a heavy stress on the revolutionary value of self-government.

Many of those early constitutions represented a strong response to a period characterized by political dependence, this is to say a period when some of the essentials of public life (i.e., basic decisions about taxation) were under the control of external or nonlocal forces. External dominion and political dependence represented, as we know, serious evils for the kind of republican political philosophy that in one way or another animated many of these early experiments (Baylin 1992; Pettit 1997; Pocock 1975; Skinner 1990). From such statements, we can infer what was the main "tragedy" that radicals tried to overcome, when they began thinking about Constitutions, namely, political dependence. In addition, as we shall immediately examine, it seems also clear what their main institutional response to that disgrace was, namely, the affirmation of a strongly majoritarian Constitution.

The 1776 Constitution of Pennsylvania may represent an interesting starting point in order to explore some of the peculiar institutional proposals that characterized radical constitutionalism. This particular Constitution was written under the influence of the British Radical Thomas Paine, and it represented an exemplar case of what a radical constitution could look like in those early years. Pennsylvania's 1776 Constitution had a generous section of rights; lifted all restrictions on voting (which was, at the time, a remarkable achievement); and also organized power in a quite untraditional way. Its power structure, in fact, included a powerful unicameral legislature, following the French Revolutionary dictum according to which "the will of the people is one and indivisible." In addition, the 1776 Constitution created a weak Executive power; established that the people themselves would be a check upon the legislature; organized a judicial system where judges were appointed for a term of seven years; and defined a political system of constitutional review.

In order to get a more complete approach of how radical constitutionalism looked like during this Founding Period, it may be worth also exploring the writings of members of the antifederalist group, this is to say the group of authors and activists that opposed the 1787 Constitution.[19] Many of them, for

---

[19] It is clear, however, that such a group included people from very diverse ideologies: from old conservative politicians who were strong at the local level and were afraid of losing their own power, to radical activists that denounced the new 1787 Constitution as an aristocratic project. In spite of this, the term is still associated with a more democratic and radical (or perhaps better, anti-liberal) approach to constitutionalism. Many of these more radical texts have been collected in excellent compilations that allow us to have a good idea of what their understanding of the Constitution was (see, for instance, Borden 1965; Allen and Gordon 1985; Kenyon 1985; Storing 1981a, 1981b).

instance, advocated federalism; rejected the central government's attempts to interfere with the local affairs; defended in one or another way for majoritarian politics; worked against political elitism; spoke the language of the "sovereignty of the people," the "general will" and the "social contract"; and took the politics of "civic virtue" seriously.

In Latin America, the history of political and legal radicalism was different than in the United States, among other reasons because radicals did not find the social bases and social conditions they found in the United States. Simplifying a very long story, we could say that in the United States, local communities composed of by British immigrants were somehow required to explore forms of self-government – they had no choice but to organize their public life by themselves. However, in the highly centralized and more authoritarian Latin American context, this possibility was not open to the locals. These adverse circumstances did not prevent the emergence of radical and critical Latin American thinking but did erode the social basis of political radicalism. In any case, there are a number of significant Latin American thinkers who developed radical views concerning the organization of the new nations. Those developments took place particularly at two "revolutionary" moments of this early history, namely, at the time that immediately followed the independence revolution (1810–1812); and then in the mid-nineteenth century (1848–1850), after the "democratic revolutions" that emerged in Europe at that time (this "wave" or European radicalism had a significant impact in the region, and particularly in Colombia, Chile and Peru).

One of the most articulated and influential branches of Latin American radicalism is the one that appeared in Chile, in 1848, around the *Sociedad de la Igualdad*. This "society" was founded by Chilean activists who had taken part in the "democratic" uprisings of the period, in France. The main figure of that social movement was Francisco Bilbao, who wrote what was, perhaps, the best piece of radical constitutionalism for the region, namely, his pamphlet *El gobierno de la libertad* (Bilbao 2007). In that document (written in response to General Castilla's call for a reform of the dominant conservative 1839 Constitution), Bilbao reflected upon constitutionalism and the role of majority will, and made clear what the main problems and solutions required by the new nations were. For Bilbao, it was necessary to fight against political dependence in the name of self-governing ideas. As he made clear in *El gobierno de la libertad*, the French Jacobin Constitution of 1793 was the only Constitution that "deserve to be remembered." In that same pamphlet, Bilbao made a case for direct forms of democracy, against those who appeared fundamentally skeptic toward this ideal (Bilbao 2007: 321–322). Similarly, he defined the delegation of legislative powers as a "crime against humanity"

(Bilbao 2007: 326) and as "slavery disguised as sovereignty" ("the history of Congresses demonstrates this claim" – he maintained (Bilbao 2007: 322)). He also defended imperative mandates and the right to recall (Bilbao 2007: 321–322). In his opinion, the people had to choose mere delegates, which he defined as "agents who depend on the sovereign, subject to imperative mandate," with an authority that had to be "revocable," according to the will of the sovereign (Bilbao 2007: 327).

Values. Radical groups, in the Americas, fought for self-government and against political dependence in a broader sense. They were also against the undue political impositions of central governments upon local communities and (in some more extreme but not totally unusual cases), against the political dominion of the powerful upon the disadvantaged (Sandel 1996). So, in principle at least, we may say that radicals worked in favor of plausible *goals* or political ideals.

The situation is somehow different if we instead focus on the constitutional responses and institutional *means* that radicals advocated for, in the name of their valuable ideals. Let me begin this examination through a brief analysis of the radicals' proposals concerning the *organization of powers*. In principle, I would claim, they favored the adoption of means that were appropriate or adjusted to the particular political goals that they pursued (even though it seems also clear to me that their favored institutional proposals were in need of much refinement and improvement): annual elections, rotation in office, mandatory instructions, the right to recall, the banning of re-elections, short-term mandates, instances of direct democracy and popular checks upon the government were among these proposals.

Things look different if we instead focus on their approach to *legal rights*. Here, the contribution of American radicals was in part very attractive, but also problematic in part. The attractive aspect of their proposals had to do with the radicals' concern with the expansion of political rights, and the importance they gave to so-called *social question* (this is to say, the attention they put on the situation of people living in deplorable social conditions). So, again, the radicals' contribution concerning these fundamental issues is indisputable and merits historical recognition. The problem that I find, however, has to do with the high price they accepted to pay in the name of their fundamental political ideals. To put it very simply, radicals usually accepted to sacrifice individual autonomy in the name of their most cherished value, namely, collective self-government. The actual political practice, in the Americas, only helped to ratify and increase those fears.

As the historian Pérez Guilhou put it (while describing the view of Argentine radicals at the end of the nineteenth century), radicals tended to make legal "rights" and their content fully depended on what "the general will" desired (Guilhou 1997: 21). Unfortunately, the idea of subordinating individual autonomy to the will of the majority was not a marginal, but rather a structural component of the radicals' political view. A good example in this respect appears in the (symbolically very important) Mexican Constitution of Apatzingán, 1814, which employed a Rousseauean language and explored the implications of an active State committed to the principle of the "general will." In its article 20, for example, the Constitution asserts the absolute predominance of the general will upon the will of particular, calls for the "submission of citizens to the law," which is described as "a sacrifice of the particular intelligence to the general will." In the same way, in article 41 it defined the obligations of citizens, the importance of obeying constituted authorities, and made reference to the "voluntary sacrifice of personal goods and personal life, when the needs (of the country) demanded it."

Now, most of the examples of radical constitutionalism, in nineteenth-century Latin America, can only be assessed through our ex ante criteria: radicals usually did not manage to gain positions of power, control Constitutional Conventions, define the content of actual constitutions that were then put in practice etc. The Mexican Constitution of Apatzingán, for instance (one of the few examples we find of a Constitution of a radical type), was never actually put in practice. The situation is different, however, if we focus our attention on the United States, where radicals managed to obtain positions of power, or directly challenge those who were in power. Take, for example, the case of Richard Henry Lee, who was one of the most active and influential thinkers of his time, and an excellent illustration of the antifederalists' approach to actual politics. Lee maintained bitter disputes with James Madison on different issues, including the one related to State and religion. Now, unlike Latin American conservatives, Lee did not advocate for the establishment of a particular religion, as the "only truth" to be accepted. However, he did believe that the State had to play a larger role on issues of personal morality, for reasons related to his interest on the "majority will." In 1784, for instance, in a message directed at James Madison, he claimed that religion had to become the "guardian of morals." Moreover, he maintained that the State had to educate its citizens in favor of "virtue and religion" (Storing 1981a: 22–23). Notably, these claims were not based on the intrinsic value of religion (as conservatives assumed) but rather on its *instrumental* or contingent value. The association between the State and religion was then defended as a way of honoring the will of the majority. In sum, when we examine the actual practice of (in this case, United States) radicalism, we find that our ex ante fears tend to be confirmed (i.e., would radicals be able to respect individual autonomy, given their strong affirmation of a principle of collective self-government?).

For reasons as the ones that were here explored, one could conclude this section by saying that political radicals failed to properly honor the value of individual autonomy in fundamental aspects of their institutional proposals.

James Madison and the Federalist Constitution

Facts. The 1787 US Constitution, which was basically the product of the Federalist's group (and – I would add – mainly the product of James Madison's genius), probably represents the best example of a liberal Constitution in the legal history of America. Its liberalism seems apparent in both its main parts. In what regards the organization of powers, the Constitution is fundamentally concerned with the establishment of strict checks upon the exercise of power – it wanted to avoid both the evils of *tyranny* and *anarchy*, which we could here translate as an attempt to avoid both the risk of conservative oppression and also the risk of majoritarian abuses. Meanwhile, in what concerns the organization of rights, the Constitution was directed to protect individual autonomy, in a time when religious imposition was common.

In addition, the US Constitution was the object of a careful, ample, and profound justification, particularly thanks to the work of Madison. More specifically (and more relevant for our purposes) Madison offered one of the most articulated defenses of a Constitution, in terms of the evils that it wanted to prevent, the goals it pursued and the legal means that were necessary for achieving its main purposes. The best expression of this justificatory exercise appears in *Federalist Papers* n. 10. In that paper, Madison openly identified what was the social and political evil against what the Constitution was conceived, namely, the tragedy of *factions*. Madison then precisely defined the concept of factions as "a number of citizens, whether amounting to a majority or a minority of the whole, who are united and actuated by some common impulse of passion, or of interest, adversed to the rights of other citizens, or to the permanent and aggregate interests of the community." A few lines below, Madison added an important specification. He said that even though – in theory – factions could amount to "a majority or a minority of the whole," he did not think it relevant to address the problem of "minority" factions. And this was so because: "If a faction consists of less than a majority, relief is supplied by the republican principle, which enables the majority to defeat its sinister views by regular vote." In other words, the Constitution was going to direct all its energies to address the problem of a particular kind of faction, namely, majority factions.[20]

Having defined so clearly the "drama" that he wanted to confront through the Constitution, Madison immediately moved on so as to examine the specific institutional means to be used for confronting the evil of factions. His analysis in this respect was also exceptionally clear and meticulous. He said: "There are two methods of curing the mischiefs of faction: the one, by removing its causes; the other, by controlling its effects." However, he discarded the first route – the attempt to remove the "causes" of faction – because this would require solutions that he deemed overtly absurd. In his words:

> There are again two methods of removing the causes of faction: the one, by destroying the liberty which is essential to its existence; the other, by giving to every citizen the same opinions, the same passions, and the same interests. It could never be more truly said than of the first remedy, that it was worse than the disease. Liberty is to faction what air is to fire, an aliment without which it instantly expires. But it could not be less folly to abolish liberty, which is essential to political life, because it nourishes faction, than it would be to wish the annihilation of air, which is essential to animal life, because it imparts to fire its destructive agency.

So, the only available solution that he envisioned consisted of attacking the "effects" of factions. Madison – as most members of the Federalist group – did believe it was both possible and necessary to explore this route. Following this conclusion, the Federalist group offered different alternatives capable of minimizing the threats posed by factions. The proposed institutional remedies were different. In what concerns individual rights, the main proposal was the creation of a *wall of separation* between the State and the Church (or, to put it more generally, a wall of separation between the State's moral ambitions and the individuals' own conceptions of the good).[21] Meanwhile, in what concerns the

---

[20] Now, someone may claim that Madison's arguments found no real "audience" until well into our time – that they played almost no role in the shaping or ratification of the Constitution (Kramer 1999). Perhaps it is true that a concept such as "faction" resonates better today than at the "founding moment." However – I submit – that fact would not deny the existence and fundamental importance and impact of the problem that Madison was describing through the idea of "factions": Certain sections of society were ready to use the institutional tools at their disposal (i.e., majority vote, within Congress) in order to impose their demands upon the rest, even at the cost of affecting other people's rights or the country's long-term interests. For those interested in re-organizing the country's institutional structure, this problem undoubtedly (and reasonably) seemed totally crucial.

[21] The metaphor was particularly fertile at a time when many "antifederalists," such as Patrick Henry, proposed to establish taxes in favor of Anglicanism. It was at that moment that Jefferson, and his ally James Madison, decided to launch a campaign against that initiative. As M. Konvitz put it, Madison assumed that the removal of "some stones from the new wall

organization of powers, the Federalists proposed, among other things, a representative system that ensured a significant degree of "separation" between the people and their representatives (which implied a strong rejection of direct democracy);[22] and, most significantly, a schema of *checks and balances*.

These proposals, and particularly the system of checks and balances, represented a direct response to constitutional organizations such as the one that was prevalent in Pennsylvania (we have explored this alternative already), which came to symbolize the unreasonable, this is to say, the kind of institutional design that was not only unable to contain the risk of factions, but also favorable to their growth. In their criticisms to alternative models, Federalists like Madison had in mind the *paper money* crisis that exploded during the post-independence/pre-constitutional period (around the mid-1780s), which the prevalent institutional system had been unable to contain (Brown 1970; Sherman 1991; Wood 1992). In fact, that early crisis provoked tremendous political and institutional problems, of different kind. On the one hand, armed groups of debtors, such as the one leaded by Daniel Shays in Massachusetts, stood up with guns against the government, in defense of their cause (many of them could not afford the payment of their debts; many of them asked, for that reason, for the emission of paper money). On the other hand, different legislatures, at the local level, fell under the control of the debtors' groups and began to pass legislation favoring the interests of the latter (typically, by allowing the emission of money). For people like Madison, this institutional outcome was even more worrisome than those earlier armed revolts: Now, the "factious" groups were obtaining by legal means what they had previously claimed through the use of violence. Those original episodes of armed violence could be confronted by the State through the use of its coercive powers, but the question was: What to do in the face of irrational legislative actions (which, in some cases, like that of Rhode Island, implied the "encroachment" of other branches)?

---

of separation between the church and the state of Virginia" could make the entire wall to collapse, and finally work for the state's support of one particular church" (Konvitz 1957: 24). Time went by, but the metaphor of the "wall of separation" continued to be useful and fruitful in the thinking about the limits of justified State action. Liberals continued to say that the State had to be prevented from using its coercive force and economic resources in order to impose its favored conception of the good.

[22] Madison defined democracy as a system where "a small number of citizens . . . assemble and administer the government in person," which – he assumed – admitted "no cure for the mischiefs of faction." And this explains his defense of a particular understanding of representation, which for him implied a system that would "refine and enlarge the public views, by passing them through the medium of a chosen body of citizens, whose wisdom may best discern the true interest of their country, and whose patriotism and love of justice will be least likely to sacrifice it to temporary or partial considerations."

Madison dedicated a lot of time to reflect upon that question. For instance, in his paper *Vices of the political system*, which appeared in 1787, he examined the main problems affecting the nation's institutional organization, underlying the "multiplicity," "injustice," and "mutability" of the laws. The system of checks and balances then appeared as the main response to the factious behavior of majority groups and the "irresponsible" responses of the legislature: The new schema of controls would prevent the passing of irrational laws.

Values. Madison's suggestion concerning the issue of factions as the main national *tragedy* to be confronted with the help of the Constitution may be considered a reasonable choice. Of course, as in other cases, one could say that their choice was not totally justified (they faced other much more relevant problems at their time, which they explicitly decided not to address, such as the problem of slavery). However, it was (as it still is) undoubtedly true that political systems need to be able to tackle the problem of majority oppression. In addition, it seems also clear that the then prevalent institutional machinery was under stress and in need of repair (also in this respect, the institutional system seemed fragile concerning the checks it established upon those in power). Finally, it seems clear that factions (and, I would add, particularly armed factions) represent a serious political problem for any political system. So, even in spite of certain reasonable disagreements, I think that it is perfectly reasonable to take Madison's suggestion as an acceptable one.

At the time of examining the institutional *means* that the Federalists offered for confronting the evil of factions, the conclusion can be different. In part, what we can say about the liberal constitutional response is the opposite of what we said about the radical project: The liberals' institutional suggestions seem quite appropriate in what regards the protection of individual autonomy, but rather poor in what concerns the value of self-government. In order to support this claim, let me examine their proposed means with a little more detail. We can start from one of the most interesting parts of their project, namely, their proposal for separating the State and the Church. In principle, the idea of building a "wall of separation," where legal rights play the role of the "bricks" of that wall, looks very attractive, and the historical practice that followed that constitutional decision tends to support it.[23]

What the US Constitution does in regard to the organization of powers seems also reasonable, at least in part. On the one hand, the Constitution created an ample system of checks upon power, which undoubtedly helped to prevent both the feared risks of tyranny and anarchy. The actual practice of the

---

[23] Of course, the picture is much more complex than described. In my opinion, it also includes an exaggerated concern with certain individual rights (particularly property rights) and a lack of concern with other rights, particularly of an economic or social type.

1787 Constitution seems to support this point, and thus provide us with good (ex post) reasons for praising its design. However, it seems also clear (although I will not press with this point here) that such a practice (perhaps unexpectedly) made some of its shortcomings evident (i.e., one could, for instance, argue that the Civil War was at least partially related to a Constitution that did not know how to deal with the issue of slavery properly, and from an early time).

On the other hand (and contrary to what happened in the case of radicalism), the liberal constitutional model seemed to be prepared to sacrifice collective self-government for the sake of protecting individual autonomy, which is obviously problematic. One may recognize this problem, first, in the Federalists' approach to political representation. Contrary to what many of their adversaries did (some antifederalists defended representation merely as a second best, given the practical impossibilities of exercising direct democracy), the Federalists tended to understand political representation as a first, desired option, given the people's difficulties for rational political deliberation. One interesting illustration of this view appears in the same *Federalist Paper* n. 10, when Madison refers to the issue of representation by stating: "(through representation we) refine and enlarge the public views, by passing them through the medium of a chosen body of citizens." In other words, representatives, for him, were supposed to modify the "will of the people," which was assumed to be unrefined and only concentrated on the defense of partial, biased interests. What comes after this line is still more illuminating and worrisome. Madison described the foreseeable result of this mechanism of refinement by stating: "Under such a regulation, it may well happen that the public voice, pronounced by the representatives of the people, will be more consonant to the public good than if pronounced by the people themselves, convened for the purpose." This is to say, for Madison – and, again, contrary to what many antifederalists claimed – representation was a desired option (rather than a "necessary evil") because – allegedly– the people tended to systematically misunderstand the requirements of the public good.

Similar assumptions, and similar distrust to the people's intervention in politics appear reflected in the organization of the system of checks and balances, this is to say the "core" of the institutional machinery.[24] The mechanisms of checks and balances – carefully discussed in *Federalist Papers* n. 51 – are based on a clear preference for "internal," rather than "external" or popular controls, as

---

[24] However, it seems clear to me that – more generally – one find clear traces of this elitist, counter-majoritarian approach in the entire *Federalist Papers*, all through the complete debates on the Federal Convention, and obviously – as a consequence – in the 1787 Constitution (Farrand 1937).

many among the antifederalists had proposed.[25] Given that (as a result of the preceding history) Federalists feared democracy ("the fury of democracy"), more than anything else, they decided to build an institutional system composed of multiple mechanisms of internal political control, particularly directed to limit the capacities of majority bodies – and particularly Congress, an institution that had created so many troubles in the pre-constitutional years. Local legislatures, in fact, had promoted "tender laws" and regulations of property that – for members of the Federalist group at least – appeared to be an expression of mere passions, a result of a complete lack of careful reflection.

As a result, the institutional system that was then created eliminated most of the mechanisms that antifederalists imagined or proposed in the previous years (mandatory rotation; instructions; the right to recall; etc.), and at the same time included numerous *counter-majoritarian devices*, aimed at limiting the capacities of the legislative. These institutional choices reflect what Roberto Mangabeira Unger, a contemporary Professor of Law and Politics, described as a shared "secret," namely, a widespread "discomfort with democracy" – a profound "fear of popular action." For Unger, the "discomfort with democracy shows up in every area of contemporary legal culture: in the ceaseless identification of restraints upon majority rule, rather than of restraints upon the power of dominant minorities, as the overriding responsibility of judges of and jurists; in the consequent hypertrophy of countermajoritarian practices and arrangements; in the opposition to all institutional reforms, particularly those designed to heighten the level of popular political engagement, as threats to a regime of rights . . ." (Unger 1996: 72).

In my opinion, the picture that we presented in the lines properly describes some of the main legacies of liberal constitutionalism, both in its serious

---

[25] More particularly, the Federalists' strong preference for "internal" controls was premised on a rather impoverished description of the antifederalists' more democratic approach. In some occasions, the antifederalists were presented as activists who did not care or were totally disinterested on the establishment of (internal) checks upon power, and in other occasions as people who believed that public-spirited officers would behave like "angels," in no need of control. In Madison's terms, "the great security against a gradual concentration of the several powers in the same department, consists in giving to those who administer each department the necessary constitutional means and personal motives to resist encroachments of the others. The provision for defense must in this, as in all other cases, be made commensurate to the danger of attack. Ambition must be made to counteract ambition. The interest of the man must be connected with the constitutional rights of the place. It may be a reflection on human nature, that such devices should be necessary to control the abuses of government. But what is government itself, but the greatest of all reflections on human nature? If men were angels, no government would be necessary. If angels were to govern men, neither external nor internal controls on government would be necessary. In framing a government which is to be administered by men over men, the great difficulty lies in this: you must first enable the government to control the governed; and in the next place oblige it to control itself."

concern for the protection of individual rights, and in its discomfort with democracy.

CONCLUSION

Let me finish this chapter by adding two different sets of comments, one more general, and the other more specific. I begin with the more specific issue, which is connected to issues of constitutional history. There are two things, in particular, that I want to mention in this regard. First, I think that it is time for regional constitutionalism (and particularly, I would add, for Latin American constitutionalism) to address a crucial *drama* that it had deeply marked the political, economic, social and legal history in the Americas, but which has never been seriously addressed: the drama of inequality. It is not obvious to me what particular contribution a valuable Constitution could do, for overcoming that drama, but I believe that it represents a relevant question in the search of a proper answer. In my opinion, we should follow what many of our ancestors – like Alberdi – did, out of their particular interest in protecting certain specific rights (i.e., property rights). More to the point, we should aim at reforming the organization of powers-section of our Constitutions, rather than continue obsessively focusing on their rights-section (adding more rights to already robust and generous declarations of rights). To put it brutally: I think that (Latin) American Constitutions have opened the doors of their sections of rights to the working classes, but managed to keep the doors of the "engine room" of the Constitution closed to the disadvantaged groups (Gargarella 2013).

Second (but closely related to the first point), I would highlight the fact that the different constitutional projects that were in force in the region, during the last two Centuries, did not properly honor the two main constitutional values proposed in this work, namely, those of collective self-government and individual autonomy. As I maintained in the introduction, *conservative* conceptions dishonored both ideals; more *radical* conceptions tended to affirm the value of self-government frequently at the expense of individual autonomy; and *liberal* conceptions dishonored the value of self-government for the sake of individual autonomy. An egalitarian constitutional conception, whose contours still need to be defined more precisely (I have tried to hint some of its distinctive features in the previous pages), should remedy those imperfections, in the near future.

My final, more general conclusion refers to the project of measuring the performance of a Constitution. In this chapter, I challenged a more traditional and intuitive approach to "good performance," which ties this concept with the idea of "political/constitutional stability." This view, as I said, played a significant role in the Founding Period, in the Americas, but still seems to exercise some influence in our time. As an alternative proposal, I suggested a different test, based on the one that Juan Bautista Alberdi offered, almost two centuries ago. As the great comparatist he was, Alberdi was interested in evaluating the performance of different constitutions and, for so doing, he proposed an interesting test that took into account both contextual and theoretical aspects of these constitutions. The (qualified) Alberdian test that I proposed showed to be properly sensitive both to theory (and thus to some fundamental normative values) and historical context. I have illustrated the strength of this test through four examples (two related to conservative con-stitutionalism, and the other two related to radical and liberal constitutional-ism), which showed both the potential of this approach and the difficulties of the enterprise. This alternative test allowed us to examine and compare different Constitutions; determine when they were doing better or worse; distinguish what particular aspects of the Constitution were performing better; etc.

I understand that the Alberdian test, in spite of its potential and its historical pedigree, may be of little interest for those simply concerned in adding numbers to the idea of "constitutional performance." However, as I said at the beginning, I am not sure that we can find an alternative proposal that is, at the same time, measurable and interesting. Some facts, such as the stability of a Constitution may somehow be measured, but it is not obvious that, by getting those numbers, we will be quantifying the "performance" of a Constitution.

REFERENCES

Albarracín, Rodríguez et al. (eds.) 1988. *La filosofía en Colombia. Historia de las ideas*, Bogotá.

Alberdi, Juan. 1954. *Sistema económico y rentístico de la Confederación Argentina*. Buenos Aires, Argentina: Editorial Raigal.

    1981. *Bases y puntos de partida para la organización política de la República Argentina*. Buenos Aires, Argentina: Plus Ultra.

Alemparte, J. Arteaga. 1870. *La reforma*. Santiago de Chile: Imprenta La Libertad.

Allen, William and Gordon, Lloyd (eds.) 1985. *The Essential Antifederalist*. New York, USA: University Press of America.

Ayala, E. 1995. *Lucha política y origen de los partidos en Ecuador*. Quito: Corporación editora nacional.

Basadre, J. 1949. *Historia de la República del Perú*. Lima: Editorial Cultura Antártica.

Baylin, B. 1992. *The Ideological Origins of the American Revolution*. Cambridge, USA: Harvard University Press.

Bilbao, Francisco. 1886. *Obras completas*, vol. I. Buenos Aires, Argentina: Imprenta de Buenos Aires.

    2007. "El gobierno de la libertad." en *Francisco Bilbao, 1823–1865*. Santiago de Chile: Editorial Cuarto Propio.

Bolívar, Simón. 1950. *Bolívar. Obras Completas*. La Habana, Cuba: Editorial Lex.

    1951. *Selected Writings of Bolívar*. New York, USA: The Colonial Press.

    1976. *Doctrina del Libertador*. Caracas: Biblioteca Ayacucho.

Borden, Morton. 1965. *The Antifederalist Papers*. Michigan, USA: Michigan State University Press.

Borja y Borja, R. 1951. *Las Constituciones del Ecuador*. Madrid: Ediciones Cultura Hispánica.

Bossano, G. 1959. *Evolución del derecho constitucional ecuatoriano*. Quito.

Brown, Robert. 1970. *Revolutionary Politics in Massachusetts*. Cambridge, USA: Harvard University Press.

Donoso, R. 1967. *Las ideas políticas en Chile*. Santiago: Facultad de Filosofía y Educación.

Egaña, J. 1969. *Juan Egaña. Antología*, ed. Por Raúl Silva Castro. Santiago de Chile: Andrés Bello.

Farrand, Max (ed.) 1937. *The Records of the Federal Convention of 1787*. New Haven, Connecticut, USA: Yale University Press.

Gargarella, Roberto. 2010. *The Legal Foundations of Inequality*. Cambridge, UK: Cambridge University Press.

    2013. *Latin American Constitutionalism, 1810–2010*. Oxford, UK: Oxford University Press.

Halperín Donghi, Tulio. 1980. *Proyecto y Construcción de una Nación*. Caracas, Venezuela: Biblioteca Ayacucho.

Jaramillo Uribe, Jaime. 1964. *El pensamiento colombiano en el siglo xix*. Bogotá, Colombia: Editorial Temis.

Jefferson, T. 1984. *Writings*. New York: Literary Classics of the U.S.

    1999. *Political Writings*. Cambridge, UK: Cambridge University Press.

Kenyon, Cecilia. 1985. *The Antifederalists*. Boston, USA: Northeastern University Press.

Konvitz, Milton. 1957. *Fundamental Liberties of a Free People: Religion Speech, Press, Assembly*. Westport, Connecticut, USA: Greenwood Press Publishers.

Kramer, Larry. 1999. "Madison's Audience," *Harvard Law Review*, vol. 112, no. 3, pp. 611–679.

Lastarria, J.V. 1906. *Estudios políticos y constitucionales.* Santiago de Chile: Imprenta, Litografía y Encuadernación Barcelona, vols. 1 y 2.

Manin, Bernard. 1997 *The Principles of Representative Government* Cambridge, UK: Cambridge University Press.

Pérez Guilhou, Dardo. 1997. *Liberales, radicales y conservadores. Convención Constituyente de Buenos Aires 1870–1873.* Buenos Aires, Argentina: Plus Ultra.

Pettit, Philip. 1997. *Republicanism. A Theory of Freedom and Government.* Oxford, UK: Oxford University Press.

Pocock, John. 1975. *The Machiavellian Moment.* Princeton, New Jersey, USA: Princeton University Press.

Portacarrero, González. 1987. "Conservadurismo, liberalismo, y democracia en el Perú del siglo xix," en A. Adrianzén, *Pensamiento político peruano.* Lima: Centro de estudio y promoción del desarrollo, 87–98.

Reyes, O. Efrén. 1942. *Breve Historia General del Ecuador.* Quito.

Romero, J.L. y Romero, A. (eds.) 1977. *Pensamiento político de la emancipación.* Caracas: Biblioteca Ayacucho.

1978. *Pensamiento Conservador, 1815–1898.* Caracas: Biblioteca de Ayacucho.

Safford, Frank. 1985. "Politics, Ideology and Society in Post-Independence Spanish America." In *The Cambridge History of Latin America*, edited by L. Bethell. Cambridge, UK: Cambridge University Press, vol. III, 347–421.

Sandel, Michael. 1996. *Democracy's Discontent. America in Search of a Public Philosophy.* Cambridge, USA: Harvard University Press.

Sherman, Michael. 1991. *A More Perfect Union: Vermont Becomes a State.* Vermont, USA: Vermont Historical Society.

Skinner, Quentin. 1990. "The Republican Ideal of Political Liberty." In *Machiavelli and Republicanism*, edited by G. Bock, Q. Skinner and M. Viroli, Cambridge, UK: Cambridge University Press.

Storing, Herbert. 1981a. *The Complete Anti-Federalist.* Chicago, USA: The University of Chicago Press.

1981b. *What the Anti-Federalists Were For.* Chicago, USA: The University of Chicago Press.

Unger, Roberto. 1996. *What Should Legal Analysis Become?* London, UK: Verso.

Wood, Gordon. 1969. *The Creation of the American Republic.* New York, USA: W.W. Norton & Company.

1992. *The Radicalism of the American Revolution.* New York, USA: Alfred Knopf.

5

Parties and constitutional performance

Martin Shapiro

An enterprise that seeks to compare the written provisions of all existing constitutions in terms of varying real-world outcomes is necessarily a highly complex one. Unfortunately there is yet a further complexity. The real workings of all constitutions depend in part not only on the institutional patterns they specifically provide but also on the nature of the party systems and the electoral arrangements of their polities, yet political parties and much of the electoral rules for most states are not provided for in their constitutions. Political regime A and political regime B might have identically worded constitutions but, nevertheless, vary greatly in their actual operations because of differing party systems and electoral rules. And, of course, party systems and electoral rules reciprocally influence one another. Each to some degree "causes" the other.

In the light of these considerations, I want to very tentatively and incompletely sketch how three general types of separation of power constitutions each may operate differently depending on which kinds of party systems and electoral rules are at play. Suppose one wished to compare parliamentary, presidential, and quasi- or semi-presidential constitutions to discover which type of constitution led to greater political stability, democracy, or other real-world outcome. Or suppose we pursued a narrower goal, say, asking in which of these constitutional types was judicial review more likely to succeed. Our findings might well be confounded if two parliamentary constitutional regimes operated in quite different ways because one enjoyed a two-party and the other a multi-party system. Showing the two together as if they were the same and then comparing them with presidential regimes to see which yielded more complete democracy or interest representation or whatever would yield very unsatisfactory results. You can compare apples to oranges if all the apples are pretty much the same as one another and all the oranges are about the same. You can't if some of the apples are very different from one another as are some of the oranges. If two-party presidential regimes actually are quite different from multi-party presidential regimes, it may not be easy to compare presidential constitutions with parliamentary constitutions that may themselves vary greatly in their actual operations because of differences in party systems. Yet this, perhaps crucial, party dimension will not be picked up in a comparative analysis of written constitutions because many nations have political parties but few have written constitutional clauses providing for them.

I do not pretend that what I have just written is original in any way. Indeed it is obvious and a mainstay of the basic comparative politics course. Nor do I pretend that the following sketch of party, electoral law, and constitutional separation of powers interactions is anything more than a set of long-held, and probably far from entirely true, clichés. They are, however, a very big elephant in the room of any effort at constitutional comparison.

Let us begin with parliamentary constitutions and party systems. For many years the model was the United Kingdom. Although, inconveniently, it does not have a written constitution, its parliamentary system has been so firmly established for so long that it may be "taken as written."

In theory, in parliamentary systems, a parliamentary majority may hire and fire the prime minister and his/her "government" at will. Executive power is vested in the cabinet. Typically the cabinet is also the drafter and submitter of legislation to the parliament. The prime minister and cabinet are entirely responsible to the parliament. No law passes without its consent. No executive continues in office without its consent. The constitution typically provides for new elections whenever the parliament expresses "no confidence" in the prime minister. In addition, either the constitution itself or electoral laws provide for new elections every so many years. So constitutionally the executive appears to be fully the agent of the parliament.

For whatever reasons, the United Kingdom had a long-standing essentially two-party system, so one party almost necessarily enjoyed a stable parliamentary majority. It chose the cabinet and that cabinet would see its proposed legislation readily achieving enactment. Legislative and executive power was concentrated in the cabinet but held responsible by parliament which in turn was held responsible by the electorate. The electorate was confronted by a clear choice between two differing party platforms. The party that won the election had a clear policy mandate and full authority to govern.

As we all know, in reality the prime minister and cabinet were not really the agents of parliament but vice versa. Members of parliament of the majority party could hardly vote against any cabinet-proposed legislation because to do so would be a vote of no confidence, triggering a new election in which their party might lose power and they their own seats. The prime ministers ruled not because they were prime ministers but because they were the leaders of their party. Real political struggle and compromise actually occurred within whatever political party held the parliamentary majority and within both parties as they chose their leaders who might become prime ministers.

Nevertheless the British experience clearly indicated that a parliamentary constitution combined with a two-party system yielded a government that could efficiently enact legislation and a politics in which the voters knew exactly whom to hold accountable.

This two-party system rested upon electoral laws providing for single member district, plurality, winner-takes-all elections. (I will forebear repeating the standard and probably correct explanation of why such electoral arrangements encourage two-party and discourage multi-party systems. I will also forebear detailing the various electoral arrangements that can be installed to give the winning party a larger proportion of parliamentary seats than its proportion of the total votes in a particular election.)

Of course the system is not foolproof. From time to time third parties emerge to contest and sometimes win UK parliamentary seats, and, horror of horrors, sometimes even a coalition cabinet becomes necessary in order to construct a parliamentary majority. But these things are usually seen as an aberration to be overcome in time by Anglo-Saxon common sense.

As night follows day, we can now move on to France, the very model of parliamentary constitution but multi-party system. We are speaking now of the France of the third and fourth republics, pre De Gaulle France. A parliamentary constitution with three or four more relatively large parties, with or without some smaller parties as well, will necessitate coalitions of several parties in order to form a parliamentary majority needed to select a prime minister. Unlike the two-party parliamentary governments, here the parliament really is the master of the prime minister who keeps the job only so long as the parliamentary coalition survives. There is, however, the standard paradox of all parliamentary systems. In theory the prime minister's cabinet is the agent of the parliament, but, because the parliament members must submit themselves to the peril of a new election if they vote no confidence in the "government," they tend to leave the cabinet coalition a good deal of elbow room.

In such a multiple large-party situation the parliament finds it difficult to find legislative proposals that all the member parties of the coalition are prepared to support, and the voters cannot easily identify which party to credit or blame for the passage and particularly the non passage of new legislative proposals. The fewer and stronger the parties, usually the more easy it is to form a majority coalition and for it to survive. Old France tended to have relatively stable governments but little legislative innovation and great trouble in responding to emergencies.

The most extreme, or perhaps purest, case is the parliamentary system with many small parties. Large parties must, of course, in order to be large, attract large numbers of voters and thus, typically, will seek to further relatively broad policy agendas that appeal to relatively widely held popular preferences. Thus, they are likely to have sufficiently large overlays in policy preferences to form parliamentary coalitions relatively easily. If there are many small parties, typically each will represent a relatively narrower range of voter preferences, interests, or ideologies. Every special interest can have its own party. So it is quite difficult to form the parliamentary majority coalition necessary to govern because each party holds fewer or no preferences that overlap with those of other parties.

Yet here again parliamentarians are reluctant to vote no confidence even in the weak coalitions that can form out of multiple parties with sharply opposing policy preferences because of the standard paradox that to do so subjects each member to the risk of a new election. Thus many small-party parliamentary regimes are likely to achieve some level of coalitional cabinet stability but typically at the cost of proposing almost no new legislation. For any new legislative proposal is likely to offend more parties in the current parliamentary coalition than it pleases and thus risks a breakdown of the existing coalition, a vote of no confidence, and a new election. Parliamentary members are most likely to avoid reelection risks if the cabinet proposes no new legislation. Government may be stable but at the cost of legislative stasis.

Yet a third variation is parliamentary systems with two large parties but one or more small ones with each of the large parties seeking to appeal to the widest spectrum of voters and the small ones representing quite narrow special interests. Such regimes are likely to function like two-party parliamentary systems except that one or two special interests in the society will achieve special legislative favors for themselves at the cost of recruiting the small party that represents them to a governing coalition of one of the two main parties plus one or two of the small parties needed to add up to a parliamentary majority. Israel comes to mind as a typical example that generally proceeds in a two-party way but with special policy treatment of ultraorthodox religious interests engendered because each of the big general parties needs the vote of one or more of the small religious parties to come up to a parliamentary voting majority.

There are, of course, a further spectrum of variations, for instance two large, general appeal parties and one smaller general appeal party seeking to become a big one or representing some regional or other slight variation from the general. Current German politics is a ready example.

Now we come to a recent and globally popular form of constitution, the quasi- or semi-presidential one. This hybrid mix of parliamentary and presidential forms arose to prominence out of a very particular and peculiar French political emergency and has become very popular among recent constitution makers. It involves a division of both legislative and administrative powers between president and prime minister *cum* cabinet. Typically the president gets foreign policy, but as to the rest, the details of the split vary from country to country. In some of these constitutions, the president appoints the prime minister but must choose one that can win majority parliamentary approval, á la the British "constitutional monarchy." In others, the arrangement varies, including parliamentary appointment of the president.

To further complicate this picture, it must be noted that in some instances it may be difficult to differentiate between a straight parliamentary system with a "head of state" presidency with no real legislative and administrative powers, and a quasi-presidential system with some power sharing between president and cabinet. Some constitutions may lie at the very edge between the two, giving only slight real powers to the president but nevertheless a modicum of such powers. And, in any given country the distribution of powers may change fairly frequently, particularly in "developing democracies."

With this on the edge phenomenon, if changes in it occur by constitutional amendment, they are not my concern here in dealing with political parties. Such changes, however, in some instances may occur due to shifts in the relative political power of political parties and, therefore, may not show up on the radar screens of those looking only to constitutional texts.

Even further off that screen will be quasi-presidential systems with two major parties in which the personality of both party leaders is so dominant in the perception of the electorate that when voting for parliamentary seats, the voters actually vote for or against a particular party leader. With Russia as an example, in such countries it may not matter whether that leader is prime minister or president, and the real constitution is not quasi-presidential, but concentrates all powers in the hands of that leader no matter which office he holds. This situation is surely the very opposite of a constitution that divides powers between prime minister-parliament and a presidency, although in form it may be quasi-presidential.

Hence again, above and beyond variations in the particular semi-presidential constitutional texts, this form can vary enormously in actual operation depending on the party structure of the particular country. Obviously, in roughly two-party systems, sometimes both presidency and parliament/prime minister/cabinet will be of the same party and, at other times, of opposing parties. So sometimes government is likely to be proactive and at other times deadlocked. The electoral arrangements, some in the constitution, some not, are likely to have some effect on which happens how often. Of course in quasi-presidential states with multiple parties, frequent and unstable coalition deals must be struck to win presidential elections, to form parliamentary majorities needed for prime ministerial appointment of the president, and to achieve parliamentary majorities to pass legislation. Sometimes enough ducks will fall in line, but probably often not. Hence again, the more parties, the more likely each is to be extreme in ideology and policy preferences, thus the less likely to be willing to compromise with others and highly unlikely to help build governing coalitions.

Having marched through this familiar history of the effects of constitutionally unwritten party structure on the natural operation of constitutionally written, government institutional structure, two final complications should be added. Albeit clichés, they almost certainly are true to some degree and significant. What form of constitution is chosen tends to have some effect on whether a two-party or multi-party system arises in a newly formed constitutional state. The necessarily winner-take-all nature of presidential elections tends to discourage the growth of third, fourth, and so on parties in presidential states. Potential voters for the presidential candidate of such parties know that they will be "wasting" their votes because only the candidate of one of the big parties has a real chance of winning. Yet this tendency toward two partyism in presidential states may be overcome or mitigated temporarily or permanently by skillful coalition building among small parties. That skill, and the complex conditions necessary for its successful exercise, may or may not be present at any particular time and place.

Parliamentary constitutions obviously are somewhat more favorable to the creation and maintenance of multiple parties. Any party with enough votes in the right places to win even a few seats in parliament receives at least some policy voice, perhaps some chance of winning some of what it wants through the bargaining necessary to build a majority parliamentary coalition, and even some chance at a seat in a coalition cabinet. So some voters at least may not feel their votes will be wasted if cast for a new or small party.

As to their effect on party structure, quasi-presidential constitutions remain, at least to me, an enigma.

The second well-known complication lies in the interaction among constitutions, party systems, and election rules. Here the cliché is that single-member district plurality election arrangements for the legislature encourage two partyism while proportional representation arrangements favor multipartyism. Single-member district majority with runoff systems face both directions, encouraging large parties but leaving some hope for smaller ones. As in presidential elections, which are actually single-member district plurality elections, such legislative elections tend to discourage the creation of new, small parties because their candidates have little or no chance of winning and so votes for the small party are wasted.

However, if regional or other loyalties concentrate a large number of like-minded voters in even a few districts, and if their like minds are at odds with the policy goals of the major parties, even single-member plurality districts may yield some representation in the legislature for small parties representing such concentrated like minds. Similarly single-member, majoritarian elections will, where there is a runoff between front winners if no majority is achieved on the first round, somewhat encourage small parties. If such a party shows enough strength in the first round to prevent a majority for any one candidate in the first round, but, its swing to one or another of the leading first-round candidates will assure that candidate's victory in the second round, it may be able to gain policy commitments it desires from one of those candidates in exchange for its second-round votes. Those favoring the small party will vote for its candidate in the first round because their votes in that round will prove to a major party candidate that their party is worth courting for the second round; on the other hand, such voters risk having their first-round votes wasted if a majority winner emerges in the first round. Even worse, they risk the big party candidate they like least winning on the first round because they cast their votes for a third party rather than helping the big party candidate they prefer to win a first-round majority. Thus the compromise between two-party and multi-party tendencies created by single-member district majority with runoff systems. Straight PR election rules favor the creation of multiple parties because even small parties may get some legislative seats.

Perhaps in some nations all or most of the electoral arrangements are spelled out in the constitutional text. Typically some are and some aren't. In some a new constitution is introduced into a polity in which two partyism or multipartyism is long established and so the party system will determine the actual workings of the constitutional text and/or election laws. In others the new constitutional text and/or election laws may heavily influence whether two or multiple parties emerge.

Why this long march through the introductory comparative politics course? To go back to where we started, a project that simply compared constitutional texts is useful as a descriptive start but only as a start. A project that seeks to align differences in the constitutional texts of various polities with differences in the real-world governing processes or general politics of those states is courageous and again perhaps a necessary beginning step. It is so often true, however, that interactive differences in political party alignments and electoral laws not directly provided for in constitutional text significantly shape the actual workings of constitutional governments, that some kind of next step is necessary. Let me offer two obvious entries in a possible party-regarding typology of constitutions. First, parliamentary constitutions with two-party systems versus parliamentary systems with multiple parties (e.g., the United Kingdom of 1930 versus France of 1930). Second, quasi-presidential constitutions with multiple parties in which the most likely outcome most of the time is likely to be truly "quasi," that is very fragmented government versus quasi-presidential two-party polities in which concentrated government is likely to alternate with deadlocked "cohabitation."

In conclusion, let me repeat that I have offered here not new and original insights but rather commonplaces to be found in any introductory political science course in comparative politics. Parties matter. Exactly the same constitutional text may trigger very different real-world outcomes in any given country depending on whether it enjoys a two-party or multi-party system or one with two dominant parties and one or more other, marginal parties. How are we to incorporate this reality into whatever typology of constitutions we may wish to establish?

PART II

MANAGING SPECIFIC CONSTITUTIONAL CHALLENGES

6

Constitutional performance in transitions from military to civilian rule

Ozan O. Varol

In the late 1990s, former Turkish president and prime minister Suleyman Demirel was asked to comment on an ongoing crisis between the civilian and military leadership in his coup-prone country. Demirel replied with a joke. There was an experiment in an English zoo, he explained, to place lambs and wolves in one cage in order to teach them how to live together. The zoo director was asked if the experiment was working. The director replied: "Yes, but from time to time, we have to replace the lambs."

A transition from military to civilian rule often forces military and civilian leaders to live together as wolves and lambs in one cage for a period of time. Among other things, they must agree on a framework for the transition, which often, but not always, includes the amendment or replacement of the existing Constitution to govern the new civilian regime. During the constitutional-design process, the military often attempts to entrench into the revised Constitution provisions that protect its institutional autonomy and perpetuate its influence in civilian governance.[1]

Constitutional entrenchment of the military's prerogatives creates a wealth of theoretical and empirical questions about constitutional performance. Depending on context, constitutional entrenchment can be a reliable method of protecting the autonomy and privileges of the military and its civilian allies, at least in the short term. Even from the perspective of other relevant actors, entrenchment may be a second-best outcome. Although immediate and complete ouster of the military from domestic politics may be possible in some transitions, in others, any attempts to swiftly force the military back to the barracks can prompt a backlash from the military, which might dig in, rather

For insightful comments, I thank José Antonio Cheibub, Tom Ginsburg, and Aziz Huq. Philip Thoennes and Elisabeth Rennick provided excellent research assistance.
[1] The sub-constitutional means that the military may employ to entrench its prerogatives are beyond the scope of this chapter.

than give in, and derail the transition process. And in some cases, some level of military involvement may be desired in the initial stages of the transition so that the military can maintain stability and act as an arbiter of constitutional bargains between competing political groups.

Entrenchment of the military's prerogatives, however, can also undermine long-term democratic development. As a result of entrenchment, the military may emerge as a de facto, if not de jure, separate branch of government from the transition process. For democracy to persist, the military must ultimately retreat to the barracks and become subordinate to democratically elected civilian leaders.

From the perspective of the military's opponents, therefore, the constitutional choices during the transition process can generate a seeming conflict between short-term and long-term goals. The short-term goal of abandoning military rule – which, in many cases, is possible only through the entrenchment of the military's prerogatives – may hamper the long-term goal of promoting democratic progress. Despite this apparent tension, however, a certain synergy exists between these two goals. By providing the military with some constitutional prerogatives, the military's democratic opponents can prevent backlash from the military or a rebound to military rule, which itself serves a democracy-promoting function. While permitting the entrenchment of the military's prerogatives for the short term, the military's opponents can also attempt to negotiate a constitutional framework that will permit the gradual eradication of those prerogatives.

As the discussion so far implies, constitutional performance is often in the eye of the beholder. What might be optimal performance for one group may constitute failure for the other. In the world of constitutional design, which entrenches one group's preferences into a relatively durable document, finishing second does not count for much. As a result, the chapter applies divergent metrics for constitutional success and discusses performance from two perspectives. After Section I provides theoretical preliminaries, Section II analyzes constitutional performance from the perspective of the military and its allies and describes the primary forms of constitutional entrenchment.

Section III then switches perspectives. It discusses the metrics of constitutional success from the perspective of the military's democratic opponents. I argue that many transitions from military rule require an incremental process, where the military's prerogatives are gradually eliminated as an institutionalized political marketplace and a healthy civil society develop. I also discuss how the use of temporal limitations on the military's constitutional prerogatives can promote their elimination.

I THEORETICAL PRELIMINARIES

Transitions from military to civilian rule often occur in order to orient or reorient the polity toward democracy. To be sure, democracy is not the inevitable – or even the probable – outcome in these transitions. Although transitions are highly context dependent, where democratization occurs, it can be conceptualized in three phases. At the risk of oversimplification, and necessarily painting with a broad brush, these phases often proceed as follows.

The first phase is transition, which begins with the breakdown of the military regime and ends with the election of civilian leaders (Agüero 1995). At the end of this first phase, a "protected democracy" often emerges (Collier & Levitsky 1997). Although civilian leaders assume power, for the reasons I discuss in the next section, the military may continue to enjoy constitutional prerogatives. The second phase, consolidation, is the phase between transition and democratic persistence. During consolidation, the military's constitutional prerogatives are reduced until they are eliminated, though this does not necessarily happen through a linear process (Valenzuela 1992). There is also a possibility, of course, that the military's prerogatives will gradually increase, rather than decrease, which in turn may foment a rebound to military rule. The final stage, democratic persistence, is reached when the major political actors expect democracy to last indefinitely and do not consider any nondemocratic alternatives – including military coups – to assume power (Linz 1990). For democracy to persist, the military must ultimately retreat to the barracks.

Persistence does not require, however, the total elimination of the military's prerogatives. Democracy can persist with some level of prerogatives for the military as long as they do not interfere with democratic notions of hierarchical civilian control over the military. For example, the military may enjoy such limited prerogatives as the appointment and removal of military personnel and the adjudication of cases involving military personnel through courts-martial, without meaningfully weakening civilian control. The focus of this chapter, as elaborated more fully later, is on prerogatives that substantially hamper the subordination of the military to civilian authorities.

I frequently refer to "the military" throughout the chapter, but the military is not a homogenous, unitary actor. Although the military displays a higher degree of coherence than many other institutions due to its hierarchical command structure, depending on context, there may be opposing factions within the military and divisions within, and between, the senior officers, the junior officers, and even the rank-and-file soldiers. The interests of these individuals are also not static and may change as the polity progresses through the transition process. Divisions may also exist within the relevant social and political actors, some of whom may oppose military rule and others support it. As a result, this chapter focuses not on the entrenchment of these particular interests, which vary over space and time, but on the entrenchment of the military's autonomy and decision-making prerogatives – however they may be exercised. Where appropriate, I also highlight instances of fissures within the military during the transition process and how they affected constitutional performance.

Relatedly, the military is not necessarily united in its entrenchment attempts. Depending on context, some factions within the military may oppose entrenchment. They might believe, for example, that entrenchment will force the military into the domestic political fray, force it to take sides on contentious issues, and undermine the military's standing and credibility, which, in the long term, may damage their personal and institutional interests. Other factions, however, may view constitutional entrenchment as a mechanism for protecting and advancing their power, constraining demo- cratic actors, and rewarding their civilian loyalists.

Even where factions within the military attempt entrenchment, they are not always successful. Constitutional design involves bargaining, and where the bargaining power of the military is low and the civilian political marketplace is sufficiently institutionalized, the military may be unable to extract any constitutional privileges. Internal conflicts within the military can also undermine the military's attempt to entrench its preferences or obtain concessions. Entrenchment is also less likely to happen where the military does not have credible partners in the political marketplace. In Greece in the 1970s and in Argentina in the 1980s, for example, the outgoing military establishment was unable to impose any significant conditions for its relinquishment of power. In both countries, the collapse of the military governments resulting from significant military defeats, combined with their internal disunity and low prestige, did not permit constitutional entrenchment (Linz & Stepan 1996).

In the next two sections, I discuss constitutional performance in transitions from military rule from two different perspectives. First, I analyze the consti- tutional entrenchment of the military's prerogatives, which often amounts to success, at least to some degree, from the perspective of the military and its allies. Second, I switch perspectives and discuss two interrelated metrics of constitutional success in the curtailment of the military's prerogatives.

II CONSTITUTIONAL ENTRENCHMENT

Where it occurs, entrenchment can take place through two primary avenues. First, where the military supervises, or directly participates in, the constitutional-design process, it can ensure the inclusion of its prerogatives in the new constitution. For example, the constituent assembly may include members of the military or loyalists appointed by the military who might protect its prerogatives, or the military may have a veto power over the new constitutional text. Second, even where the constitutional design occurs without direct military involvement, the military can condition its surrender of power on obtaining certain constitutional rewards, or, as explained below, can structure the transition process to indirectly influence substantive constitutional outcomes.

Various different constitutional configurations can protect the military's institutional prerogatives. In the sections that follow, I consider three types of entrenchment: direct, institutional, and procedural. These categories are admittedly not airtight, and some types of entrenchment straddle more than one category. They are nevertheless useful in considering the available design options and their consequences. Although I describe the advantages and disadvantages of each design option, I refrain from reaching any abstract conclusions on which type of entrenchment is likely to be more successful, given the highly context-dependent nature of the inquiry.

A Direct entrenchment

At the most direct level, entrenchment can take the form of substantive constitutional powers for the military. Because direct entrenchment appropriates constitutional powers to the military itself, it can provide the military with more certainty over the protection of its prerogatives. Its direct nature, however, can also hinder its adoption and cause more resistance during constitutional design from the military's opponents than other forms of entrenchment.

One form of direct entrenchment is to authorize the military to enact laws or review legislation adopted by the political branches. Two examples from Portugal and Turkey are illustrative. The 1976 Portuguese Constitution was drafted following a military coup in 1974 that ousted the authoritarian New State (*Estado Novo*) regime, with the promise of a transition to democratic civilian rule. The Constitution, drafted under military supervision, authorized the Council of the Revolution, composed predominantly of members of the military,[2] to serve as an "advisory body" to the president and, exclusive of the other branches, "make laws concerning the organization, functioning, and

---

[2] Specifically, the Council was chaired by the president and composed of the chief of the general staff and his vice-chief, the three branch chiefs of the military, the prime minister, and fourteen officers to be selected by the Army, Air Force, and the Navy.

discipline of the Armed Forces." These laws would have the same validity as legislation passed by the parliament. The Constitution further authorized the Council to act as a de facto constitutional court and judge the constitutionality of all laws passed by the parliament. The Council also could invoke "unconstitutionality by omission" and call for the passage of legislation to further the purposes of the Constitution where the parliament did not pursue such legislation. Likewise, the 1982 Turkish Constitution, drafted during a transition to civilian rule after a 1980 coup, also created a Presidential Council comprising the leaders of the military coup. The Council was authorized, among other things, to provide advice to the president upon his request and to examine legislation adopted by the Parliament concerning a rather extensive list of subjects specified in the Constitution.[3]

Constitutions drafted during transitions from military rule may also establish a quota for the military in the parliament or the cabinet. For example, the 2008 Burmese Constitution, which was drafted as part of a roadmap for democracy, reserves for military delegates a maximum of 56 of 224 seats in the National Assembly (*Amyotha Hluttaw*) and a maximum of 110 seats of 440 in the People's Assembly (*Pyithu Hluttaw*). The Constitution is surprisingly transparent about the purpose of the quota, which is to enable "the Defense Services to be able to participate in the National political leadership role of the State." The quota gives the military an effective veto power over any constitutional amendments, which require a three-fourths supermajority in the People's Assembly. In addition, government ministries that concern national security – Ministries of Defense, Home Affairs, and Border Affairs – are also reserved for military officers. These ministers are not required to resign their positions within the military, and at the time of this writing, the current ministers have not done so. Likewise, the 2014 Egyptian Constitution requires the Minister of Defense to be a military officer and provides the military a veto power over its appointment for two full presidential terms after the Constitution goes into effect.

Another form of direct entrenchment is the constitutional authorization to try civilians in military courts. This allows the military to wield its authority through its judicial arm by imposing criminal sanctions against those who threaten the military's interests. Some constitutions define the jurisdiction of

---

[3] The subjects included "the fundamental rights and freedoms and duties, the principle of secularism, the preservation of the reforms of Ataturk, national security and public order set forth in the Constitution, the Turkish Radio and Television Corporation, International Treaties, the sending of Armed Forces to foreign countries and the stationing of foreign forces in Turkey, emergency rule, martial law and the state of war, and other laws deemed necessary by the President of the Republic."

military courts in fairly broad and vague terms, whereas others impose more specific limitations. The two most recent versions of the Egyptian Constitution illustrate both types. The 2012 Constitution created an autonomous military judiciary and defined its jurisdiction over civilians rather broadly, encompassing "crimes that harm the armed forces" and authorized the legislature to define such crimes. In contrast, the 2014 Constitution attempted to rein in the military judiciary's broad jurisdiction with a specific list of circumstances that permit the trial of civilians in military courts.[4]

Finally, the Constitution may also include a "guardian of the nation" clause, expressly declaring the military to be the protector of the state, as in the cases of Chile, Ecuador, and Turkey (Croissant et al. 2010). The military can invoke its authority under this clause to protect what it deems to be the fundamental principles of the state from democratically elected governments. For example, the Turkish military, invoking the "guardian of the nation" clause in the Turkish Constitution, has directly or indirectly intervened in political affairs on numerous occasions.

B   Institutional entrenchment

In transitions from military rule, the military leaders, by definition, will hand over power to civilians. As a result, the military may have an incentive to establish counter-majoritarian institutions to indirectly protect its prerogatives after it relinquishes power. These institutions, whose structure and membership can be designed to protect the military's prerogatives, can be more reliable partners than the elected branches, particularly where the elected branches are dominated by the opponents of the military. Institutional entrenchment is conceptually distinct from direct entrenchment (discussed above) in that the former delegates constitutional authority to a separate counter-majoritarian institution whereas the latter provides the military itself with substantive constitutional authorities.[5] Compared to direct entrenchment, institutional entrenchment is often more palatable to the opponents of the military since the mission of these institutions is likely to be more innocuous and its protection of military prerogatives more uncertain. The next two subsections illustrate institutional entrenchment through two institutions: (1) a constitutional court and (2) a national security council.

---

[4]   As several commentators have noted, because the list is rather long, it is unlikely to be meaningfully different from its previous iteration (Al-Ali 2013).

[5]   The line between direct and institutional entrenchment blurs with respect to institutions such as the National Security Council, which includes members of the military.

1 Constitutional court

One option for institutional entrenchment is the establishment of a constitutional court. A constitutional court comprising judges loyal to the military may strike down democratically enacted legislation that threatens the military's prerogatives (Ginsburg 2003; Hirschl 2004). Unlike an institution such as a national security council composed partly of military officers, a constitutional court often has no military members. The creation of a constitutional court thus allows the military to constrain the political branches through a separate institution with no overt military involvement. By establishing a constitutional court, the military can demonstrate its commitment to constitutional rules, let a different branch of government protect its prerogatives, allow the judiciary to issue controversial decisions that it approves but cannot publicly champion, and insulate itself from accountability in the process (Stepan 1988).

To be sure, a constitutional court may disappoint its military founders by acting contrary to their interests, as discussed below in the case of the Turkish Constitutional Court. Although the military cannot directly control the constitutional court, it can indirectly influence its decisions by providing to loyalist institutions the authority to appoint judges to the court. In addition, the military may grant friendly institutions standing to seek judicial review before the constitutional court.

The Turkish Constitutional Court (*Anayasa Mahkemesi*) was one of the counter-majoritarian institutions established by the military following a 1960 coup. The coup overthrew the authoritarian Adnan Menderes government with the promise of swift return to civilian rule after the adoption of a new liberal Constitution and democratic elections. The initial draft of the Constitution was prepared by a panel of law professors handpicked by the military junta that staged the coup, and the panel frequently consulted the junta during the drafting process (Varol 2012). The constituent assembly that ratified the final draft likewise comprised primarily members of the military and other loyalist groups (Belge 2006).

Among other things, the Constitution created a Constitutional Court authorized to engage in both abstract and concrete judicial review of legislation and to try high-ranking government officials. The Court consisted of fifteen permanent and five substitute members. Eight of the fifteen permanent members would be selected by other appellate courts (Council of State, Court of Cassation, and Court of Accounts), two by the president of the Republic, three by the National Assembly, and two by the Senate, but the Senate had to draw one of its appointees from three nominations by the Military Court of Cassation. The authority to select a majority of the members on the Court was thus given to the unelected judiciary, ensuring that professional judges would dominate the Court. At the time, the judiciary was more likely to be aligned with the coup leadership than the elected branches because the merit-based promotion system for judges largely insulated them from political influence and recycled a relatively homogenous group of elites across the judicial system (Shambayati 2004).

Reflecting the military's trust in sympathetic unelected guardians, the new Constitution also adopted a liberal definition of standing. A wide range of persons and institutions could petition the Court for constitutional review of legislation: The president of the Republic, political parties that were represented in the Parliament, political parties that had obtained at least 10 percent of the votes in the last general election, and one-sixth of the members of either the National Assembly or the Senate. Universities, the High Council of Judges, and other appellate courts (Court of Cassation, Council of State, and Military Court of Cassation) could also petition the Court for constitutional review "in cases concerning their duties and welfare." In practice, this broad definition of standing provided the Constitutional Court with extensive opportunities to engage in judicial review and strike down constitutional amendments, laws, and regulations passed by the political branches (Belge 2006; Shambayati 2008).

The Constitution also empowered the Constitutional Court with the authority to permanently dissolve political parties whose "statutes, programs, and activities" did not "conform to the principles of a democratic and secular republic, based on human rights and liberties, and to the fundamental principle of the State's territorial and national integrity." Furthermore, the authority to bring a case for party dissolution was provided to the chief public prosecutor of the Republic, a democratically unaccountable lawyer appointed by the president from a short list of nominees prepared by other prosecutors. After its establishment, the Court exercised with zeal its authority to shut down political parties (Shambayati 2008). The Court wielded its dissolution power primarily against Islamist parties, such as the Welfare Party (*Refah Partisi*) and the Virtue Party (*Fazilet Partisi*), and separatist Kurdish political parties, such as the People's Democratic Party (*Halkin Demokrasi Partisi*) and the People's Labor Party (*Halkin Emek Partisi*) (Kogacioglu 2003). The Court's targeting of Islamist and separatist parties is in line with the principles – in particular, secularism and national unity – that can be considered the common denominators espoused by the military leadership that created the Constitutional Court (Aydinli et al. 2006; Belge 2006; Shambayati 2004).

As the Court grew more powerful following its establishment, however, it began to issue opinions antagonistic to the military (Shambayati & Kirdis 2009). For example, in 1972, the Court found unconstitutional a law that established martial law courts staffed with military judges. In 1975, the Court struck down a law establishing State Security Courts, staffed in part with military judges, authorized to try crimes against the state. And in 1977, the Court invalidated a constitutional amendment adopted by a military-appointed cabinet that had exempted disciplinary decisions about judges from judicial review.

The case of the Turkish Constitutional Court illustrates the uncertainty associated with institutional entrenchment through the judiciary. Despite the military's efforts to ensure the appointment of loyalist judges, the Court turned out to be an unreliable partner in protecting the military's interests. It would take another coup and a new constitution to bring the Court to heel. Partially in response to the Court's increasingly defiant stance, the 1982 Constitution, drafted following a coup in 1980, restructured the Court. Among other things, it completely abolished the authority of the legislature to make appointments to the Court, which further insulated the Court from political influence. Instead, it granted to the president (who, from 1982 until 1989, was the leader of the 1980 coup) the authority to appoint all judges based on nominations by other institutions. At the time, many of the institutions responsible for nominating judges to the Court were under the direct or indirect influence of the military (Choudhry et al. 2014).

Consider also the Constitutional Tribunal in Chile in its 1980 Constitution, which was drafted as part of its transition from military rule. Several authors have argued that the outgoing military government established the Tribunal to serve as a guardian over the civilian institutions (Heiss & Navia 2007). Like its Turkish counterpart, the Tribunal was authorized to declare unconstitutional political movements or parties that violated the military's vision of a protected democracy. In addition, the military-dominated National Security Council was authorized to appoint two judges to the seven-judge court, directly guaranteeing the military's influence in the Tribunal's membership.

2   National security council

A national security council, designed as a forum for exchange of views between civilian and military leaders, is another common method for institutionalizing the military's influence in civilian policy-making. Because it often includes military officers, the Council can be effective in protecting the military's prerogatives and serving as a formal, constitutional conduit for the expression of the military's views to civilian policymakers. The Council can be particularly effective where it has substantive decision-making or veto powers on certain subject matters, as in the case of Burma and Egypt discussed below.

For example, the 1961 Turkish Constitution established a National Security Council (*Milli Guvenlik Kurulu*) to serve as an advisory body and facilitate the exchange of views between the military and the civilian leaders on national security matters. Notwithstanding its facially advisory mission, the National Security Council became the primary institutional avenue for the Turkish Armed Forces to influence the nation's political affairs (Shambayati 2008). Although the Constitution limited the Council's role to advice on matters of "national security and coordination," the military members of the Council interpreted that phrase broadly to encompass many matters of domestic and foreign policy unrelated to security (Shambayati 2004). The Council's decisions covered an extensive array of internal policy matters, including, for example, regulating broadcasting hours for television stations, outlining the substance of laws on terror and capital punishment, and determining whether to offer Arabic as an elective in schools (Sakallioglu 1997).

The Turkish military's influence over the Council grew over time, as the number of military representatives on the Council increased steadily. With the revisions brought by the 1982 Constitution, which was drafted following a 1980 coup, the Council consisted of five military members and five civilians, with the Council's civilian president frequently voting with the military (Aydinli et al. 2006). The 1982 Constitution also required the Cabinet to give "priority consideration" to the Council's "decisions" (which no longer were mere "recommendations"). What was originally conceived as an advisory body thus became an instructing body, whose views were given priority over other government agencies (Aydinli et al. 2006). Military representatives on the Council also gained control of the Council's Secretary General, giving them the power to set the Council's agenda (Aydinli et al. 2006).

Burma is also illustrative. The 2008 Burmese Constitution was drafted as part of a roadmap for transition from a twenty-one-year military rule (Bünte 2011). Among other things, the Constitution established a military-dominated National Defense and Security Council.[6] In conjunction with the president, the Council participates in various executive functions, including the power to grant amnesty and the power to sever diplomatic relations. Further, the president has the authority to commence military action or declare a state of emergency only in coordination with the Council. A declaration of

---

[6] The Council comprises the president, two vice-presidents, the speaker of each chamber of the legislature, the commander-in-chief and deputy commander-in-chief of the defense services, and the ministers of defense, foreign affairs, home affairs, and border affairs. The Council is military-dominated since, in addition to the active military personnel that serve on the Council, the ministers of defense, home affairs, and border affairs must also be members of the military. The military also elects one of the three vice-presidents on the Council.

emergency dissolves national and local legislative bodies and allows the president to transfer all executive, legislative, and judicial functions to the commander-in-chief, with the approval of the Council. After the state of emergency ends, the Council is responsible for exercising executive and legislative powers until a new election can be held, which itself is organized by the Council. The Council also enjoys wide-ranging powers in the administration of military affairs. For example, the Council can authorize the military to require mandatory participation of "the entire people" in the "security and defense" of the nation.

Consider also the case of Egypt. The most recent iteration of the Egyptian Constitution establishes a military-dominated National Defense Council.[7] The Council has exclusive oversight over the military's budget, and its opinion must be sought on pending legislation relevant to the armed forces. The president must also consult with the Council before declaring war, sending armed forces to combat outside national territory, or dissolving the House of Representatives.

Chile is also illustrative. Before revisions in 2005, Article 45 of the Chilean Constitution authorized the military-dominated National Security Council to appoint designated senators. After Chile's democratic transition, the coalition of political parties that resisted the military junta (collectively known as the *Concertación*) controlled the presidency, the lower legislative chamber, and a majority of the elected Senate seats (Landregan 2002). But the Senators appointed by the National Security Council often combined forces with those elected senators representing right-wing minority parties that sympathized with the former military junta, which created a de facto policy veto for the opposition and inhibited policy changes favored by the *Concertación* (Landregan 2002; Meyer 2014).

C   Procedural entrenchment

The military may also design the transition process so that it produces a favorable substantive constitutional outcome. Procedural entrenchment is particularly likely to occur where the constitution-drafting process lacks military participation. In that case, the military may not have the power to directly dictate the content of the new Constitution and may thus resort to procedural entrenchment to indirectly influence the constitution's content. Procedural entrenchment is the weakest form of the entrenchment methods considered

---

[7] Although there are an equal number of civilians and military officers on the Council (seven each), one of the civilian ministers (the minister of defense) must be a military officer.

here – and I hesitate to call it entrenchment – but I nonetheless consider it because the extent to which procedural decisions can influence constitutional content has been underappreciated in the literature. I also recognize that the choices discussed later may be motivated – not by strategic considerations related to self-interest – but unrelated factors such as the status quo bias.

For example, the military may decide to hold democratic elections within a short time frame, making it very difficult for new parties to effectively organize and mount an electoral campaign. The military may have an incentive to protect established political parties where the military believes that they will better preserve the military's prerogatives than new and unfamiliar ones. Various commentators argued, for example, that the Egyptian military held elections under a relatively short timetable after Mubarak's ouster in 2011, in part because the military leadership anticipated that the principal beneficiaries of quick elections – the pre-existing political groups – would oppose fundamental constitutional changes and protect the Mubarak-era political structures that benefit the military's interests (Ajami 2011).

In addition to controlling the timeline for the elections, the military may also alter their sequence. Depending on the type of government, three types of elections may take place in various orders during the transition process. Presidential elections may be held first, with the newly elected president holding power for a fixed period of time (Shain & Linz 1995). Alternatively, parliamentary elections may be held first, with the legislature giving its confidence to a government executive such as a prime minister and a cabinet (Shain & Linz 1995). Finally, elections for a constituent assembly may be held before presidential or parliamentary elections (Shain & Linz 1995).

The determination of which institution is elected first can affect constitutional substance. For example, if presidential elections occur first and a popularly elected president is in place during constitutional design, the constitutional drafters have to work with an elected leader who is not accountable to the legislature and whose term is fixed and may extend beyond the ratification of the new Constitution (Shain & Linz 1995). In that case, it will be more difficult to alter the constitutional status quo and opt for a parliamentary, as opposed to a presidential, system (Shain & Linz 1995). The president may also exert pressure on the constituent assembly to retain the presidential system, as President Sarney did in Brazil (Shain & Linz 1995). In contrast, if elections for a constituent assembly or the parliament are held first, then the establishment of a parliamentary system remains a possibility (Shain & Linz 1995).

In some contexts, the military may favor presidentialism over parliamentarism because a strong president may better preserve the military's prerogatives.

If the military expects a loyalist candidate to win the presidential elections, it may prefer presidentialism. In addition, in a presidential system, the military would need the cooperation of only one civilian officeholder – who is often unaccountable to the parliament – to exert its influence on political affairs. The military may also benefit from the increased autonomy that might result from the division of power between the executive and the legislative branches created by presidentialism. For example, in Brazil, the military supported the existing presidential system in part because of its desire to not be subject to votes of no confidence by the parliament and to retain its direct relationship with the president (Linz & Stepan 1996).

In other contexts, a strong parliament may be more likely to protect the military's prerogatives. For example, if the military has the constitutional authority to appoint members of the parliament, it might be incentivized to structure the transition process to favor a stronger legislature. Likewise, where the president is unfriendly to the military's interests, the military may have an incentive to limit presidential powers. For example, the outgoing military dictatorship in Chile sought to curb presidential powers and increase the authorities of the legislature because a presidential victory for the *Concertación* in the 1989 elections was virtually guaranteed (Heiss & Navia 2007).

III   CURTAILMENT OF CONSTITUTIONAL ENTRENCHMENT

To varying degrees, constitutional entrenchment often amounts to success from the perspective of the military and its allies. At least in the short term, entrenchment can permit the military to exert its influence on political affairs and safeguard its autonomy at the expense of its opponents. In contrast, entrenchment may appear, at first blush, to be a design failure from the perspective of others because the preservation of constitutional prerogatives for the military can impede long-term democratic development and hinder the adoption of policies favored by elected representatives.

In some transitions, however, entrenchment can be a second-best constitutional outcome. Attempts by civilian leaders to preclude entrenchment and force the military's immediate confinement to the barracks may provoke backlash from military leaders who might dig in, rather than give in, and force a rebound to military rule. Backlash is particularly likely to occur where the civilian political marketplace is perceived as weak or unstable.

The recent transition process in Egypt provides a cautionary tale. In the immediate aftermath of the coup that toppled the Hosni Mubarak regime in February 2011, the Egyptian military's interests were aligned to a large extent with those of the Muslim Brotherhood. From the military's perspective, the Muslim Brotherhood promised stability after a tumultuous revolution and a turbulent transition period, and the two institutions appeared to be in a tacit partnership (Varol 2012). But as the democratic transition progressed and the Muslim Brotherhood grew to be more ambitious and opportunistic, the military's position also shifted. Instead of supporting the Brotherhood's electoral prospects, the military began to oppose them. Concerned with the growing threat to its own prerogatives from the Brotherhood, the military launched a campaign to hinder the Brotherhood's attempts to dominate the Constituent Assembly and the Parliament. The Brotherhood's continued consolidation of power eventually prompted a military coup in July 2013 against President Mohamed Morsi.

In addition to avoiding backlash, in some contexts, the relevant actors may have good reasons to provide a supervisory constitutional role to the military in the initial stages of the transition process. The 1974 coup in Portugal is illustrative. The coup overthrew the nearly five-decades-old New State (*Estado Novo*) regime, which was Western Europe's oldest dictatorship, with the promise to institute political and socioeconomic reforms to establish democracy. That was a formidable task, given the long authoritarian legacy of the *Estado Novo*, the revolutionary turbulence, and the ongoing global economic recession. The military leadership played a significant stabilizing role during the transition process (Varol 2012). Political actors looked primarily to the military to serve as an arbiter of political disputes and enforcer of bargaining rules in the newly formed, fragile, and uncertain political marketplace. As a result, many political actors believed it would be impracticable, even undesirable, to immediately exclude the military from Portuguese politics (Rato 2002). The drafters of the 1976 Constitution therefore provided a supervisory constitutional role to the military to safeguard its functions as the guarantor of Portugal's newly established democracy.

Finally, the institutions created by the military to protect its interests can be reconfigured to serve other purposes. For example, a constitutional court, initially established as a tool of political insurance or hegemonic preservation, can also serve the legitimate function of reviewing the constitutionality of legislation. The structure, the appointments process, and rules of standing may be altered to remove the military's influence, without abolishing the institution. For example, the authority of the Turkish Constitutional Court to dissolve political parties was curbed significantly by constitutional amendments ratified in October 2001 to advance Turkey's candidacy to the European Union (Shambayati 2008). In addition, a constitutional amendment package adopted by referendum in September 2010 altered the appointments process to the Court to bolster the authorities of the elected branches.

Likewise, a national security council, initially established for the purpose of institutionalizing the military's influence on domestic politics, may be reconfigured to serve as an advisory body on national security policy. Turkey, for example, adopted a number of constitutional amendments in 2001 that curbed the military's role in the National Security Council. Among other things, the amendments increased the number of civilians on the Council, emphasized the Council's advisory role, deprived the Council of its executive powers, replaced the Council's military secretary-general with a civilian leader, and abolished the requirement of the civilian government to give "priority consideration" to the Council's recommendations (Varol 2013).

Although entrenchment is not necessarily a design failure for the opponents of the military, for democratic consolidation and persistence, the prerogatives of the military must eventually be curtailed. As noted above, curtailment may happen immediately where the opponents have sufficient bargaining leverage to force the military into the barracks without awarding them any prerogatives. In many cases, however, curtailment occurs in an incremental fashion, as an institutionalized political marketplace and civil society develop and the civilians renegotiate the military's constitutional prerogatives from a position of relative strength.

In the next two sections, I discuss two salient metrics of constitutional success in eradicating the military's constitutional prerogatives: (1) the imposition of temporal limitations on the military's prerogatives and (2) the formation of an institutionalized political marketplace. As discussed later, these metrics are interrelated in that the former can promote the latter.

A   *Temporal limitations on the military's prerogatives*

A temporary constitution or constitutional provision limits its own term and automatically lapses at its expiration date unless reenacted through regular constitutional amendment procedures (Varol 2014). In the context of transitions from military to civilian rule, temporary provisions can serve two primary purposes: (1) promoting the incremental elimination of the military's constitutional prerogatives and (2) reducing decision costs in constitutional negotiations.[8]

---

[8]   Although most constitutional prerogatives of the military are amenable to temporal limitations, there are some exceptions. For example, the constitutional designers may refrain, for good reason, from putting a temporal limit on a constitutional court even if it was created as a form of

The use of temporary provisions can permit incremental change through minor modifications to the existing constitutional configuration. Abrupt, large-scale changes to the status quo may face significant resistance, derailing the alteration attempt; in contrast, small-scale incremental change may be more palatable. With incremental constitutional evolution, each change represents only a minor modification to the status quo, which diminishes the costs and biases that impede constitutional change (Varol 2016).

The 1976 Portuguese Constitution is illustrative. As discussed above, the Constitution entrenched certain direct prerogatives for the military. But the political actors also did not want the military's constitutional authorities to stick and were cognizant of the need to eventually abolish them (Varol 2014). A temporal limit was therefore placed on the constitutional amendment rule, which prohibited the amendment of the Constitution for six years following its ratification without the consent of the military-dominated Council of the Revolution. After the six-year period, revision was possible with a two-third parliamentary majority. The temporary provision proved effective when a coalition of the existing political parties obtained the requisite supermajority to abolish the military's prerogatives after the amendment rule expired. The amendments also established a legal framework for democratic civilian control of the military (Varol 2012).

In the Portuguese case, the use of a temporary provision served several purposes. An attempt to immediately abolish the military's constitutional authorities may have provoked backlash from the military leaders and cemented the military's role in Portugal's constitutional order (Rato 2002). In granting temporally limited powers to the military, the Constitution preempted any tensions that may have arisen had the newly formed political parties attempted to eject the military from politics immediately or otherwise curtail the military's autonomy (Rato 2002). The temporal limitation thus allowed the constitutional framers to respond to a social problem that was itself temporary without etching the military's role into a durable constitution. It also relaxed the handcuffs placed on future political actors and allowed them to consolidate democracy after evolving societal conditions obviated the need for the military to serve a constitutional role. Finally, as discussed in the next section, the temporal limitation also allowed the political parties to institutionalize and gather sufficient popular backing from the electorate before moving to a new equilibrium.

Other examples also illustrate the use of temporary provisions in this context. For example, the 2014 Egyptian Constitution placed a temporal

---

institutional entrenchment. Yet, authorities given to the military or military-friendly institutions to appoint members to the court can be temporally limited.

limitation of two presidential terms on the military's veto power over the appointment of the defense minister. Under the 1982 Turkish Constitution, the military-dominated Presidential Council, and its authorities to review legislation in certain areas, terminated after six years. During the 1984 transition from military rule in Uruguay, the military was able to extract certain guarantees concerning its authorities, but the bargaining power of the political parties was sufficient to impose a one-year limitation on them (Linz & Stepan 1996).

The use of temporal limits can also have the benefit of reducing decision costs, which refer to the costs associated with reaching a constitutional decision. Constitutional design in transitions from military rule, which pits the wolves against the lambs, is a delicate exercise in consensus building. Consensus, however, is often difficult to achieve since the parties at the bargaining table will have competing visions for the document and will often disagree, and do so vehemently, about its content. The placement of temporal limitations on the military's prerogatives can reduce decision costs and make the contested provisions more palatable by lowering the political stakes. The temporary nature of the provision may mollify, at least to some extent, the opponents of the provision who fear that the entrenchment of the military's autonomy in a durable document will make it prohibitively difficult to remove thereafter.

The military, on the other hand, may acquiesce to a temporal limitation if it lacks the bargaining power and leverage to entrench a more durable status for itself. Where the bargaining power of the military is relatively low, the civilians may deny any temporally unlimited prerogatives to the military. From the military's perspective, the use of a temporal limitation can also signal to domestic and global audiences that the military views the term of its prerogatives to be temporary and its eventual exodus from politics to be permanent. In some cases, the imposition of temporal limitations can also support the long-term interests of the military as an institution. Depending on context, prolonged military presence in domestic politics can force the military to repeatedly take sides on contentious domestic issues and undermine the military's status and credibility domestically and globally. Put differently, the benefits of temporal limitations can exceed their costs, at least from the perspective of some factions within the military. Finally, logrolling may also prompt the military to accept temporal limitations. In exchange for agreeing to temporal limitations, the military may extract other compromises, such as an increased defense budget.

To extract temporal limitations, constitutional designers can also exploit the gap between the individual interests of the military elite and the interests of the military as an institution. A long line of constitutional thinkers dating back to James Madison have assumed that personal and institutional motivations largely overlap. A more recent scholarship has called this assumption into question, arguing that government officials tend to care more about their own self-interest, which may not necessarily overlap with the interests of the institution to which they belong (Levinson 2005). This gap between individual and institutional motivations also exists within the military, as the personal interests of the military elite may diverge from the interests of the military as a durable institution of government. The military's democratic opponents can take advantage of this gap and appeal to the individual interests of the decision-makers within the military elite by providing them privileged "exit" benefits. These individual benefits may in turn allow the military's opponents to extract compromises (such as temporal limitations) that allow the eventual eradication of the military's institutional prerogatives.

To be sure, the use of temporal limitations is not necessary to abolish the military's prerogatives. As noted above, entrenchment with temporal limits can itself reflect some lack of bargaining power and institutional weakness on the military's part, in which case the civilians might, in some contexts, be able to force the military back to the barracks without using temporary provisions. Put differently, temporal limitations may be possible precisely where they are not necessary.[9] This is a tempting narrative that may match the empirical reality in some, but certainly not all, cases. To return to the examples discussed above, the militaries in Egypt, Portugal, and Turkey – despite their institutional strength and bargaining power during constitutional design – accepted temporal limitations on some of their constitutional authorities. In other words, temporal limitations may be useful and palatable even where the military has significant institutional leverage.

Of course, even without temporal limitations, civilians can amend the existing Constitution to subordinate the military to the political branches. But most constitutions impose supermajority requirements for amendment, and depending on context, it may be prohibitively costly to put together the required coalition for the abolishment of the military's prerogatives. The use of temporary provisions reduces the costs associated with constitutional amendment or replacement because they expire automatically on their sunset date.

The use of temporal limitations can also provide the opportunity for the political marketplace to grow and stabilize, which in turn permits the civilian leaders to challenge the military's constitutional prerogatives from a position

---

[9] I thank José Antonio Cheibub for this point.

of relative strength. In the next section, I discuss the formation of an institutionalized political marketplace as another metric of success.

B　*The formation of an institutionalized political marketplace*

The creation of a competitive, multiparty, and institutionalized political marketplace is critical to the advancement of a nascent democracy (Issacharoff & Pildes 1998; Lai & Melkonian-Hoover 2005). Institutionalization can be conceptualized on a spectrum between inchoate party systems and fully institutional party systems. Most polities in transition from military to civilian rule are closer to the inchoate side of this spectrum since military rule, particularly where prolonged, tends to have an adverse affect on the health of the political marketplace.

In institutionalized party systems, "actors develop expectations, orientations, and behavior based on the premise that [the democratic party system] will prevail into the foreseeable future" (Mainwaring & Scully 1995). Characteristics of an institutionalized party system include stability in rules and the nature of interparty competition, stable linkages between parties and their constituents, expectations among major political actors that elections are the primary route to alternation of government power, and firmly established party organizations that are not subordinated to the interests of ambitious leaders (Mainwaring & Scully 1995). All relevant actors are less likely to resort to extra-constitutional sources, including their allies in the military, and more likely to play the democratic game, if they have the opportunity to compete – and win – in a healthy political marketplace. And military interventions in politics tend to occur when political institutions lack autonomy or coherence (Janowitz 1964; Rustow 1964). Where military bureaucracy is more developed than political parties, it will be easier for the military to create or coopt political parties to support its prerogatives or fill the power vacuum by staging a coup (Huntington 1965; Negretto 2013). That pattern has been common in Latin America, including in Guatemala, El Salvador, Peru, and Argentina (Huntington 1965).

In addition to promoting a competitive democracy, a stable and institutionalized political marketplace can also play an important role in eliminating the military's constitutional prerogatives. Indeed, if the political marketplace is sufficiently institutionalized in transitions from military rule, the military may be unable to extract any constitutional prerogatives. Even where the level of political institutionalization is low during constitutional design, if political parties take the time to empower themselves, obtain popular support, and subsequently challenge the military's prerogatives from a position of institutional strength, their attempts to curtail the military's authorities are often more likely to succeed. For example, elected leaders in Portugal waited until they formed stable and popular political parties in the early 1980s before attempting to abolish the military's constitutional prerogatives. The same move may have been derailed by the military in the immediate aftermath of the 1974 coup, but the military eventually acquiesced to the constitutional reforms advocated by the stable civilian government in power.

Although the existence of an institutionalized political marketplace is an important factor in promoting both democratic consolidation and the elimination of the military's institutional prerogatives, it guarantees neither. Other variables, which are difficult to control through constitutional design, can hinder democratic consolidation even where the political marketplace is sufficiently institutionalized. For example, if the military has powerful allies within the civilian political establishment, they can derail any civilian attempts to curb the military's prerogatives. In many cases, however, the institutionalization of democratic politics will provide the civilians more leverage to curtail the constitutional authorities of the military.

Although institutionalized political competition is important, excessive political competition can also produce undesirable consequences. As Robert Dahl has lamented, "one perennial problem of [political] opposition is that there is either too much or too little" (Dahl 1966). Excessive political competition can spawn factionalism, legislative deadlocks, and instability and lead to the breakdown of a democratic state (Lai & Melkonian-Hoover 2005; Linz 1978). The proliferation of political parties can disperse political institutionalization and spawn a large number of weak parties (Huntington 1965). Weak political institutionalization, in turn, renders a regime vulnerable to frequent power vacuums, political instability, collapse of governments, and further military interventions (Huntington 1965). The institutionalization of the "right" amount of political pluralism is therefore a formidable challenge for constitutional design in transitions from military rule.

What is more, depending on context, constitutional design may not significantly affect political institutionalization. The emergence of an institutionalized marketplace may depend more on sub-constitutional norms (e.g., election laws) and the socio-political environment that cannot be controlled through constitutional design. This does not mean, however, that constitutional design is irrelevant to political institutionalization. Although an extended discussion of the constitutional variables conducive to a robust political marketplace is outside the scope of this chapter, I offer some preliminary observations here through two case studies: Portugal and Turkey.

Portugal performed relatively well in generating an institutionalized political marketplace following the 1974 coup. In part because the Constitution was drafted in the aftermath of the anti-party *Estado Novo* dictatorship, it sought to establish strongly institutionalized parties. The Constitution retained the system of proportional representation in the legislature that had led to the election of four major political parties to the Constituent Assembly (Rato 2002). That achieved two ends. First, the exclusion of significant political powers from the parliament could have led them to adopt an anti-democratic agenda (Rato 2002). Second, the existence of four political parties ensured that no single party became too powerful to endanger democratic governance (Rato 2002). The political parties, uncertain of their prospects at the polls, readily acceded to a system that prevented the exclusion of any significant political party from the parliament (Rato 2002). A system of proportional representation also meant, however, that single-party majority governments might be difficult to form and portended bargaining, compromise, coalitions, and impasses – a potential recipe for political combustion and instability (Rato 2002).

But, as time would show, the Portuguese system of proportional representation posed no serious impediment to democratic consolidation (Rato 2002). Rather, the centralized party structures of the main political parties led to the expulsion of anti-democratic factions (Rato 2002). Each of the four major parties that won seats in the Constituent Assembly elections became an integral part of the newly established democracy, which was confirmed in the first parliamentary elections of April 1976 in which all four parties obtained representation (Magone 1997; Rato 2002). The December 1979 and the October 1980 parliamentary elections handed a landslide victory to the Democratic Alliance coalition (Rato 2002). These electoral triumphs ignited a period of stability and process of institutional change that ended with the abolishment in 1982 of the military's constitutional prerogatives (Magone 1997; Rato 2002).

In contrast to post-1974 Portugal, post-1960 Turkey did not generate a robust and stable political marketplace. Unlike the 1976 Portuguese Constitution, which sought to bolster political institutions, the drafters of the 1961 Turkish Constitution sought to end the supremacy of the single-chamber parliament. As a result, the Constitution established a plethora of counter-majoritarian checks on the parliament, which significantly weakened it and strengthened the bureaucracy. In addition to creating a constitutional court and a national security council, the Constitution also created a second legislative chamber, the Senate, and required bills to be approved by both chambers in order to become law. The Constitution also increased the authorities and autonomy of the Council of State, Turkey's highest administrative court. It created a State Planning Organization to guide "economic, social, and cultural development" and a Supreme Council of Judges with the authority to appoint and remove judges. The Supreme Council of Judges was largely divorced from political control since two-thirds of its members were elected by other judges and the remaining one-third by the Parliament. Universities and the Turkish Radio and Television Corporation were also divorced from government control and granted autonomy.

This constitutional arrangement, which favored the bureaucracy at the expense of the elected branches, was partially responsible for producing decades of weak coalition governments and legislative impasses in Turkey. The distribution of constitutional authority across a wide spectrum of counter-majoritarian institutions also created power vacuums. As the elected branches remained unable to form stable governments – let alone effectively conduct legislative affairs – the military began to stage further interventions to fill the resulting power vacuums, presenting serious impediments to democratic consolidation. It was not until the 2000s, with the ascension to power of stable governments and the legal-constitutional reforms brought by Turkey's accession process to the European Union, that the Turkish military retreated to the barracks.

Although significant political instability also existed in post-authoritarian Portugal, the resulting political coalitions were much stronger than the weak and fragile coalitions in post-1961 Turkey. After the 1974 coup in Portugal, political parties "successfully infiltrated so many aspects of Portuguese society that one can imagine few public offices or social institutions not subject to their dictates" (Bruneau & Macleod 1987). In stark contrast to Turkey, it was the political parties, not military leaders, that filled any resulting power vacuums in Portugal (Bruneau & Macleod 1987). And struggling to overcome internal conflicts, the Portuguese military was not as effective as the Turkish military in filling political power gaps (Bruneau & Macleod 1987).

IV CONCLUSION

Transitions from military rule often require civilian and military leaders to live together in one cage as lambs and wolves as they negotiate a framework for the transition and design a new constitution. The wolves, by virtue of their strength, are often able to extract constitutional prerogatives through direct, institutional, and procedural means. For democratic consolidation and persistence, however, these prerogatives must eventually be eliminated. A key, and difficult, challenge is to design the constitution to ensure democratic progress without causing a backlash from the military or prompting a rebound to military rule. To achieve that end, the chapter explored the use of temporal limitations on the military's constitutional prerogatives and discussed the importance of designing the constitution to promote the development of an institutionalized political marketplace to permit the lambs to challenge the wolves from a position of relative strength.

REFERENCES

Agüero, Felipe. 1995. Democratic Consolidation and the Military in Southern Europe and South America. In *The Politics of Democratic Consolidation*, edited by Richard Gunther, P. Nikiforos Diamandouros, and Hans-Jürgen Puhle. Baltimore, MD: The Johns Hopkins University Press.

Al-Ali, Zaid. 2013. *Egypt's Missed Constitutional Moment*. Available at http://foreignpolicy.com/2013/12/17/egypts-missed-constitutional-moment/.

Aydinli, Ersel, et al. 2006. The Turkish Military's March toward Europe. *Foreign Affairs* 85: 77–85.

Belge, Ceren. 2006. Friends of the Court: The Republican Alliance and Selective Activism of the Constitutional Court of Turkey. *Law and Society Review* 40: 653–692.

Bruneau, Thomas C. and Alex Macleod. 1987. *Politics in Contemporary Portugal: Parties and the Consolidation of Democracy*. Boulder, CO: Lynne Rienner Publishers.

Bünte, Marco. 2011. *Burma's Transition to "Disciplined Democracy": Abdication or Institutionalization of Military Rule?* German Institute of Global and Area Studies.

Choudhry, Sujit et al. 2014. *Constitutional Courts after the Arab Spring: Appointment Mechanisms and Relative Judicial Independence*. New York: NYU Law School Center on Constitutional Transitions.

Collier, David and Steven Levitsky. 1997. Democracy with Adjectives: Conceptual Innovation in Comparative Research. *World Politics* 49: 430–451.

Croissant, Aurel et al. 2010. Beyond the Fallacy of Coup-ism: Conceptualizing Civilian Control of the Military in Emerging Democracies. *Democratization* 17: 950–975.

Dahl, Robert A. 1966. *Political Oppositions in Western Democracies*. New Haven, CT: Yale University Press.

Fouad, Ajami. 2011. Egypt and the Fruits of the Pharaohs. *Wall Street Journal*, November 29, at A19.

Ginsburg, Tom. 2003. *Judicial Review in New Democracies: Constitutional Courts in Asian Cases*. Cambridge, UK: Cambridge University Press.

Heiss, Claudia and Patricio Navia. 2007. You Win Some, You Lose Some: Constitutional Reforms in Chile's Transition to Democracy. *Latin American Policy and Society* 49: 163–190.

Hirschl, Ran. 2004. *Towards Juristocracy: The Origins and Consequences of the New Constitutionalism.* Cambridge, MA: Harvard University Press.

Huntington, Samuel P. 1965. Political Development and Political Decay. *World Politics* 17: 386–430.

Issacharoff, Samuel and Richard H. Pildes. 1998. Politics as Markets: Partisan Lockups of the Democratic Process. *Stanford Law Review* 50: 643–717.

Janowitz, Morris. 1964. *The Military in the Political Development of New Nations: An Essay in Comparative Analysis.* Chicago, IL: University of Chicago Press.

Kogacioglu, Dicle. 2003. Dissolution of Political Parties by the Constitutional Court in Turkey: Judicial Delimitation of the Political Domain. *International Sociology* 18: 258–276.

Lai, Brian and Ruth Melkonian-Hoover. 2005. Democratic Progress and Regress: The Effect of Parties on the Transitions of States to and Away from Democracy. *Political Research Quarterly* 58: 551–564.

Landregan, John. 2002. Appointment, Reelection, and Autonomy in the Senate of Chile. In *Legislative Politics in Latin America*, edited by Scott Morgenstern and Benito Nacif. Cambridge, UK: Cambridge University Press.

Levinson, Daryl. 2005. Empire-Building Government in Constitutional Law. *Harvard Law Review* 118: 915–972.

Linz, Juan J. 1978. Crisis, Breakdown and Reequalibration. In *The Breakdown of Democratic Regimes*, edited by Juan J. Linz and Alfred Stepan. Baltimore, MD: The Johns Hopkins University Press.

    1990. Transitions to Democracy. *Washington Quarterly* 13: 143–164.

Linz, Juan J. and Alfred Stepan. 1996. *Problems of Democratic Transition and Consolidation: Southern Europe, South America, and Post-Communist Europe.* Baltimore, MD: The Johns Hopkins University Press.

Magone, Jose M. 1997. *European Portugal: The Difficult Road to Sustainable Democracy.* Palgrave Macmillan.

Mainwaring, Scott and Timothy R. Scully. 1995. Introduction. Party Systems in Latin America. In *Building Democratic Institutions: Party Systems in Latin America.* Redwood City, CA: Stanford University Press.

Meyer, Peter J. 2014. *Chile: Political and Economic Conditions and U.S. Relations.* Available at www.fas.org/sgp/crs/row/R40126.pdf.

Negretto, Gabriel. 2013. Authoritarian Constitution Making: The Role of the Military in Latin America. In *Constitutions in Authoritarian Regimes*, edited by Tom Ginsburg and Alberto Simpser. Cambridge, UK: Cambridge University Press.

Rato, Vasco Fernando Ferreira. 2002. *Reluctant Departure: The Politics of Military Extrication in Portugal, 1974–1982*, unpublished dissertation.

Rustow, Dankwart A. 1964. The Military: Turkey. In *Political Modernization in Japan and Turkey*, edited by Robert E. Ward and Dankwart A. Rustow. Princeton, NJ: Princeton University Press.

Sakallioglu, Umit Cizre. 1997. The Anatomy of the Turkish Military's Political Autonomy. *Comparative Politics* 29: 151–166.

Shain, Yossi and Juan J. Linz. 1995. Timing of First Democratic Elections. In *Between States: Interim Governments and Democratic Transitions*, edited by Yossi Shain and Juan J. Linz. Cambridge, UK: Cambridge University Press.

Shambayati, Hootan. 2004. A Tale of Two Mayors: Courts and Politics in Iran and Turkey. *International Journal of Middle East Studies* 36: 253–275.

2008. The Guardian of the Regime: The Turkish Constitutional Court in Comparative Perspective. In *Constitutional Politics in the Middle East*, edited by Saïd Amir Arjomand. Oxford, UK: Hart Publishing.

Shambayati, Hootan and Esen Kirdis. 2009. In Pursuit of "Contemporary Civilization": Judicial Empowerment in Turkey. *Political Research Quarterly* 62: 767–780.

Stepan, Alfred. 1988. *Rethinking Military Politics: Brazil and the Southern Cone*. Princeton, NJ: Princeton University Press.

Valenzuela, Samuel J. 1992. Democratic Consolidation in Post-Transitional Settings: Notion, Process, and Facilitating Conditions. In *Issues in Democratic Consolidation: The New South American Democracies in Comparative Perspective*, edited by Scott Mainwaring, Guillermo O'Donnell, and J. Samuel Valenzuela. Notre Dame, IN: University of Notre Dame Press.

Varol, Ozan O. 2012. The Democratic Coup d'État. *Harvard International Law Journal* 53: 291–356.

2013. The Turkish "Model" of Civil-Military Relations. *International Journal of Constitutional Law* 11: 727–750.

2014. Temporary Constitutions. *California Law Review* 102: 409–464.

2016. Constitutional Stickiness. *U.C. Davis Law Review* 49: 899–961.

7

Constitutional permissiveness, constitutional restrictiveness, and religious freedom

Hanna Lerner

INTRODUCTION

Constitutional ambiguity, vagueness, and indecision have been recently recognized by growing number of scholars and practitioners as a useful tool for mitigating conflicts over ideational issues during constitution-drafting processes (Bali and Lerner 2016; Brown 2008; Dixon and Ginsburg 2011; Lerner 2011; Shankar Forthcoming; Sunstein 2001). Under conditions of deep disagreements over the religious/national identity of the state or when the drafters are polarized around other ideological questions, it had been argued, drafters managed to craft democratic constitutional arrangements by using a variety of incrementalist or permissive constitutional strategies such as the use of vague and ambiguous language, the deferral of decisions to future parliaments, or even defining certain provisions as non-justiciable (Jacobsohn 2010; Lerner 2011). Yet what is the long-term impact of such incrementalist/ permissive strategies? To what extent do they allow, for example, for the emergence or consolidation of a stable democratic order? Do they manage to promote or rather impede the protection of human rights, gender equality, or minority rights?

The long-term consequences of formal constitutions have become an emerging topic of interest in the field of comparative politics and comparative constitutionalism. Most works tend to explore the influence of particular provisions within formal constitutions, such as electoral rules or bill of rights (e.g. Horowitz 1985; Law and Versteeg 2013). By contrast to these studies,

I would like to thank Alfred Stepan, Asli Bali, Mirjam Künkler, Amaney Jamal, Bajeera McCorkle, Shylashri Shankar, Murat Somer, Alison LaCroix, Tom Ginsburg, and Aziz Huq as well as the participants at the conference on "How Do Constitutions Succeed? Defining and Assessing Constitutional Performance," University of Chicago, for helpful comments and suggestions. This article partly draws on my study published in "Permissive Constitutions, Democracy and Religious Freedom in India, Indonesia, Israel and Turkey," World Politics 65, no. 4 (October 2013).

which look at the impact of formal written constitutional provisions, this chapter aims at exploring the consequences of decisions made by constitutional drafters which in many cases did not have a clear formal manifestation within a written constitution. In other words, the chapter aims at exploring the effect of framers' decisions to leave clear choices on controversial issues outside the formal constitution by, for example, deferring these issues to future political deliberation, or by including ambivalent and opaque wording, or even conflicting provisions, in the constitutional text. Such permissive strategies were rarely employed by constitutional drafters when institutional issues, concerning the structure and mechanisms of government, were at stake, yet were often used in order to mitigate ideational conflicts, namely when the constitution was written under conditions of deep division over the basic values and norms that should underpin the state.

The chapter takes first steps in examining the impact of constitutional permissiveness in the area of one particular type of ideational conflicts – religious conflicts. It explores four cases where questions of religion were at the heart of the constitutional debate – Indonesia, India, Israel, and Turkey – and examines the various ways through which permissive strategies were employed in order to mitigate tensions over the religious identity of the state or the role of religious law in the democratic order. As the following sections demonstrate, the drafters during the formative years in three of the countries – Indonesia, Israel, and India – preferred a permissive constitutional approach in order to allow the political system greater flexibility in future decision-making regarding controversial religious issues. By contrast, the Turkish drafters preferred a different model and adopted restrictive constitutional approach where specific constitutional constraints were designed to limit the range of possibilities available to future decision-makers when addressing religion–state relations.

More specifically, the chapter proposes directions for comparative analysis of the long-term consequences of constitutional permissiveness in the area of religion by focusing on two specific criteria: the ability of permissive/restrictive arrangement (a) to promote the democratic functioning of future governments and (b) to guarantee religious freedom. This study suggests that permissive arrangements – more than restrictive arrangements – are likely to facilitate the emergence of democratic institutions. On the question of religious freedom, I argue that the two approaches differ in their impact on freedom *of* religion (that is, protection of the rights of religious groups) and freedom *from* religion (that is, the right of individuals to opt out of religious practices and affiliations). Constitutional permissiveness for the most part allowed for greater freedom *of* religion than did restrictive constitutions. By contrast, freedom *from* religion was limited under permissive constitutional arrangements, compared with the restrictive constitutions studied here.

Before delving into the details of the four case studies, the next section will present the definitions of constitutional permissiveness and restrictiveness used in this chapter.

CONSTITUTIONAL PERMISSIVENESS/RESTRICTIVENESS

The permissive constitutional approach allows drafters to circumvent direct conflicts and to reconcile the deep disagreements regarding religious identity with the principles of democracy. Through strategies of indecisiveness, ambiguity, and vagueness, permissive constitutional arrangements afford the political system greater flexibility for future decisions on controversial religious questions. Constitutional flexibility, in this context, does not refer to amendment rules or to the level of entrenchment or rigidity of the written constitutional provisions. Rather, flexibility relates to the degree to which the formal constitution limits the range of political possibilities to be decided by ordinary legislation.

By refraining from setting definitive principles that would guide and restrict decisions of future generations on religious issues, permissive constitutions are often criticized for relinquishing the distinction between "higher lawmaking" and "lower lawmaking," which is a central pillar of liberal constitutional thinking (Ackerman 1991). By sidestepping substantial decisions on controversial religion-related issues, the framers of permissive arrangements transferred these decisions from the legal/constitutional level to the realm of ordinary parliamentary politics. This transfer rests on the assumption that the greater flexibility afforded in the domain of ordinary legislation could better accommodate the demands of the conflicting camps, providing, perhaps, more room for innovative and nuanced solutions.

In contrast to the permissive approach, the *restrictive* constitutional approach aims to limit the range of options for future political actors. While permissive constitutions allow political actors greater flexibility to reform policies surrounding religion at the level of "normal lawmaking," restrictive constitutions, by contrast, constrain future decision-making. Such restrictions may be included either formally in constitutional provisions or informally through authoritarian means.

While the chapter attempts to make a clear distinction between permissive and restrictive constitutional arrangements, the political reality tends to be more complicated. In some cases, the exportation of controversial issues from the constitution-drafting process does not rest on a genuine intention to pursue further political deliberation but rather represents an instrumental strategy aimed at guaranteeing favorite decisions in a more politically convenient setting. Given predictions on how political forces will congeal into the institutional arrangements in the post-drafting phase, drafters may prefer to transfer decision-making to political bodies which would favor their positions. By that, they pursue in fact a strategy of restriction of future political choices rather than aim at permitting flexibility. Similarly, constitutional deferral may go hand in hand with strict negotiations concerning the structure of future judicial institutions (e.g. nomination procedures for the supreme/constitutional court) which would guarantee certain judicial interpretations on issues left open by the constitutional drafters. Indeed, whether drafters' choices are underpinned by a genuine intention for further deliberation or by a more instrumental/strategic motivation is a question often difficult to investigate by empirical means. Furthermore, even when the adoption of vague constitutional formulations or the deferral of choices was initially motivated by instrumental intentions, the political or legal outcomes may not meet the intended consequences predicted by the drafters. As the following sections illustrate, in some cases the indecision on the constitutional level yielded an unintended institutional trajectory that was difficult to change in later decades.[1]

Among the countries discussed in this chapter, in three cases the constitutional drafters adopted permissive constitutional arrangements in the area of religion: in India in 1950, in Israel in 1950, and in Indonesia in 1945. Restrictive constitutional arrangements have been adopted by Turkey during the formative stage of the state, as well as in the later reiterated in 1961 and in 1982. Similarly, in 1959 the political leadership of Indonesia embraced a restrictive rather than a permissive constitutional approach. In both cases, as further illustrated later, constitutional restrictiveness was adopted in order to promote secular ideologies. However, restrictive constitutional arrangements may be used in order to advance a wide variety of preferences concerning the relations between religion and state. For example, the constitution of post-1979 Iran as well as that of Saudi Arabia may be defined as restrictive constitutions, aiming at limiting the range of options for future political actors. Similarly, liberal constitutions, which include strict protections for individual rights, may be considered restrictive in the way the category is used in this discussion.

From that liberal perspective, permissive constitutional arrangements may be considered normatively inferior. Permissive constitutional arrangements

---

[1] This was the case, for example, in Israel, where the legislation of Tribunals of Rabbinical Courts (Marriage and Divorce) Law in 1953 created an Orthodox monopoly over Jewish marriage and divorce which is very difficult to reform for over six decades. See Lerner (2014).

tend to refrain from providing a definitive set of norms and values that would serve as the legal tool for crafting future judicial and legislative decisions in religious affairs. They also tend to tolerate nonliberal worldviews and often provide weaker protections for fundamental rights. In the absence of clear and unequivocal liberal constitutional statements, the religious institutions and the regulations that emerge tend to be conservative and traditional. However, as the rest of the chapter demonstrates, under circumstances of deep disagreements over the state's religious character, permissive arrangements facilitate the enactment of a democratic order. While it may limit the citizen's freedom from religion, it often encourages state policies which protect citizen's freedom of religion.

The next section will briefly present the constitutional discussion that lead to the adoption of permissive/restrictive arrangements in India, Israel, Indonesia, and Turkey. To clarify, the selection of cases to be analyzed in this chapter did not intend to represent a range of secular/religious ideologies or a variety of relationships between freedom of and freedom from religion. Rather, as the following section further elaborates, the four countries have been selected for this study since in all four of them religion stood at the center of the constitutional debate during the foundational stage of the state and because democracy and religious freedom were defined as explicit goals of their governments. Moreover, the four countries debated their constitutions in the first part of the twentieth century, which allows enough time for retrospective analysis of the consequences of the choices made by the constitutional drafters.

THE CASE STUDIES

The four states under discussion in this chapter differ greatly in size, history, and geopolitical conditions, as well as in the social and religious composition of their populations. The differences are striking in terms of sheer numbers: after the partition in 1947, the population in India was approximately 250 million, of which 85 percent were Hindus and 10 percent were Muslims; in Indonesia, at the time of constitution writing in 1945, 88 percent of the population of approximately 77 million, were Muslims, with large Christian and Hindu minorities; the Israeli population at independence, in 1948, comprised of 600,000 Jews and about 180,000 Palestinians (18 percent), mostly Muslim; and in Turkey in 1924, 99 percent of the population of twenty million were Muslims. Nevertheless, there were striking similarities in the constitution-writing projects undertaken by these states. In all four cases, constitutional drafting took place in the first half of the twentieth century in the wake of a colonial or imperial past (Turkey had reinvented itself as a modern nation-state). In each case, the ensuing constitutional debates addressed issues beyond the framework of regime change, government structuring, or power allocation. Instead, the constitution-making process was seen as a foundational moment in which "the people" had to be defined. In all four cases, the drafters of the constitution had a sense of operating as "founding fathers" and were engaged in debates over the identity of the emerging state: what does it mean to be Indian? What is Indonesia's Dasar Negara (philosophy of state)? What is modern Turkey? What is a Jewish state? In all of these debates, the question of religious identity was central and the disagreements between the framers were intense. The disputes extended beyond questions of religious symbolism and centered on the role of religious law in the new states. For example, in all four cases family law was based on religious traditions from the preindependence era, and the question of maintaining legal pluralism was central to the constitutional debate.

The constitutional debates on religious identity addressed two types of tensions, interreligious and intrareligious. In Indonesia and India, interreligious tensions predominated and the objective of the constitution was to create a sense of unity amid religious diversity. Intrareligious arguments characterized the religious–secular conflict between Jews in Israel, the dispute over the role of religion in Turkey, and the debate on Hindu personal law in India.

In India and Israel, as well as in Indonesia in 1945, the drafters preferred to overcome divisions on religious questions by consensual means. Despite the differences between the three cases, they all debated and drafted the constitutional arrangements in assemblies or committees representing the various identity and ideological groups in their societies, and they all adopted permissive constitutional arrangements through a process of deliberation, negotiation, and compromise. In contrast, at the foundational stage of Turkey, religious differences were addressed by radical reforms based on exclusionary ideology that were imposed top-down by authoritarian means. Similarly, in Indonesia in 1959, an authoritarian government replaced the inclusionary ideology of the state with an exclusionary one.

India: formal permissiveness

The process of constitution writing in India began in December 1946, seven months before Indian independence and the partition with Pakistan. The constitutional draft took three years to complete. From the very beginning the debate over India's religious identity was twofold. It revolved around interreligious issues between the Hindu majority and Muslim minorities and around intrareligious issues, regarding the question of state interference in religious practices. What is India and to what extent is it exclusively Hindu? Should the state intervene in religious practices of either majority or minority religions that conflict with basic principles of equality and liberty? These questions were vigorously debated by the Constituent Assembly (Constituent Assembly Debate II, Rao 1966, Austin 1999: ch. 3). Personal law became a focal point for both the intrareligious and interreligious debates. At the intrareligious level, the Constituent Assembly debated whether Hindu family laws should be secularized by the state or maintain its traditional and often inegalitarian practices.[2] While Nehru viewed the reform of Hindu traditional family laws essential to advancing India's development and modernization (Som 1994), conservative hard-liners and Hindu fundamentalists within the Congress Party objected to such reforms (Jaffrelot 1996). At the interreligious level, the Assembly was harshly divided over the question of the Uniform Civil Code, namely, whether personal law should be unified for all citizens, regardless of the individual's religious affiliation (Constituent Assembly Debated VII: 540–550).

Ultimately, the Constituent Assembly refrained from making clear-cut decisions on either one of these issues. On the intrareligious front, it avoided the constitutionalization of a Hindu Code (Som 1994). In the question of the Uniform Civil Code, the decision was to include it in the constitution. However, in order to pacify the Muslim minority that remained in India after partition with Pakistan and feared cultural Hindu homogenization, the article was included in the Directive Principles for State Policy section and was defined as nonjusticiable, meaning that it would not be enforceable by the courts.[3] The drafters, who preferred to follow an evolutionary rather than a revolutionary constitutional approach, directed the constitution's potential power to rule on the secular identity of the state back to the political arena, leaving future parliamentarians to decide whether and how to implement the recommendations set forth in the constitution (Jaffrelot 1996: 102–104). Indeed, in the 1950s the legislature continued debating the Hindu Code and eventually split the law into four different pieces of legislation that were passed between 1955 and 1961, introducing reforms regarding issues such as marriage and divorce, inheritance laws, and adoption. By contrast, the Uniform Civil Code was never implemented. The result was the maintenance of a separate

---

[2]   The debate over codification of reformed Hindu law goes back to the Hindu Women's Rights to Property Act (1937) and the 1941 Hindu Law Committee appointed under the British rule.

[3]   Article 44 of the Indian constitution states: "The state shall endeavor to secure for the citizens a uniform civil code throughout the territory of India."

personal law system in India for each religious group and the implementation
of only minor reforms in the traditional Muslim and Christian personal laws
(Subramanian 2010).

Overall, the set of ambiguous and ambivalent provisions included in the
Indian constitution with regard to religion–state relations amounts to what
Rajeev Bhargava termed "political secularism" or "contextual secularism."
According to this model, the state is not separated from religion but rather
keeps a "principled distance" from all religions, by providing equal protection
and support for all religions and by selectively interfering in religious practices
that conflict with the state's goals of promoting equality, liberty, and socio-
economic development.[4] While supporters of this approach have emphasized
the advantage of such ambiguous arrangements for the purpose of maintaining stability and democracy at the foundational stage of the state (Austin 1999;
Bhargava 2010; Hardgrave 1993; Jackobsohn 2006; Khilnani 1999), its critics
have pointed to the tendency of such arrangements to perpetuate – rather than
mitigate – conflicts over issues of religion and secularism, which ultimately
resulted in overburdening India's political and judicial institutions (Hasan
1994; Needham and Rajan 2007).

Israel: informal permissiveness

While in India constitutional drafters faced the challenge of advancing
national unity in the face of interreligious (as well as linguistic, social, and
cultural) diversity, in Israel the most heated debates during the constitutional
discussion concerned internal divisions within the Jewish majority over
a religious or secular definition of the state. The issue of interreligious relations was barely addressed by the drafters. The Palestinian minority in Israel,
which constituted 18 percent of the total population (of less than 800,000), was
able to exercise some political rights but was consistently excluded from Israeli
nationhood, defined in terms of Jewish identity. Until 1966, large part of the
Palestinian population in Israel lived under military rule. In the early years of
the state, the Palestinian minority was excluded from the constitution-drafting
process and from efforts to define the state's basic tenets and credo (Peled and
Shafir 2005).

The secular Zionist leadership of the state, dominated by the socialist
Mapai Party, perceived the Jewish character of the state in national-secular
terms. By contrast, Orthodox groups objected to the secular character of the

---

[4] For example, state regulation intended to reduce inegalitarian caste practices are thus justified
     as part of the overall secular identity of the state (Bhargava 1998, 2002; Jacobsohn 2006).

state and sought to grant Jewish religious law precedence over state law (Knesset Records 1950: 744, 812). Under the fragile circumstances of a newly independent state, many in the Knesset feared that writing a constitution would require clear-cut choices regarding the vision of the state and would stir up conflict between religious and secular Jews (Lerner 2011: chap. 3). The government already faced serious challenges to its sovereignty from various underground nationalist and young religious zealots (Friedman 1991: 60–66; Sprinzak 1999: 62–65). Hence, the threat of destabilization was not taken lightly by the drafters. Moreover, the government believed that the most urgent task during the state-building period would be the absorption of immigrants. The Jewish population in Israel in 1948 was less than 10 percent of world Jewry and the immigrants that were expected to arrive from the Jewish Diaspora were generally religious. Thus, despite a significant majority of secular Jews in the Knesset[5] and a formal commitment in the Declaration of Independence to draft a constitution, the Knesset decided in 1950 to avoid drafting a constitution. Instead, the constitution was to be enacted in a gradual manner, through a series of Basic Laws (Knesset Records 1950: 1743). Among the chief reasons for the decision was the wish to avoid a greater division between religious and secular Jews.[6]

In the absence of a written constitution, religion–state relations in Israel evolved through ordinary legislation or through informal means during the early years of the state. These arrangements, known as "the religious status quo," stipulate the nonseparation between religion and state in various areas of life: a religious monopoly on marriage and divorce and the institutionalization of a pluralist personal law system (following the Ottoman Millet system),[7] kosher food in state institutions, prohibition of public transportation on the Sabbath, autonomy for religious schools, and exemptions from military service for Orthodox yeshiva students and religious women. This religious status quo was never clearly defined. Yet a commitment to maintain it was included in most governing coalition agreements. Thus, although the religious status quo was criticized by both the religious and the secular-liberal camps, by and large the core religion-state arrangements that were formulated in the first decade of the state were preserved.[8]

The characterization of the State of Israel as "Jewish and democratic" was introduced in the 1994 amendments to the Basic Laws on Human Liberty and

---

[5] Only 16 out of 120 Knesset members in 1950 represented religious parties.
[6] On the debates that led to this decision, see Lerner (2011: 60–70).
[7] Civil marriages are recognized only if performed outside of Israel.
[8] The Supreme Court intervened in some minor issues but never challenged the core arrangements of the religious status quo (Corinaldi 2004; Wood 2008).

Dignity (Article 1a) and to the Basic Law on Freedom of Occupation (Article 2). Yet the debate over the meaning and interpretation of what many consider a self-contradictory definition continues to divide Israeli society (Mautner 2011).

Indonesia: shifting from religious constitutional permissiveness to constitutional restrictiveness and back

The constitutional trajectory of Indonesia demonstrates the possibility of a religious type of permissive constitution. It also represents a case in which permissive constitutional arrangements intended to address religious conflicts at the time of independence (1945) were replaced by a restrictive constitutional approach almost a decade and a half later (1959). The restrictive constitution was itself replaced by a permissive constitution as part of subsequent demo-cratization efforts (1998).

The first Indonesian constitution was drafted between May and August of 1945. The drafting process was initiated by the Japanese just three months before their surrender to the Allied Forces. Recognizing the imminent end of their rule in Indonesia, the Japanese formed the Investigative Committee for Preparatory Work for Indonesian Independence (BRUPK), comprising sixty-two members selected mainly from the older generation of Indonesian leadership from Java.[9] The main debates in the committee revolved around the role of Islam in the new state. The dispute was between the Islamists, who wished Indonesia to be an Islamic state, and the nationalists, who envisioned an all-inclusive Indonesian national identity rather than an exclusively Islamic identity. Due to Indonesia's sprawling geographical organization, its large non-Muslim minorities, and the different ways Islamic law may be understood and interpreted, the committee advocated a "state which will unite itself with the largest group but which can stand above all groups" (Ramage 2002).

The disagreements were bridged by the doctrine of *Pancasila* (literally, five principles) laid down by Sukarno in a famous speech on June 1, 1945, and later included in the constitutional preamble (Feith and Castles 2007: 40–49). The first of these five vague principles was "belief in God."[10] In addition, Article 29 of the constitution states that "the state is based upon the belief in

---

[9] Some claim that committee membership had a strong majority of those who are "known to favor a religiously neutral form of territorial nationalism," while advocates of Islamic ideology constituted about a quarter of committee members (Elson 2009: 109; Ricklefs 2008: 245).

[10] The additional four principles are Indonesian unity, humanism, democracy based on deliberation and consensus, and social justice. For detailed discussion of their meaning, see Ramage (2002: 12–14).

one supreme God." By avoiding the name of a particular God, Indonesian identity is defined in religious but not in Muslim terms (Hosen 2007: 64, 194; Künkler Forthcoming; Künkler and Sezgin 2015).[11]

The draft preamble to the constitution, known as the Jakarta Charter, included, in addition to *Pancasila*, two short statements: a seven-word sentence according to which all Muslims are obliged to follow Islamic law[12] and a requirement that the president must be Muslim. However, just before the constitution was enacted, these two Islamic statements were removed from the constitution. The decision was driven by a concern that predominately Christian eastern Indonesia would not join the unitary republic if the constitution characterized it as an Islamic state. There was concern as well about the internal division among the Muslim leaders, between those who believed Islamic law should be legislated at the national level and those who opposed state-enforced Islamic law (Ramage 2002: 15; Ricklefs 2008: 247).[13]

For the first fourteen years following independence, the exact meaning of *Pancasila* and the question what should be the "philosophy of the state" (Dasar Negara) continued to be at the heart of public and political debates. The ambiguous character of *Pancasila* was preserved in the two constitutions that replaced the 1945 constitution and were formally in force between 1949 and 1957.[14] Like the 1945 constitution, the 1950 constitution, which established Indonesia's parliamentary system, was enacted as a provisional arrangement meant to stand until such time as a democratically elected constituent assembly (the Konstituante) drafted a permanent and legitimate constitution. The debate about the meaning of *Pancasila* and over the philosophy of the state continued during the two and a half years of Konstituante discussions regarding the new constitution (1956–59).[15]

---

[11] As one observer noted, the first principle of *Pancasila* is a "multi-interpretable formula and must be appreciated as providing a real possibility for people to agree while disagreeing" (Boland 1982: 39).

[12] Some analysts argue that even Muslim members of BRUPK did not agree on the practical implications of the famous seven words (Elson 2009: 113n59).

[13] For various alternative explanations, see Elson (2009: 122–26).

[14] The first, a federal constitution of the United States of Indonesia, was adopted as part of the Hague Agreement between Indonesia and the Netherlands. It survived only few months, until the summer of 1950, when Indonesia withdrew from the Agreement and enacted a unitary constitution of the Republic of Indonesia.

[15] The Konstituante comprised 544 members, of which 514 were elected by free and open elections in December 1955. Thirty-four parties participated in the elections, as did forty million Indonesian citizens (about 90 percent of the registered voters). An additional thirty members of the Konstituante represented minority groups (Chinese, Indo-European, and the Dutch occupied territories of West Irian) (Nasution 1992: 30–35).

Yet the permissive constitutional framework established by the Indonesian leadership at its foundational stage was short-lived. It was replaced by the restrictive constitutional approach of Sukarno's regime of Guided Democracy, which was imposed by extraconstitutional means. The deterioration of the economy, the increase in national conflicts, and the apparent inability of the government to deal with the crisis caused support for the parliamentary system to diminish dramatically. It also led Sukarno to declare martial law in May 1957 and to begin creating the institutional framework of Guided Democracy, with the intent of restoring stability and preventing the disintegration of the republic. The army increased its interference in politics and in the economy and in 1958 demanded a return to the 1945 constitution, which allegedly provided a legal basis for greater military involvement in civilian affairs (Lev 1966). On June 2, 1959, in what became its final session, the Konstituante voted against the proposal, which was supported by the president and the National Council, to reinstate the 1945 constitution (Nasution 1992: chap. 2). Sukarno subsequently published a presidential decree dissolving the Konstituante and reinstating the constitution.

The formal wording of the 1945 constitution was not altered. However, upon the establishment of Guided Democracy in 1959, *Pancasila* would begin to represent a substantively new conception. In 1945, it had been proposed as a vague set of inclusivist principles. It was viewed as a "forum, a meeting point for all the different parties and groups, a common denominator of all ideologies and streams of thought existing in Indonesia" (Nasution 1992: 421). By contrast, in 1959, *Pancasila* became part of the authoritarian regime's justifying ideology, much like Turkey's Kemalism. Invoking the "integralist state," the nationalist camp in the late 1950s presented *Pancasila* as the only political ideology that would guarantee national unity. Rather than serve as a common platform for the different political ideologies in Indonesia, *Pancasila* was reconfigured as an exclusivist ideology standing in opposition to other ideologies and streams of thought. Moreover, it was imposed by the military and by the government through authoritarian means (Assyyaukanie 2009; Nasution 1992: 65; Ramage 2002: 17–22, 26).

During the years of Sukarno's Guided Democracy (1959–65), as well as under Soeharto's New Order (1966–98), the government maintained its monopoly on the interpretation of *Pancasila* as an ideology of the state that guarantees national unity through various means of indoctrination.[16] While already during the 1980s Soeharto' regime was more tolerant toward public

---

[16] For example, by establishing "The Guidance of Conscientization and Implementation of Pancasila," which was a national-scale program of indoctrination courses for members of the bureaucracy, armed forces, political leaders, businessmen, students, and religious leaders.

expressions of Islam, as late as 1998, the government forbade any public debate on the place of religion in the constitution.[17]

After Soeharto's resignation in 1998, the new political leadership attempted to restore the inclusivist interpretation of *Pancasila* and return to a permissive constitutional approach. The 1945 constitution was amended in a series of reforms enacted from 1999 to 2002. These reforms established new democratic institutions and strengthened the protection of human rights. During the open and free debates, several Islamic parties renewed the demand to restore the Jakarta Charter and to insert Sharia law into the constitution. Yet the debate ended with Parliament's decision to retain the wording of Article 29 and refrain from modifying the definition of the state's religious identity expressed in the constitution (Hosen 2007). The amended democratic constitution of Indonesia enhanced religious permissiveness through additional ambiguous formulations, such as Article 28J (2), which guaranteed the protection of "religious values" (Hosen 2007: 127–28). Whether the original ambiguous moderate character of *Pancasila* can be fully restored through the process of democratization is still a controversial question in Indonesia. Some observers argue that once the five principles of *Pancasila* had been exploited by the authoritarian regime, it would never be possible to restore the term's original meaning (Jones 2010).

Turkey: imposed secularism through restrictive constitution

Modern Turkey's first constitution was drafted in 1924,[18] one year after the establishment of the republic, by the Grand National Assembly, which was largely controlled by the RPP, Mustafa Kemal's "People's Party."[19] The constitution-writing project played a central role in the establishment of the Kemalist state. Kemalism was designed to advance a particular modernizing ideology based on three tenets: Westernization, Turkish nationalism, and a scientific approach to religion (Hanioglu 2013). Kemal and his fellow founders aimed at constructing a prosperous, rational, and irreligious modern society (Hanioglu 2013). Secularizing Turkish society and consolidating a homogenous national identity from its diverse ethnic and religious groups were the central goals of the state (Bali 2011a; Horowitz 2013: 120–22; Yavuz 2009: 25).

---

[17] For example, through the 1963 Anti-subversion Law.
[18] The first Ottoman constitution was enacted in 1876. In 1921 the first Grand National Assembly adopted a short and provisionary constitutional document, yet it was never expected to serve as the republic's permanent constitution (Özbudun and Genckaya 2009: 8–10).
[19] Many of the 1923 Grand National Assembly were members of the first Grand Assembly (1920–23), yet none of those who opposed Ataturk (some of them Islamists) were allowed to be reelected (Özbudun and Gencckaya 2009: 10–11).

At the same time, Mustafa Kemal realized that Islam was deeply embedded in Ottoman culture and could not be eliminated by the stroke of a pen. For that reason, the 1924 constitution included the statement that "the religion of the Turkish Republic is Islam"; in 1937, however, this statement was removed from the constitution and Turkey was defined as a secular state.

In contrast to the consensus-based approach of decision-making on religious issues adopted by the drafters in India and Israel, the Turkish constitution represented a revolutionary model of imposed secularism. The founding elite's vision of a Kemalist revolution lacked the necessary broad social basis (Anderson 2009: 414–17). So, although attempts were made to introduce *Laikik* as a particular form of secularism,[20] ultimately, the transformation of Turkish society was promoted through a set of top-down policies enforced by powerful state institutions. Between 1924 and 1937, the republic introduced a series of radical reforms designed to advance state control of religion as well as the secularization and homogenization of Turkish society. These reforms included: the abolition of the caliphate and the subordination of all religious institutions to the state through the establishment of a Directorate of Religious Affairs, the replacement of Sharia personal status laws with a European-inspired civil code, the outlawing of traditional dress, the adoption of a Western calendar, and the replacement of the Arabic alphabet with the Latin alphabet (Bali 2011a: 28–34; Kuru 2007).

The revolutionary constitution was not designed to establish a truly democratic order. As some commentators observed, instead of a system of checks and balances, it envisioned a "Rousseauist" version of democracy, in which the legislature represents the "general will" of the people (Özbudun and Genckaya 2009: 12). The constitution provided the conditions for the emergence of a single-party system (until 1946) and allowed for the establishment of tutelary state institutions, intended to safeguard the core commitments of the founding elite, particularly the security apparatus, civilian bureaucracy, and the judiciary system. These institutions, formed during the constitutive moment of state formation, generated a legacy of repressive strategies, which is "now embedded in Turkish constitutional culture [and] provides the context against which to understand the state's institutional defensiveness in the face of contemporary demands for further liberalization" (Bali 2011a: 9).

In the eight decades since independence, the Turkish political and constitutional trajectory has been characterized recurring authoritarian interventions by the military in the enduring conflicts over the state religious and

---

[20] Influenced by the French *laïcité*, the Kemalist project of secularism – *Laikik* – aimed at controlling religion and limiting it to the private sphere of personal belief and worship (Kuru 2007; Yavuz 2009).

national identity. Two of these coups were followed by a rewriting of the constitution by the military (1961 and 1982), reestablishing the Kemalist foundational ideological orthodoxy (Akan 2011; Özbudun and Genckaya 2009: 14–29; Zürcher 1997).[21] Since 1982 the Turkish constitution has added seventeen amendments, introducing elements of democratization and liberalization into the document. Moreover, the more recent electoral successes of Muslim political parties have generated a more ambiguous relationship between state and religion (for example, by introducing compulsory religious education in schools and allowing prohibitions on alcohol in certain municipalities) (Kuru 2009). Nevertheless, the formal constitution is still commonly viewed as representative of the authoritarian and tutelary legacy of the National Security Council regime under which it was drafted (Hale and Özbudun 2010). In 2007, an attempt to draft a civilian constitution by the Özbudun committee failed. Yet expectations that a new constitution would be drafted after the June 2011 elections gave rise to numerous constitutional drafts proposed by think tanks and NGOS. Whether the next Turkish constitution will adopt a permissive rather than a restrictive approach to address the internal tensions regarding religion–state relations is a question that will be resolved by future developments.

LONG-TERM CONSEQUENCES

From a normative perspective, the constitutional arrangements adopted by the four religiously divided societies studied here, whether restrictive and permissive, seem inferior to the ideal-type of liberal constitutionalism. The restrictive constitutions adopted in Turkey and in Indonesia (1959) were imposed by authoritarian means and the constitutions infringed upon citizens' basic human and political rights. Yet even the permissive constitutional arrangements in India, Israel, and 1945/1998 Indonesia, which were adopted by more consensual and democratic methods, are often criticized as normatively inferior to liberal constitutions for their failure to guarantee the type of human rights protection advocated by liberal constitutionalists (Agnes 2011; Kremnitzer 2005; Needham and Rajan 2007; Raday et al. 1995).

I would like to argue, however, that viewing permissive constitutional arrangements as merely failed projects compared with the liberal constitutional ideal oversimplifies the picture and precludes a more nuanced understanding of the risks and opportunities offered by ambiguous constitutional

---

[21] In the 1982 constitution the inalterable Article 2 states that "the Republic of Turkey is a democratic, secular and social state."

strategies. In this section, I explore variation in the long-term impacts of the different constitutional models adopted by India, Indonesia, Israel, and Turkey. Such an investigation would have not only normative but also practical significance. It may provide guidance for current and future constitutional drafters and advisers, who struggle with questions about the role that constitutions should play in defining religion–state relations.

The following discussion proposes a preliminary framework for analyzing the consequences of permissive and restrictive constitutions. First, I examine the implications of constitutional choices made by political actors at the foundational stage of the state with regard to the emergence or endurance of democracy. Second, I explore the impact of constitutional permissiveness/ restrictiveness on the attainment of religious freedom. I propose to unpack the conception of religious freedom, which is usually measured in general terms, to draw a distinction between institutions and regulations that promote freedom *of* religion and those that promote freedom *from* religion.

Democratic institutions

While permissive constitutions by definition deviate from the ideal of liberal democracy, such instruments are compatible with a consensual conception of democracy and thus are more likely to allow for the emergence of democratic institutions, characterized by open and free elections and the guarantee of civil and political rights to all citizens. Table 7.1 shows a correlation between ambiguous permissive constitutional arrangements and the emergence of democratic institutions, as measured by Freedom House and by Polity iv project until 2012.

The correlation between permissive constitutional arrangements in the area of religion and democracy is demonstrated in all cases examined in this chapter. In Israel and India, permissive constitutions go hand in hand with a relatively stable democratic order.[22] In Indonesia, the 1945 constitution, which defined *Pancasila* as an ambiguous principle in order to overcome deep disagreements regarding the religious character of the state, facilitated the emergence of a parliamentary system that functioned under difficult security and economic conditions a little more than a decade following independence.[23] By contrast, Indonesia's authoritarian period (1959–98) was accompanied by a decisive interpretation of *Pancasila* along "integralist" anti-Islamic lines. As discussed

---

[22] Except for the period of emergency rule in India. For a critical discussion of Israeli democracy, see, e.g., Smooha (1997) and Jamal (2009).

[23] While formally the parliamentary system was established in the 1950 constitution, the commitment of the Indonesian government to democracy was already expressed with independence (Nasution 1992: 4, 15–27; Ricklefs 2008: 273).

TABLE 7.1 *Permissive/restrictive constitutional arrangements and measures of democracy*

Country and year of const. formation	Type of constitutional arrangements in the area of religion	Freedom House[a]				Polity IV project[b]		
		Year	Political rights	Civil liberties	Status	Year	Score	Type of regime
India 1946–50	formal permissiveness					1950	9	democracy
						1962	9	democracy
		1972	2	3	free	1972	9	democracy
		1982	2	3	free	1982	8	democracy
		1992	3	4	partly free	1992	8	democracy
		2002	2	3	free	2002	9	democracy
		2012	2	3	free	2010	9	democracy
Israel (1950)	informal permissiveness					1948	10	democracy
						1962	10	democracy
		1972	2	3	free	1972	9	democracy
		1982	2	3	free	1982	9	democracy
		1992	2	2	free	1992	9	democracy
		2002	1	2	free	2002	10	democracy
		2012	1	2	free	2010	10	democracy
Indonesia 1945, 1959, 1998–2002	1945–59: religious ambiguity; 1959–98: restrictive					1947	2	open anocracy
						1957	0	open anocracy
		1972	5	5	partly f	1962	−5	closed anocracy
		1982	5	5	partly f	1972	−7	autocracy
		1992	6	6	partly f	1982	−7	autocracy

TABLE 7.1 (Cont.)

Country and year of const. formation	Type of constitutional arrangements in the area of religion	Freedom House				Polity IV project		
		Year	Political rights	Civil liberties	Status	Year	Score	Type of regime
	post-1998: religious ambiguity	2002	3	4	partly f	1992	−7	autocracy
		2012	2	3	free	2002	6	democracy
						2010	8	democracy
Turkey 1924–37; 1961, 1982	restrictive constitution					1946	−7	autocracy
		1972	3	4	partly f	1956	4	open anocracy
		1982	5	5	partly f	1972	−2	closed anocracy
		1992	2	4	partly f	1982	−5	closed anocracy
		2002	3	4	partly f	1992	9	democracy[c]
		2012	3	3	partly f	2002	7	democracy
						2010	7	democracy

[a] Freedom in the World Country Rating 1972–2012, Freedom House. At www.freedomhouse.org/template.cfm?page=439.
[b] Polity IV Individual Country Regime Trends, 1946–2010. At www.systemicpeace.org/polity/polity4.htm. Polity IV scores are based on coding of governmental institutions. While according to this institutional measure Turkey is defined as a democracy since the 1990s, it is still rated as "Partly Free" according to levels of political rights and civil liberties protection rated by Freedom House.

above, *Pancasila* thus lost its ambiguous, all-inclusive nature, and its enforcement depended on repression, rather than on consensus. After 1998, Indonesia's return to democracy was accompanied by an attempt to return to a more ambiguous definition of *Pancasila*, which resulted, for example, in a de facto (and partial) decentralization of regulations in the area of religion in several provinces and regions.[24]

Similarly, Turkey's trajectory reflects a correlation between restrictive constitutional arrangements in the area of religion and authoritarian regime. As discussed above, a decisive Kemalist secular ideology was imposed during Turkey's foundational stage and reinforced in subsequent military coups (1960, 1981, and the "soft coup" of 1997). As in Indonesia, Turkey's gradual transition toward democracy over the past two decades has been accompanied by a growing ambiguity surrounding the definition of its secular identity. The departure from the decisive Kemalist ideology and the relaxation of the repressive secularism were reflected in electoral terms in the increasing influence of moderate Islamic parties (from DP to AKP) on religious legislation (for example, compulsory Muslim education in schools and prohibition of alcohol in certain municipalities), as well as in the growing demand to redraft the constitution and redefine religion–state relations (Köker 2010; Özbudun and Genckaya 2009).

While a permissive constitution may be more likely to allow for the emergence of democratic institutions, such constitutional arrangements may pose a potential danger to democratic stability arising from long-term conflict over religion–state issues. The political inability to settle controversies over the state's religious identity tends to invite judicial intervention. Such interventions may create tension between the legislative and judicial branches. While an interinstitutional tension is common – and even welcomed – in any democracy, such tension may be particularly problematic if the Supreme Court and the Parliament hold opposing ideologies regarding controversial foundational issues, such as religion–state relations. A direct conflict between the two branches of government may lead to the delegitimization of both

---

[24] In addition to the special autonomy granted for Aceh, the 2004 Law on Regional Government allowed for the rise of what is usually termed "Sharia by-laws" (*perda syari'ah* literally mean Sharia Regional Regulations) issued by provisional or district-level administrations. Formally, the Law on Regional Government restricts regional/provisional regulations in the area of religion, yet because of ambiguities in the law, as well as in the constitutional order, more than 200 regulations that contain some elements of Islamic law have been passed in recent years (at both district and provincial levels). These include, for example, the mandatory headscarf for women in civil service, the requirement to prove ability to read the Quran for applicants for government jobs or marriage licenses, a ban on prostitution in the name of "religions and morals," requirements to pray at certain times or to recite the Quran in schools, and mandatory religious tax collection (Bowen 2013; Parsons and Mietzner 2009; see also Horowitz 2013).

institutions in the eyes of the public. The court might lose its legitimacy as a neutral arbitrator in legal issues and the Parliament might lose its legitimacy as a representative body of the various interests in society.

Such developments have occurred in Israel: given the Knesset's legislative preference for the religious worldview, the secular-liberal camp turned to the Supreme Court to rule against the existing and growing religious arrangements. However, the court's increasing intervention in the religious status quo led to the public refusal on the part of religious leaders to abide by the Supreme Court's decisions and ultimately resulted in the obstruction of the constitution-making process. According to ongoing polls, public trust in the Supreme Court dropped from 88 percent in 1990 to 49 percent in 2010. And trust in the Knesset dropped from 45 percent in 1990 to 39 percent in 2010 (Arian and Hermann 2010).

In contrast to Israel, in India the Supreme Court has refrained from playing a contentious role in the struggle over the state's religious definition by maintaining a more ambivalent position in the religious–secular debate (Jacobsohn 2010). For example, in a series of rulings addressing the question of the Uniform Civil Code, the Supreme Court was inconsistent in its explicit call for the implementation of Article 44 (Agnes 2011).

Freedom of religion and freedom from religion

To what extent do permissive constitutions allow for religious freedom? Most large-N comparative studies define religious freedom in terms of limited constraints imposed on religious organizations, institutions, beliefs, and practices (Marshal 2008: 441).[25] Constraints on freedom of religion are generally perceived to be imposed by governments[26] and are usually linked to a tenuous separation of religion and state (Fox 2008). Some studies distinguish between various types of limitations on religious freedom, such as those imposed directly by governments, indirectly by government favoritism toward particular religions, or by social regulation of religion (Grim and Finke 2006).[27]

By grouping together various types of state regulation of religion and focusing on broad and all-encompassing definitions of limitations on religious freedom,

---

[25] The term usually used is "restrictions on religious freedom." However, to avoid confusion with restrictive constitutions, I will use alternative terms such as constraints, limitations, and violations of religious rights/freedom.

[26] See, for example, the US Department of State's International Religious Freedom Report. At www.state.gov/g/drl/rls/irf/2010/148659.htm. Similarly, see Center for Religious Freedom (CIRI Human Rights Data Dataset).

[27] By social regulation of religion, they mean attempts of established religious groups to monopolize the arena and effectively shut out new religions and discourage other faiths from proselytizing.

large-N studies tend to overlook an important distinction within the category of "religious freedom" – between two different types of rights. What most of these studies miss is the difference between the advancement of freedom *of* religion (guaranteeing the survival of and providing state support for religious groups) and the advancement of freedom *from* religion (providing individuals with protection from coercion to participate in religious customs and ceremonies). Whereas the former is concerned with the rights of religious *groups* to advance or protect their own culture, the latter is mostly concerned with the right of *individuals* to opt out of a religious affiliation.[28] In the religiously divided societies discussed in this chapter, this distinction is particularly notable in the debate over secularism, which involves a conflict over the rights of atheists or nonbelievers to refrain from practicing any religion and the demands of religious groups to exert influence over the public sphere. Moreover, the distinction is important because the two types of freedoms (of and from religion) can generate policies that conflict with rather than complement each other. Often, by allowing freedom of religion for particular groups, governments may support policies which might stifle or impede freedom of conscience for others. For example, freedom of religion may imply state funding for religious education institutions that limit the students' ability to opt out of the religious groups after graduation.[29] Alternatively, under the principle of freedom of religion the state may refrain from intervening in religious practices and traditions that violate freedom from religion for individual members of these religious groups.[30]

As Table 7.2 demonstrates, comparing the impact of permissive and restrictive constitutions on freedom of religion and on freedom from religion is a complex task. The complexity partly stems from the fact that state policies towards religion evolve over the years. For the sake of comparison, the Table takes a snapshot of existing policies in 2012. Overall, permissive constitutions for the most part allowed for state policies that better protect freedom *of* religion as compared with state policies toward religion that evolved under restrictive constitutions. Freedom *from* religion, by contrast, appeared to be less protected under permissive constitutional arrangements.

---

[28] The relations between freedom of/freedom from religion are clearly more complicated and deserve more nuanced discussion than the operative definition used here. For example, in the American constitutional context it is mostly discussed as the difference between implications of the "the establishment clause" and the "free exercise clause" in the First Amendment to the US Constitution (Eisgruber and Sager 2007; Greenawalt 2009). See also Sapir and Statman (2005).

[29] For example, due to insufficient general education which allows them to make a living outside their religious communities (Bowen 2013; Künkler and Lerner 2016).

[30] For discussion of this problem in the context of gender equality and multiculturalism, see, for example, Okin (1999).

TABLE 7.2 *Freedom of religion and freedom from religion in Indonesia, India, Israel, and Turkey, 2012*

	Type of regulation	Indonesia	India	Israel	Turkey
Freedom OF religion	state recognition of religions	six officially recognized religions: Islam (86.1% of population), Protestantism (5.7%), Catholicism (3%), Hinduism (1.8%), Buddhism, and Confucianism[a]	no limitations	fourteen recognized religions	Islam (99.8% of the population), and three religious minorities recognized by the 1923 Lausanne Treaty: Greek Orthodox, Armenian, and Jewish (in total less than 0.2% of population)
	state funding of religious education	yes	yes	yes	yes
	funding religious institutions	yes	yes	yes	yes
	presence of religious courts with jurisdiction over personal law	yes	yes	yes	yes
	restrictions on religious practices	unrecognized religious groups can be registered only as social organizations	restrictions on Hindi discriminatory practices	no	no religious expression (including headscarf) in government offices unrecognized religious groups cannot form a foundation/association
	restrictions on conversions	no	in practice in some provinces	no	no
	linking particular religion to citizenship	ID states religion (one of the six recognized)[b]	no	automatic citizenship for Jews	only recognized religions are listed on national ID

Freedom FROM religion				
monopoly of religious authorities on marriage and divorce	yes for Muslim alone	yes in practice, especially for Muslims	yes	no
mandatory religious education	religious instruction is required in student's faith	no; religious education is forbidden in public schools	no	yes for Muslims; recognized religious minorities are exempted
mandatory prayer in school	no	no	no	no
restrictions on business on holidays/Sabbath	no	no	yes	no
dietary laws/restrictions on alcohol	yes in some regencies	restriction on cow slaughter in some provinces	yes	no
religious rules regarding inheritance	no (since 2008)	in practice yes	no	no
Others	atheism is a-legal; government employees must declare belief in God			

TABLE 7.2 (Cont.)

Type of regulation	Indonesia	India	Israel	Turkey
Summary	FOR no FFR	FOR FFR mostly for Hindus FFR limited for Muslim	FOR no FFR	1924–81: FFR FOR limited 1982–2011: FFR limited FOR limited

SOURCES: US Department of State, 2010 Report on International Religious Freedom; Global Study of Islamic Family Law, The Law and Religion Program of Emory University. At www.law.emory.edu/ifl/legal/; Marshal 2008; Fox 2008; Dahne Barak-Erez, "Symbolic Constitutionalism: On Sacred Cows and Abominable Pigs." Law, Culture and the Humanities, 6:3, 420–35: CIA The World Factbook. At www.cia.gov/library/publications/the-world-factbook/index.html.
a Confucianism is recognized as a faith, rather than a religion.
b Legally, this issue is not formally regulated. Yet there are contradictory interpretations of the law.

To be sure, the net effect of a constitutional regime on the type of religious of/from religion does not depend solely on whether the constitution was considered permissive or restrictive. Nevertheless, we can learn from the comparative analysis below that the level of permissiveness/restrictiveness adopted by the constitutional drafters is associated with particular types of freedoms guaranteed by state policies in the area of religion in the following decades.

Freedom *of* religion for all religious groups is by and large guaranteed in Israel and in India. Religious groups enjoy complete autonomy under Israeli law, and in India the government tends to intervene in Hindu religious practices and activities when they violate the principle of equality, most notably in the case of caste discrimination (Bhargava 2010; Jacobsohn 2006). Thus, for example, the Indian constitution abolished the status of "untouchables" and disallowed prohibitions on entry into Hindu temples. In Indonesia, while only five religions are formally recognized by the state,[31] these five religions encompass over 97 percent of the population. By contrast, freedom of religion in Turkey was relatively constrained. Respect for religious expression in the public sphere is limited. Until 2011, Muslim women were prohibited from wearing headscarves in universities and public schools (Elver 2012; Kavakci 2010). The prohibition on wearing headscarves for women in the civil service was lifted in 2013. Moreover, those in the 12–27 percent of the population that identifies as Alevis[32] were not recognized as a religious minority. Consequently, their places of worship (*cemevleri*) were not officially recognized by the state and were not eligible for the same benefits received by mosques. Likewise, their demand to be exempted from compulsory Sunni religious teachings in public schools was disregarded (Hale and Özbudun 2010: 79).

While permissive constitutional arrangements tend to guarantee freedom *of* religion, they are more likely to result in reduced protection of freedom *from* religion, compared with restrictive constitutional arrangements, such as those that exist in Turkey. In Israel, for example, religious marriage and divorce are the only options for all citizens, including nonbelievers and atheists. Consequently, the religious monopoly on marriage and divorce violates the right to marry for hundreds of thousands of citizens, including interreligious couples or those who are not affiliated with any religion (comprising about 4 percent of the population). Similarly, in India legal pluralism in the area of personal law results in greater freedom from religion for Hindus, while religious law is de facto applied to Muslim and Christian minority groups.

[31] Confucianism is recognized as a faith.
[32] The difference in the estimated number stem from vagueness in the self-definition of members of the Alevi community (Hale and Özbudun 2010: 78).

The controversy over the *Shah Bano* case in India, followed by the legislation of the Muslim Women (Protection of Rights on Divorce) Act in 1986, demonstrated the persistence of legal pluralism in the area of family law (Engineer 1995; Hasan 1989). At the same time, recent interpretations by the Indian Supreme Court (especially in the *Daniel Latifi* case) have arguably expanded the freedom of Muslim women from religious personal status laws (Hasan 2003; Menski 2001; Subramanian 2010). Among the three countries that adopted permissive constitutional arrangements, freedom from religion is most constrained in Indonesia, where religious instruction is required, where citizens must formally state their religion on their identification card, where government employees must declare their belief in god, and where atheism is not recognized by the state. By contrast, in Turkey freedom from religion was strictly protected by the secular Kemalist ideology for over half a century following independence. Limitations on freedom from religion began in 1982, when compulsory religious education was introduced in the public schools. However, members of the three religious minorities recognized by the 1923 Lausanne Treaty, namely, Greek Orthodox and Armenian Christians and Jews, are exempted from this requirement (Article 24).

It is interesting to note that while freedom from religion is more limited under the permissive constitutional arrangements of India, Israel, and Indonesia, none of these countries institutionalized compulsory religious education. To a large extent, the constitutional enforcement of compulsory religious teachings in primary and secondary schools in Turkey continues the restrictive constitutional tradition developed by the Kemalist secular ideologists, who prohibited any kind of religious education during the first two and a half decades of the republic (1924–49). The 1982 introduction of mandatory religious education should be understood as part of a larger process of the state's recognition of the central and legitimate role of religion.[33] The new education policy was designed to introduce a form of state-led Islamization, imposed from above through the synthesizing of conservative elements of Turkish nationalism with Islam (Bali 2011: 11; Hale and Ozbudun 2010: xx). By returning to a "homogenizing and nationalist model of Islam reminiscent of the early republican period" (Bali 2011b: 12), this new state-led approach to religion was meant to prevent processes of social and political fragmentation, which in the 1970s had led to direct violent confrontations.

---

[33] Such as the creation of unofficial and private religious education networks and private sector Islamic enterprises during the 1983–90 ANAP government.

CONCLUSION

From a liberal, secular constitutionalist perspective, incrementalist or permissive constitutional arrangements are perceived as normatively inferior, as they allow for the endurance of conservative and nonegalitarian policies and institutions in the religious sphere. Moreover, by blurring the distinction between higher lawmaking and normal lawmaking, ambiguous constitutional arrangements forgo the educative role that constitutions are usually expected to play at both the judicial and the societal levels. However, as this chapter demonstrated, permissive constitutional arrangements in the area of religion may also enable societies deeply divided over the religious identity of the state to enact a democratic constitution or function with informal constitutional arrangements. Ambiguous constitutional formulations in the area of religion allow controversial decisions on these divisive issues to be deferred to some future time and direct and even violent conflict to be averted. Further, they promote a consensual, rather than a majoritarian, perception of democracy, by reflecting the competing religious/secular visions held by "the people."

An important question that remains open is whether a permissive constitutional approach facilitates or hinders the evolution of a liberal "overlapping consensus" over time. While further comparative research is required, the Israeli and Indian experience seems to suggest that the drafters were misguided in their expectation that constitutionalizing secular principles in the future would be easier. Illiberal policies and institutions that were adopted in the state's formative stage were difficult to change in later years through procedures of ordinary politics because their reforms were easily blocked by simple majorities.[34] In retrospect, some form of time-limiting constitutional mechanism, such as a sunset clause, might have helped prevent the long-term entrenchment of inegalitarian or illiberal religious policies and institutions (Arato 2010; Sunstein 2001). However, whether instating sunset clauses at the time of constitution writing was politically feasible or whether such a mechanism would have been effective in preventing the perpetuation of illiberal religious arrangements are both questions difficult to resolve in a retrospective study.

REFERENCES

Ackerman, Bruce. 1991. *We the People: Foundations*. Cambridge, Mass.: Belknap Press of Harvard University Press.

---

[34] This is the case, for example, in Israel, where the legislation of civil marriage is constantly blocked by the religious parties (Lerner 2014).

1992. *The Future of Liberal Revolution*. New Haven, Conn., and London, UK: Yale University Press.

Agnes, Flavia. 2011. *Family Law. Vol. 1: Family Law and Constitutional Claims*. New Delhi, India: Oxford University Press.

Akan, Murat. 2011. "The Infrastructural Politics of Laikik in the Writing of the 1961 Turkish Constitution." *Interventions: International Journal of Postcolonial Studies* 13, no. 2: 190–211.

Anderson, Perry. 2009. *"Turkey" in the New World Order*. London, UK, and New York, N.Y.: Verso.

Arato, Andrew. 2010. *Constitution Making under Occupation*. New York, N.Y.: Columbia University Press.

Arian, Asher and Tamar Hermann. 2010. *Auditing Israeli Democracy – 2010: Democratic Values in Practice*. Jerusalem, Israel: Israel Democracy Institute.

Assyyaukanie, Luthfi. 2009. *Islam and the Secular State*. Singapore: Institute of Southeast Asian Studies.

Austin, Granville. 1999. *The Indian Constitution: Cornerstone of a Nation*. Oxford, UK, and New York, N.Y.: Oxford University Press.

Bali, Aslı. 2011a. "The Paradox of Judicial Independence: Constitutional Transition and the Turkish Example." *Virginia Journal of International Law* 52, no. 2: 235–320.

        2011b. "Modernity, Secularity and the Headscarf Debate in Turkey." Paper presented at the workshop on "Comparative Sociolegal Processes of Secularization," Onati, Spain, May.

Bali, Aslı Ü. and Hanna Lerner. 2016. "Constitutional Design without a Constitutional Moment: Lessons from Religiously Divided Societies." *Cornel International Law Journal* 49, no. 2.

Barak, Aharon. 1992. "The Constitutional Revolution: Protected Human Rights." *Mishpat Umimshal: Law and Government in Israel* 1, no. 1: 9–35 (in Hebrew).

Bhargava, Rajeev. 1998. *Secularism and Its Critics*. Delhi, India, and New York, N.Y.: Oxford University Press.

        2002. "What Is Indian Secularism and What Is It For?" *India Review* 1, no. 1: 1–32.

        2010. *The Promise of India's Secret Constitution*. New Delhi, India: Oxford University Press.

Boland, B. J. 1982. *The Struggle of Islam in Modern Indonesia*. The Hague: Nijhoff.

Bowen, John R. 2013. "Contours of Shari'a in Indonesia." In Mirjam Künkler and Alfred Stepan, eds., *Indonesia, Islam and Democratic Consolidation*. New York, N.Y.: Columbia University Press.

Brown, Nathan J. 2008. "Reason, Interest, Rationality, and Passion in Constitution Drafting." *Perspectives in Politics* 6, no. 4: 675–89.

Corinaldi, Michael. 2004. *Personal, Family and Inheritance Law – Between Religion and State: New Trends. Jerusalem.* Israel: Nevo.

Dixon, Rosalind and Tom Ginsburg. 2011. "Deciding Not to Decide: Deferral in Constitutional Design." *International Journal of Constitutional Law* 9, no. 3/4: 636–72.

Eisgruber, Christopher L., and Lawrence G. Sager. 2007. *Religious Freedom and the Constitution.* Cambridge, Mass.: Harvard University Press.

Elson, R. E. 2009. "Another Look at the Jakarta Charter Controversy of 1945." *Indonesia* 88 (October): 105–30.

Elver, Hilal. 2012. *The Headscarf Controversy:* Secularism and Freedom of Religion. Oxford: Oxford University Press.

Engineer, Asghar Ali., ed. 1995. *Problems of Muslim Women in India.* Hyderabad, India: Orient Longman.

Feith, Herbert and Lance Castles. 2007. *Indonesian Political Thinking 1945–1965.* Singapore: Equinox.

Fox, Jonathan. 2008. *World Survey of Religion and State.* Cambridge, UK: Cambridge University Press.

Friedman, Menachem. 1991. *The Haredi (Ultra-Orthodox) Society: Sources, Trends and Processes* (in Hebrew). Jerusalem, Israel: Jerusalem Institute for Israel Studies.

Greenawalt, Kent. 2009. *Religion and the Constitution: Free Exercise and Fairness.* Princeton, N.J.: Princeton University Press.

Grim, B. J. and R. Finke. 2006. "International Religion Indexes: Government Regulation, Government Favoritism, and Social Regulation of Religion." *Interdisciplinary Journal of Research on Religion* 2, no. 1: 1–40.

Hale, William and Ergun Özbudun. 2010. *Islamism, Democracy and Liberalism in Turkey: The Case of the AKP.* London, UK: Routledge.

Hanioglu, M. Sükrü. 2013. *Atatürk: An Intellectual Biography.* Princeton: Princeton University Press.

Hardgrave, Robert L. 1993. "India: The Dilemmas of Diversity." *Journal of Democracy* 4, no. 4 (October): 54–68.

Hasan, Zoya. 1989. "Minority Identity, Muslim Women Bill Campaign and the Political Process." *Economic and Political Weekly.* January 7.

1994. *Forging Identities: Gender, Communities, and the State in India.* Boulder, Colo.: Westview Press.

2003. "Shah Bano Affair." In Suad Joseph, ed., *Encyclopedia of Women and Islamic Cultures.* Leiden: Brill.

Horowitz, Donald. 1985. *Ethnic Groups in Conflict.* Berkley and Los Angeles, Calif.: University of California Press.

Horowitz, Donald. 2013. *Constitutional Change and Democracy in Indonesia.* Cambridge: Cambridge University Press.

Hosen, Nadirsyah. 2007. *Shari'a and Constitutional Reform in Indonesia.* Singapore: Institute of Southeast Asian Studies.

Jacobsohn, Gary. 2006. *The Wheel of Law: India's Secularism in Comparative Constitutional Perspective*. Princeton, N.J.: Princeton University Press.

2010. *Constitutional Identity*. Cambridge, Mass.: Harvard University Press.

Jaffrelot, Christophe. 1996. *The Hindu Nationalist Movement in India*. New York, N.Y.: Columbia University Press.

Jamal, Amal. 2009. "The Contradictions of State-Minority Relations in Israel: The Search for Clarifications." *Constellations* 16, no. 3: 493–508.

Jones, Sidney. 2010. "Second Thoughts about Violence: Evolution within the Indonesian Jihadi Community." Luce Speakers Series on Religion, Democracy and Conflict, Princeton University, December.

Kavakci, Merve. 2010. *Headscarf Politics in Turkey: A Postcolonial Reading*. New York: Palgrave Macmillan.

Khilnani, Sunil. 1999. *The Idea of India*. New York, N.Y.: Farrar, Straus and Giroux.

Knesset Records (Divrei Ha'Knesset). 1949–50. Jerusalem. Vols. 4–5 (in Hebrew).

Köker, Levent. 2010. "Turkey's Political-Constitutional Crisis: An Assessment of the Role of the Constitutional Court." *Constellations* 17, no. 2: 328–44.

Kremnitzer, Mordechai. 2005 "Between Progress towards and Regression from Constitutional Liberalism: On the Need for Liberal Constitution and Judicial Review of Knesset Legislation." In Yoav Dotan and Ariel Bendor, eds., *Zamir Book: On Law, Government and Society*. Jerusalem, Israel: Sacher Institute for Legislative Research and Comparative Law, Hebrew University.

Künkler, Mirjam. Forthcoming. "Constitutionalism, Islamic Law, and Religious Freedom in Post-Independence Indonesia." In Asli Bali and Hanna Lerner, eds., *Constitution Writing, Religion and Democracy*. Cambridge, UK: Cambridge University Press.

Künkler, Mirjam and Hanna Lerner. 2016. "A Private Matter? Religious Education and Democracy in Indonesia and Israel." *British Journal of Religious Education* 38, no. 3.

Künkler, Mirjam and Yüksel Sezgin. 2015. "Regulation of 'Religion' and the 'Religious': The Politics of Judicialization and Bureaucratization in India and Indonesia." *Comparative Studies of Society and History* 56.

Kuru, Ahmet T. 2007. "Passive and Assertive Secularism: Historical Conditions, Ideological Struggles, and State Policies toward Religion." *World Politics* 59, no. 4 (July): 568–94.

2009. *Secularism and State Policies toward Religion: The United States, France and Turkey*. New York, N.Y.: Cambridge University Press.

Law, David S. and Mila Versteeg. 2013. "Sham Constitutions." *California Law Review* 101: 863–952.

Lerner, Hanna. 2011. *Making Constitutions in Deeply Divided Societies*. Cambridge, UK: Cambridge University Press.

2014.

Lev, Daniel. 1966. *The Transition to Guided Democracy: Indonesian Politics 1957–1959.* Ithaca, N.Y.: Cornell Modern Indonesia Project.

Marshal, Paul A. 2008. *Religious Freedom in the World.* Lanham, Md.: Rowman and Littlefield and the Center for Religious Freedom, the Hudson Institute.

Mautner, Menachem. 2011. *Law and Culture in Israel.* Oxford: Oxford University Press.

Menski, Werner F. 2011. *Modern Indian Family Law.* London: Curzon Press.

Nasution, Adnan Buyung. 1992. *The Aspiration for Constitutional Government in Indonesia: A Socio-Legal Study of the Indonesian Konstituante 1956–1959.* Jakarta, Indonesia: Pustaka Sinar-Harapan.

Needham, Anuradha Dingwaney, and Rajeswari Sunder Rajan, eds. 2007. *The Crisis of Secularism in India.* Durham, N.C., and London, UK: Duke University Press.

Okin, Susan. 1999. *Is Multiculturalism Bad for Women?* Princeton, N.J.: Princeton University Press.

Özbudun, Ergun and Ömer Faruk Genckaya. 2009. *Democratization and the Politics of Constitution-Making in Turkey.* Budapest, Hungary, and New York, N.Y.: Central European University Press.

Parsons, Nicholas and Marcus Mietzner. 2009. "Sharia By-Laws in Indonesia: A Legal and Political Analysis." *Australian Journal of Asian Law* 11, no. 2: 190–217.

Peled, Yoav and Gershon Shafir. 2005. *Being Israeli: The Dynamics of Multiple Citizenship.* New York, N.Y.: Cambridge University Press.

Raday, Frances, Carmel Shalev, and Michal Liban-Kooby, eds. 1995. *Women's Status in Israeli Society and Law.* Jerusalem: Shocken.

Ramage, Douglas. 2002. *Politics in Indonesia: Democracy, Islam and the Ideology of Tolerance.* London, UK: Routledge.

Ricklefs, M. C. 2008. *A History of Modern Indonesia since 1200,* 4th ed. Stanford, Calif.: Stanford University Press.

Sapir, Gidon and Daniel Statman. 2005. "Why Freedom of Religion Does Not Include Freedom from Religion." *Law and Philosophy* 24, no. 5: 467–508.

Shankar, Shylashri. Forthcoming. "Cross Cutting Rifts in Constitutions and Minority Rights: India, Pakistan and Sri Lanka." In Aslı Ü. Bali and Hanna Lerner, eds., *Constitution Writing, Religion and Democracy.* Cambridge, UK: Cambridge University Press.

Smooha, Sammy. 1997. "Ethnic Democracy: Israel as an Archetype." *Israel Studies* 2, no. 2: 198–241.

Som, Reba. 1994. "Jawaharlal Nehru and the Hindu Code: A Victory of Symbol over Substance?" *Modern Asia Studies* 28, no. 1: 165–94.

Sprinzak, Ehud. 1999. *Brother against Brother: Violence and Extremism in Israeli Politics from Altalena to the Rabin Assassination*. New York, N.Y.: Free Press.

Subramanian, Narendra. 2010. "Making Family and Nation: Hindu Marriage Law in Early Postcolonial India." *Journal of Asian Studies* 69, no. 3: 771–98.

Sunstein, Cass R. 2001. *Designing Democracy: What Constitutions Do.* New York, N.Y.: Oxford University Press.

Wood, Patricia. 2008. *Judicial Power and National Politics: Courts and Gender in the Religious-Secular Conflict in Israel*. Albany, N.Y.: State University of New York Press.

Yavuz, M. Hakan. 2009. *Secularism and Muslim Democracy in Turkey.* Cambridge, UK: Cambridge University Press.

Zürcher, Erik J. 1997. *Turkey: A Modern History*. London, UK, and New York, N.Y.: I. B. Tauris.

8

Performance of constitutions
Transitional provisions

Sumit Bisarya

As detailed throughout this volume, assessing the performance of a constitution is a complex and subjective task, and perhaps even an impossible one. Problems include determining the objectives against which performance is to be measured, what can be positively and negatively attributed to the constitution, and what the counter-factual in any given case might be. We focus here on one aspect of constitutional implementation which is crucial to nearly all constitutional stories, and an issue which we often observe[1] as a key practical challenge which does not receive the attention it deserves – that of constitutional transitional provisions ("transitional provisions").

Transitional provisions provide a series of directions through which the new constitutional regime is established, and the old order is phased out. During this state of "interregnum" between one constitutional order (or in some cases, a lack thereof) and the new order, transitional provisions must cover a series of issues including, *inter alia*, the establishment of new institutions and reform of continuing institutions; continuity of law and the status of the current law on the books, transitional justice processes and the timing and procedures for the first elections.

The argument that more attention should be paid to the performance of transitional provisions is threefold. Firstly, as mentioned by Ginsburg and Huq in the introductory chapter, transitional provisions provide a "threshold bundle of steps" set forth by a constitution in the process of institutional development. As they rightly observe, these steps are generally methodologically simple to measure, and cannot only reveal how well implementation is progressing, but might also reveal where blockages might lie, and afford an opportunity to address such obstacles.

Many thanks to the research support of Katalin Dobias in preparing this chapter.
[1] International IDEA is engaged in providing research and technical assistance in the field of constitution building throughout the world.

Secondly, without the establishment of the fundamental building blocks of the new constitutional order, the performance of the constitution in terms of fulfilling its own goals and objectives is immediately subject to question. Cracks in the foundations will more often than not lead to significant challenges in constructing the new house. Thus, transitional provisions are an important bellwether in determining early in the constitutional life cycle how a constitution will fare among the four mid-range criteria suggested by Ginsburg and Huq, because non-compliance or underperformance can quickly become a pattern and lead to de-legitimization of the constitution as the supreme law of the land. In this way, transitional provisions can function much in the same way that we see a "100-day plan", or similar, for a new government.[2] Deliver immediately on a series of promises, particularly those that result in visible changes, and support for the new constitutional order will increase. Failure to deliver, or lack of demonstrable change, can see the new order lose support and legitimacy before it is born. In keeping with the notion that broad-based support and legitimacy is fundamental to successful performance of the constitutional order (e.g. Michelman, 2003), effective implementation of transitional provisions can thus maintain momentum for change, which is likely at its high-water mark during promulgation.

Lastly, while transitional provisions may vary to a certain extent as to their ends, there is also a great deal of commonality among constitutions. Fundamentally, transitional provisions must achieve two first-order, institutional objectives: set up the institutions of the new constitutional order and provide a legal and political framework for governance while those institutions are being established. In this chapter, we also add three second-order,[3] sociological objectives: to maintain political stability, to bring about change in without undue delay (particularly in transitional contexts) and to build legitimacy for the new constitutional order.

Similar to Ginsburg/Huq's division of external/internal criteria to measure the performance of constitutions in general (see introduction), transitional provisions too may have objectives specific to the constitutional project at hand which may or may not overlap with the common secondary objectives detailed here. Attention to such context-specific objectives is important in understanding the performance of the transitional provisions as it might be perceived by the general citizenry or political stakeholder groups, and thus

---

[2] A recent example would be President Sirisena of Sri Lanka who announced a 100-day plan for reforms following his election to power in December 2014.

[3] I use the term "second-order" here in its mathematical sense, meaning these functions are derivative of the first-order functions. Thus, how the first-order objectives are achieved will affect the success of achieving the second-order objectives.

a close study of the context and the text is needed to discern any specific objectives under the transitional period.

This chapter provides a survey of transitional provisions in two recent constitutions and some comment on the considerations behind their inclusion based on conversations with actors involved with the respective constitution-making bodies. Each case will include a brief description of the constitutional moment in question, its objectives and the major relevant issues and parties to the negotiations and will then examine the following questions: (a) How did the transitional provisions seek to address the two primary objectives of establishing the institutions of the new constitutional order and providing for a transitional constitutional framework? (b) How well were these provisions implemented? (c) How did implementation affect the secondary objectives of maintaining momentum for reform and building legitimacy for the constitution.

The chapter is divided as follows. The first section defines transitional provisions and establishes a framework for assessing performance. The second section applies the framework to two recent cases: the Tunisian Constitution of 2014 and Somalia's Provisional Constitution of 2012. The third section provides some tentative conclusions on the performance of transitional provisions in each of these cases in terms of how the different approaches used might be adapted in other contexts and provides some questions constitutional designers should ask themselves when thinking through the design choices related to transitional provisions.

THE FUNCTIONS OF TRANSITIONAL PROVISIONS

Transitional constitutional provisions ("transitional provisions") govern the processes and mechanisms through which the new constitutional order is established and the existing order is phased out (DRI, 2014). Of central importance is articulating the process by which key institutions will be created – including provisions governing the timing and sequencing of elections and the sequencing of the establishment of political institutions vis-à-vis non-elected institutions – as well as laying out how the country will be governed in the period until the new institutions can take over. This latter concern may include issues such as the governing law and governance framework during the transition, transitional structures of governance such as national unity governments and transitional justice processes.

Often found towards the end of constitutional texts, transitional provisions represent an important, yet understudied, aspect of constitutional transitions.

Their long-term significance is of course diminished by their limited temporal effect, and also their narrow scope – they rarely contain many details relating to constitutional rights, identity of the state, divisions of powers amongst levels of government or amongst organs of government. However, the choices transitional provisions make regarding timing of elections and how/when key institutions such as constitutional courts will be established are not only crucial to the healthy establishment of the new constitutional order but are also of great short-term significance to negotiating parties who may develop firm positions over timing and sequencing of elections based on their immediate electoral expectancies. Indeed, design choices for transitional provisions – in particular the timing of the first elections – can in turn affect negotiating positions over allocation of powers between state institutions in the "permanent" constitutional order (e.g. see Negretto, 2013 on Latin American cases).

In seeking to assess the performance of transitional provisions, we must first be clear on their purpose. What might successful performance look like? In answering this question, it is helpful to recognize their distinguishing characteristics as compared with the rest of the constitution. While an inherent goal of most of the constitution is to endure (Elkins et al., 2009), by their nature transitional provisions have "performed" once they no longer endure. This fundamental teleological difference implies we need a bespoke approach to measuring the performance of transitional provisions, rather different from that we use to assess the performance of constitutions in general.

We can also distinguish transitional provisions from "temporary constitutional provisions" as defined by Ozan Varol in his paper "Temporary Constitutions" (Varol, 2014) which covers interim constitutions (zulueta-Fülscher, 2015), sunset clauses and incremental constitutional design. In some respects, transitional provisions can be seen as a subset of those "temporary constitutional provisions" which seek to address the legal and governance challenges of a period of constitutional transition, in particular the need for a temporary legal and governance framework to avoid any "interregnum" in which uncertainty over who has the power to make laws, and which laws are in force can lead to constitutional and political crisis.

However, one should note an important distinction between transitional provisions and interim constitutions, or other temporary constitutional provisions.

Temporary constitutional provisions, as discussed by Varol, make a decision about a certain rule (or rules) for a limited period of time. The destination point – in terms of the final rule – is unknown, or at least uncertain as the temporary rule may be replaced, confirmed, extended or modified once the time limit expires. Transitional provisions, on the other hand, are rules that are only applicable for a limited duration of time until the final (already-decided) rule comes into place. They do their work and then cease to apply – they are neither substituted nor extended, they simply cease to have function or relevance as they have brought about a new order which can now take effect.[4] Thus, they can be compared to a catalytic enzyme whose job it is to initiate a metabolic chain-reaction. The destination point in this case is known – it is the starting-point of the chain reaction (or the constitutional order), the transitional provisions "transition" us from the current state to the destination. Unlike the temporary constitutional provisions, such as interim constitutions or review and sunset clauses, they have a clear vector-quality which takes us in the direction of the already-determined new constitutional order.

Thus, the first function of transitional provisions is to set up the game. Just as we can inspect a chessboard to see if all the pieces are in the right places at the start of the game, we can assess the transitional provisions to see if they have indeed set up the constitutional order completely intact and in-line with the directions of the constitution.

However, unlike the setting up of a chessboard, the sequencing of establishing institutions can matter greatly (see, for example, Negretto, 2013 on the effect of timing of elections on constitutional negotiations, or Shugart and Carey, 1997 on the effects of sequencing on presidential and parliamentary elections). In particular, a key set of questions surrounds whether to hold elections for the political institutions first (and if so, in what order if there is a directly elected presidency). This would allow key state institutions (for example, a constitutional court and judicial service mechanism) to be established under the body elected under the new constitutional order. Alternatively, state institutions may be established ahead of elections, such that they are in place to oversee the legitimacy and regularity of the ballot.

The two cases covered in this chapter come down on opposite sides of this question: in Tunisia elections were held first, while in Somalia the transitional provisions called for a host of state institutions to be established before elections are scheduled. Another recent example – Kenya – also provided for the establishment of the new court, various independent commissions and a raft of implementing legislation to be in place before elections were held three years

---

4   Indeed, in some constitutions they call for their own removal from the text once their work is done, thus vanishing as if they were never there (see, e.g., the Ireland Constitution as it appears on the statute book today: www.irishstatutebook.ie/en/constitution/ (last accessed 24 August 2014). "(T)he Transitory Provisions are omitted as required by their terms." While I use the analogy of the foundations of a house in some places of this article, perhaps scaffolding might be more appropriate in cases such as Ireland.)

after the promulgation of the constitution. There is, of course, no recipe in determining the correct sequencing but the successful performance of transitional provisions is likely to be highly dependent on the correct sequencing for the context at hand. Key considerations are likely to be the viability of the existing political institutions (moderately high in the case of the power-sharing government of Kenya, low in the case of Tunisia) and the feasibility of early elections (impossible in the case of Somalia). According to the case studies presented by Gabriel Negretto (Negretto, 2013) delayed elections may be normatively preferable as they encourage cooperative bargaining during constitutional negotiations, but the reality is that sequencing is likely to be determined by the relative strengths of those negotiating the transitional provisions, and their level of interest in holding early elections or keeping the current institutions in place.

However, unlike the ten minutes it might take to set up a board game, or the millisecond it takes to catalyse a metabolic reaction, the setting up of the constitutional order will take months, or more likely years. Thus, we need to know what the rules of the game are during this transitional period. This is the second function of transitional provisions.

Transitional provisions take effect during the period between the moment of promulgation of the constitution and the establishment of the full constitutional order. During this period, the previously existing constitution, or interim constitution, is no longer de facto in effect, but the institutions of the new constitutional order may take time to be established. Elections take time to prepare, organic laws take time to negotiate and draft and it may be preferable to have key institutions such as constitutional courts established by newly elected political institutions rather than the existing institutions. Therefore, in the meantime transitional provisions must avoid an "interregnum crisis" by establishing the rules which apply in the time between the two constitutional orders – where "the old is dying, and the new cannot be born" (Gramsci, 1975). In this way, the transitional provisions are a second, temporary constitution within a larger, more enduring constitution.

One should acknowledge that with regard to this second function, the weight carried by all transitional provisions is not the same. In many cases, the transitional provisions need only to state that the existing law continues to function, and existing institutions continue until they are replaced under the new constitutional arrangements. Nevertheless, there is always a decision to be made regarding the "rules of the game" between the moment the new constitution comes into effect (promulgation) and the time when the institutions it provides for have been set up. Promulgation is not contemporaneous with the realization of the new constitutional order.

These then are two fundamental purposes of transitional provisions: setting up the constitutional order and providing for the legal and governance framework during the transitional period. But why do they matter? Why should we be concerned with measuring the performance of transitional provisions at all?

First, if we are at all interested in knowing whether a constitution is performing or not, measuring performance early in a constitutional life might be particularly important. Firstly, it is early in the constitutional life that general public interest in the constitution is at its zenith, particularly following broadly participatory constitution building processes where expectations for change are heightened. Further, Elkins et al. (2009) show that the most fragile point of a constitution's life in determining if it will endure or not comes early in the lifespan. This fragility may be due to general instability at a time of transition, but may also be caused by the aftermath of heated debates whereby the losers refuse to accept the constitutional design choices made and continue to contest those decisions (see example of Brazil given later).

If any adjustments are to be made, therefore, those in a position to do so should know earlier, rather than later. But what can be measured in the first years of a constitution's existence? For example, consider the analysis in this volume by James Gathii of the 2010 Constitution of Kenya, looking in particular at the role of the Kenyan judiciary. As Gathii acknowledges, how do we really know at this point whether the work is being done by the constitution, or whether Kenya is just lucky to have an excellent leader currently occupying the seat of chief justice? At such an early point we can't yet assess the full constitutional system as we need time to see how it might work in different economic climates, under different political leaders and parties and generally how resistant it is to societal change over time.

However, the transitional provisions do all of their work in the first years of a constitution, and thus a full assessment of their performance can be made. If the constitutional system has not been set up as was intended, we can interrogate why this is, and how it might affect the workings of the system in the coming years. Examining the constitutional foundations should give us a good indication whether the constitutional construction will be a stable one, or whether it is already showing fatal cracks which need to be addressed.

In this way, certain transitional provisions have actually themselves provided for mechanisms through which certain decisions made in the design of the constitution can be reviewed, and in this way either corrected or reaffirmed. For example, after significant debate between proponents of a parliamentary or presidential system of government, the 1988 Constitution of Brazil decided on the latter, but Article 2 of the Transitional Provisions called for a referendum to decide whether Brazil should have a republic or a monarchy, and (if a republic) whether it should be parliamentary or presidential. When it was held in 1993, the referendum reaffirmed the decision to create a presidential republic, thus ending what could have become a corrosive and destabilizing debate. Interestingly, this confirmation of the choice of a directly elected president came in the immediate aftermath of the resignation of the sitting president during the course of impeachment proceedings, thus accentuating the choice of the constitutional system in place, rather than the individual leader (Linz and Stepan, 1996).

Second, the performance of transitional provisions is methodologically easy to assess. One could envision the assembly and completion of a simple checklist against which to measure whether the new constitutional order has been established as designed (T. Ginsburg. (2013). *Assessing the Performance of Constitutions – Concept Note for International IDEA*. Unpublished). The Commission for the Implementation of the Constitution of Kenya (CIC, 2011–2015) has developed such reports, to provide a quarterly assessment of, *inter alia*, the establishment of constitutional organs and offices as provided for in the transitional provisions of the 2010 Constitution. The relative ease of such an exercise, coupled with the foundational nature of the performance of transitional provisions for the constitutional system as a whole, makes their assessment an attractive and cost-efficient exercise.

Third, I posit that transitional provisions – in addition to the first-order, institutional objectives described already – have important second-order, more broadly sociological functions related to the temporal context in which they operate, which can determine the success, or failure, of the transition as a whole. These include maintaining momentum for reform, promoting stability and building legitimacy. These three effects are linked, but I briefly describe each one in turn here and all form part of the following assessment of performance of transitional provisions.

A common aspiration during constitutional transitions is for a "durable agreement ... and within a *short period of time*" (Widner, 2008, emphasis added). Expectations for change are high at the moment of transition, and at the moment of constitutional promulgation in particular. Excessive delay in realizing the new constitutional order may result in frustration among the public and reduced support for and interest in the constitutional project, which in turn can jeopardize the chances of the project's success (Ginsburg, Elkins, and Blount, 2009).

At the same time, in particular in post-authoritarian transitions, there is a need for political stability lest uncertainty and instability bring about calls for a return to less democratic, but more secure times. Research shows that the economy generally suffers in the immediate aftermath of a democratic transition (Acemoglu et al., 2014) and large-scale violence is also likely to increase before the new institutions are fully formed and operational (Mansfield and Snyder, 1995), which perhaps explains the high fragility observed by Elkins et al. in early moments of a constitution's lifespan. Political stability is crucial to steer the country through the rough waters of the transition to the comparatively safe seas of democratic consolidation.

Lastly, building legitimacy for the constitution – as discussed by Ginsburg and Huq with regard to the constitutional project as a whole – is a key criterion of "good performance". Transforming the text into the development of a constitutional culture whereby the constitution is "worthy of respect, so that people living in legitimate legal systems have reason to accept the use of state coercion to enforce laws that they do not necessarily agree with and may even find quite unjust" (Michelman, 2003). Legitimacy among the broad public is important, but equally if not more so in the early years of the constitutional lifespan is legitimacy among political elites. Transitional provisions must seek to build this legitimacy through beginning the process of "converting the spoilers" (Widner, 2008) by bringing all groups inside the constitutional project. This function cannot be understated in its importance. In situations of major political transition, failed states or the creation of new states in particular, a critical function of constitutions is as part of a nation-building project, to define the political community (Ghai, 2010). However, in many cases the polity will be either nascent, divided, or both and thus the new constitution risks being artificial or ornamental if it cannot develop an attachment to the polity. Transitional provisions will play a key role in ensuring this process of developing ownership of, and attachment to, the constitution and defeating any lingering contestations of spoilers to the process.

In this regard, perhaps we can paraphrase Adam Przeworski's characterization of when we know a democratic transition is over (Przeworski, 1991) by saying that transitional provisions have achieved their goal in terms of legitimacy if all parties agree that the constitution is "the only game in town".

These three second-order functions of transitional provisions are, as stated above, linked. Transitional provisions which set short timelines in order to quickly establish the new constitutional order may maximize the pace, and thus momentum, for reform but at the same time may create political instability if there is not enough time for adequate care and consideration in the development of legislation, or enough time for inclusion and participation of different political and societal groups. Similarly, short time frames may increase legitimacy of the constitution in generating visible signs of reform, but if such time frames are unreasonably tight they may be impossible to meet, resulting in immediate violation of constitutional provisions, and an accompanying de-legitimation of constitutional rules as a whole (the Somali case discusses this scenario). Regardless of the overlap of these functions, it is useful to consider them separately because, as I posit in the conclusion, they are considerations constitutional designers should keep in mind when making choices about transitional provisions.

I now apply the criteria for assessment to two recent cases – Tunisia and Somalia.

CASES

Tunisia

Constitution building process

The Tunisia constitution building process of 2011–2014 was triggered by the "Jasmine Revolution" which forced President Zine el-Abidine Ben Ali from power and into exile in January 2011. Mass protests took place across the Arab region, resulting in the peaceful overthrow of President Hosni Mubarak in Egypt, civil war resulting in the death of President Muammar Qadaffi in Libya, ongoing civil war in Syria and concessions from governments, including constitutional reforms, in Jordan, Algeria, Morocco, and Bahrain.

In Tunisia, events moved quickly after the revolution. Without delving into too much detail regarding the path towards the establishment of the National Constituent Assembly in October 2011, it is important to note some key aspects of the early transition as indicative of the power of civil society organizations to mobilize citizens and to participate in political decision-making, the impatience for reform amongst the masses and an introduction to the protagonists who would still be negotiating their roles on the political stage during the negotiations and implementation of the transitional provisions of the 2014 constitution.

Mohamed Ghannouchi – prime minister of Tunisia for over eleven years at the time of the revolution – formed a new government, but soon the Tunisian street made its voice heard again, taking to protest at the slow pace of reform (Pickard, 2015) and forcing Ghannouchi to resign, to be succeeded by Beha Caid Essebsi, former foreign minister in the early 1980s under President Habib Bourguiba. (Essebsi would later be elected president in the November 2014 elections.)

At the same time, different institutions were created to plan and coordinate the post-revolution reforms. Ghannouchi created a High Commission for Political Reform while, following the mass protests which led to Ghannouchi's demise, civil society organizations established the Committee to Safeguard the Revolution. These two bodies were soon merged to form the High Commission for the Realization of the Goals of the Revolution, Political Reform and Democratic Transition (or the "Ben Achour" Commission, after its Chairman Prof. Yadh Ben Achour). The Commission soon suspended the 1959 Constitution and called for elections for a National Constituent Assembly (NCA) which would be tasked with negotiating and drafting a new Constitution.

Lastly, it is important to note that the Tunisian government sought to establish some measure of legality for the transition through the quasi-constitutional decrees of 23 March and 16 December of 2011. The decree-law of 23 March 2011 met the immediate post-revolutionary needs of the nation. Just two months after the ousting of Ben Ali, it formally acknowledged the revolution and that the people of Tunisia expressed their will to exercise their "full sovereignty within the framework of a new constitution".[5] The decree introduced dramatic changes, such as the dissolution of the legislature and the constitutional council,[6] giving assurance to the people that a break from the old regime was underway. For continuity, the decree left the judicial powers to be exercised according to the laws and regulations in force.[7] At this early stage the main objective was to maintain (or conform to) the constitutional moment and to keep the transition within the legal/constitutional framework. Thus, the 2011 March provisional arrangement was a decisive step towards a new constitutional order without a complete breakaway from the centralism of the Ben Ali regime.

The 16 December 2011 decree-law, sometimes called the "small constitution", was passed by the newly established NCA. The law provided for the respective powers of the NCA – with regard to both its constituent and legislative capacities – the presidency, the government and the judiciary. In short, it acted as an "interim constitution" (International IDEA, 2015) which provided for the road map to a new constitution, while establishing the framework for governance in the interim period. Much of the decree was kept in force by the transitional provisions of the 2014 Constitution, and we will return to this document later in the chapter.

The National Constituent Assembly

On 23 October 2011, the Tunisian people participated in large numbers in the elections to the NCA. The plurality winner was Ennahda, an Islamic party which had been hitherto banned as a political organization, but importantly did not win a majority. The result was an uneasy governing coalition of three

[5]   www.constitutionnet.org/files/decree_law_english.pdf.
[6]   Article 3.
[7]   Article 17.

parties – the Islamist Ennahda with the secular Ettakatol and Congress for the Republic (CPR) parties. On 12 December 2011, the NCA elected CPR leader Moncef Marzouki as interim president, who appointed Ennahda leader Hamadi Jebali as prime minster. The interim government, known as the Troika, took office on 24 December 2011.

The envisioned one-year drafting process lasted for three years, with four different drafts[8] and two political assassinations, which brought the country close to crisis. Contentious issues could be divided into two groups: the role of religion – its relationship with the state, in defining the national identity of Tunisia and with traditional liberal democratic values; and the structure of government – specifically whether the system of government should be parliamentary, or semi-presidential, and if the latter how the power of the bi-cephalous executive should be divided. In this regard, Ennahda argued for a parliamentary system, or failing this for a strong parliament in a semi-presidential system, while the secular parties were keen on a directly elected president with strong powers (Pickard, 2015). As one might expect (Negretto, 2013), this positions were very much based upon the electoral expectancies of the respective parties.

The second political assassination in July 2013 – of opposition leader Mohammed Al-Brahimi – led to the defining moment of the constitution building process. Unable to reach consensus, and with high levels of suspicion and mistrust between the negotiating coalition partners, the government was in paralysis. A quarter of four civil society organizations, led by the trade union alliance UGTT (Union Générale Tunisienne du Travail) – convened a "national dialogue" where political parties were convened to resolve the impasse. The National Dialogue formed a parallel constitution making body with the four civil society organizations acting as mediators between the political parties. Each of the twenty-one parties was represented by one member, regardless of electoral strength (Redissi, 2014). The result was an agreement that the government would resign, to be replaced by a caretaker government whose members would not stand in the next elections, the establishment of an independent electoral commission and a process to finalize the constitution before the end of the year (International IDEA, 2014). This informal body continued to meet on a periodic basis both before and after the promulgation of the constitution in January 2014 and was responsible for many of the decisions regarding transitional provisions described below.

---

[8] www.constitutionnet.org/country/constitutional-history-tunisia.

Tunisia – transitional provisions

First let us examine what the constitution sought to achieve in terms of the two primary functions of transitional provision – setting up the new constitutional order and providing for the transitional legal and governance framework:

Establishing the new constitutional order

The key transitional provisions of the Tunisia Constitution are found in Articles 148 and 149. In terms of their primary function of establishing the new constitutional order, the key issues were the establishment of an electoral commission, the holding of elections for legislature and president (Article 148.3), the establishment of the Superior Judicial Council (SJC) and of a Constitutional Court (Article 148.5).

These institutions were to be set up sequentially. An electoral commission was to be established first and was given a minimum of four months to prepare elections. Elections for both president and legislature were to be held by the end of 2014. The new legislature was then to create the SJC within six months of the elections, and the Constitutional Court was to be established within one year of elections.

The legal and governance framework in the transitional period

The transitional provisions provided that the sitting NCA and president would continue to work until the election of the new legislature, and used the existing constitutional decree of December 2011 as a basis for their continuing powers with the important exception of limiting the NCA's mandate to legislate only on the electoral process, the transitional justice system and constitutional bodies to be established (Article 148.1).

Importantly, the transitional provisions also provided for a means to challenge/validate the constitutionality of the laws passed by the NCA in the transitional period. Article 148.7 directing the NCA to pass a law establishing a "provisional authority" which would determine the constitutionality of laws until the Constitutional Court was established.

Assessing performance

Establishing the new constitutional order

The electoral commission, legislature and presidency were all established in accordance with the transitional provisions. Elections were widely perceived to be free and fair and were conducted without major controversy (Carter

Center, 2014). There was disagreement between Ennahda and the secular parties regarding whether legislative and presidential elections should be held simultaneously, and if not which should be held first, as this was not made explicit in the transitional provisions. Agreement was reached through the National Dialogue, resulting in parliamentary elections taking place in October, while the two-round presidential election took place in November and December, thus meeting the constitutional deadline. If there was one criticism of the implementation of these provisions, it was in the passing of the electoral law, which took place with the NCA under great pressure resulting in a number of ambiguous provisions, including those regarding compliance with the constitutional provision on gender parity in elected assemblies, Article 46 (Carter Center, 2014, p. 22).

However, at the time of writing there is delay over the establishment of the SJC. Initially, there was controversy over whether the "six months from the date of elections" meant six months from the elections date or six months from the date election results were announced. This controversy went to the provisional authority on constitutional determination, and will be discussed below, but for purposes of assessing the establishment of the constitutional order it suffices to say that this delay will mean missing the constitutional deadline.

Legal and governance framework

In terms of the transitional legal and governance framework, the transitional provisions contained two major decisions: the continuation of the NCA and the creation of the "provisional authority". With regard to the former decision, the NCA – while imperfect and unpopular – was the only real choice in terms of a body to prepare for elections. However, the limitation of the scope of the NCA's mandate to the bare essential functions necessary to move the transition forward proved to be a sound decision given the NCA's unpopularity at the time of promulgation.

One way in which the NCA's scope of work was limited was by postponing the creation of the Constitutional Court until after elections. However, this decision meant that an interim body was needed to judge the constitutionality of the few, but crucial, laws that were to be passed in the meantime. The creation of the provisional authority can be judged a mixed success. Firstly, it is important to note that the composition of the provisional authority detailed in the transitional provisions (Article 148.7) left no room for political negotiations, and thus no room for disagreement or delays. Three members were selected *ex-officio* as presidents of the courts of cassation, of audit and administration, and three more were appointed, one each by the president, the president of the NCA and the head of government.

Determining the composition of the provisional authority in this way was a small but important point. There was an understanding that appointments to key bodies would be subject to political dispute, but that for a body that must be established quickly in order to avoid legal uncertainty prolonged disputes were to be avoided at all costs.[9] Thus, in this regard the establishment and design of the provisional authority must be assessed positively.

The provisional authority has been called into duty several times during the transitional period. Most notably, with regard to the electoral law and with regard to the law establishing the SJC. The electoral law was upheld against appeals from deputies of the NCA in a timely fashion that allowed the elections to proceed with a fair degree of certainty over their constitutionality. However, the bill establishing the SJC was found to be unconstitutional on procedural grounds, although the court's precise reasoning is unclear. At the time of writing, the NCA is yet to pass a law establishing the SJC, resulting in delays regarding the establishment of not only the SJC but also the Constitutional Court, whose composition depends in part on nominations from the SJC. Despite these delays, the recourse to the constitution and its reaffirmation as the supreme law of the land has resulted in increased legitimacy of the constitution and support for the provisional authority – albeit at the cost of frustration with the government and NCA (interview with Zied Boussen).

In sum, the assessment of transitional provisions in defining the transitional legal and governance framework is positive. The decision to continue the NCA for a limited amount of time and conduct elections as soon as reasonably possible in terms of ensuring adequate time for organization was received well by Tunisians, and the quick establishment of the provisional constitutional authority helped ensure legal certainty, and as a consequence lend broader legitimacy to the first elections.

Momentum for reform

Promising and then holding elections within 2014 was essential in maintaining support in the reform processes.[10] The NCA had already outlived its mandate by over a year, had been elected in very different circumstances for a specific task of drafting the constitution. Further, the political infighting had made governing from the NCA impossible, necessitating the periodic renewal of the National Dialogue into 2014. Allowing elections as soon as possible was important so that both the Tunisian people felt directly their influence in

---

[9] Interview with Zied Boussen, Al Bawsala, 19 August 2015.
[10] Ibid.

the new constitutional order, and so that there would be a better chance of forming a coalition capable of governing. In this regard, the transitional provisions can be assessed positively as delaying elections into 2015 would have risked significant delusion with the constitutional project.[11]

Political stability
Political stability was perhaps the crucial imperative in the context in which the transitional provisions were to operate. The crisis caused by the political paralysis of July–October 2013 had been survived, but for most Tunisians the country was still teetering on the brink of collapse. Events in the region – from the collapse of the reform process in Libya, to the rise of ISIS in Syria and Iraq and the overthrow and prosecution of the regime of Muhammed Mursi in Egypt – added to the sense of fragility in Tunisia.

Indeed, given the regional context, it is impressive that Tunisia has managed to remain relatively stable politically, if not from a security perspective. Continuation of the NCA in some ways perhaps contributed to political stability as one might speculate that rushed and disputed elections could have pushed the country in the other direction. However, the truth is that political stability post-promulgation of the constitution was maintained primarily through the National Dialogue – an informal body outside the constitutional order – than any consequence of the constitutional provisions for the transition.

Building legitimacy
Under the implementation of the transitional provisions, Tunisians have seen three national elections (one legislative, two rounds of presidential elections) take place in free and fair conditions (Carter Center, 2015), with genuine political choice at the polls. They have seen constitutional disputes resolved through the mandated authority, and institutions established according to constitutional deadlines. Where a constitutional deadline has been missed – in the case of the establishment of the SJC – it has been due to debates over the constitutionality of the establishing law, rather than any wanton and deliberate violation of the constitution.

For most Tunisians, the constitution may be irrelevant to their daily lives but amongst political groups it seems that all actors have accepted that it is "the only game in town" and are not questioning its legitimacy as the supreme law of the land. This is due, of course, to the negotiated consensus which underlay the finalization of the constitution drafting process, but by delineating a manageable and orderly transition to the new constitutional order, providing means for political minorities to challenge the constitutionality of laws and also by limiting the mandate of the NCA to not stray from the necessary thereby limiting questions about its own legitimacy to continue, the transitional provisions can be assessed to have contributed to the critical task of building legitimacy for the new constitution.

Summary

The transitional provisions of the 2014 Tunisia Constitution can be easily misread as having done nothing more than provided for some almost automatic steps which would establish the new constitutional order. What should be clear from this brief analysis is that there were a series of questions and options which the transitional provisions had to respond to, and how they delineated these responses would have serious implications for the health in which the new constitutional order would be established. Should the NCA continue? If so, for how long and what should be its powers? When would the Constitutional Court be established? Soon, in order to oversee the constitutionality of the entire process? Or after elections, so a body with a clear democratic mandate could be responsible for the establishment of the necessary legislative framework. If the latter, how will the constitutionality of laws in the meantime be determined? Should timelines be set for the establishment of key institutions, and if so how should they be determined? There were a series of choices to be made, and we can assess the impact of these choices against the criteria of the establishment of the new constitutional order, the transitional legal and governance framework and the impact of these processes on momentum for reform, political stability and the building of legitimacy for the constitution.

With the exception of the laws establishing the SJC and the Constitutional Court,[12] thus far the key deadlines have been respected and key constitutional events – specifically presidential and parliamentary elections – have taken place as planned. Political institutions were established reasonably early, in response to the delegitimization of the NCA, but with adequate time to prepare the ground for elections. Key constitutional bodies such as the Constitutional Court and the SJC were scheduled to be formed only after

---

[12] Following the completion of drafting this chapter, these two laws and the institutions they establish suffered from further delay and some degree of frustration among limited numbers of Tunisian stakeholders, but this does not change the overall assessment of the performance of the transitional provisions in the author's assessment.

the newly elected institutions were in place, but interim arrangements were made to rule on the constitutionality of the all-important electoral law.

While there is no way to determine what the impact of a counterfactual design choice may have been, and any attribution of impact to the constitution can be made only with a host of reservations given the complex context and number of contributing factors to outcomes such as "political stability", conducting even this brief assessment of the performance of the transitional provisions gives a positive reading of the care and thought which went into the transitional provisions, which bodes well for the future performance of the constitution as a whole.

Somalia

Constitution building process

The Republic of Somalia gained independence in 1960 and adopted a national constitution by referendum the same year. The constitution was replaced, again through national referendum in 1979 but following increased resistance to, and the 1991 overthrow of, President Siad Barre's authoritarian regime, the country descended into civil war in the 1990s and any semblance of constitutional order has since been lost (Mubarak, 1996).

The current constitution building process finds its roots in the peace processes of the early 2000s, in particular through the Somali National Peace Conference where a Transitional National Charter was adopted under the auspices of the governments of Djibouti and Egypt, as well as the United Nations, seeking to share power amongst the four major clans of Somalia. National unity was elusive and a group of decentralized Somali authorities led by Puntland president Abdulahi Yusuh established a rival coalition to the Transitional National Government (Kouroutakis, 2015).

The Inter-Governmental Authority for Development (IGAD) mediated a new political settlement which included the replacement of the Transitional National Charter with the Transitional Federal Charter which established a federal form of government (Article 11.1) and directed the Transitional Federal Government to establish an Independent Federal Constitution Commission (IFCC) to draft a new constitution to be approved through a national referendum.

National security, however, remained a significant challenge as the Transitional Federal Government struggled to maintain control over any significant share of its territory. The most significant opposition came from the Alliance for the Re-liberation of Somalia (ARS), an Islamist association linked to the deposed Islamic Courts Union (Ainte, 2014), which necessitated a new political settlement to bring them inside the constitutional project.[13]

In 2010, the IFCC was expanded to accommodate ARS interests, and in 2011, the Road map to End the Transition[14] was negotiated. The agreement was critical in the constitution building process not only as it reframed the timeline for finishing the constitution (it set a deadline of 1 July 2012, which was missed by one month) but more significantly because it represented political agreement between a group of national, subnational, regional and international actors who would then, known as "the roadmap signatories", become the core political decision-making group to resolve all details regarding how the constitution would be finalized.

By 2012, then, progress towards a draft new constitutional text and political settlement had been made, albeit slowly, but the Transitional Federal Government had long passed the expected deadline to end the transitional period through the promulgation of a new constitution.

At the same time, it is important to note that progress in maintaining security was almost non-existent outside the capital city (International Crisis Group, 2012), primarily due to the emergence of Somali Islamist terrorist group Al Shabaab. While forces operating under the African Union Mission to Somalia (AMISOM) began to weaken Shabaab to an extent, the lack of security made holding a national referendum – as required by the Transitional Federal Charter and the Road map – impossible.

At this time, in February 2012, political leaders and international partners gathered for a meeting in Garowe, Puntland, to agree on the final steps for the constitution. The meeting resulted in agreements on several aspects of both the constitution's content and the process for approval.[15] The outcomes included firstly the confirmation of Puntland and Galmadug as two federal states in the new federal republic and the reaffirmation of the federal system as outlined in the Transitional National Charter. Secondly, agreement on a parliamentary system of government and a bicameral legislature, with the upper house being representative of the states. Thirdly, the establishment of an Interim Independent Electoral Commission which would, *inter alia*, verify nominations for a National Constituent Assembly to approve the constitution, and nominations for the first federal parliament. Fourthly, the procedures for

[13] "Djibouti Agreement" available here: http://unpos.unmissions.org/Portals/UNPOS/Repository %20UNPOS/080818%20-%20Djibouti%20Agreement.pdf (last accessed 23 August 2015).

[14] Road map text available here: www.somaliareport.com/index.php/post/1519/TFG_Agrees_To _End_Transition (last accessed 23 August 2015).

[15] "Garowe II Principles" available here: http://unpos.unmissions.org/LinkClick.aspx?filetic ket=RhnQqHTAfCA%3D&tabid=9705&mid=12667&language=en-US (last accessed 23 August 2015).

the establishment of the National Constituent Assembly, and the new parliament.

The National Constituent Assembly met for eight days at the end of July, and then adopted the Provisional Constitution with overwhelming majority on 1 August 2012.

The transitional provisions

It should be noted that the task of the transitional provisions was made significantly more complex by the fact that the provisional nature of the constitution and the need to progress towards a final constitution, as well as the fact that Somalia was more building an entirely new constitutional order, rather than transitioning from one order to the next. This was of particular importance with regard to the establishment of a federal structure for the new republic.

Establishing the new constitutional order

The transitional provisions are found in Chapter 15 of the text.[16] The delineated objectives in terms of establishing the new constitutional order include: review of the provisional constitution including proposals for amendments where necessary (Articles 133 and 134, and Schedule 1C), the promulgation of a raft of legislation to implement the constitution (Schedule 1D), the establishment of key institutions and independent commissions such as the Constitutional Court, Judicial Service Commission and Electoral Commission within set deadlines (Article 135) and preparation for elections by the end of the assembly's term (set at four years under Article 60).

Underlying all of these objectives was the paramount task in terms of founding the new constitutional order: that of the delineation of the federal structure of Somalia, including the defining of the number of states, state boundaries, and the establishment of state institutions and the Upper House of the Federal Parliament. Not only was a federal state structure necessary to form many of the institutions of the new constitutional order (e.g. the Upper House of Parliament and the Independent Provisional Constitution Review and Implementation Committee) but a federal bargain (Riker, 1964) was also needed to ensure the very viability of the constitutional project itself.[17]

---

[16] English translation of the text available here: www.constituteproject.org/constitution/Somali a_2012.pdf?lang=en.

[17] Interview with Adam-Shirwa Jama, country director, International Development Law Organization, 24 August 2014.

Transitional legal and governance framework

Under the agreement reached at Garowe,[18] a federal lower house of parliament would be formed through a nomination process whereby clan elders would select individuals as their representatives in parliament. These would be vetted against some basic qualifying criteria (e.g. age, Somali citizenship, no criminal record). The federal parliament would be given a full term to implement the transitional provisions and prepare for elections for 2016.

Importantly, Article 138(2) provides that any provisions relating to the Upper House are suspended until all Federal Member States are formed and their representatives have taken their seats in the Upper House, with the Lower House (House of the People) responsible for all Upper House duties and functions in the interim period.

Article 139 rather vaguely states that all laws in force continue to be in force, but should be interpreted with any adaptations or exceptions as may be necessary to bring them into compliance with the constitution until said laws are formally amended or repealed.

Perhaps because the tight timelines were expected to force the creation of key institutions such as the Constitutional Court within a short period of time, there was no provision similar to the Tunisian Constitution in providing for a transitional body to judge the constitutionality of laws before the Court was established.

Assessing performance

The transitional provisions of the Provisional Constitution of Somalia cannot be said to have performed well. Many of the specific tasks they required of the government have not been implemented, those that were implemented were almost uniformly late and there has been little formal progress on the central process of negotiating and agreeing the federal structure of the state. What progress has been made on state structure has been through extra-constitutional processes as discussed later.

Establishing the new constitutional order

A quick glance at Article 135, which provides for timelines for establishing ten constitutional institutions, gives the reader a clear idea of how wanting the performance of the transitional provisions has been:

---

[18] See Article 3.3 of operationalizing principles under Garowe agreement, see note (iii) supra.

Institution	Deadline (from formation of government – 13 November 2012)	Status as of August 2015
Judicial Service Commission	30 days	Established July 2014, Disbanded March 2015. Reconstituted May 2015
Constitutional Court	60 days	Not formed. Bill has been drafted.
Human Rights Commission, Ombudsman, National Security Commission, Civilian Oversight Sub-Committee	45 days	Not established
National Independent Electoral Commission and Boundaries and Federation Commission	60 days	Established May 2015
Parliamentary Service Commission	15 days	Not established
Interstate Commission	1 year	Not established
Truth and Reconciliation Commission	30 days	Not established

The deadlines set were clearly unrealistic. Just the drafting of the nine laws required within 60 days would have been a Herculean task for the new Somali government, which had many other competing priorities including setting up the new government offices and responding to the ever-present security threat. In addition to drafting, negotiations over such key political bodies as the electoral commission, constitutional court and judicial service commission, and such a sensitive body as the truth and reconciliation commission, were never likely to be completed in the tight timeframes given.

The reasons why the deadlines were drafted in this way are unclear. According to one leading Somali participant in the process, the drafters were aware that the government would seek to delay the establishment of key constitutional institutions, and thus "needed a stick to beat them with".[19] In this view, the missed deadlines served a purpose as they showed the international community could then use them to pressure the government into action. However, according to other international advisors who were

[19] Interview with Honourable Abdirahman Jibril Hosh, former minister of constitutional affairs, 4 June 2014.

closely involved in the drafting process, the deadlines were drafted between the United Nations office in Nairobi and law professors in Boston and showed an enormous lack of understanding of the Somali context. Whatever the reason for drafting these provisions in this way, it led to instant under-performance of the constitutional transitional provisions.

Similarly, Schedule 1D provides for a list of priority laws to be enacted in the first term of the federal parliament. According to an international advisor providing assistance to the legislative process,[20] only four or five of the twenty-two laws in this list have been promulgated.

The Provisional Constitution also provides for specialized institutions, a parliamentary committee and an independent commission, to oversee the implementation of the constitution including through preparing draft legislation, as well as conducting a review of the text to suggest amendments if/where necessary. However, the independent commission was not established until June 2014 and subsequently became involved in battles with the parliamentary committee over which institution should be driving the process.[21] Another reason why the commission was unable to make progress in its tasks is that it received no funding from the government – partly because the IFCC, an institution which no longer exists, is still on the government payroll.[22]

Lastly, but most importantly, to the federal state structure where the Provisional Constitution left much work to do in defining the number of states, boundaries and balance of powers between state and federal governments. Although located outside the chapter on transitional provisions, Article 49 provides for the formation of the federal state structure and the operation of the Boundaries and Federation Commission (BFC) contained in Article 135 of the transitional provisions. Under Article 49, the House of the People is to determine the number and boundaries of states through a law based on a report submitted by the BFC.

Distracted with its many other priorities, including many of those detailed in the preceding paragraphs, the federal parliament made little initial headway in establishing the federal member states. As mentioned above, the first step in the process – the establishment of the BFC – took place over two years after the constitutional deadline. However, actors at the regional and state level decided to push forward the process by themselves, supported by the

---

[20] Interview with Adam-Shirwa Jama, country director, International Development Law Organization, 24 August 2014.
[21] Interview with Jan Schmidt, research fellow and Somalia country manager, Max Planck Foundation for International Peace and Rule of Law.
[22] Ibid.

international community[23] in general as well as specific neighbouring countries for some states. In this way, interim administrations have been set up in several states including Jubbaland, South West State and most recently Galmudug without the involvement of either the BFC or the Federal Parliament. Looking now at almost a *fait accompli*, which has the support of the international community, the federal parliament is making belated moves to bring the de facto state formation process under the umbrella of the constitutional procedures by asking the BFC to study the processes through which the states were formed, and then pass a federal law approving the decisions made.[24]

Legal and governance framework

In establishing the federal parliament to oversee the transitional period until the first elections, two key decisions were made. The first was to select members of the lower house in the manner prescribed above, the second was to allow the lower house to take over responsibilities of the upper house until the federal member states were in place to establish the upper house.

With regard to the first decision, at the time of promulgation of the constitution there was no possibility of elections due to the security situation and while there were tentative discussions over replacing the so-called 4.5 formula for sharing public offices amongst the clans, there was no time to explore any other options in detail. If nothing else, the nomination process ensured that the executive and legislature were quickly in place, and that the interests of the major power holders would be reflected through their nomination or that of their chosen designees.

Given the delays in establishing the state structure in Somalia, constitutionalizing the postponement of the role of the upper house was a wise act of foresight by the constitutional drafters without which even the minimally operational governance framework that exists in Somalia today would not be constitutionally possible.

Momentum for reform

The poor implementation of the transitional provisions, admittedly under difficult conditions and with hugely ambitious deadlines, has given little momentum to reform. Where momentum has been found, it has been mostly outside constitutional procedures in the de facto establishment of interim administrations for federal states.

---

[23] For example, see statement of the UN secretary general welcoming establishment of Interim Administration of South West State www.un.org/apps/news/story.asp?NewsID=48120 #.VeTDpLyqpHw (last accessed 29 August 2015).

[24] Interview with Jan Schmidt, supra.

Whereas the tight deadlines in establishment of constitutional institutions can be seen as an effort to ensure reform efforts moved forward, the willful and regular flouting of these deadlines has only served to diminish the sense of progress.[25]

Importantly, chances of holding elections for the next parliament seem to be receding fast[26] and discussion over another nominations process has begun. Elections – as a mechanism for citizens to interact with and exercise their voice in national governance – could have been crucial in building a sense that reform was advancing, and while given the ongoing levels of violent conflict elections were always going to be difficult, the poor performance of the transitional provisions is reflected in the fact that progress on the political and governance framework never moved quickly enough to make elections a possibility even if conflict abated.

Perhaps the biggest fault one can find in the performance of the transitional provisions is that they tried to achieve too much, including many issues which surely were not a priority for the immediate transition. For example, the long list of twenty-two "priority laws" in Schedule 1D could have been limited to a select few (e.g. a law on dumping of waste could have been postponed, Schedule 1D section 8). Commentators also note that the institutions responsible for overseeing implementation replicated the structure during the Transitional Federal Charter period, which also suffered from turf wars over mandates.[27] A lesson should have been learnt, and the process could have been simplified in the provisional constitution. Political energy could instead have been focused on three key issues – federal state structure, review of the Constitution and preparation for elections in 2016. Counterfactuals represent a core problem at the heart of the entire exercise at hand here, but those involved in the process since the drafting of the provisional constitution until today agree that more could have been done with less ambitious, and more focused, transitional provisions.[28]

Political stability

Somalia is currently under its third government since the promulgation of the constitution. The two previous governments fell due to conflicts between the prime minister and the president, with parliament siding with the president in

[25] Interview with Adam Shirwa Jama, country director, International Development Law Organization, 24 August 2014,
[26] For example, see commentary at http://sahanjournal.com/somalias-democratic -transformation-options-2016/#.VeTLobyqpHw (last accessed 29 August 2015).
[27] Interview with Jan Schmidt, see note 21.
[28] Interviews with Jan Schmidt and Adam Shirwa Jama (notes 20 and 21, respectively).

a vote of no confidence against the government on both occasions. Senior officials in key positions such as the governor of the Central Bank and the chairperson of the Oversight and Implementation Commission have resigned not long into their tenures, and as this article was being written in July 2015, a group of MPs initiated impeachment proceedings against the president.

Whether the transitional provisions themselves are connected in any way to the instability is doubtful, as both government replacements were brought about due to disputes between the president and the prime minister regarding cabinet appointments and the impeachment is called for on grounds of general incompetence.[29] All that can be said for our purposes is that the instability and political infighting certainly did not help focus energies and attention on the implementation of reforms.

Building legitimacy

The provisional constitution was promulgated in a manner unlikely to lend much legitimacy to the document. From the heavy involvement of international actors to the limited circle of Somali elites involved in the negotiations, the rushed finalization of the constitution to meet the deadline set in the road map to the non-elected body asked to ratify the text instead of a national referendum – there was little about the process to lend broad legitimacy to the constitution.

As even the limited political elites did not believe in the legitimacy of the constitution,[30] it was unlikely they would act in a way that accepted the constitutional constraints on their actions, and the missed deadlines at the outset of the process did little to build support for the document as the supreme law of the land.

Lastly, the nomination process to the Federal Parliament further hampered legitimacy: while elections were impossible, as stated above, the nomination process had few safeguards to prevent undue pressure – in the form of bribes or threats – on clan elders for their nominations.[31]

Summary

The challenge for the transitional provisions of the Provisional Constitution of Somalia was immense. Building a new constitutional order following the prolonged period of the Transitional Federal Charter, two decades of

---

[29] See www.reuters.com/article/2015/08/20/us-somalia-politics-idUSKCN0QP0KY20150820 for news report on impeachment (last accessed 29 August 2015).
[30] Interviews with Jan Schmidt and Adam Shirwa Jama.
[31] Interview with Jan Schmidt.

widespread violent conflict and little institutional capacity to build upon was perhaps the most challenging constitutional transformation in the modern world. However, the design of the transitional provisions made an extremely difficult challenge an impossible one.

Although we are admittedly judging with the benefit of hindsight, assessing the poor performance in terms of the criteria we have identified here supports the conclusion that the transitional provisions could have been improved, most obviously in the following two ways. Firstly, the deadlines for the establishment of key institutions were unrealistic and never likely to be met. Realistic deadlines for a few key institutions would have still been a "stick to beat the government with" while not diminishing constitutional legitimacy from the outset. Secondly, the transitional provisions called for a range of reforms from a raft of twenty-two priority laws to the amendment of the constitution, the establishment of key institutions and of a new federal structure. A limited mandate for the federal parliament, as with the NCA of Tunisia, may have focused political energies on the essential tasks.

Also in comparison with Tunisia, the case of Somalia shows that political consensus over the transitional provisions is as important as consensus and support for the Constitution as a whole. Due to the frustrating experience with delays under the Transitional Federal Charter, the drafting of the transitional provisions in Somalia was taken out of Somali hands, and drafted through a select few individuals in the United Nations Joint Coordination Unit, with the support of consultants in the United States.[32] This stands in stark contrast to the transitional provision of the Tunisia Constitution which were drafted after intensive negotiations in the National Dialogue.[33] As a result, the Somali political actors never took ownership over this part of the Constitution in particular, and were resistant to the idea of accepting – for example – that their legislative priorities had been set for them by Schedule 1D.

CONCLUSIONS

In writing this chapter, I have explained a set of criteria for assessing the performance of transitional provisions of Constitutions and applied those to two vastly differing cases: Tunisia 2014 and Somalia 2012.

In doing so, I seek to show that assessing performance of transitional provisions can give early insights into the performance of a Constitution as a whole, but at this early stage in the Constitution's life – when the new order is

[32] Interview with Jan Schmidt.
[33] Interview with Zied Boussen.

not yet born – we cannot use the same criteria to judge performance as we might for a "mature" constitutional order. Thus, we have examined carefully the primary purposes of transitional provisions, and proposed some second-order functions they can also be judged against.

This brief study also confirms that transitional provisions are not a given in any context, and are a worthy object of more research. A range of questions faces constitution makers at the time of drafting transitional provisions, and how they answer those questions – from a range of different options to be negotiated – will weigh a great deal on the success of the constitutional transition as a whole.

Another issue that is worth stressing is the importance of political bargaining and consensus in the transitional provisions, as with the constitution as a whole. The 2012 Provisional Constitution of Somalia in some ways replicated the Kenya 2010 Constitution[34] in setting the legislative priorities for the post-promulgation government. However, an important difference with Kenya was that the same Kenyan government that oversaw the constitution drafting process was then responsible for implementing the transitional provisions. Notwithstanding the over-involvement of international advisors in drafting the Somalia provisions, constitutionalizing a strict set of priorities for legislation for a future government, as was done in Somalia, is a practice open to question.

Lastly, without wishing to read too much into the two selected cases, a tentative hypothesis regarding the performance of transitional provisions is that more modest but focused transitional provisions provide a greater chance of success along the three second-order effects we have defined – momentum for reform, political stability and building legitimacy. Focusing political energies and attention on the essential tasks during the transitional period may give a better chance of achieving success in terms of a "batting average", thus lending legitimacy to the constitutional project through compliance with constitutional requirements, while also building momentum for reform by focusing on areas of key importance, and perhaps also lending itself to greater political stability as political energies are not wasted fighting unnecessary battles.

REFERENCES

Acemoglu, D., Naidu, S., Restrepo, P. and Robinson, James A. (2014). *Democracy Does Cause Growth*. MIT Department of Economics Working Paper No. 14-09.

[34] See Schedule Five, Kenya Constitution 2010, available here: www.constituteproject.org/constitution/Kenya_2010.pdf?lang=en (last accessed 31 August 2015).

Ainte, A. (2014). *Somalia: Legitimacy of the Provisional Constitution.* Conciliation Resources.

Carter Center. (2014). *Legislative and Presidential Elections in Tunisia – Final Report.* The Carter Center. Retrieved from www.cartercenter.org/resour ces/pdfs/news/peace_publications/election_reports/tunisia-final-rpt-2014 -elections.pdf.

Carter Center, Legislative and Presidential Elections in Tunisia – Final Report. Available at: www.cartercenter.org/resources/pdfs/news/peace_publications/ election_reports/tunisia-final-rpt-2014-elections.pdf. Last accessed 5 April 2016.

Constitution, C. f. (2011–2015). *Quarterly Reports.* Retrieved 4 August 2015, from www.cickenya.org/index.php/reports.

DRI. (2014). *Lier L'Ancien et e Nouvel Ordre Constitututionnel. Le Role des dispositions transitoires dans les constitutions.* Democracy Reporting International. Retrieved 25 July 2015, from http://democracy-reporting.org /publications/country-reports/tunisia/briefing-paper-44-january-2014.html.

Elkins, Z. et al. (2009). *The Endurance of National Constitutions.* Cambridge University Press.

Ghai, Y. (2010). "Chimera of Constitutionalism: State, Economy and Society in Africa." In Swati Deva (Ed.), *Law and (In)Equalities – Contemporary Perspectives*, 327. Westbrook, ME: Eastern Book Company.

Ginsburg, T., Blount, J. and Elkins, Z. (2012). "Does the Process of Constitution-Making Matter?" In Tom Ginsburg (Ed.), *Comparative Constitutional Design.* Cambridge University Press.

Gramsci, A. (1975). *Prison Notebooks* (Vol. II). Columbia University Press.

International Crisis Group. (2012). *Somalia: An Opportunity That Should Not Be Missed.* Africa Briefing No. 87.

International IDEA. (2014). *Constitution Building: A Global Review (2013).* The Hague, Netherlands: International IDEA.

Kouroutakis, A. (2015). "The Provisional Constitution of the Federal Republic of Somalia: Process, Architecture and Perspectives." *Cambridge Journal of International and Comparative Law* 3(4): 1195–1206.

Linz, J. J. and Stepan, J. L. (1996). *Problems of Democratic Transition and Consolidation.* Johns Hopkins.

Mansfield, E. D. and Snyder, J. (1995). "Democratization and the Danger of War." *International Security* 20(1): 5–38.

Michelman, F. I. (2003). "Constitutional Legitimation for Political Acts." *The Modern Law Review* 66: 1–15. doi:10.1111/1468-2230.6601001.

Mubarak, J. (1996). *From Bad Policy to Chaos in Somalia: How an Economy Fell Apart.* Praeger.

Negretto, G. (2013). *Making Constitutions: Presidents, Parties and Institutional Choice in Latin America.* Cambridge University Press.

Pickard, D. (2015). Al-Nahda: Moderation and Compromise in Tunisia's Constitutional Bargain. In J. O. Frosini, & F. Biagi (Eds.), *Political and Constitutional Transitions in North Africa: Actors and Factors*. Routledge.

Przeworski, A. (1991). *Democracy and the Market*. Cambridge University Press, 26.

Redissi, H. (2014). *What Role for Tunisia's National Dialogue under the Interim Unity Government*. Arab Reform Initiative: Policy Alternatives. Available at: www.arab-reform.net/sites/default/files/Redissi%20-%20National%20Dialo gue%20in%20Tunisia%20-%20EN%20-%20July%202014.pdf. Last accessed 5 April 2016.

Shugart, M. and Carey, J. M. (1997). *Presidents and Assemblies. Constitutional Design and Electoral Dynamics*. Cambridge University Press.

Varol, O. (2014). Temporary Constitutions. *California Law Review*, 102(2): 10.

Widner, J. (2008). "Constitution Writing in Post-Conflict Settings: An Overview." *William and Mary Law Review* 49: 1515–1541.

Zulueta-Fülscher, K. (2015). *Interim Constitutions Peacekeeping and Democracy-Building Tools*. International IDEA Policy Paper.

9

Time and constitutional efficacy

Zachary Elkins, Tom Ginsburg and James Melton

A standard way to think about constitutional efficacy is to compare the text of a document with reality, as captured in some empirical measure. In our experience, it is an extremely rare conversation about comparative constitutions that is not interrupted by a plaintive interjection – by well-meaning observers – that constitutional rules are not always enforced. While commentators no doubt intend such remarks as a caution against excessive formalism, we find these interjections tiresome and sometimes wish they were deterred by cruel and unusual punishment. Too harsh? Perhaps, but the interjection misunderstands the appeal of constitutions entirely. The surprising fact is *not* that constitutions are often ignored; it is that they guide the behavior of power-hungry leaders at all! Indeed, the holy grail of constitutional scholarship is the identification of those conditions that lead leaders to adhere to their prior commitments (and to those of their forbears). In this chapter, we reconsider an important condition that is central to constitutionalism: time.

Our chapter makes the observation that efficacy changes over time: Constitutional provisions can be either more or less effective over time (or the effect can be constant). In thinking about the criteria for constitutional success, it seems useful to consider whether there are general trends in efficacy over time, and whether certain provisions are more vulnerable than others to decay and desuetude. Using rights as a focus, this chapter undertakes that inquiry.

We have grappled with this question previously, mostly in an effort to speak to the normative implications of long-lived constitutions (Elkins et al. 2009) and, then, mostly in passing. Our return to the question arises in the context of our current investigation into the origins, spread, and consequences of constitutional rights. Our empirical approach, therefore, is myopically rights-centric. To be specific, our research question is, do constitutional rights become more or less effective as they age?

To emphasize our focus on rights, and since the analysis of institutional effects can be maddeningly aggregate and abstract, consider the right to health in Kenya and South Africa. Kenya entrenched the right to health when it rewrote its constitution in 2010 (Article 43). South Africa incorporated a right to health in its 1996 post-apartheid constitution (Article 27). Neither country had a right to health in its prior constitution. All else equal (counterfactually), would one expect access to, and the quality of, health care to be better in South Africa, which has had the right entrenched in its constitution for nearly thirty years or Kenya, which has had the right for only five years? Or would one expect health care provision to be about the same in South Africa and Kenya because both provide the same right in their constitutions? Does time improve or retard constitutional enforcement, or does it have no effect?

These questions disturb some normative tensions that occasionally arise from the point of view of those concerned with constitutional counter-majoritarianism. Since constitutions are designed to regulate the future on behalf of the past (Rubenfeld 2001), conventional theorists worry about empowering the "dead hand" of the past (McConnell 1988). Such normative theorizing *assumes* that constitutions will be continually efficacious. However, if the efficacy of law decreases over time, then the dead hand problem is moderated, for the past does not effectively control the future. If, on the other hand, constitutional provisions become more effective over time, then the dead-hand problem is exacerbated. Of course, one person's vice is another's virtue, and one person's dead hand is another's moral constraint on majoritarian excess. Either way, the question of time's increasing or decreasing returns to efficacy is relevant. And because constitutional law in many countries is reconsidered and reformulated with some regularity (every nineteen years on average, by our count), it is worth thinking about how this legal renewal will shape constitutional performance.

Of course, the age of a law may mean nothing at all, in which case South Africans are not any better or worse off under a 1996 provision than Kenyans are under a 2010 one. The idea of a constant effect is implicitly adopted by many cross-sectional studies of the efficacy of constitutional rights (see Camp Keith et al. 2009), which if only for empirical tractability assume invariant effects across age. Such invariance seems highly unlikely in a world in which aging has pronounced effects in nearly every realm. But, as we elaborate below, we hold two competing expectations with regard to the effects of age, each of which implicates a different mechanism of constitutional performance. On the one hand, there may be a maturation effect. As society accommodates norms that may initially be only aspirational in character, its members may find that the gap between the demands of the constitution and social reality shrinks over time. This could be because norms grow to be more venerated with age. Veneration, in turn, increases the likelihood of enforcement, which increases the costs of violating the norm and leads to greater compliance. A shrinking of the gap might also be the result of bureaucratic institutionalization, if the right implicates state agencies. Many rights do: criminal procedure protections imply the resolution of principal–agent problems within police forces, just as health and educational rights require significant investment in state infrastructure. In this sense, general features of state capacity are crucial for constitutional performance, as they are for other political goods (Fukuyama 2014).

On the other hand, there may be an effect of drift or even decay of constitutional norms, as society shifts away from norms that once made sense. If constitutional text is stable and society changes, then over time, the text may matter less and less. As successful constitutional communities of interpretation develop, there will be drift from the four corners of the text (Strauss 2010). Of course, layers of doctrine do not mean that the text is unimportant, so long as it embodies some shared understanding and continues to constitute the interpretive community in the first place. Thus, the text may be of central importance at the moment of promulgation, but over time, it may be the *existence* of text, rather than its objective content, that matters. This effect is different from the maturation hypothesis.

Of course, it is likely that the two processes occur at the same time, with regard to different systems. Consider the analogy to human aging. As people grow older, they mature. Some systems and faculties decline; none of us can run as fast as when we were twenty years old. Other systems continue to develop. Bodily decline may be inevitable, but the accumulation of wisdom and judgment is offsetting, more than compensating for reduced physical acuities (Posner 1997). Witness the persistence of the wily veteran in professional sports. Given these competing aging mechanisms, one might think of overall health as an aggregate of the quality of all the different subsystems in the body. In this sense, an individual would be considered in her prime when the aggregate quality of all her systems is at maximum.

The same may be true of constitutions. Some provisions may exhibit maturation; other systems may exhibit decay. Some provisions fall into desuetude (Albert 2014), while others may be revived. Whether or not a constitution is "working" is in fact a statement of the average efficacy of all its provisions. Of course, just as one cannot understand overall health without an understanding of the functioning of individual bodily systems, one cannot understand a constitution without focusing on its specific parts. Part of our argument is that the effect of time (and of constitutional provisions more generally) is best understood at the level of the individual provision, though we recognize there are interaction effects at work as well, so that some provisions depend on others to be effective.

This chapter is organized as follows. We begin with a skeptical review of "gap" approaches to measuring constitutional efficacy (skeptical, not because of the quality of the studies, but because of the ambitious nature of the undertaking). We then develop the maturation and decay hypotheses, and introduce, through a discussion of literature, the possibility of nonlinear patterns. Next, we conduct an empirical examination to see whether constitutional rights become more or less efficacious over time. We find a slight effect for maturation over a long period, conditional on regime type and levels of judicial independence. The results are, by their nature, aggregate, and so we close with a suggestion for more case-focused research to try to identify the precise mechanisms of maturation.

PRELIMINARIES: THE PROBLEM OF ASPIRATION AND THE INSUFFICIENCY OF GAP STUDIES

It is absolutely critical that scholars marshal data to identify clear patterns in the association between constitutional promise and performance. It is not always clear, however, what exactly to make of any observed gap in such studies. Some have argued that a gulf between promise and reality suggests constitutional non-efficacy (Finn 1991: 22–23; Law and Versteeg 2013). But as Robert Cover (1986: 1604) notes about law, constitutions project "an imagined future on reality," making aspiration a central constitutional function. Taking aspirations seriously, therefore, implies a more generous view of gaps than does one that speaks in terms of failure, fiction, or the like. If we think that one way in which constitutions work is motivational – in guiding and incentivizing future achievement – we must step back to examine a broader temporal swath.

If constitutional promises *can* motivate, then analyzing a maturation effect is the ultimate test of whether they, in fact, *do*. The motivational mechanism is intuitive. Language, especially in the form of revered higher law, can serve as a focal point for activists seeking a rhetorical "hook" for their cause. Sometimes this sort of leveraging happens during the process of constitution-making; in other instances, a group that is marginalized can appropriate constitutional terms and discourse adopted for one purpose to advance very different claims years later. This is part of the story of the African-American freedom movement, as well as the strategy of Francophone Canadians (Breslin 2009: 116). The African-American freedom struggle, in particular, took a century after the passage of the 13th, 14th, and 15th Amendments in the aftermath of the Civil War to realize anything close to freedom and equality. To examine the efficacy of these amendments in 1970 would produce a very different view than would examining them in 1867 or even in the early 1900s.[1]

Michael Dorf points out that this pattern was true more generally of the Bill of Rights. Its provisions were not effectively enforced by the courts until the rise of judicial review after the Civil War (Dorf 2009). Indeed, the founders' fear of governmental tyranny was realized with the passage of the Alien and Sedition Acts in 1798, just a few years after the passage of the Bill of Rights. The First Amendment evidently meant very little at that time, and it would be over a century before it would mean anything more.

But sometimes the temporal gap between the adoption of a constitutional promise and its implementation is narrow. The 19th Amendment to the US Constitution, ratified in 1920, was an aspirational provision in that it sought to change reality. Its narrow purpose was embodied in the text: constitutionalizing women's suffrage. Like many anti-subordination amendments, the 19th was controversial at the time of its adoption, even in its limited scope. But perhaps this narrow purpose was accompanied by broader set of background purposes even more aspirational: to signal that women were full citizens in the society, to encourage further steps in the long process of anti-subordination, and perhaps to ensure the election of female candidates (Siegel 2002).

The narrow text of the 19th amendment hardly "matters" today. Suppose, following Dorf (2009: 1645), that the 19th amendment had been time-limited and expired in 2000. Does anyone think that a state or local government would limit the franchise to men? It seems unlikely. On the other hand, the Amendment has served to inspire a broader set of changes in the status of women, and that project continues. In short, the immediate impact of the text was real and profound; the long-term change even greater (though not because of any correlation between text and practice).

These examples suggest at least two analytic insights. First, the "lag structure" of causal effects will differ across rights and depend upon conditions such as the narrowness of the right's content. Second, the right may have both direct and indirect effects on outcomes. More generally, these examples reinforce the importance of unbundling the full package of constitutional rights; rights come in different flavors and intensities, with different purposes and different time horizons.

For example, consider a constitution that promises a right to housing to address a country's chronic homelessness problem.[2] The morning after the

---

[1] The Francophones in Africa had more immediate results from their successful constitutionalization of linguistic rights. Public institutions, public education, and even public space were transformed in fairly short order. Breslin (2009 at 128).

[2] See, e.g., Constitution of South Africa, Sec. 26.

constitution is adopted, the level of homelessness is likely to be identical to that of the day before, because there are likely to be structural barriers to helping the homeless that cannot be remedied overnight: homes are not built in a day. Now, suppose one looks at the situation ten years later, after a partial decline in homelessness. One might think the constitution has been implemented but only in part because there is still a gap between a universal right to housing and the amount of homelessness in society. If, by the constitution's 50th birthday, homelessness has been eradicated, focusing on the gap between promises on paper and actual performance might lead one to the conclusion that the constitution has been effective.

However, much depends on the counterfactual. Suppose that hypothetical fifty-year period was one of phenomenal economic growth. We might then think that the level of homelessness would have declined anyway, so no additional work has been done by the constitution. Conversely, what if homelessness had actually increased over that fifty-year period? Would that indicate that the constitution has been ineffective? Possibly, but there could be some unanticipated shock that causes homelessness to increase – e.g., a natural disaster, an economic crisis, or domestic conflict – despite government's best efforts to decrease it. Knowledge of such shocks might change one's perception of a gap between constitutional promises and political reality.

Another issue is that the presence of a constitutional right can lead to claiming behavior that makes it appear that practice has actually worsened. Consider, for example, rights to a timely trial and to an appeal. Implementing these rights involves significant institutional reforms to the judiciary that take time, but the presence of the constitutional right can increase demand from the public, even before institutional reform is completed. Observing a constitutional right to appeal might lead to more appellate litigation, outstripping judicial capacity to process them. In this case, we will observe a *negative* association between the right and the practice. But it would be wrong to conclude that the constitution has really made things worse. In fact, the constitution has changed social expectations in a way that might lead to long-run pressures for better implementation.

The point is that gaps between text and practice – the usual way of approaching the question of whether rights "work" – are a poor indicator of constitutional efficacy because gaps do not indicate when or how a constitution makes a difference. Frequently, constitutional changes reveal the extent of a problem that previously was thought to be much smaller and so can motivate improvements. Methodologically, then, as an alternative to looking at gaps, we might instead see whether there was political and social mobilization around the constitution, which would indicate a causal mechanism. For example, if interest groups demanded enforcement of the constitutional right to housing, or if the government initiated a housing program in response to a court order, then one might say that the constitution has made a difference, assuming that the government program actually reduced homelessness. Thus, to say a constitution matters, one looks not only to the outcome of a reduction in the gap between text and practice but also to the channels by which it did so. *Mechanisms are essential to understand efficacy*, as they are for any causal study. Our chapter aspires to push scholars to the level of mechanism analysis, though we recognize our own current gap in promise and delivery.

With these preliminaries out of the way, let us consider the possibilities of maturation and decay.

PATTERNS OF MATURATION, DECAY, AND STASIS

Because constitutional provisions differ in the timing of their potential impact, time is an important variable to keep in mind when thinking of the impact of individual provisions. Some provisions may exhibit maturation over time; others may exhibit decay, while yet others may show neither effect. Figure 9.1 captures these three possibilities by illustrating the effect of a newly entrenched constitutional right that stays in place for some time. The horizontal axis captures time, with a new constitutional right entrenched at time t. The vertical axis captures the level of de facto rights performance, where higher values equal better protection. Intuitively, democracies would tend to be closer to the maximum, performing well in terms of de facto rights protection, while dictatorships would tend to be closer to the minimum, performing relatively poorly in terms of de facto rights protection (see Davenport and Armstrong 2004).

Each line in Figure 9.1 represents a different effect of time. Consider first the line representing what we will call provision A. At the adoption of the constitutional right (time – t), the value is near the minimum, suggesting that constitutional performance may lag between the textual promise to protect the right. One might think of this as a kind of "blueprint" provision that aspires toward change (Ginsburg and Simpser 2014). As time goes on, there is some form of investment in the implementation of the provision that causes performance to increase. Because performance increases with time, we call this maturation. Contrast this with the line representing provision B. For provision B, the line starts near the middle of the y-axis, suggesting a moderate level of de facto protection. There may still be a gap between promise and performance, since presumably the constitution promises high levels of protection, but

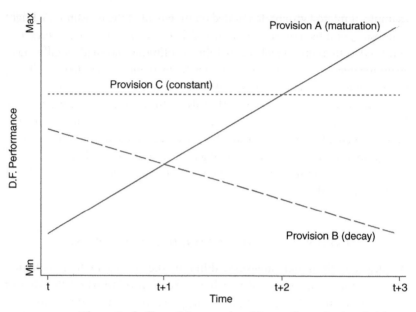

FIGURE 9.1 Theoretical effect of time on the efficacy of constitutional rights

unlike for provision A, there is no investment in performance, so over time the gap becomes larger for provision B. This is decay.

Note that one's assessment of the performance of these two provisions depends entirely on the point in time at which one observes their respective trajectories. If one is assessing the relative performance of provisions A and B at time t, one might think that provision B is more efficacious, since de facto performance is higher for provision B than provision A. However, if one were to make the assessment at time t+3, one would have exactly the opposite view. At this later point, the constitution has fulfilled its promise with respect to provision A but has witnessed a widening gap between promise and performance with respect to provision B.

Now consider provision C. In this case, when the constitutional right is adopted at time t, de facto performance is relatively high, and no change from the status quo is intended. Some constitutions entrench existing practices, providing "operating manuals" to codify understandings. At whatever point one makes the assessment of performance, provision C will appear to be "implemented," even though there was no required investment and, thus, no sense in which the constitution had any visible impact on it. Note that a crude assessment at time t would make it appear as if the performance on this provision was better than for either of the others. At t+3, however, it becomes quite apparent that the performance on provision A is better, and that the constitution made more of a difference than for the others. (Note that the year-on-year change for provision A is better throughout.)

MECHANISMS OF MATURATION

There are several plausible mechanisms by which maturation may occur. Citizens play a strong role in what we view as the most plausible explanation (one popularized by Weingast 1997 and his work with various co-authors; see also Ordeshook 1992; Carey 2000) for how constitutions constrain leaders. Under this view, constitutions serve as important coordinating devices that allow citizens to act en masse to punish a leader's transgression. Such a coordinating device relies (or at least works better) if citizens know it and are attached to it. Thus, a first mechanism is that there may be increased awareness of the provision over time, which might support people *mobilizing* around it.

Think for a moment how and when citizens learn about the constitution, or at least anything that would be useful as operators in enforcement. In some (though probably not most) countries, constitutional awareness is transmitted in schools. Some educational systems, especially state-financed ones, include a fair degree of civic instruction in their curriculum at the primary and secondary level, and in some countries this might focus on the structure and guarantees of the national constitution. Citizens receive this crucial instruction at exactly the phase in their life cycle in which it will have its maximal impact. We know from the rich literature on political socialization that political knowledge and attitudes form (and often crystallize) during their adolescent years.

For those raised and socialized (indoctrinated even) with a sense of what is constitutional, updates later in life may not stick. Our music collections are dominated by bands and genres that captured us in our 20s. Our bookshelves and syllabi are filled with titles that inspired us in graduate school. Generations and socialization early in the human life cycle imply that the bite of constitutions might lag their introduction. New constitutions may simply not register immediately with those raised with other constitutions. One can think of new constitutions as stimulating a change in constitutional culture. Cultures change as generations turn over, which allows hardened and crystallized ideas of right and wrong to shift. This sort of shift is most obvious with identity rights, whether for women, racial minorities, or gays.

Consider, then, the Tunisian Constitution of 2014. Citizens awoke on January 28, 2014, with a new set of rights, including the explicit mention of gender in the equality clause.[3] Gender was a major issue in constitutional drafting, leading to street protests when the dominant Ennahada party insisted in one draft to refer to women's traditional roles in the family. After the adoption of the new provision, those in elementary school could look forward to a full educational program with the new constitution as a background text, which would help to cement the new vision of gender equality. Some of those older than twenty-one may never think of the right to non-discrimination as part of the fabric of their polity or, if they do, it will not be until a critical mass of the younger generation brings them around.

Second, even if *awareness* of constitutional provisions were constant across generations, there may be increased respect for the document over time, perhaps even leading to something we might call veneration. Over time, the mere survival of a text could lead people to impute wisdom to its contents, which might mean that the cost of violating the provision increases.

Thirdly, there may be increased capacity among enforcers as the constitution ages. Law works, in part, through institutionalization. The judiciary, for example, is obviously a critical enforcer of constitutional rights. But in many situations, particularly in new democracies, the judiciary lacks the institutional capacity to serve as a perfect enforcer. The public may not respect its decisions, or trust its judgment. The literature on judicial capacity suggests that, like most other institutions, courts develop over time (see, e.g., Ginsburg 2003). The same is likely true of police, prosecutors, ombudsmen, health bureaucracies, and teachers. When new enforcement institutions are created as part of a constitutional reform, they will need time to develop. As bureaucratic capacity grows over time, so too does the possibility of implementing constitutional promises. To be sure, bureaucratic capacity creates a Hobbesian dilemma: any state strong enough to protect rights is also strong enough to violate them (Weingast 1997). Yet it is also the case that the increasingly dense set of commitments found in modern constitutions is unachievable *without* significant state capacity.

Beyond an expansion in capacity, time may increase the shared understandings of rules among enforcers. Even if a constitution is adopted in a context of established institutions, they may need time to learn the new constitutional rules. Individual cases may arise that establish important precedents for what the constitution means. This information can spread to government institutions and the public, increasing the probability that the rules will be enforced. For all of these reasons, maturation is thus a real

---

[3] Article 21 replaced article 6 of the prior constitution, adding the words in italics: "All citizens, *male and female,* have equal rights and duties, and are equal before the law *without any discrimination.*"

possibility, though far from a certainty. The next section provides an initial test.

TESTING THE EFFECT OF MATURATION

There is a small empirical literature that assesses the efficacy of constitutional rights (Pritchard 1986; Fruhling 1993; Blasi and Cingranelli 1996; Davenport 1996; Cross 1999; Camp Keith 2002a and 2002b; Camp Keith et al. 2009; Camp Keith 2012; Chilton and Versteeg 2014; Melton 2014). In general, this literature has found that constitutional rights have very little effect on countries' rights practices. For instance, Linda Camp Keith (2002a and 2002b) compares the provision of rights, both substantive and procedural, and actual human rights protection, and finds that provisions for judicial independence improve human rights protection, as do due process provisions such as guarantees of public and fair trials. These process rights seem to be more important than the presence or absence of the substantive provisions themselves. Frank Cross (1999) finds that judicial independence is correlated with the presence of political rights and protection against unreasonable searches and seizures. Christian Davenport's (1996) more comprehensive analysis covers thirty-nine countries over a thirty-five-year period and distinguishes de jure provisions on rights, limitations on rights, state of emergency clauses, and limitations thereof. Davenport finds that countries with a state of emergency clause have lower levels of repression and that the freedom of the press is a crucial variable for reducing repression. Camp Keith et al. (2009) confirmed many of the findings from earlier studies using a longer time period and larger sample of countries. Most recently, Camp Keith (2012), Melton (2014), and Chilton and Versteeg (2014) find that the effect of constitutional rights varies across categories of rights. Entrenchment of civil and political rights seems to be more effective than entrenchment of other classes of rights. However, even when constitutional rights are shown to be statistically associated with rights practices, the average effect of entrenchment is substantively insignificant when compared with other factors associated with the protection of constitutional rights.

Given all the complexity laid out above, one should not be surprised that the empirical literature that assesses the effectiveness of constitutional rights provisions finds that those provisions have, on average, only a small effect. Although it is convenient to think about constitutional rights as either entrenched or not, in a binary fashion, this masks the conditions under which those rights are enforced, and there are strong theoretical reasons to believe that political leaders will only abide by constitutional rights when they are forced to do so. This fact has prompted some to look for the conditions under which constitutional rights are enforced (Davenport 1996; Camp Keith 2012; Melton 2014). The primary condition that has been identified in the literature is judicial independence. As one might expect, constitutional rights seem to have little (or no) effect in countries that lack an independent judiciary. Other conditions have been tested – for example, regime-type (Davenport 1996; Melton 2014), domestic conflict (Davenport 1996; Melton 2014), and the presence of NGOs (Camp Keith 2012), – but the effect of these other conditions is not robust.

The conceptualization of judicial independence in the literature is static, perhaps because of the cross-sectional nature of these empirical analyses. As noted above, however, judicial capacity is likely to improve over time with institutionalization (Ginsburg 2003). This implies that, within any particular country, one would expect increasing levels of rights performance over time as the judiciary improves. Other mechanisms of constitutional performance may also become more effective over time. This implies that there may be some maturation, and it is this condition – untested in the previous literature – that we explore here.

As described earlier, rights provisions often require a very sharp move from current baseline levels of protection, and sometimes require extensive institutional reforms for effective enforcement. As a result, one should not expect an immediate association between de jure and de facto rights protection. Note that all previous studies (implicitly) expect an immediate effect by using a binary variable to operationalize implementation of constitutional rights after adoption. Our own hypothesis is that, on average, constitutional rights that have been entrenched for a longer period of time are more likely to be observed by political leaders in practice. Although decay is certainly possible (see above), we believe that most constitutional rights are like provision A in Figure 9.1, so that when we look across rights, we will observe a positive relationship between duration of entrenchment and efficacy. Note that this relationship could be exhibited in at least two ways. We might observe that rights practices improve over time in countries where a constitutional right is entrenched. Alternatively, we might observe that rights practices decline over time in countries that fail to entrench a right in their constitution. We will try to tease out these two effects in the analysis below.

RESEARCH DESIGN

One must overcome two major challenges when analyzing the empirical effect of constitutional rights. The first is lack of quality data. Data on de facto human rights protection only extends back to about 1980, so at best, we have data on de facto rights protection for only about thirty years. Given the complex interactions that we intend to test below and the fact that we are probably looking for a relatively small effect, we worry that these data do not provide sufficient power for the tests conducted below, increasing the odds of committing an inferential error. The second challenge is endogeneity. To be specific, one worries that states' motivations for entrenching constitutional rights are related to the probability that they protect rights in practice.

Our imperfect solution for both of these problems is to pool the data available to us into one large data set. The result is a data set with variance across fourteen rights for up to 194 countries and thirty years. Not only does this approach dramatically expand the power of the analyses below, but if one is willing to assume that states' motivations for protecting rights is uniform across rights, then this approach allows us to rule out the more obvious source of endogeneity as well. The risk of this approach is that it masks potential heterogeneity in the efficacy of constitutional rights. Recall that Camp Keith (2012), Melton (2014), and Chilton and Versteeg (2014) find that some categories of rights are more effective than others. The theory outlined above also suggests that the effect of some rights might decay over time. In short, there are both empirical and theoretical reasons to suspect heterogeneity, which we will not be able to detect by pooling rights. That said, we think a pooled analysis is a good starting point for analysis.

OPERATIONALIZING PERFORMANCE

The dependent variable in the analysis below is de facto rights protection. We use fourteen different rights from three sources (see Table 9.1). The CIRI Human Rights dataset (Cingarelli and Richards 2011) provides data on freedom of association, freedom of expression, freedom of movement, freedom of religion, the right to join political parties and trade unions, and the prohibition of torture.[4] Freedom House provides data on freedom of the press. Lastly, we use data from Hathaway (2002) to measure the right to appeal, the right to counsel, the presumption of innocence in trials, the right to public trial, the right to a timely trial, and the right to a trial in the language of the accused. Each de facto right can take on three values: 0 means many de facto rights

---

[4] For freedom of movement and freedom of religion, we combine the old and new versions of these variables from the CIRI dataset. In each case, we primarily rely on the new version and use the old version to fill in missing data.

TABLE 9.1 *De jure and de facto rights data*

Right	Countries	Years	De jure variable name	De facto source
Right to appeal	113–159	1985, 1988, 1991, 1994, 1997, 2000	appeal	Hathaway (2002)
Freedom of association	133–193	1981–2011	assem; assoc	Cingarelli and Richards (2011)
Right to counsel	113–159	1985, 1988, 1991, 1994, 1997, 2000	couns	Hathaway (2002)
Freedom of expression	133–193	1981–2011	express	Cingarelli and Richards (2011)
Freedom of movement	133–193	1981–2011	freemove	Cingarelli and Richards (2011)
Freedom of religion	133–193	1981–2011	freerel	Cingarelli and Richards (2011)
Right to unionize	133–193	1981–2011	jointrde; strike	Cingarelli and Richards (2011)
Right to political parties	133–193	1981–2011	partrght	Cingarelli and Richards (2011)
Presumption of innocence	113–159	1985, 1988, 1991, 1994, 1997, 2000	presinoc	Hathaway (2002)
Freedom of press	153–194	1980–2012	press	Freedom House (2010)
Right to a public trial	113–159	1985, 1988, 1991, 1994, 1997, 2000	pubtri	Hathaway (2002)
Right to a timely trial	113–159	1985, 1988, 1991, 1994, 1997, 2000	speedtri	Hathaway (2002)
Prohibition of torture	133–193	1981–2011	torture	Cingarelli and Richards (2011)
Trial in language of accused	113–159	1985, 1988, 1991, 1994, 1997, 2000	trilang	Hathaway (2002)

violations, 0.5 means a few de facto rights violations, and 1 means minimal or no known de facto rights violations.[5]

There is significant variance in state's performance on these fourteen rights. Most countries score pretty well on the legal process rights. In fact, virtually all countries protect the right to appeal, right to a public trial, and the right to a trial in the language of the accused in practice, with around 90% of country-years scoring a one for these three rights. The distribution of scores is more

---

[5]   Freedom of the press takes on five values, ranging from −1 to 1. We lump −1 and −0.5 together and 0.5 and 1 together in the analysis below.

normal for other rights. For instance, for freedom of expression, 27% of country-years are scored 0, 47% are scored 0.5, and only 26% are scored 1. Many of the civil and political rights have a similar distribution of scores. Lastly, there are two rights for which a plurality of country-years are scored 0: freedom of the press and the prohibition against torture. Thirty-nine percent of country-years are scored 0 for freedom of press, and 41% of country-years are scored 0 for the prohibition of torture.

OPERATIONALIZING CONSTITUTIONAL RIGHTS

The main independent variable in the analysis is de jure rights protection. These data are from the Comparative Constitutions Project (CCP), which catalogs the contents of constitutions in force in independent states since 1789.[6] One or sometimes two variables from the CCP are matched with each of the twelve de facto rights discussed in the previous paragraph (see Table 9.1). This is a departure from much of the extant literature, which tends to estimate the effect of many constitutional rights on a single omnibus measure of de facto rights protection, such as the political terror scores (for exceptions, see Melton 2014 or Chilton and Versteeg 2014). Our approach provides a more direct test of constitutional efficacy because it is assessing the effectiveness of de jure rights on the same de facto rights that they were meant to protect.

Each right has two de jure variables associated with it. The first is simply a binary variable that is coded one when that right is entrenched in a country's constitution. This variable should be positive if entrenchment improves countries' rights practices. Like the de facto variables introduced previously, there is significant variance across rights in this simple indicator of de jure rights protection. A number of civil and political rights are protected in the vast majority of constitutions. For instance, freedom of religion is entrenched in 90% of the country-years analyzed, freedom of expression is entrenched in 87% of the country-years analyzed, and freedom of association is entrenched in 86% of the country-years analyzed. Other rights are far less popular. Most of these less popular rights are legal process rights, such as the right to a timely trial, which is only entrenched in 32% of country-years, and the right to a trial in the language of the accused, which is only entrenched in 26% of country-years. Many of the remaining rights are entrenched in roughly 50% of national constitutions in force in our sample.

---

[6] For more information about the Comparative Constitutions Project and its coding strategy, see Elkins et al. (2009) or the project's website (www.comparativeconstitutionsproject.org).

The second de jure variable measures maturation, which is simply a counter for the number of consecutive years that the de jure rights variable has been in the same state. For instance, freedom of the press was introduced in Brazil by its 1988 constitution, so the de jure right variable from freedom of press would take a value of 1 starting in 1988 and the maturation variable would take a value of 0 in 1988, 1 in 1989, and so on. The counter would continue until the de jure rights variable for freedom of press switches to a value of 0, at which point the counter would start over at zero. The 1988 constitution did not provide the accused a right to a timely trial. Actually, none of Brazil's constitutions provided for the right to a timely trial, so in 1988, the de jure right variable for a timely trial takes a value of 0 in 1988 and the maturation variable takes a value of 164 in 1988, 165 in 1989, and so on. Notice that the maturation variable represents the number of consecutive years that the de jure variable takes a value of 0 since Brazil's first constitution was entrenched in the early 1800s, not since its most recent constitution was put into force.

Given the importance of maturation in the analysis below, it is worth describing this variable in some detail. We should start by noting that the entrenchment status of constitutional rights does not change frequently, a reflection of what we and others have called the stickiness of constitutions (Elkins et al. 2009: 3; Varol 2016). Across the fourteen rights in our sample, in independent states from 1789 to 2013, we observe only 1,580 changes in entrenchment status out of 192,528 observations, putting the average probability of change at only 0.008. Consistent with previous work in this area, entrenchment is slightly more likely than removal, at least within the set of rights we analyze here. Overall, we observe 1,083 entrenchments (probability of entrenchment equals 0.011) and 497 removals (probability of removal equals 0.006). Notably, most entrenchments and removals occur through constitutional replacement. Only 117 rights were entrenched through constitutional amendment (roughly 11%), and only thirty-four were removed by the amendment process (roughly 7%).[7]

As should be clear from the previous paragraph, the status of constitutional rights in constitutions is remarkably stable, even across constitutional systems. This fact is further illustrated in Figure 9.2, which plots the survival rate and smoothed hazard rate of constitutional rights by entrenchment status. The top

---

[7] We likely miss some changes in entrenchment status because we have not coded all of the constitutional events for every country. Although, after interpolating our data across constitutional systems, we have data covering 89% (14,172) of country-years from 1789 to 2013, we still need to code a number of events. To be specific, we are entirely missing data from 220 constitutional systems, and in systems for which we do have data, we still need to code 1,523 amendments. We have coded over 1,200 amendments.

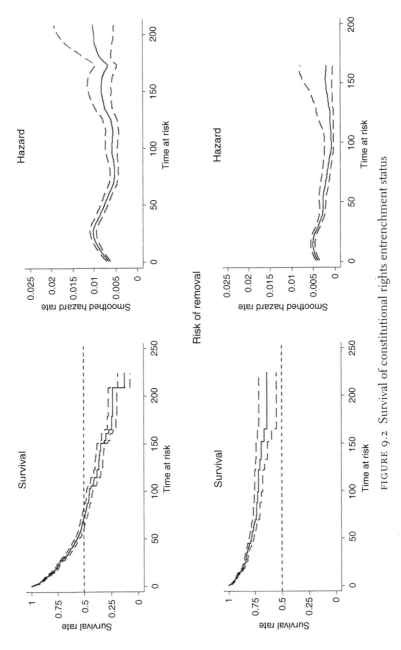

FIGURE 9.2 Survival of constitutional rights entrenchment status

two plots in the figure represent country-right-years at risk of entrenchment, where a right is absent from the constitution and is waiting to be entrenched. The bottom two plots represent country-right-years at risk of removal, where a right is entrenched in the constitution and is waiting to be removed. For each of these states, we plot the survival rate (i.e., the proportion, at time t, of right states that are unchanged since their observation began) and the smooth hazard rate (i.e., an estimate of the probability that a right state will change in time t, conditional on a right surviving until time t).

The plots largely confirm the descriptive statistics above, although there is some variance over time in the probability of entrenchment and removal. Starting with the risk of entrenchment, we find that most countries that did not entrench these rights in their first constitution, had entrenched these fourteen rights within seventy-five years, (where the solid line crosses the dashed reference line in the top left figure). We observe that countries were most likely to entrench the right within the first twenty-two years of not having it entrenched. There is also an increase in the rate of entrenchment after about 125 years, but given the small number of constitutions in this sample, we do not entirely trust those estimates (notice the large 95% confidence intervals after one hundred years).

The risk of removal plots on the bottom of Figure 9.2 are less interesting than those on risk of entrenchment because rights are rarely removed from constitutions once they are entrenched, a ratchet effect we have identified in earlier work. This is apparent in the survival plot in the bottom left. Even after 225 years, more than 50% of the rights entrenched in a country are still entrenched. Rights are most at risk of removal in the first thirty years of entrenchment. After thirty years, the risk of removal decreases until there is virtually no risk at age 100. In other words, once a right is entrenched, our expectation is that it will never be removed from the constitution, an expectation that grows stronger the longer a right is entrenched. This is unsurprising. As we noted in previous work (Elkins et al. 2009), there are likely few drafters who would be willing to stand up in a constituent assembly and argue that some right, which was entrenched in a country's previous constitution, should not be in the new constitution.

To summarize, the addition and removal of rights from constitutions is extremely rare. So, while most countries undergo constitutional change relatively frequently, these changes often leave the bills of rights untouched. One does not even observe much change in bills of rights following a constitutional replacement, and if a change does occur, then the change is most likely the addition of a right. This means that the maturation variable used in the analysis below can take very high values. For example, freedom of expression and freedom of association have been continuously entrenched in the United States' constitution for more than 200 years. Similarly, the United Kingdom has a long history of guaranteeing timely court proceedings, and France has had a number of rights entrenched in its many constitutions since the late eighteenth century. On average, rights that are absent from constitutions have been that way for fifty-four years (standard deviation = 53 years), and rights that are present in constitutions have been entrenched for thirty-five years (standard deviation = 38 years). Thus, even though we only have data on de facto rights for thirty years, we can test our maturation hypothesis across a wide range of levels of maturation.

CONTROL VARIABLES

In addition to the de jure rights variables, we include a number of other independent variables in the models below. These variables are based on what Camp Keith (2012) refers to as the "standard" model of state repression, which is based on the variables that have been demonstrated in the existing literature to affect de facto rights protection (Poe et al. 1999; Camp Keith et al. 2009). According to the standard model, democracy, judicial independence, veto players, and economic development are all expected to increase de facto rights protection. Domestic conflict and large populations are both expected to decrease de facto rights protection. Aside from these traditional variables, we also include a few variables known to be associated with de jure rights protection, which may also affect de facto rights protection, especially for some rights. We include variables on the religious composition of the countries as well as variables for colonial history, fixed effects for rights, and fixed effects for region.[8] In addition, we include a number of different year counters to ensure that our maturation variable is really measuring maturation and not some other effect. To be specific, we include a variable for state age to account for the fact that older states tend to be more economically and politically developed, and as a result are likely to have better de facto rights protection. Similarly, we include a variable on the age of the in-force constitution to control for the effect of institutional stability on de facto rights protection. Lastly, we include year since it is well

---

[8] We have also estimated the models with fixed effects at the country-level. The results do not change much, except for a few models that have a small number of observations.

TABLE 9.2 *Description of control variables*

Variable	Description	Source
Democracy	Binary variable indicating democratic country-years	Cheibub et al. (2010)
Judicial independence	Level of judicial independence	Linzer and Staton[a]
Veto players	Number of veto players based on the political constraints index	Henisz (2013)
Domestic conflict	Binary variable indicating the presence of domestic conflict (e.g., a strike, a riot, or guerrilla warfare)	Banks and Wilson (2014)
GDP (ln)	Log of real GDP	Heston et al. (2009)
Population (ln)	Log of population	Heston et al. (2009)
Christians (%)	Percent of population that is Christian	ARDA
Muslims (%)	Percent of population that is Muslim	ARDA
British Colony	Binary variable indicating British colonies	Geopolitical Database
French Colony	Binary variable indicating French colonies	Geopolitical Database
Spanish Colony	Binary variable indicating Spanish colonies	Geopolitical Database
Other Colony	Binary variable indicating colonies of other countries	Geopolitical Database
State age (100 years)	Number of years of continuous independence of the state	Gleditsch and Ward (2013)
Constitution age (100 years)	Age of the in force constitution	CCP
Year (100 years)	Year	CCP
Right	Binary variables indicating the right being assessed (right to appeal is the reference category)	CCP
Region	Binary variables indicating the region to which the country belongs (Latin America is the reference category)	CCP

[a] Drew A. Linzer and Jeffrey K. Staton. 2011. "A Measurement Model for Synthesizing Multiple Comparative Indicators: The Case of Judicial Independence." Unpublished manuscript.

known that measures of de facto rights protection have declined over time as monitoring has increased. A description of all these variables is provided in Table 9.2. Descriptive statistics for all of the variables are provided in Table 9.3.

TABLE 9.3 *Descriptive statistics*

Variable	Mean	St. dev.	Range	N
D.F. Right	0.51	0.42	(0–1)	34,221
D.J. Right	0.73	0.45	(0–1)	34,221
Maturation (100 years)	0.42	0.44	(0–2.23)	34,221
Democracy	0.53	0.50	(0–1)	34,160
Judicial independence	0.52	0.32	(0–1)	29,965
Veto players	0.25	0.21	(0–0.72)	33,477
Domestic conflict	0.40	0.49	(0–1)	32,647
GDP (ln)	10.19	2.17	(4.38–16.49)	31,796
Population (ln)	8.82	1.87	(2.85–14.10)	32,081
Christians (%)	0.57	0.38	(0–0.98)	34,084
Muslims (%)	0.22	0.34	(0–0.99)	34,084
British Colony	0.31	0.46	(0–1)	34,221
French Colony	0.17	0.38	(0–1)	34,221
Spanish Colony	0.13	0.33	(0–1)	34,221
Other Colony	0.23	0.42	(0–1)	34,221
State age (100 years)	0.78	0.67	(0–2.23)	34,221
Constitution age (100 years)	0.28	0.38	(0–2.23)	34,221
Year (100 years)	19.97	0.09	(19.80–20.12)	34,221

RESULTS

Table 9.4 provides the estimates from six ordinary least squares regression models. The coefficient estimates are provided in the table with robust standard errors in parentheses. Since these are ordinary least squares models, the coefficient estimates can be interpreted directly, so the 0.79 coefficient estimates for judicial independence means that a one unit increase in judicial independence leads to an average increase in the level of de facto rights of 0.79.

The first thing to note about the table is that most of the control variables have signs in the expected direction. Judicial independence, veto players, and GDP all increase de facto rights protection, while domestic conflict and population decrease de facto rights protection. The one variable that is not in the expected direction is democracy. There are a couple of possible explanations for this, some which are artifacts of the analytic design. One is that we are using a binary measure of democracy that essentially captures whether states have competitive elections, or not. There is some evidence that its horizontal accountability, which is measured more precisely by veto players and judicial independence, is more important than vertical accountability when it comes to improving de facto

TABLE 9.4 Main model estimates

Variables	(1)	(2)	(3)	(4)	(5)	(6)
D.J. Right	0.04***	0.05***	0.08***	0.02***	0.01	0.00
	(0.00)	(0.01)	(0.01)	(0.00)	(0.01)	(0.01)
Maturation (100 years)	0.01***	0.02***	0.10***	0.02***	0.01	−0.07***
	(0.00)	(0.01)	(0.02)	(0.01)	(0.01)	(0.02)
D.J. × Maturation		−0.02***	−0.13***			0.02
		(0.01)	(0.02)			(0.02)
Maturation²			−0.04***			0.04***
			(0.01)			(0.02)
D.J. × Maturation²			0.06***			0.01
			(0.01)			(0.01)
Democracy				−0.03***	−0.03***	−0.03***
				(0.01)	(0.01)	(0.01)
Judicial independence				0.79***	0.79***	0.80***
				(0.01)	(0.01)	(0.01)
Veto players				0.04***	0.04***	0.04***
				(0.01)	(0.01)	(0.01)
Domestic conflict				−0.02***	−0.02***	−0.02***
				(0.00)	(0.00)	(0.00)
GDP (ln)				0.01**	0.01**	0.01***
				(0.00)	(0.00)	(0.00)
Population (ln)				−0.03***	−0.03***	−0.03***
				(0.00)	(0.00)	(0.00)
Christians (%)				0.00	0.00	0.01
				(0.01)	(0.01)	(0.01)
Muslims (%)				0.03***	0.03***	0.03***
				(0.01)	(0.01)	(0.01)

	(1)	(2)	(3)	(4)	(5)
British Colony			−0.03***	−0.03***	−0.04***
			(0.01)	(0.01)	(0.01)
French Colony			0.01	0.01	0.00
			(0.01)	(0.01)	(0.01)
Spanish Colony			−0.03***	−0.03***	−0.03***
			(0.01)	(0.01)	(0.01)
Other Colony			−0.02***	−0.03***	−0.03***
			(0.01)	(0.01)	(0.01)
State age (100 years)			−0.02***	−0.02***	−0.02***
			(0.00)	(0.00)	(0.00)
Constitution age (100 years)			0.00	0.00	−0.01
			(0.01)	(0.01)	(0.01)
Year (100 years)			−0.60***	−0.60***	−0.59***
			(0.02)	(0.02)	(0.02)
Association	−0.39***	−0.39***	−0.36***	−0.36***	−0.36***
	(0.01)	(0.01)	(0.01)	(0.01)	(0.01)
Rt. to Counsel	−0.27***	−0.27***	−0.26***	−0.26***	−0.26***
	(0.01)	(0.01)	(0.01)	(0.01)	(0.01)
Expression	−0.45***	−0.45***	−0.41***	−0.41***	−0.41***
	(0.01)	(0.01)	(0.01)	(0.01)	(0.01)
Free movement	−0.31***	−0.31***	−0.29***	−0.29***	−0.29***
	(0.01)	(0.01)	(0.01)	(0.01)	(0.01)
Freedom of religion	−0.29***	−0.29***	−0.26***	−0.27***	−0.26***
	(0.01)	(0.01)	(0.01)	(0.01)	(0.01)
Join trade unions	−0.48***	−0.48***	−0.43***	−0.42***	−0.42***
	(0.01)	(0.01)	(0.01)	(0.01)	(0.01)

TABLE 9.4 (*Cont.*)

Variables	(1)	(2)	(3)	(4)	(5)	(6)
Form political parties	-0.36***	-0.36***	-0.36***	-0.33***	-0.33***	-0.33***
	(0.01)	(0.01)	(0.01)	(0.01)	(0.01)	(0.01)
Presumption of innocence	-0.09***	-0.10***	-0.10***	-0.09***	-0.08***	-0.09***
	(0.01)	(0.01)	(0.01)	(0.01)	(0.01)	(0.01)
Freedom of press	-0.45***	-0.45***	-0.44***	-0.44***	-0.44***	-0.44***
	(0.01)	(0.01)	(0.01)	(0.01)	(0.01)	(0.01)
Rt. to public trial	-0.01	-0.01	-0.01	-0.00	-0.00	-0.00
	(0.01)	(0.01)	(0.01)	(0.01)	(0.01)	(0.01)
Rt. to speedy trial	-0.38***	-0.38***	-0.38***	-0.38***	-0.38***	-0.38***
	(0.02)	(0.02)	(0.02)	(0.02)	(0.02)	(0.02)
Freedom from torture	-0.55***	-0.55***	-0.55***	-0.53***	-0.53***	-0.53***
	(0.01)	(0.01)	(0.01)	(0.01)	(0.01)	(0.01)
Trial in own language	0.05***	0.05***	0.05***	0.05***	0.05***	0.05***
	(0.01)	(0.01)	(0.01)	(0.01)	(0.01)	(0.01)
W. Europe/U.S./Canada	0.18***	0.18***	0.18***	-0.09***	-0.09***	-0.09***
	(0.01)	(0.01)	(0.01)	(0.01)	(0.01)	(0.01)
E. Europe	-0.21***	-0.22***	-0.22***	-0.09***	-0.09***	-0.10***
	(0.01)	(0.01)	(0.01)	(0.01)	(0.01)	(0.01)
Sub-Saharan Africa	-0.24***	-0.24***	-0.24***	-0.02***	-0.02***	-0.03***
	(0.01)	(0.01)	(0.01)	(0.01)	(0.01)	(0.01)
Middle East/N. Africa	-0.44***	-0.44***	-0.44***	-0.15***	-0.15***	-0.14***
	(0.01)	(0.01)	(0.01)	(0.01)	(0.01)	(0.01)
South Asia	-0.26***	-0.26***	-0.26***	-0.05***	-0.05***	-0.05***
	(0.01)	(0.01)	(0.01)	(0.01)	(0.01)	(0.01)

	(1)	(2)	(3)	(4)	(5)	(6)
East Asia	−0.28***	−0.28***	−0.29***	−0.07***	−0.07***	−0.06***
	(0.01)	(0.01)	(0.01)	(0.01)	(0.01)	(0.01)
Oceania	0.17***	0.17***	0.16***	0.05***	0.05***	0.05***
	(0.01)	(0.01)	(0.01)	(0.01)	(0.01)	(0.01)
R²	0.34	0.34	0.34	0.50	0.50	0.51
Observations	43,557	43,557	43,557	36,409	36,409	36,409

Notes: Estimates are from OLS models with robust standard errors. Statistical significant is denoted as follows:
* = $p < 0.1$; ** = $p < 0.05$; *** = $p < 0.01$.

rights (Davenport 2007). Another explanation is that we have included a number of rights that are not traditionally included in studies of rights protection, such as legal process rights. It is possible that democracy has a different effect on these rights than on physical integrity rights or civil and political rights, which are typically the rights assessed in the extant literature. In either case, the effect is small, so even though the effect is statistically significant, it is not substantively significant. The most substantively significant variable, by far (!), is judicial independence, which improves rights protection.

The only other variable that has a large effect is year. Over the thirty years for which data are available, de facto rights protection has decreased by about 0.18, on average, across the rights being analyzed. Like others before us (Fariss 2014), we suspect this is the result of increased monitoring, and not that countries are actually repressing rights more than they were thirty years ago.

Moving to the de jure variables, we test the effect of de jure rights in three ways, with and without covariates. The first model specification (models 1 and 4) assesses the independent effect of de jure rights and small maturation. The second model specification (models 2 and 5) includes an interaction between de jure rights and maturation. The third model specification (models 3 and 6) also includes an interaction, but this specification also allows the effect of maturation to be non-linear. In general, there is support for a small maturation effect. Actually, neither de jure rights nor maturation has a very strong effect. Both are statistically significant in models 1 and 4, but their effects are small (~0.02) and the model fit is slightly better for models 2 and 5 (AIC = 11784 for model 5 versus 11848 for model 4).

Focusing on model 5, we estimate that each additional year a right is entrenched increases de facto rights protection by 0.0003 (i.e., (0.01 + 0.02)/ 100 = 0.0003). So, if a country had the "average right" entrenched in its constitution in 1980, by the end of the period under observation in 2010, we would expect that country's level of de facto protection of the average right to increase by about 0.0096. Conversely, if a country lacked that right in its constitution in 1980, then its protection of that right in practice is expected to increase by only 0.0024. Thus, across thirty years, one might say that the total effect of entrenchment is about 0.014.

There are a variety of reasons why the effect of maturation might be so small. One possibility is that the effect is non-linear. We test this in models 2 and 6. We do find some evidence of a non-linear effect in model 6, which is illustrated in Figure 9.3. In the figure, the black lines illustrate the effect of maturation when the average right is present in a country's constitution, and the gray lines illustrates the effect of maturation when the average right is

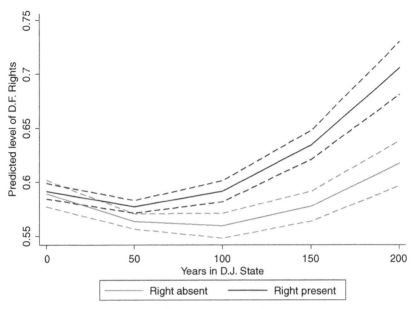

FIGURE 9.3 Effect of maturation ($N = 36,409$)
Notes: The figure is based on the estimates from Table 9.1, model 6.

absent in a country's constitution. The solid line is the predicted level of de facto rights protection, and the dashed lines represent the 95% confidence interval around that prediction. Notice that, initially, de facto protection is about the same when the de jure right is absent from the constitution as when it is entrenched. However, over the first fifty years, de facto protection decreases pretty dramatically when the de jure right is absent, such that, by year 50, the level of de facto rights protection is higher when the right is entrenched. After those first fifty years, de facto rights protection starts to increase in both states, but it increases faster when the right is entrenched. So, by 200 years, the difference in the two lines is about 0.1, which is about twice the effect predicted by model 5 and just less than the effect of year in models 4–6.

Another reason that we might observe such a small effect is that we have pooled all countries together, regardless of their level of de facto rights protection. As noted earlier, some constitutional rights are meant to commit to the status quo, while others are more aspirational. The effect of entrenchment in the former can only be negative because such countries that seek to entrench current practice will by definition already have high levels of de facto

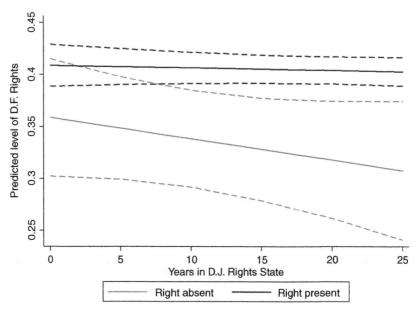

FIGURE 9.4 Effect of maturation on aspirational constitutional rights (N = 1,696)

rights protection.[9] By pooling such countries with those countries that have more aspirational constitutions, we are attenuating our estimates of the effect of entrenchment. To address this problem, we analyze a subsample of the observations that received the lowest score on a given de facto rights variable in the five years leading up to the entrenchment (or removal) of some right from a country's constitution. Re-estimating model 5 on this subsample yields the results illustrated in Figure 9.4.

The results suggest that aspirational constitutions do have an effect, but the effect is to prevent decay. Notice that simply making a constitutional change seems to increase the average level of rights in this subsample of countries because, despite the fact that all countries had a history of rights protection of 0, the initial level of protection is about 0.42 in countries with the right entrenched and 0.35 in countries without the right in their constitutions. Thus, the events that prompted the constitutional change led to some improvement in the level of de facto rights protection (~0.05, p(t = 0) = 0.08). However, in constitutions that did not entrench those gains, the level

---

[9] In our case, these are countries that have a history of 1's on de facto rights protection. Since this is the maximum allowable score on the crude measures of de facto rights that we are using, such countries' scores can literally only decrease after entrenchment.

of de facto rights protection decayed back toward its starting point within fifteen or twenty years. In constitutions that did entrench the right, though, the level of de facto rights protection remained relatively constant. This is not to say that the level of de facto rights protection will never increase. Recall that Figure 9.3 suggested that maturation does not start to take hold until a right has been continuously in force for about fifty years, but due to lack of data, we can only analyze the first twenty-five years of entrenchment in Figure 9.3. As these newly entrenched rights continue to age, it is possible that we may be able to observe some maturation.

Lastly, the effect of maturation might be conditional on other variables. In particular, maturation might be dependent on some actor to enforce those rights, and this enforcement might strengthen over time, as discussed earlier. Here, we replicate the analysis of Melton (2014), who finds that the effect of de jure rights is condition on the presence of an independent judiciary to enforce them. He further finds that the effect of judicial enforcement is strongest in dictatorships. Here, we test whether the effect of maturation is conditional on the independence of the judiciary by interacting judicial independence with our variables for de jure rights and maturation. In addition, like Melton (2014), we stratify the sample by regime type to see if the conditional effect of judicial independence is indeed stronger in non-democratic settings. The results of these models are illustrated in Figure 9.5. The top four panels represent the relationship between maturation and de facto rights in democracies, and the bottom four panels represent that same relationship in dictatorships. Within each subplot, four levels of judicial independence are plotted: 0 in the top left, 0.33 in the top right, 0.67 in the bottom left, and 1 in the bottom right. The interpretation of each panel is the same as the interpretation of Figures 9.3 and 9.4.

The results illustrated in Figure 9.5 are largely consistent with those presented by Melton (2014). Regardless of the level of judicial independence, de facto rights protection tends to be a bit stronger in democracies than in dictatorships, and in general, as judicial independence increases, so does the level of de facto rights protection. For constitutional rights, the effect is positive if the black line is higher than the gray line, which is true in democracies when the level of judicial independence is highest (at 1) and in dictatorships as long as the level of judicial independence is below the minimum.

The effect of maturation is indicated by the slope of the lines in the panels. In democracies, there is basically no maturation effect. If anything, there seems to be decay when the level of judicial independence is low because the black line has a negative slope, suggesting that de facto rights protection

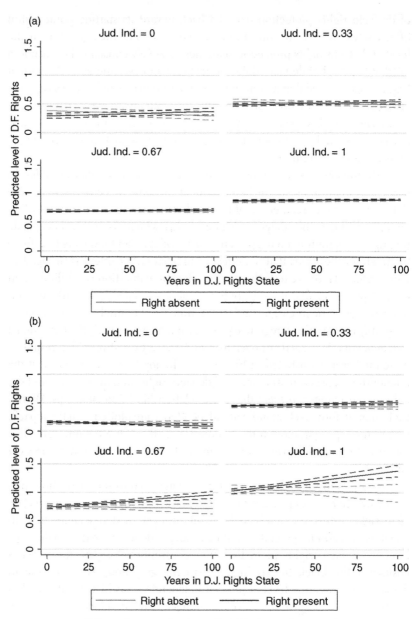

FIGURE 9.5 Effect of maturation by judicial independence and regime type

decreases as rights age in democracies with low levels of judicial independence. As the level of judicial independence increases, the slope of the black line increases to near zero and largely overlaps the gray line. Our interpretation of these results is that democracies already have high level of de facto rights protection, so there is simply no room for protection to increase further, at least on the measures of de facto rights used here. Furthermore, since there are very few democracies with low levels of judicial independence, it is hard to trust the results in the top row of subplots in plot A.

If we consider dictatorships, the effect of maturation is much stronger. When judicial independence is low, the black line is negatively sloped, and the gray line is just about flat. As judicial independence increases, the slope of the gray line stays about the same, but the slope of the black line, representing countries with a right entrenched in their constitution, increases relatively quickly. As a result, by the time judicial independence is 0.67, the black line is significantly higher than the gray line, indicating a strong maturation effect. To be precise, when judicial independence is at 0.67, the initial level of the average de facto right is expected to be 0.74 in countries with the right entrenched in their constitution and 0.76 in countries that lack the right. After twenty-five years, the level of de facto rights has actually decreased by about 0.01 in countries that lack the right and increased by 0.05 in countries that have entrenched the right. So, what started as a modest negative effect of 0.02 from de facto rights protection has increased a positive effect of 0.04 after twenty-five years and 0.12 after fifty years. Compared to the other variables in the model, these are relatively large increases in de facto rights protection, and the effect is even stronger if the level of judicial independence is higher.

In summary, we do observe a maturation effect. When looking across the entire sample, that effect is relatively small, only about 0.014 over thirty years. However, the effect does vary over time, with the strongest effect of maturation felt after fifty years. In addition, the effect is conditional on both regime type and the level of judicial independence. There seems to be very little maturation effect in democracies, but in dictatorships, constitutional rights become more effective as they age, provided they have an independent judiciary to enforce them. Lastly, it is worth noting that these results are remarkably stable across groups of rights. In analyses available from the authors upon request, we re-estimated the models presented above on only civil and political rights and only legal process rights. The estimates from these models were substantively the same as those presented in Figures 9.3 and 9.5.

CAVEATS AND COMPLICATIONS

These aggregate results do not fully adjudicate the theoretical question of whether maturation or decay dominates. The small effect we find for maturation could have myriad causes. It might be, for example, that ineffective constitutions die out from the sample, so that only efficacious documents are left in the population. Thus the observed effect would reflect a correlation between age and efficacy, but the causality would be reversed. It could also be the case that there is a substantial amount of maturation in some observations, offset by decay in others, so the aggregate effect is small. Drilling down on conditional effects will help us to tease out the particular sources of change over time.

The discussion so far has set aside another potentially complicating factor. Provisions may be designed and analyzed in isolation; but they operate as part of institutional systems in which the whole is more than the sum of its parts. Constitutional provisions interact with each other. Consider the structural priority thesis, the Madisonian idea that structural design was the key to ensure liberty. As Federalist 51 says, "different governments will control each other, at the same time that each will be controlled by itself." Breaking up political power is a design choice that serves to advance liberty. It is obvious that interpreting institutional provisions related to one government body cannot be understood without understanding the provisions related to other institutions. This point implies that we ought to control for some features of government structure which might enhance the efficacy of rights protection, beyond simply judicial independence.

CONCLUSION

One of the central roles of the constitution is to limit government. Yet, most scholars are skeptical about the ability of the constitution to fulfill this role, which recalls James Madison's famous view of bills of rights as mere parchment barriers. There is plenty of empirical evidence to support this skepticism (see, for example, Camp Keith et al. 2009), but in our minds, the extant literature has been asking the wrong question. Rather than asking *do* constitutional rights matter, we should be asking *how* and *where* they matter. Rather than treating efficacy as black and white, our focus should be on the conditions under which constitutional promises are transformed into political reality.

In this chapter, we have assessed the effect of time on the efficacy of constitutional rights. Although we identified three possible theoretical effects of time – maturation, decay, and stasis – the statistical analysis suggests that the primary effect of time on the efficacy of constitutional rights is maturation. As constitutional rights get older, the constitutional promises tend to improve performance. The average maturation effect is relatively small, but there are some conditions under which the effect is more pronounced. To be specific, the effect of maturation is strongest in contexts where the right has been in existence more than fifty years, when a country has a history of poor performance, and in authoritarian regimes with a relatively high level of judicial independence.

Contrary to much of the existing literature on the efficacy of constitutional rights, this study has demonstrated that, over time, constitutional rights do improve countries' human rights practices. Perhaps the most surprising result is that constitutional rights seem to be the most effective in authoritarian regimes, where their limits are needed most. While these findings alone are unlikely to dispel hundreds of years of skepticism toward the effectiveness of texts, they should at least provoke more careful inquiry before constitutions are dismissed as mere parchment barriers.

REFERENCES

Albert, Richard. 2014. "Constitutional Disuse or Desuetude: The Case of Article V." *Boston University Law Review*. 94: 1029–1085.

Banks, Arthur and Kenneth A. Wilson. 2014. "Cross-National Time-Series Data Archive." Jerusalem: Databanks International. Available at www.databanksinternational.com.

Blasi, Gerald and David Cingranelli. 1996. "Do Constitutions and Institutions Help Protect Human Rights?" In *Human Rights and Developing Countries*, ed. David Cingranelli. Greenwich: JAI Press.

Breslin, Beau. 2009. *From Words to Worlds: Exploring Constitutional Functionality*. Baltimore: Johns Hopkins University Press.

Camp Keith, Linda. 2002a. "Judicial Independence and Human Rights Protection around the World." *Judicature*. 85: 194–200.

2002b. "Constitutional Provisions for Individual Human Rights (1976–1996): Are They More than Mere 'Window Dressing?'" *Political Research Quarterly*. 55: 111–143.

Camp Keith, Linda. 2012. *Political Repression: Courts and Law*. Philadelphia: University of Pennsylvania Press.

Camp Keith, Linda, C. Neal Tate and Steven C. Poe. 2009. "Is the Law a Mere Parchment Barrier to Human Rights Abuse?" *Journal of Politics*. 71(2): 644–660.

Carey, John. 2000. "Parchment, Equilibria, and Institutions." *Comparative Political Studies*. 33: 735–761.

Cheibub, Jose Antonio, Jennifer Gandhi and James Vreeland. 2010. "Democracy and Dictatorship Revisited." *Public Choice.* 143(1–2): 67–101. Data available at https://net_les.uiuc.edu/cheibub/www/DD page.html.

Chilton, Adam and Mila Versteeg. 2014. "Do Constitutional Rights Make a Difference?" Chicago: University of Chicago Coase-Sandor Institute for Law and Economics Working Paper No. 694 (2D Series).

Cingranelli, David L. and David L. Richards. 2011. "The Cingranelli-Richards Human Rights Dataset." Available at http://ciri.binghamton.edu/index. asp.

Cover, Robert. 1986. "Violence and the Word." *Yale Law Journal.* 95: 1601–1629.

Cross, Frank. 1999. "The Relevance of Law to Human Rights Protection." *International Review of Law and Economics.* 20: 87–98.

Davenport, Christian A. 1996. "'Constitutional Promises' and Repressive Reality: A Cross-National Time-Series Investigation of Why Political and Civil Liberties Are Suppressed." *The Journal of Politics.* 58(3): 627–654.

   2007. *State Repression and the Domestic Democratic Peace.* Cambridge: Cambridge University Press.

Davenport, Christian A. and David A. Armstrong. 2004. "Democracy and the Violation of Human Rights: A Statistical Analysis from 1976 to 1996." *American Journal of Political Science.* 48(3): 538–554.

Dorf, Michael C. 2009. "'The Aspirational Constitution.' George Washington University." *Law Review.* 77: 1631–1671.

Elkins, Zachary, Tom Ginsburg and James Melton. 2009. *The Endurance of National Constitutions.* New York: Cambridge University Press.

Fariss, Christopher. 2014. "Respect for Human Rights Has Improved over Time: Modelling the Changing Standards of Accountability." *American Political Science Review.* 108(2): 297–318.

Finn, John. 1991. *Constitutions in Crisis.* New York: Oxford University Press.

Freedom House. 2010. "Freedom of the Press Country Ratings." Available at https://freedomhouse.org/template.cfm?page=16.

Fruhling, Hugo. 1993. "Human Rights in Constitutional Order and in Political Practice in Latin America." In *Constitutionalism and Democracy: Transitions in the Contemporary World,* ed. Douglas Greenberg et al. New York: Oxford University Press.

Fukuyama, Francis. 2014. *Political Order and Political Decay: From the Industrial Revolution to the Globalization of Democracy.* New York: Farrar, Straus and Giroux.

Ginsburg, Tom. 2003. *Judicial Review in New Democracies.* New York: Cambridge University Press.

Ginsburg, Tom and Alberto Simpser. 2014. "Introduction: Constitutions in Authoritarian Regimes." In *Constitutions in Authoritarian Regimes,* ed.

Tom Ginsburg and Alberto Simpser. New York: Cambridge University Press.

Gleditsch, Kristian S. and Michael D. Ward. 2013. *List of Independent States.* Last modified March 14, 2013. Available at http://privatewww.essex.ac.uk/~ksg/statelist.html.

Hathaway, Oona. 2002. "Do Human Rights Treaties Make a Difference?" *Yale Law Journal.* 111(8): 1935–2042.

Henisz, Witold. 2013. "The Political Constraint Index." Available at www-management.wharton.upenn.edu/henisz/POLCON/ContactInfo.html.

Heston, Alan, Robert Summers and Bettina Aten. 2009. "Penn World Table, Version 6.3." Available at http://pwt.econ.upenn.edu.

Law, David and Mila Versteeg. 2013. "Sham Constitutions." *California Law Review.* 101: 863–952.

McConnell, Michael. 1988. "Textualism and the Dead Hand of the Past." *George Washington University Law Review.* 66: 1127–1209.

Melton, James. 2014. "Do Constitutional Rights Matter? The Relationship between De Jure and De Facto Human Rights Protection." Working Paper. University College London, London.

Ordeshook, Peter C. 1992. "Constitutional Stability." *Constitutional Political Economy.* 3(2): 137–175.

Poe, Steven C., C. Neal Tate and Linda Camp Keith. 1999. "Repression of the Human Right to Personal Integrity Revisited: A Global Cross-National Study Covering the Years 1976–1993." *International Studies Quarterly.* 43 (2): 291–313.

Posner, Richard. 1997. *Aging and Old Age.* Cambridge, MA: Harvard University Press.

Pritchard, Kathleen. 1986. "Comparative Human Rights: An Integrated Explanation." *Politikon: South African Journal of Political Studies.* 13 (2): 24–37.

Rubenfeld, Jeb. 2001. *Freedom and Time: A Theory of Constitutional Self-Government.* New Haven: Yale University Press.

Siegel, Reva. 2002. "She the People: The Nineteenth Amendment, Sex Equality, Federalism and the Family." *Harvard Law Review.* 115: 947–1046.

Strauss, David. 2010. *The Living Constitution.* New York: Oxford University Press.

Varol, Ozan. 2016. "Constitutional Stickiness." *UC Davis Law Review.* 49: 899–961.

Weingast, Barry. 1997. "The Political Foundations of Democracy and the Rule of Law." *American Political Science Review.* 91: 245–263.

10

Competitive democracy and the constitutional minimum core

Rosalind Dixon and David Landau

A central function of a written constitution is to enhance the stability of the political system that underpins it. Constitutions often do this by adopting formal norms of entrenchment, or imposing formal barriers to constitutional change that depend on more than mere legislative majority support. In some systems, political conventions and practices may serve the same function and create effective informal barriers to constitutional change. These formal and informal barriers to change help to protect institutions and values by entrenching them. Thus, recent literature has suggested that one key metric for the success of a constitutional order is its overall "endurance", or capacity to withstand pressures for constitutional change (Elkins, Ginsburg, and Melton 2009).

We argue in this chapter that for those constitutions with a democratic starting point, one important criterion for constitutional success is the degree to which the constitution preserves a minimal or thin conception of competitive democracy. We do not argue that this is the sole criterion for success, but it does allow for relatively structured comparisons across countries and it would be difficult to argue that a constitution failing this criterion has been successful. Thus, constitutional designers and scholars working from a democratic starting point should be most concerned with the endurance of those parts of a democratic constitution protecting this thin version of democracy: what one might call the minimum core of a democratic constitution. The endurance of the minimum core is normatively important in determining constitutional success because the failure to protect the minimum core will lead to the erosion of democracy. However, the desirability of change to the rest of a democratic constitution is more ambiguous from a normative perspective; such change may be harmful, neutral, or even affirmatively beneficial from the standpoint of constitutional theory.

This point has consequences for both the conceptualization and measurement of constitutional change. From a conceptual perspective, it suggests that constitutions are heterogeneous documents with different kinds of levels of provisions, and changes at these different levels have different normative consequences. We distinguish at least two different levels at which constitutions operate: the minimum core and more ordinary law. We define the minimum core of a democratic constitutional order as the set of institutions, procedures, and individual rights that are necessary to maintain a system of multiparty competitive democracy. Modern democratic constitutional design often responds to the importance of this concept by placing certain key provisions of a constitution on a higher tier, requiring more stringent amendment thresholds in order to change those provisions. Constitutional judges also respond to this understanding via doctrines such as the "basic structure", or substitution of the constitution doctrine. Thus, modern constitutional practice recognizes that those parts of the constitution associated with a democratic minimum core have a higher need for protection from change than other parts of the constitution. A major focus of constitutional theory should be on improving the effectiveness of these defences against increasingly sophisticated attacks.

Our point about the contingency of the value of stability on a minimum core of democracy also suggests directions for scholars interested in measuring constitutional change. The relationships between the changes to the democratic minimum core of a constitution and changes to other parts of a constitution are difficult to determine *ex ante*. In some cases, ordinary constitutional changes may be positively correlated with changes to the democratic minimum core via a "coat-tails" effect, but in other cases, negatively correlated due to a "safety valve" effect. The broad quantitative measures found in most existing work, which count any act of constitutional replacement or any constitutional amendment during a given time period, may thus fail to measure relationships between constitutional change and the democratic minimum core.

We therefore suggest ways in which additional measures, some of which have already been used and others of which could be developed, might be used as direct measures of change to the democratic minimum core in quantitative work. At the same time, we recognize that quantitative work on changes to the minimum core will need to be supplemented by qualitative work that focuses on teasing out the complex ways in which change to the constitutional minimum core occurs. Put more broadly, a fully fleshed out theory and measure of constitutional change will need to recognize the different levels at which constitutional change can operate and grapple with the consequences of changes to these different constitutional levels.

The remainder of the chapter is divided into five sections. Section I surveys the existing literature on normative value and measurement of constitutional endurance. Section II defends the use of a minimal or thin conception of competitive democracy as a useful criterion for assessing constitutional success and introduces the constitutional minimum core as a defence of this type of democracy. Section III explores the complex ways in which the constitutional democratic minimum core can be attacked, while Section IV examines the uncertain relationships between changes to the minimum core and broader forms of constitutional change. Finally, Section V considers some ways in which changes to the minimum core might be measured. The chapter concludes by discussing the utility of our criterion of constitutional success – the preservation of a thin notion of competitive democracy through protection of the constitutional minimum core – for related projects.

I THE VALUE OF CONSTITUTIONAL ENDURANCE

Since the writings of James Madison, the endurance of a written constitution is often thought to carry with it a range of benefits: it can facilitate valuable forms of pre-commitment by political actors; help create social and political stability, in a way that helps unify an otherwise divided society; promote the development of ordinary democratic institutions; and promote various instrumental goals such as economic growth and prosperity, by encouraging economic investment (Elkins, Ginsburg, and Melton 2009: 22). Elkins, Ginsburg, and Melton find support for several of these claims in their study of global constitutional endurance. Formal constitutional endurance, they find, is in fact positively correlated with GDP per capita, democracy, and political stability, and (modestly) negatively correlated with crisis propensity (Elkins, Ginsburg, and Melton 2009: 31–32).

Normatively, the attractiveness of constitutional endurance is thus in helping to stabilize a political system, potentially contributing to a range of other goods. In contrast, short-lived constitutions may destabilize political systems and therefore undermine other social and political goods. One might think of this stabilization function as working in two distinct but interrelated ways. First, constitutional stability serves a coordination function – it stops politicians and citizens from constantly needing to suffer the costs of basic redesigns of the political order, which may distract from the achievement of other political and economic goals. Second, constitutional stability serves a preservation function – at least where the starting point is a normatively good one, written constitutions may help to protect institutions and values against destructive forms of change.

Put this way, the argument that constitutional endurance equals constitutional success is at least in part a contingent one. Most obviously, it may depend on starting points. For political systems that are democratic in nature, a commitment to competitive democracy suggests that it will be highly desirable for constitutions to help entrench, or stabilize, existing political arrangements. Doing so will help reduce the transaction costs associated with the process of democratic competition (Eisgruber 2001; cf. Tushnet and Khosla 2015: ch. 1). It will also help guard against the risk that temporary political majorities may seek to use their access to legislative or executive power to insulate themselves from the effects of future competition or create a form of political "monopoly". Constitutional endurance, in this sense, will be a clear normative good.

For authoritarian or hybrid constitutions, in contrast, a commitment to competitive democracy might suggest the opposite normative conclusion. Such systems do not generally allow meaningful competition amongst political parties or elites; hold regular elections, the results of which are decisive of who subsequently holds political power; or allow citizens to vote free from harassment and intimidation and on terms of universal adult suffrage (Ginsburg and Moustafa 2008). In many cases, the text of the constitution itself will also entrench – not simply authorize – such practices (e.g., *Constitution of the Republic of the Union of Myanmar* 2008). Attempts to change a constitution so as to remove such provisions will often be normatively good from a democratic perspective.

Thus, a high degree of entrenchment of constitutional norms – and particularly core provisions – may be a normatively positive feature if one starts from a democratic starting point but a normatively negative feature if one starts from an authoritarian starting point. The challenge of constitutional designers or reformers seeking to democratize an authoritarian regime may instead be in finding the best ways to change core parts of an authoritarian constitution. Often, although not inevitably, formal mechanisms of constitutional change will play an important role in this process, both by serving as a way to remove anti-democratic constitutional features and by preserving newly won democratic gains.

It may also be important to recognize a distinct category of "transitional" constitutions. Many constitutions that help establish the conditions for competitive democracy will be adopted against the backdrop of a history of authoritarian rule. In many countries, authoritarian rulers will also remain formally in control at the time constitutional negotiations take place, or even when final constitutional changes are adopted (Ginsburg and Moustafa 2008). For constitutions to promote democratic outcomes in these circumstances, they will thus need to perform both an important stabilizing and de-stabilizing function. They will need to *stabilize* or entrench the terms of the original political deal to create such a transition, but at the same time ensure that outgoing authoritarian rulers do not themselves attempt to entrench a power sharing-arrangement intended to be temporary in nature. Constitutional endurance in this setting will thus generally be a clear normative good – but only for as long as was agreed to by the original drafters of the transitional context. Sometimes, there may be truly exogenous "shocks", or unanticipated events, that require a modest extension of the timeframe or lifespan of such a constitution. But for the most part, endurance will be a good for such constitutions only for a limited time frame.

The broader point is that the normative value of constitutional stability or endurance depends on starting points. For purposes of the remainder of this chapter, we bracket the distinct challenges posed by authoritarian or transitional constitutions. Following the work of others (Negretto 2012), we focus on the normative assessment and measurement of constitutions which have a democratic starting point.

Analysts also face a distinct problem of measurement. This is because constitutions can change formally both through processes of constitutional amendment and replacement and through processes of informal change. A formal process of amendment will generally involve reliance on a set of defined procedures for change set out in the text of the existing constitution. Elkins, Ginsburg, and Melton (2009: 74) note that more than 90 per cent of constitutions written since 1789 have included formal procedures for constitutional amendment. For something to count as an "amendment", it is generally agreed that it must conform to such procedures. Constitutional replacement, on the other hand, is often carried out by procedures quite different to those required by an existing constitution. Sometimes these procedures may simply involve a raw exercise of political power, by a military leader or would-be autocrat. In other cases, they will involve widespread popular participation, so that the claim to legitimacy for a new constitution lies in the exercise of an ultimate form of "constituent power" by the people themselves (cf. Sieyés 1963; Schmitt 2008; Colon-Rios and Hutchinson 2011).

A simple baseline measure of endurance, used by Elkins, Ginsburg, and Melton, is to say that a constitution has endured in a given year whenever it has not gone through a process of formal replacement. But there are good reasons to think that this measure is both over- and under-inclusive from the standpoint of constitutional endurance. A constitution – or at least its most important provisions – can effectively be "replaced" by masquerading as a process of constitutional amendment. Take the processes of constitutional change that occurred in Indonesia in 1999–2002 and in Egypt in 2012 or 2014. In Indonesia, the "shell" or packaging of the constitution was retained almost entirely unchanged, while a series of amendments to the constitution fundamentally altered the constitutional system, from one based on a highly authoritarian form of executive control to one based on diffuse presidential, parliamentary, judicial, and *popular* control (as well as sub-regional government).[1] Recent episodes of abusive constitutionalism like Fidesz's actions in Hungary likewise suggest that constitutional amendment and replacement are complementary mechanisms, which are often used to achieve similar goals – both pro- and anti-democratic (Bánkuti, Halmai, and Lane Scheppele 2012; Rupnik 2012).

At the same time, the fact of constitutional replacement may tell us relatively little about changes in the content of constitutions, since recent work has suggested that constitutional provisions themselves are often "sticky" even when the constitution itself has been replaced (Varol 2016). In Egypt, for example, the 2012 and 2014 constitutions were both heralded as major constitutional changes in the wake of a democratic revolution (2012) and restoration of military government (2014), but had significant substantive similarities with each other, and with the prior 1971 constitution (Fedtke 2014: 8–9).

For some purposes related to the normative goals of constitutional endurance, there may still be reasons to focus on formal constitutional replacement as an important variable. For example, constitution-making processes themselves may be particularly destabilizing, irrespective of changes in constitutional content. For example, constitution-making processes can be traumatic events that exacerbate political and social cleavages in ways that may be avoided through either constitutional amendment or informal processes of constitutional change (Landau 2013 on Bolivia). Formal constitutional replacement may also encourage changes to fundamental constitutional norms – essentially opening a kind of Pandora's Box – in ways that can be avoided by more pedestrian forms of change. But this is a different argument than the one normally made in the literature, which focuses instead on the content of the constitution rather than on the process by which it was achieved.

Scholars have responded to the problems with the baseline measure by proposing alternatives. One possibility is to measure constitutional endurance or stability by measuring any constitutional change in a given year, rather than simply focusing on replacements (Mila Versteeg and Emily Zackin. 2014.

---

[1] The only change was to their immediate legal significance and interpretation (Butt and Lindsey 2012: 13–14). Another example is Chile, where a range of constitutional amendments were passed between 1989 and 2009 which facilitated and entrenched the transition to democracy, but those changes did not touch the shell of the 1980 authoritarian constitution, or some scholars argue, some of its other important aspects, such as its approach to the role of markets (Couso 2011: 410–414) (arguing that the relevant changes did not touch important areas of ordinary constitutional law in alluding various economic rights and liberties and the "principle of susbsidiarity" which gave priority to private over state action).

Towards an Alternative Theory of Constitutional Design. Unpublished manuscript, University of Maryland). This measure fixes the under-inclusiveness problem, but at the potential cost of being more over-inclusive, for example by defining routine or ministerial constitutional changes as sources of instability. Recent work has also suggested ways to measure the scope or extent of constitutional change, thus potentially moving towards a more refined measure of how much formal constitutional content endures through time.

A more troublesome problem is the issue of informal constitutional change. The most obvious mechanism for this kind of change is judicial: courts can effectively change the effect of a wide variety of constitutional provisions by adopting a new, or altered, interpretation of their meaning. This may be more likely under some conditions, such as older constitutions and more abstract (rather than specific and rule-like) language (Strauss 1996). But informal change can also be carried out through the work of the other branches of government. An increasing body of work in the United States recognizes the role of particular key statutes, or "super-statutes", in creating quasi-constitutional or small "c" forms of constitutional change (Ackerman 2014; Eskridge and Ferejohn 2001). Statutes of this kind not only address key issues of the allocation of government power, fundamental rights, but also tend to have the same capacity as formally entrenched constitutional provisions to stabilize certain political arrangements or understandings.[2]

Finally, a range of executive actions may affect important informal changes to the constitutions. In many countries, constitutions allow the executive to impose a state of emergency and impose varying degrees of checks on this power. Where the executive declares an emergency it will also often have broad freedom to suspend the operation of the range of constitutional structures and guarantees. In some cases, these changes may only be temporary: after the relevant emergency ends, ordinary constitutional norms may revive, and the emergency period simply be treated as a period of "exception" with no impact on the meaning or operation of the constitution in ordinary times (e.g., Jackson J in *Youngstown Sheet & Tube Co v. Sawyer*, 343 U.S. 579, 1952). But in other cases, the emergency declaration itself – and accompany policies – may serve to create long-term changing constitutional norms.

---

[2] In some cases, the formal text of a constitution will explicitly authorize this kind of legislative change from the outset: as one of us notes with Tom Ginsburg in prior work, many constitutions contain certain "by law" clauses, which expressly delegate power to determine (and thus change) constitutional norms to the legislature (Dixon and Ginsburg 2011). Changes are made to statutes authorized or contemplated by law causes of this kind; there will thus so often be an argument that the relevant change is constitutional in nature.

Similarly, executive actors or ordinary circumstances may sometimes attempt to achieve certain forms of "workaround" in respect of formal constitutional requirements, which if successful can create new informal understandings as to the scope of permissible executive action under the constitution (Tushnet 2009). A good example in the United States is the creation by the executive of the idea of a congressional-executive agreement: the difficulty of obtaining the two-thirds majority of votes in the Senate necessary to ratify an international treaty in the United States led to the creation of a new category of international agreement, extremely similar to a treaty but different in name, which the executive can obtain ratification for with only an ordinary majority vote in both houses of Congress.

Informal change suggests an important challenge from the standpoint of measuring endurance: it is extremely difficult to track, at least through large-N quantitative methods. In some cases, the presence of informal change may suggest that constitutional norms have effectively shifted despite the absence of formal amendment or replacement. In other cases, informal change may work together with formal amendment or replacement to alter the significance or scope of those formal changes.

In the remainder of this chapter, we argue for an additional mechanism that ought to affect the normative assessment and measurement of constitutional change: constitutions are not homogenous documents, but rather contain different types or kinds of provisions. This point raises some familiar challenges, like the link between formal and informal change, as well as some new ones.

II THE MINIMUM CORE OF A DEMOCRATIC CONSTITUTION

Recent work in constitutional theory suggests that constitutions operate at a number of different levels of layers, and we suggest that constitutional change should be theorized differently across these distinct layers. The argument that certain elements of a constitutional text are a more fundamental form of higher law than others is now well established in comparative constitutional law and doctrine. This assumption is embodied in the doctrine of unconstitutional constitutional amendment, which as noted by Roznai (2013) has been one of the most successful exports in comparative constitutional theory. In Colombia, the Constitutional Court has held that there is a clear distinction between amendments to the constitution, which can be passed by referendum or a constituent assembly under Articles 374–378, and a "substitution" of the constitution, which the Court has suggested is an original exercise of constituent power (Bernal 2013). In India, Supreme Court has held that the power of amendment under Article 368 of the Indian Constitution does not allow Parliament to alter the "basic structure" of the constitution, in part because such a change would amount to a wholescale "revision" or replacement, rather than mere amendment, of the constitution (Jacobsohn 2006; Neuborne 2003).

This assumption is also embodied in the increasingly widespread practice of tiering constitutional provisions through constitutional design. Some constitutions make certain provisions unamendable; many others include different processes by which different pieces of the constitution might be changed. The California Constitution, for example, draws a clear distinction between "amendments" and "revisions": amendments can be passed by way of popular initiative; whereas revisions require additional legislative approval. The way in which the California Supreme Court has defined this distinction is also in terms of the breadth of the relevant change, or the degree to which it departs from the "fundamental principles" implicit in a free society. Other constitutional texts explicitly identify certain provisions or parts of the constitution as requiring a more demanding procedure for change.

Constitutional theory suggests that the basic structure of a constitution is defined by those provisions, values, and principles seen as fundamental to the constitutional order by those who are designing and interpreting it. What we call the minimum core of a democratic constitution is a related (but not identical) concept: the minimum core is composed of those elements of a democratic constitution that are required to preserve competitive democracy. The minimum core of a democratic constitution is thus almost invariably bound to be a part of that constitution's basic structure. The Colombian Constitutional Court, for example, in Decision C-141 of 2010, struck down an attempt by President Alvaro Uribe to amend the constitution and allow three consecutive presidential terms on the ground that that amendment "substituted" the Colombian Constitution by practically eliminating horizontal checks on the power of incumbent presidents and making the electoral playing field much less equal. At the same time, the basic structure may contain other elements that are idiosyncratic to particular national traditions and are not necessary to maintain competitive democracy.

Defining the minimum core of a democratic constitution of course depends on one's conception of democracy, which is itself a notoriously complex and contested idea. For some political theorists, democracy involves a thick set of commitments to processes of deliberation. For "deliberative democrats", the exercise of public power will only be legitimate where it is the product of processes of deliberation that are held in public, and open to all citizens on terms of substantive equality (Ackerman and Fishkin 2005; Gutmann and

Thompson 2004; Habermas 1994; Habermas 1998). For others, democracy entails an equally thick, but more substantive, set of commitments, to individual rights and political equality (Dworkin 2008), or a set of "constitutional essentials" which include basic liberties for all citizens, and substantively equal political rights or liberties (Rawls 1999; Rawls 2013). Other theorists, in contrast, reject these ideas as implicit in the idea of democracy itself, and suggest that they are better treated as a separate set of substantive political ideas or commitments, related to notions of *liberal* or constitutional democracy, rather than democracy *per se* (Posner 2005).

Almost all democratic theorists, however, agree that, at a minimum, the idea of democracy entails a basic set of commitments to regular free and fair elections, in which rival political elites compete for access to democratic office, and citizens have the ultimate right to decide the relevant context – by casting a vote, free of intimidation or harassment, on the basis of universal adult suffrage.[3] This is the basic idea of democracy implicit in Schumpeter's (2013) notion of "competitive democracy", and Schumpeter himself clearly saw it as sufficient for meaningful democracy (see Issacharoff, Karan, and Pildes 2012; Issacharoff and Pildes 1998; Schleicher 2006). Other theorists directly challenge this claim of sufficiency: but few, if any, challenge the claim that these conditions are at least necessary for democracy.

A minimalist, competitive understanding of democracy therefore provides a useful *normative* benchmark for making judgements about constitutional performance across a wide variety of constitutional systems. It not only has the advantage of being based on normative commitments or understandings that are widely shared amongst political theorists with otherwise quite different perspectives, but is also sufficiently "thin" in content to allow for relatively objective empirical judgements about constitutional "success" or "failure" (Rawls 1999 on transparency as a criterion for constitutional and political theory). For constitutions with a democratic starting point, the preservation of this minimalist conception of democracy is therefore a useful and important criterion of constitutional success. It seems at least to be a necessary (if not sufficient) criterion for constitutional success.

From this perspective, the minimum core of the constitution likely includes the core set of institutions, procedures, and individual rights that are necessary to maintain a system of multiparty competitive democracy itself. The contents of this aspect of a constitution will, of course, necessarily vary from one country

---

[3] It is worth noting that not all theorists agree about the goal of even minimal conceptions of democracy. For example, while some theorists may seek to maximize party competition, others may emphasize alignment between the policy preferences of the electorate and their representatives (Stephanopoulos 2014). For our purposes, these distinctions are unimportant.

to the next. But we have suggested elsewhere that it will often have a strong degree of commonality across countries or include some international, or at least regional, constitutional "minimum core" (Dixon and Landau 2015; Landau and Dixon 2015). On a global scale, it is possible to identify provisions that almost all constitutional democracies seem to regard as fundamental, or include within the scope of either capital "C" or small "c" constitutional norms. Together, such provisions might be regarded as constituting something like an international democratic "minimum core", or an overlapping consensus amongst countries as to the minimum content of any "basic structure" of a domestic constitution.

A good example of the kinds of provisions that will be included in this category are those that European Union (EU) member states have agreed to, as part of the Copenhagen principles, as necessary preconditions for accession to the EU. The EU accession criteria include a commitment to democracy, the rule of law, human rights, and respect for and protection of minorities. But in respect of democracy itself, the EU has held that, at minimum, this requires: free elections with a secret ballot, the right to establish political parties without any hindrance from the state, fair and equal access to a free press, free trade union organizations, freedom of personal opinion, and executive powers restricted by laws and allowing free access to judges independent of the executive (Emerson 2005; Pridham 2002; Raik 2004).

Constitutional law in a democracy will also comprise a vast array of other kinds of provisions, many of which have little direct connection to competitive democracy. What one might call the "shell" or outer packaging of a constitution will often have important symbolic or expressive value for citizens, without those values being part of the constitution's basic structure (on expressive values, see Anderson and Pildes 2000; Albert 2013). A constitution's shell can also play a key role in setting the procedural rules for legislative, judicial and executive action, and for constitutional change: but the substance of the particular rules adopted in this context will not be fundamental to democracy, only the existence of some set of rules that can provide the basis for effective political co-ordination (Ginsburg 2013; Hardin 1989; McAdams 2015). Democratic constitutions will also often contain a range of provisions designed to promote the rule of law and individual rights, or more "maximal" conceptions of democracy. While important, many of these provisions will also go beyond what is necessary to preserve a system of competitive democracy.

The endurance of these different layers of a constitution will have quite different significance from the perspective of a commitment to competitive democracy. In a democratic system, the endurance of the minimum core of the constitution will generally be critical to protecting a competitive democratic system: preserving the stability of this layer of the constitution will not only be instrumental to promoting or protecting democracy, it will actually be necessary to preserve democracy itself in most cases. But the same does not necessarily apply to ordinary aspects of constitutional law. In a deliberative understanding of democracy, there will often be intrinsic reasons to value stability (or change) at all levels of a democratic constitution, particularly in the overall "packaging" of a constitution. If a constitution, for instance, is drafted via inclusive and participatory processes, there may be good reason to preserve the results of that deliberation – because the understanding is that deliberation may only be possible in such "constitutional moments", and not in ordinary politics (Ackerman 1993; Ackerman 2000). Conversely, in some cases, there may be good reason for allowing amendment as a means of trumping or overriding decisions of courts, which interpret existing constitutional language in ways that a majority (or super-majority) of citizens deem unreasonable or unworkable. Often, there will be few other formal mechanisms that can allow such democratic input to occur, and the premise of deliberative democratic theory is that such input is necessary for legitimacy, in the context of issues open to a range of reasonable viewpoints.

In a thinner, competitive view of democracy, however, these concerns are largely irrelevant: the concern is to ensure that the constitution provides for, and entrenches, the minimum requisites for effective political competition. To go beyond that, and insist that constitutions should promote and enshrine citizen deliberation or participation, is to build in the kind of contested assumptions about the nature of democracy, or political consent and legitimacy, that as a thin or "consensus" theory of democracy, a competitive theory of democracy seeks to avoid. In a competitive theory of democracy, therefore, the only layer of a democratic constitution where we can make confident claims about the desirability of constitutional endurance is at the level of the constitution's minimum core. For other layers of the constitution, the question will be far more contingent – and instrumental. In this setting, the key question will be whether a particular constitutional change respects the outer bounds of what is reasonable and necessary to preserve the minimum core of the constitution; and if it does, whether allowing the particular change is ultimately likely to increase, or decrease, the chances of future change to the more fundamental level of the minimum core of the democratic system as a whole.

III   THE VARIETY OF THREATS TO THE CONSTITUTIONAL MINIMUM CORE

Modern constitutions respond to the importance of the minimum core of the constitution in a variety of ways. As noted earlier, constitutional designers often place certain constitutional provisions or principles on higher tiers, making them more difficult to change by constitutional amendment. In the extreme, a provision may be made completely unamendable (Albert 2010). In alternative, or in addition, judges may develop variants of a "basic structure" doctrine and thus block constitutional amendments that are perceived to impinge on the minimum core (Roznai 2013). In a more inchoate form, some scholars have suggested variants of ex ante and ex post protections as ways to defend the minimum core against certain forms of constitutional replacement. We have argued elsewhere that the choice between ex ante and ex post protections is a trade-off – more specific, ex ante protections may be easier for judges to enforce, but ex post doctrines like the basic structure doctrine may prove more flexible against unexpected threats (Landau and Dixon 2015). At any rate, the mechanisms can be complementary, and it may be wise for constitutional designers and judges to use both.

An important question in the field involves measuring and assessing the extent to which these tools are actually effective at limiting attempts to alter the minimum core. The answer to these questions is complicated by two factors. First, constitutional changes that impact the minimum core can be carried out in a number of different ways: by combinations of constitutional amendment and replacement, and through combinations of formal and informal change. Second, these attacks often rely on the aggregative effect of different changes, and it is the interaction effect (rather than any single change) that produces the impact on the minimum core.

In Venezuela, for example, President Chavez upon taking power in 1998 used a constitutional replacement process controlled by him to sweep the institutional order clean and to shut down institutions still allied with the opposition, as well as to entrench more power in the presidency (Segura and Bejarano 2004). The Constituent Assembly elected in 1999 claimed to wield "original constituent power" and used this power to shut down the Supreme Court and most of Congress and remove local and union officials while ratifying Chavez in office (Brewer Carias 2010a). The constitution also increased presidential power at the expense of other institutions (particularly the Congress). President Chavez subsequently used amendment to increase presidential power further, for example by holding a referendum to eliminate presidential term limits in 2009.

There were potential constitutional limits on both of these efforts. During the 1999 constitutional replacement, for example, the Supreme Court issued several rulings holding that Chavez could go forward with the replacement because the people held "constituent power", but that he would need to be guided by limits or principles derived from the existing constitution (see Caso:

Gerardo Blyde, contra la Resolucion N. 990217–32 del Consejo Nacional Electoral (17–2–99), March 18, 1999 (Supreme Court of Justice, Political-Administrative Chamber)). These rulings ultimately did not succeed in imposing meaningful limits on the constitutional replacement process: The Assembly, for example, was selected through an electoral rule picked by Chavez and which allowed him to gain over 90 per cent of seats with under two-thirds of votes (Segura and Bejarano 2004). Subsequently, the successful referendum eliminating term limits was challenged using the "tiering" provisions found in the new text. These provisions suggested that changes to the fundamental principles of the constitution would need to follow at least a more demanding method of change (most likely, a Constituent Assembly) rather than the simpler procedure for "constitutional amendment". But the Court rejected that argument and allowed the amendment procedure to be used (Brewer-Carias 2010b).

The fact that these checks failed was caused in part by another aspect of Chavez's undermining of Venezuelan democracy: it depended on combinations of formal and informal methods of change. He often used corruption and other methods to undermine aspects of the institutional order that were designed to check his power. For example, the civil society commission that was supposed to select members of the judiciary under the 1999 Constitution was effectively never set up, and Chavez controlled those appointments directly (Brewer-Carias 2010a). Further, Chavez used both formal and informal methods to control the media, making it more difficult for the opposition to mobilize effectively against the referendum. Thus, the 2009 referendum was decided on a playing field tilted towards Chavez, and with a court that was controlled by him.

President Correa's actions in Ecuador have been somewhat similar. After winning election, he replaced the constitution in 2008 in an assembly that he controlled, which allowed him to pack key institutions, strengthen the presidency, and pursue ideological goals (Conaghan 2008). Correa is in the process of passing a constitutional amendment eliminating term limits, after deriding such a measure as "absurd" during the constitutional replacement process. And his actions, as in the Venezuelan case, rest on complex combinations of formal and informal change. For example, Correa has used his power over electoral institutions and the media to marginalize opposition groups. And he used his hegemony in the Constitutional Court to gain a ruling that the elimination of term limits could be pursued using the standard amendment procedures, rather than a more demanding procedure, despite a constitutional text requiring that constitutional changes that alter the basic structure or undermine fundamental rights utilize the more demanding routes of constitutional revision or constituent assembly (Landau 2015).

A second problem is that constitutional changes often impact the minimum core through a series of complex interaction effects. The process of constitutional change in Hungary under the Fidesz party (which took power in 2010) is a paradigmatic example (Bánkuti, Halmai, and Scheppele 2012). The process of change in Hungary bears many of the hallmarks pointed out elsewhere – it combined amendment and replacement, as well as formal and informal methods of constitutional change. After gaining power with a simple majority of votes but over two-thirds of seats, the party began amending the constitution to undermine key institutions like the Constitutional Court. It then engaged in wholesale constitutional replacement; the new constitution weakened checking institutions designed to rein in electoral majorities and made it harder to dislodge the party from power. Further, Fidesz has again relied on a combination of formal and informal methods of change to undermine institutions like the judiciary and to take control of the media.

The Hungarian case is also noteworthy because the new constitutional order in Hungary constitutes what Kim Lane Scheppele (2013) calls a "frankenstate" – the erosion of democracy is dependent not on any single institution but in the combination of elements into a whole. That is, the new Hungarian institutional order contains a number of elements, such as a reduced judicial retirement age, more limited jurisdiction for the Constitutional Court, and gerrymandered districts, that are seen as somewhat problematic for democracy, but are all, on an individual basis, found elsewhere. Indeed, Fidesz has defended these changes on precisely that basis. Scheppele (2013) argues that it is not any one of these changes, working in isolation, that is producing democratic erosion in Hungary, but rather the combination of effects produced by all of these changes.

These elements pose a challenge both of democratic design and of measurement. From the standpoint of designers interested in protecting the minimum core, it suggests the potential limitations of constitutional defence mechanisms. Would-be authoritarian actors may be able to shift between different forms of change – amendment, replacement, and informal methods – and to rely on complex interaction effects in order to evade limitations. There is thus great uncertainty about the effectiveness of constitutional defences like the unconstitutional constitutional amendment doctrine against these threats. From the standpoint of measurement, these problems made it difficult to assess how a given program of change is actually impacting the minimum core. We return to these difficulties, and suggest some modest solutions, below.

IV   CONSTITUTIONAL CHANGE AND THE MINIMUM CORE

A related question, linked to the problem of measurement, is determining how changes to the minimum core are linked to broader programs of constitutional change to other parts of the constitution. Here too, there is significant uncertainty, since from a theoretical perspective, the relationship between broader constitutional changes and the constitutional minimum core is indeterminate. Change to a constitution's ordinary provisions, or packaging, and change to its basic structure may be positively correlated due to a "coat-tails" effect or negatively correlated due to a "safety valve" effect. There is no reliable way to determine which of these two effects is likely to dominate in any given case.

In democratic elections, a "coat-tails effect" is the tendency for a particular popular individual candidate to help win votes for other candidates, from the same political party, or for issues supported by that party (Samuels 2000). In some settings, successful constitutional changes may have the same capacity to increase chances of other constitutional change: change in one context may help increase support for change in other contexts, either simultaneously or over time. Where constitutional changes are proposed simultaneously, this form of spillover effect will follow exactly the same logic as for ordinary democratic elections: support for a popular candidate may have an indirect capacity to increase support for a less popular candidate running on the same political "ticket". Democratic actors may attempt to exploit this effect in order to increase support for otherwise unpopular constitutional changes. In some cases, this kind of strategic "bundling" of proposed constitutional changes may be used by political elites to erode a democratic constitution's minimum core: political leaders seeking to increase their power may combine changes to a constitution's minimum core with more routine – and popular – changes to other aspects of a constitution, such as provisions dealing with individual rights. The 2008 Constitution of Ecuador perhaps offers an example: President Correa packaged symbolically important provisions on individual and environmental rights with a much more controversial – but important – set of provisions altering the structure of the state, entrenching presidential power, and marginalizing the opposition (Whittemore 2011).

Where changes are more spread out or sequential, the logic of this kind of spillover effect may be somewhat different. Some forms of constitutional change may pave the way for later change by lowering the formal threshold for amendment. Others may encourage proponents of constitutional change to increase their efforts at political mobilization: their initial success may increase their sense that other changes are actually achievable, and thus worth expending time and resources campaigning for in the medium to long term. Alternatively, some types of constitutional change may increase the dependence of government actors on particular interest groups in a society, so that the government is then under increased pressure to respond to demands from those groups for further constitutional change, while others may reduce the power of existing players to "veto" further constitutional change.[4] In democratic systems in particular, successful instances of constitutional change may also have the capacity to alter public attitudes towards constitutional amendment processes generally – by making the process of amendment itself seem more routine, familiar, or legitimate.[5] All of these connections may support a positive correlation between ordinary constitutional changes and changes to the constitutional minimum core.

However, some variant of a "safety valve" dynamic seems equally plausible, and such a dynamic suggests a negative rather than positive correlation between forms of constitutional change. Many scholars suggest that constitutions that provide for relatively flexible processes of constitutional amendment are less likely to be subject to formal constitutional replacement, because the ability to update the constitution lessens political pressure for new constitution-making. Large-N studies support this hypothesis: Elkins, Ginsburg, and Melton, for instance, find that constitutions that are relatively easy to amend are less likely to be replaced, across both democracies and non-democracies, than those that are more difficult to amend (Elkins, Ginsburg, and Melton 2009).[6] The same kind of dynamic may also operate across different levels of constitutional change: change to ordinary forms of constitutional law may forestall or lessen demands for change to a constitution's basic structure, whereas failure to achieve such change may increase pressure on the basic structure (what one might call a "pressure cooker" effect).

How these two effects likely balance out, in any given context, will be hard to predict. Each dynamic depends on political conditions that are highly local

---

[4] This was perhaps part of the logic of the initial Hungarian constitutional amendments that aimed to contract the jurisdiction of the Constitutional Court, thus making it less able to stop subsequent statutory and constitutional changes. Bánkuti, Halmai, and Scheppele (2012).

[5] For example, Ginsburg and Melton (2015) find that the frequency of amendment under the prior constitution in a given country (what they call "amendment culture") has a more significant impact on current frequency of amendment than the difficulty of the current formal constitutional amendment rule. This finding has a number of possible interpretations, but might suggest that over time, frequent amendments alter public consciousness in a way that makes subsequent amendments more likely.

[6] Consistent with our hypothesis, however, the effect is not entirely linear: constitutions that are both extremely easy and hard to amend are less likely to endure, than those that are moderately flexible: Elkins, Ginsburg, and Melton (2009: 140). In contrast, Negretto in a study of Latin American constitutions finds a linear relationship that more frequently amended constitutions are less likely to be replaced (Negretto 2012: 771).

and contingent and open to rapid evolution or change. In many cases, they will also be the subject of deliberate manipulation by non-democratic actors seeking to retain or gain greater power, so that there are significant information asymmetries, or imbalances, between non-democratic and democratic actors as to the likely operation of these dynamics. Because the nature of these correlations is so unclear, broad measures of constitutional change cannot be considered reliable measures of change to the minimum core.

V MEASURING CHANGE TO THE MINIMUM CORE

As we have noted above, scholars interested in competitive democracy should not view all changes to democratic constitutions equally. Some kinds of constitutional change – those to what we call the constitutional minimum core – are indeed deeply threatening to democracy, regardless of whether they are carried out formally or informally, or by constitutional amendment or replacement. The normative impact of other kinds of constitutional change is more difficult to evaluate. This insight complicates the measurement of constitutional change.

It suggests first that the homogenous measures of constitutional change which make up much of the existing empirical literature are not effectively measuring changes to the constitutional minimum core. As noted above, most existing work focuses on broad measures of amendment or replacement, say by counting incidents of formal replacement or years in which constitutional amendments have occurred. These different measures embody a complex mix of trade-offs about how to measure the magnitude of constitutional change. But a key problem with all these approaches from the perspective of a constitution's minimum core is that it is hard to predict how general changes to a constitution will relate to more specific changes to its minimum core. As a formal matter, the replacement of a constitution only requires change to a constitution's shell or packaging, and may or may not involve change to the constitutional minimum core. Similarly, formal constitutional amendments may be directed to ordinary constitutional laws or to a constitution's minimum core. And as noted above, the cross-cutting nature of coat-tails versus safety-valve effects makes it dangerous to theorize about the relationship between broader constitutional change and change to the constitutional minimum core.

One helpful approach would be to seek more refined versions of these broader or indirect measures. It may be possible to code the degree of constitutional change in an amendment or replacement rather than just coding amendment or replacement as a binary variable. For example, Ginsburg and Melton (2015) measure the extent of constitutional change by asking whether a constitution's coding on a large number of different dimensions is the same or different after an amendment has been passed. They find that many amendments result in little or no change to the different dimensions on which they are coding constitutions, while others result in changes to at least a significant subset of those dimensions. The utility of such an approach, for our purposes, depends on the mechanisms used both to divide constitutions into different bins and to code changes to those bins, and to the theoretical relationship between broad constitutional changes and changes to the minimum core.

Other indirect measures may also prove fruitful. For example, one could imagine constructing a "frequency model", which seeks to predict the normal rate of amendment for a constitution with given characteristics, in order to identify instances in which a constitution is being amended more frequently than is average in ways that might suggest some potential attempt at revisionary, rather than merely "ordinary", constitutional change. Such an approach would pose similar challenges at the level of coding and theory.

An alternative approach is to measure changes to the minimum core of a constitution more directly. To do this, one would need to code various provisions of a constitution belonging inside or outside the minimum core. Such a task would clearly go beyond the existing efforts at coding global constitutions and would involve difficult exercises of evaluative judgment. These objections, however, need not be overwhelming. As we noted earlier in Section II, the constitutional minimum core is one that can be gleaned from the regional and international practices of organizations like the Venice Commission. Some examples of relevant provisions would include those defining the form of government, the method of election and term of the chief executive, and the method of selection and jurisdiction of the high court. Comparative constitutional scholars could attempt to track changes to this particular subset of provisions. Scholars could then track whether a particular set of amendments changed these provisions or whether a formal constitutional replacement actually affected them. The Ginsburg and Melton approach noted above, which measures changes along a large number of different dimensions or bins, could be very useful for this purpose. In the political science literature, a number of scholars have also already begun the task of coding constitutional provisions according to their relationship to democracy (e.g., Cheibub 2011; Cheibub and Chemykh 2007).

All of these approaches have promise in measuring change to the democratic minimum core.[7] They would potentially help to test important

---

[7] For some purposes, an alternative measure of the state of the minimum core may be to look at changes in a country's level of democracy directly. Many such measures exist in political science. See, e.g., *Uniform Democracy Scores*, at www.unified-democracy-scores.org/.

hypotheses within the field, for example the question of whether mechanisms of democratic defence like the banning of undemocratic parties (militant democracy), the placement of certain provisions on higher constitutional tiers or unamendable tiers, or the basic structure doctrine actually protect the core institutions of competitive democracy in practice. However, the complex ways in which constitutional change of this type occurs suggest that quantitative work in this area must be supplemented by in-depth qualitative case studies. This is chiefly because of two characteristics of change to the minimum core, noted above in Section III: it often depends on a mix of formal and informal means, and it often depends on the interaction of a number of different constitutional provisions or areas, which vary across time and place. Neither of these two problems is likely to be effectively captured even by more refined data collection or quantitative measures.

VI   CONCLUSION

Unlike many chapters in this volume, we suggest that it is possible to identify a broadly shared criterion for assessing constitutional performance – i.e., the degree to which a constitution has served to promote some relatively thin or minimal concept of democracy, which involves free and fair elections and competition between rival political parties. Such a competitive notion of democracy certainly does not exhaust what is necessary for democratic success. But it does provide a relatively thin criterion for measuring constitutional success, which we believe most reasonable citizens (or constitutional scholars) could reasonably be expected to endorse.

Utilizing this kind of commitment to competitive democracy as a criterion for judging democratic success, or failure, however, necessarily requires distinguishing different forms of constitutional starting points, as well as disentangling different parts of a constitution. It is impossible to measure success according to this criterion without first understanding whether a constitution begins life as democratic, authoritarian, or transitional in nature. And even for democratic constitutions, it requires distinguishing the minimum core of a constitution from its other parts, since the minimum core is vital for the persistence of competitive democracy while the remaining parts of the constitution may not be.

This modest point also has broader significance both for the measurement of constitutional change and at the theoretical level. From the perspective of measurement, it suggests that broad measures of constitutional change may miss the relationship between constitutional change and democracy and point towards plausible refinements, both qualitative and quantitative, that could be implemented by researchers. And at the theoretical level, the disentangling of constitutional provisions into more refined pieces helps to draw attention to those aspects of constitutional design that are fundamental for success and may allow us to test the effectiveness of those features. For example, we still know too little about whether constitutional tiering and the unconstitutional constitutional amendment doctrine actually work to ward off threats to the minimum core.

Finally, a focus on more precise measures of success forces us to consider the relationship between constitutionalism and different forms of democracy. Constitutional designers may make different recommendations, or at least emphasize different features, depending on whether they are seeking to achieve a more minimal or more maximal conception of democracy. Thus, adopting more nuanced definitions both of constitutional change and of constitutional success will help scholars to develop richer theories of the relationship between constitutionalism and social and political goals.

REFERENCES

Ackerman, Bruce and James S. Fishkin. 1993. *We the People: Transformations*, vol. 1. Harvard, US: Harvard University Press.
   2000. *We the People: Transformations*, vol. 2. Harvard, US: Harvard University Press.
   2005. *Deliberation Day*. Yale, US: Yale University Press.
   2014. *We the People: The Civil Rights Revolution*, vol. 3. Harvard, US: Harvard University Press.
Albert, Richard. 2010. Constitutional Handcuffs. *Arizona State Law Journal* 42: 663–716.
   2013. The Expressive Function of Constitutional Amendment Rules. *McGill Law Journal* 59: 225–281.
Anderson, Elizabeth S. and Richard H. Pildes. 2000. Expressive Theories of Law: A General Restatement. *University of Pennsylvania Law Review* 148: 1503–1575.
Bánkuti, Miklós, Gábor Halmai and Kim Lane Scheppele. 2012. Hungary's Illiberal Turn: Dismantling the Constitution. *Journal of Democracy* 23: 138–146.
Bernal, Carlos. 2013. Unconstitutional Constitutional Amendments in the Case Study of Colombia: An Analysis of the Justification and Meaning of the Constitutional Replacement Doctrine. *International Journal of Constitutional Law* 11(2): 339–357.
Brewer-Carias, Allan R. 2010a. *Dismantling Democracy in Venezuela: The Chávez Authoritarian Experiment*. Cambridge, UK: Cambridge University Press.

2010b. Reforma constitucional y fraude a la Constitution: el caso de Venezuela 1999–2009. In *La Reforma Constitucional: Sus implicaciones juridicas y politicas en el context comparado*, edited by Pedro Rubén Torres Estrada and Michael Núñez Torres. Mexico City, Mexico: Editorial Porrua.

Butt, Simon and Tim Lindsey. 2012. *The Constitution of Indonesia: A Contextual Analysis*. Oxford, UK: Hart Publishing.

Caso: Gerardo Blyde, contra la Resolucion N. 990217-32 del Consejo Nacional Electoral (17-2-99), March 18, 1999 (Supreme Court of Justice, Political-Administrative Chamber), *in* REVISTA DEL DERECHO PUBLICO, nos. 77–80, January–December 1999.

Cheibub, Jose Antonio. 2011. Economic Development and Democratization. In *The Dynamics of Democratization: Dictatorship, Development, and Diffusion*, edited by Nathan J. Brown. Baltimore, US: John Hopkins University Press.

Cheibub, Jose Antonio and Svitlana Chernykh. 2007. Constitutions and Democratic Performance in Semi-Presidential Democracies. *Japanese Journal of Political Science* 9(3): 269–303.

Colon-Rios, Joel and Allan C. Hutchinson. 2011. Democracy and Constitutional Change. *Theoria: A Journal of Social and Political Theory* 127: 43–62.

Conaghan, Catherine M. 2008. Ecuador: Correa's Plebiscitary Presidency. *Journal of Democracy* 19(2): 46–60.

Couso, Javier. 2011. Trying Democracy in the Shadow of an Authoritarian Legality: Chile's Transition to Democracy and Pinochet's Constitution of 1980. *Wisconsin International Law Journal* 29(2): 393–415.

Dixon, Rosalind and David Landau. 2015. Transnational Constitutionalism and a Limited Doctrine of Unconstitutional Constitutional Amendment. *International Journal of Constitutional Law* 13: 606–638.

Dixon, Rosalind and Tom Ginsburg. 2011. Deciding Not to Decide: Deferral in Constitutional Design. *International Journal of Constitutional Law* 9: 636–672.

Dworkin, Ronald. 2008. *Is Democracy Possible Here? Principles for a New Political Debate*. Princeton, US: Princeton University Press.

Eisgruber, Christopher L. 2001. *Constitutional Self-Government*. Harvard, US: Harvard University Press.

Elkins, Zachary, Tom Ginsburg and James Melton. 2009. *The Endurance of National Constitutions*. Cambridge, UK: Cambridge University Press.

Emerson, Michael (ed.). 2005. *Democratisation in the European Neighbourhood*. Brussels, UK: Centre for European Policy Studies.

Eskridge, William N. and John Ferejohn. 2001. Super-Statutes. *Duke Law Journal* 50: 1215–1276.

Fedtke, Jörg. 2014. *Comparative Analysis between the Constitutional Processes in Egypt and Tunisia – Lessons Learnt – Overview of the Constitutional Situation in Libya.* Belgium: European Union.

Ginsburg, Tom. 2013. Constitutions as Contract, Constitutions as Charter. In *Social and Political Foundations of Constitutions,* edited by Denis J. Galligan and Mila Versteeg. Cambridge, UK: Cambridge University Press.

Ginsburg, Tom and James Melton. 2015. Does the Constitutional Amendment Rule Matter at All? Amendment Cultures and the Challenges of Measuring Amendment Difficulty. *International Journal of Constitutional Law* 13: 686–713.

Ginsburg, Tom and Tamir Moustafa (eds.). 2008. *Rule by Law: The Politics of Courts in Authoritarian Regimes.* Cambridge, UK: Cambridge University Press.

Gutmann, Amy and Dennis Thompson. 2004. *Why Deliberative Democracy.* Princeton, US: Princeton University Press.

Habermas, Jürgen. 1994. Three Normative Models of Democracy. *Constellations* 1(1): 1–10.

   1998. *Between Facts and Norms: Contributions to a Discourse Theory of Law and Democracy,* translated by William Rehg. Cambridge, UK: MIT Press.

Hardin, Russel. 1989. Why a Constitution? In *The Federalist Papers and the New Institutionalism,* edited by Bernard Grofman and Donald Wittman. New York, US: Agathon Press.

Issacharoff, Samuel and Richard H. Pildes. 1998. Politics as Markets: Partisan Lockups of the Democratic Process. *Stanford Law Review* 50: 643–717.

Issacharoff, Samuel, Paula S. Karan and Richard H. Pildes. 2012. *The Law of Democracy: Legal Structure of the Political Process,* 4th edition. Westbury, Australia: Foundation Press.

Jacobsohn, Gary. 2006. An Unconstitutional Constitution? A Constitutional Perspective. *International Journal of Constitutional Law* 4: 460–487.

Landau, David. 2013. Constitution-Making Gone Wrong. *Alabama Law Review* 64: 923–980.

   2015. Term Limits Manipulation across Latin America – And What Constitutional Design Could Do about It. Constitutionnet, July 21. At: www.constitutionnet.org/news/term-limits-manipulation-across-latin-america-and-what-constitutional-design-could-do-about-it.

Landau, David and Rosalind Dixon. 2015. Constraining Constitutional Change. *Wake Forest Law Review* 50: 859–890.

Lane Scheppele, Kim. 2013. The Rule of Law and the Frankenstate: Why Governance Checklists Do Not Work. *Governance* 26: 559–562.

McAdams, Richard A. 2015. *The Expressive Powers of Law: Theories and Limits.* Harvard, US: Harvard University Press.

Negretto, Gabriel. 2012. Replacing and Amending Constitutions: The Logic of Constitutional Change in Latin America. *Law & Society Review* 46: 749–779.

Neuborne, Bert. 2003. The Supreme Court of India. *International Journal of Constitutional Law* 1: 476–510.

Posner, Richard A. 2005. *Law, Pragmatism, and Democracy*. Harvard, US: Harvard University Press.

Pridham, Geoffrey. 2002. EU Enlargement and Consolidating Democracy in Post-Communist States – Formality and Reality. *JCMS* 40(5): 953–973.

Raik, Kristi. 2004. EU Accession of Central and Eastern European Countries: Democracy and Integration as Conflicting Logics. *East European Politics and Societies* 18(4): 567–594.

Rawls, John. 1999. *A Theory of Justice*, revised edition. Harvard, US: Belknap Press.

2013. *Political Liberalism*, expanded edition. Columbia, US: Columbia University Press.

Roznai, Yaniv. 2013. Unconstitutional Constitutional Amendments – The Migration and Success of a Constitutional Idea. *American Journal of Comparative Law* 61: 657–719.

Rupnik, Jacques. 2012. How Things Went Wrong. *Journal of Democracy* 23: 132–137.

Samuels, David J. 2000. The Gubernatorial Coattails Effect: Federalism and Congressional Elections in Brazil. *The Journal of Politics* 62: 240–253.

Schleicher, David. 2006. "Politics as Markets" Reconsidered: Natural Monopolies, Competitive Democratic Philosophy and Primary Ballot Access in American Elections. *Supreme Court Economic Review* 14: 163–220.

Schmitt, Carl. 2008. *Constitutional Theory*, translated by Jeffrey Seitzer. Durham, US: Duke University Press.

Schumpeter, Joseph A. 2013. *Capitalism, Socialism and Democracy*. Hoboken, US: Routledge.

Segura, Renata and Ana Maria Bejarano. 2004. Ni una asamblea mas sin nosotros! Exclusion, Inclusion, and the Politics of Constitution-Making in the Andes. *Constellations* 11: 217–236.

Sieyés, E. J. 1963. *What Is the Third Estate?* London, UK: Pall Mall Press.

Stephanopoulos, Nicholas O. 2014. Elections and Alignment. *Columbia Law Review* 114: 283–365.

Strauss, David. 1996. Common Law Constitutional Interpretation. *University of Chicago Law Review* 63: 877–935.

Tushnet, Mark. 2009. Constitutional Workarounds. *Texas Law Review* 87: 1499–1516.

Tushnet, Mark and Madhav Khosla. 2015. Introduction: Unstable Constitutionalism. In *Unstable Constitutionalism: Law and Politics in South Asia*, edited by Mark Tushnet and Madhav Khosla. Cambridge, UK: Cambridge University Press.

Uniform Democracy Scores, www.unified-democracy-scores.org/.

Varol, Ozan O. 2016. Constitutional Stickiness. *UC Davis Law Review* 49: 899–961.

Whittemore, Mary Elizabeth. 2011. The Problem of Enforcing Nature's Rights under Ecuador's Constitution: Why the 2008 Environmental Amendments Have No Bite. *Pacific Rim Law & Policy Journal Association* 20: 659–691.

PART III

CASE STUDIES

11

Ambedkar's constitution
Promoting inclusion, opposing majority tyranny

Martha C. Nussbaum

So rigorous is the enforcement of the Social Code against the Depressed Classes that any attempt on the part of the Depressed Classes to exercise their elementary rights of citizenship only ends in provoking the majority, to practice the worst form of social tyranny known to history. It will be admitted that when society is itself a tyrant, its means of tyrannizing are not restricted to the acts which it may do by the hands of its functionaries and it leaves fewer means of escape penetrating much more deeply into the details of life, and enslaving the soul itself.

B. R. Ambedkar, 1928

Our society often ridicules and abuses the Transgender community and in public places like railway stations, bus stands, schools, workplaces, malls, theatres, hospitals, they are sidelined and treated as untouchables, forgetting the fact that the moral failure lies in the society's unwillingness to contain or embrace different gender identities and expressions, a mindset which we have to change.

Supreme Court of India, *National Legal Services Foundation* v. *Union of India*, 2014

I CURBING MAJORITY TYRANNY, PROMOTING SOCIAL INCLUSION

India's Constitution, like others the world over, was ratified by a constitutional assembly. Unlike many or even most, however, it is to a considerable extent the creation of one dominant legal intellect, B. R. Ambedkar (1891–1956), who, as Nehru's law minister, had considerable latitude in drafting it and who has told history a great deal about what he wanted to achieve and at times had to

I am very grateful to Tom Ginsburg and Aziz Huq for their extremely helpful comments on an earlier draft, to Madhav Khosla for marvelous comments, to Zoya Hasan and to faculty at the National University of Juridical Sciences, Kolkata for related discussions, and to Vasujith Ram for painstaking and most helpful comments at a near-final stage.

fight to achieve. He argued extensively for a particular conception of the Constitution, one in which a central purpose was protecting vulnerable minorities from majority tyranny and promoting their full social inclusion. He focused centrally on the evils of the Hindu caste hierarchy, but he was also passionately concerned with the situation of India's women and its religious minorities. Although he did not address the problems faced by sexual minorities and transgender people, his name and his principles have been central to recent legal activism in these areas. In a very general way, Ambedkar saw the practice of stigmatizing and excluding groups of people as a major obstacle to India's success as a nation, and one that law could productively address. Leaving the management of the economy to others (although he himself had two Ph.D. degrees in Economics, one from Columbia and one from LSE, and insisted that economic progress was essential to his central goals), he set himself, as Nehru's law minister, to use constitutional drafting to address the problem of inclusion.

Who was Ambedkar? Centrally, he was a *dalit*, that is, from a caste (the Mahars) formerly called "untouchable," and viewed by most Hindus, during his childhood and youth, in that light. (Since a recent high-quality survey showed that 30 percent of Hindu households in India still practice untouchability, we can add that were he alive today, 30 percent of Hindu Indians would refuse to have physical contact with him.[1]) His good luck was that his father was an employee of the British East India Company, an organization full of moral defects, but the practice of untouchability was not among them. So his father made a good income, and Ambedkar and his sisters did well – so long as they did not have to encounter other Hindus. But of course B. R. did have to encounter them often. Here's what a day at school was like:

> I knew that I was an untouchable and that untouchables were subjected to certain indignities and discriminations. For instance, I knew that in the school I could not sit in the midst of my class students according to my rank but that I was to sit in a corner by myself. I knew that in the school I was to have a separate piece of gunny cloth for me to squat on in the class room and that the servant employed to clean the school would not touch the gunny cloth used by me. I was required to carry the gunny cloth home in the evening and bring it back the next day. While in the school I knew that children of the touchable classes, when they felt thirsty, could go out to the water tap, open it and quench their thirst. All that was necessary was the permission of the teacher. But my position was separate. I could not touch the tap and unless it was opened for me by a touchable person, it was not possible for me to quench my thirst. In my case the permission of the teacher was not enough.

---

[1]   The India Human Development Survey, see below Section III.

The presence of the school peon was necessary, for, he was the only person whom the class teacher could use for such a purpose. If the peon was not available I had to go without water. The situation can be summed up in the statement – no peon, no water. (Ambedkar 1993: 670–1)[2]

Such experiences shaped, not surprisingly, his view of the world. Also not surprisingly, when the time came for legal education, he sought it far from India – at Columbia University, where he became a protégé of John Dewey. He developed an intense admiration for American achievements in both politics and law, and the US Constitution, with its explicit protections for a set of fundamental rights, became an inspiration, even before he met and conferred with distinguished US jurists, for example Felix Frankfurter (Ambedkar 1993).[3] Not surprisingly either, he left Hinduism for Buddhism, a religion seen by Indians for centuries as a haven of equal respect.[4] The Buddhist emperor Ashoka (3rd–2nd CBCE), also a convert from Hinduism, favored equal respect for all people (and also for many animals!), and Ashoka, a hero of Nehru as well as Ambedkar, became a mythic presence in the Indian founding. His symbol, the Buddhist wheel of law, occupies the center of the Indian flag. We could do worse than to think of Ambedkar, albeit a far less poetic man than Nehru, as inspired by that vision of law: a wheel with equal spokes.

This much is clear: Ambedkar was a great man whose example continues to inspire. His name and thought are a rallying point for the despised and dispossessed. But Ambedkar was first and foremost a lawyer. My question in this paper is: how far did he succeed in drafting a constitution whose normative vision was such as to promote the realization of his aims?

Of course this sounds like an originalist question, but it really isn't: I am not advancing any doctrine of constitutional interpretation or constitutional

---

[2] Ambedkar, "Waiting for a Visa," in Ambedkar (1993: 670–1). This fragment probably dates to the mid-1930s and was left incomplete at Ambedkar's death. For more on Ambedkar's life and work, see Nussbaum (2015).

[3] In fact it was actually the "Constitutional Advisor" B. N. Rau, who met with Frankfurter and relayed his views about substantive due process to Ambedkar. Ambedkar's view of the United States was too rosy: in an essay published posthumously, he argues that slavery was less bad than untouchability. See Ambedkar (1993).

[4] Ambedkar's conversion took place in 1956, after the debut of the Constitution and shortly before his own death, but his interest in Buddhism was lifelong, and he wrote copiously about it. In 1936, he already announced that he had ceased to be a Hindu (Ambedkar 2014). His conversion spurred a mass conversion by members of his caste. Buddhism in India stands more generally for the value of inclusion: A recent revival of the ancient Buddhist university Nalanda has been supported by an international team committed to ideas of inclusion and equality, and led by economist Amartya Sen, who as a child declared his identity as Buddhist because of its ideas of equal respect and nonviolence. Unfortunately Sen has recently resigned his post as chancellor of Nalanda on account of pressures by the present government: see Sen (2015).

meaning. And therefore, I am not advancing any view of what the Indian Constitution means, which would have to precede and ground any more general inquiry into how well "it" has succeeded. Because I do not know how to answer these difficult questions of constitutional meaning, and to defend my answer, in the course of such a brief paper (although I do have views about them), I'm just asking the historical question: how far did a man with some definite aims succeed in promoting those aims through constitutional law?

Parenthetically, let me note that the question posed by this volume involves great theoretical indeterminacy, and it seems hard to proceed unless these theoretical questions are addressed first. If ours is the question, "How far has the constitutional text been implemented?" that question cannot be seriously confronted without first getting clear about a theory of constitutional meaning/ interpretation, since without that the "constitution" is just a set of symbols on paper (or computer screen). There is (as yet) no there there. Even if the assessor assumes or argues for a given type of theory, originalist or anti-originalist, and puts that out front for all to see, still, such abstract theories often leave many hard questions about constitutional meaning undecided, so the interpreter will have to decide those somehow, before assessment can begin. If one's theory is textualist, furthermore, one would first need an exhaustive linguistic inquiry into meaning in the language(s) of the nation at the time of the constitutional framing, and sometimes it is not even clear what that language (or those languages) might be.[5] If one's theory of meaning allows open-endedness and tailoring to changing conditions, as many do, then the assessment can hardly begin at all, since in advance of knowing the conditions life and the law will throw up, we can't even spell out what a successful implementation of "the constitution," according to our theory of meaning, would look like. Another indeterminacy is created by *stare decisis*, to which even ardent originalists give some role: interpretation in a given case will involve both textual meaning and precedent.

To be sure, there are practices out there, in the world of international and comparative law: people routinely talk about whether a constitution has "succeeded." One possible role for a conference such as ours is to understand these practices and evaluate them. But if these practices leap over the thorny

---

[5] India has twenty-two official languages, and the Constitution is available in all of them; thus though English is the default option it would not be safe to assume that it is the only language relevant for constitutional meaning. An argument has to be offered. Moreover, the Indian dialect of English is subtly different from the UK and US dialects, just as they are from each other. The fact that Indian judges routinely allude to Webster's and the OED does not mean that they are doing what a good textualist should.

questions of constitutional meaning that I have just identified, and if the practitioners simply assume that they somehow understand without further ado what a given constitution "is" or "means," I'm afraid that I know how I would evaluate those practices: they are question-begging and theoretically inadequate. Perhaps because empirical comparatists are not always also deeply interested in the theoretical questions of constitutional meaning that preoccupy scholars of constitutional law, some of them can become more confident than they have any right to be about the putative clarity of the meaning of the constitutions about whose success or lack of success they make claims.[6]

An example will, I hope, make my worry clearer. Suppose one were to pose the question: has the free speech guarantee in the US Constitution been successful? Everyone in any US law school, and many foreign legal scholars, would quickly realize that this question involves enormous theoretical complexity, since, as is well known, the meaning of the speech clause of the First Amendment is multiply contested. We could not even begin to approach the question of success without first arguing for a position on the question of meaning. And even members of the same general theoretical school may differ about such all-important questions as whether the speech of corporations is protected by the First Amendment, or whether the First Amendment protects political speech more stringently than artistic and/or commercial speech. Hardly any two scholars agree on all details of the meaning of the guarantee. John Rawls, who holds that the *Brandenberg* test is much too restrictive, involving an incorrect view of the First Amendment's meaning, would conclude, for that reason, that the free speech clause has not been successfully implemented: it hasn't been correctly understood. And, for reasons that he also gives, he would regard the current protection of corporate speech and the consequent striking down of campaign finance laws as a further, and very grave, failure to understand, and hence to implement, the true meaning of the speech clause (Rawls 1986: 340–56). The late justice Thurgood Marshall, who held (and I agree) that a right to education was inherent in the free speech clause, arguing that a decent level of education is a prerequisite for meaningful political speech, would say that the failure to recognize and implement

---

[6] Such is rarely the case with historical scholarship that also poses questions about implementation and, in a way, of "success": thus the work of Alison LaCroix and Laura Weinrib on our faculty, just to mention two cases that exemplify the best norms of the profession, never make normative claims about success or failure without also confronting the thorny questions of meaning and interpretation. Indeed, the project devised by Alison LaCroix and linguist Jason Merchant and funded by the Neubauer Collegium, concerning the importance of linguistics for constitutional theory, can be seen as one instance of proceeding in an intellectually correct order, and putting these questions prior to normative assessment.

such a right (since his view did not prevail) means that the correct meaning of the speech clause of the First Amendment has been neither recognized nor implemented.[7] However, since theirs are minority views, many other scholars, judges, and citizens think differently and would come to different conclusions about the First Amendment's success accordingly.

Again, Catharine MacKinnon argues that the First Amendment should not be interpreted in such a way that the test for (unprotected) obscenity focuses on a concept of "the prurient interest," as in current law; instead, the focus should be humiliation and violence.[8] Her views have not prevailed, and current obscenity doctrine is to her a failure to implement the real meaning of the Amendment. Other scholars have a different critique of current doctrine: they hold that the whole idea that some artistic materials may forfeit protection by being obscene is a misunderstanding of the First Amendment's scope: they hold that it protects artistic speech as stringently as political speech. Given that a majority of legal scholars object to current obscenity doctrine in one way or another (starkly opposing ways, as we see), these people would all say that in respect of obscenity the First Amendment has not been successfully implemented because the text has been wrongly construed. Others, those who uphold the current doctrine, disagree, thinking current doctrine a success.

In short, we cannot hope to give an intelligent answer to the success question about free speech without first settling who is right about meaning, in a variety of contested areas. In this case, because the debates about meaning are so familiar, this problem would be evident to most or all US scholars, and to many scholars abroad. But of course it is highly problematic to acknowledge such problems in the case of the US Constitution and to bypass them in the case of the constitutions of other nations. Surely it would be most ungenerous to ascribe to the bypasser a belief that other nations, and their documents, are somehow simpler than Americans and their documents. Rather than such an objectionable thought, the bypasser's procedures are much more likely to be explained by a general reluctance to get involved in theoretical questions of great complexity. I believe, however, that this reluctance is intellectually mistaken and that such questions cannot be avoided.

There is, further, a second difficult problem of a very different sort. This question, unlike my first, is normative: questions of constitutional success cannot be resolved without a normative theory of what a constitution can be expected to achieve, and in what time frame. Anything such a document does

---

[7] See *San Antonio School District* v. *Rodriguez*, 411 U.S. 1 (1973).

[8] Thus the common tendency to call MacKinnon an "enemy of the First Amendment" is frivolous: she offers a different account of what it means and protects.

achieve requires not just courts who use it, but also a social and economic background against which a particular set of judicial directives operates, and which may facilitate or impede. Suppose we are clear that the constitution says that such and such should happen (we've solved the question of meaning somehow, and arrived at a determinate understanding of the constitutional text, whether we think its recommendations are good or bad), and we see that it doesn't happen: in what situations do we say that the constitution (or the courts) bear the blame, and in what circumstances do we say, well, they did the best they could, but it really was not in their hands? (Furthermore we also have a correlation-causation problem: for the reasons that lead a group to include something in a constitution might be reasons that are already at work in culture and in the economy helping to explain progress on such matters, in which case the constitution would be epiphenomenal.)

In short, I believe that the larger question or questions this volume is posing requires or require a prior theoretical inquiry into meaning and a concurrent economic/historical inquiry into other factors that may contribute to the fate of the norms embodied in the text (as somehow interpreted). This prior inquiry, in the case of the Indian Constitution, would be a task of enormous difficulty, and the "meaning" part would require me to resolve issues that scholars of constitutional law debate endlessly, and without clear resolution, in the case of the US Constitution – something that I do not believe to be doable by me without ten years of theoretical work, since there is no consensus view on these matters, to put it mildly, and I do not feel able at present to offer knock-down arguments in favor of the (non-originalist) view that I favor. (My second question, about economic and other forces, seems more doable by me, given the state of my knowledge, but it would require a book-length treatment to do it right.) Progress, in short, cannot be achieved by empirical work without theory, and theory of more than one type.

So I shall not try to answer the larger questions posed by this volume. I shall do something that I think can be done by me at the present time, a modest historical inquiry. I think that we know enough about B. R. Ambedkar to know what he was after in seeking to draft particular sections of the constitution as he did, and what his most salient aims were in areas pertinent to the text. He tells us very clearly and he repeated himself often. So, forgetting about theories of interpretation for the moment (for courts might go against his wishes and yet be interpreting the text quite properly, and we'll see at least one case where someone could argue this), how far did he achieve his own goals, through the means available to him? This question is at an oblique angle to the larger question of constitutional meaning, but I think it is an interesting question.

If one should ask, why the focus on Ambedkar, I would reply: because he is a very significant historical figure whose views can be known; because he expressed some aspirations that were at least prominent in the founding and relevant to the larger question of constitutional meaning, though not determinative of any particular answer to that question; and because his name is constantly invoked by courts today on behalf of a set of goals and aspirations that are a significant part of India's fraught and deeply conflicted political/judicial reality. In short, he stands for something, and this something is at least one part of India's Constitution. Finally, I am fascinated by his ideas, and I think that it is productive to see today's India through his eyes.

How should we perform such an assessment? Clearly we cannot expect, and he did not expect, the document all by itself to achieve social inclusion for groups that have experienced not only stigma and discrimination but also related deficiencies in nutrition, health care, education, employment opportunities, and political influence. Even effective implementation of non-discrimination guarantees depends, as he knew well, on the work of courts, of the police, and other institutional actors. Furthermore, people don't stop stigmatizing others just because the law tells them to. As I shall later emphasize, almost seventy years after the Indian Constitution outlawed untouchability and forbade its practice "in any form," 30 percent of Hindus still say frankly that they practice it, at any rate in their homes. It would indeed have been astonishing if legal elites had succeeded in ending discrimination, just as we know well that US racism has not been ended by our courts. Moreover, no formerly subordinated group can make progress in the absence of effective policies in areas such as education, health, and employment. All we can do, then, is to study closely the normative vision embodied in the constitution itself, asking both how it has held up over time and how its textual choices have played out in the realm of law. We can then examine as best we can the ways in which law has been either assisted or thwarted by other political choices.

I shall argue that the specific normative commitments of the Constitution, as subsequently understood, had some legal value and a broader social expressive value in connection with Ambedkar's announced goals – though they have proven insufficient to counteract social tyranny in the absence of a wide range of social and economic measures, which have not exactly been forthcoming. In a few respects, however, Ambedkar's legal choices were less helpful than others he might have made. And in some respects choices that have been and are extremely productive at the same time created new problems.

In the area of caste, Ambedkar's drafting squarely outlawed untouchability and explicitly approved of affirmative action programs, permitting the nation to adopt sweeping such measures without the distraction of continual constitutional challenges to them, US style. Those measures, however, have had a mixed track record, as have the economic ideas outlined in the aspirational section of the Constitution. Nor could they be expected to be very successful in the absence of effective primary education, not to mention maternal and child nutrition. Moreover, the social attitudes described by Ambedkar remain extremely prevalent, imposing barriers to progress. Finally, the very programs that Ambedkar promoted to end caste have in some ways backfired, entrenching caste identities and promoting a type of identity politics that he abhorred.

In the case of Muslim and Christian minorities, the same educational and health-related shortfalls have kept them deeply poor, and, due to Ambedkar's deliberate choice (supported by most at the time), they do not even get the benefit of affirmative action. Moreover, saying people have religious freedom is not very helpful, if religious violence is condoned by public officials and people not only do not stop those officials but overwhelmingly elect one of them to the prime ministership. That's majority tyranny for you, showing that when an overwhelming majority of the citizens of a nation share a prejudice, democracy is a very uncertain instrument of equal respect and inclusion.

As for women, it's obvious that gender equality involves multiple factors, of which law is only one. Ambedkar was bold in setting sex equality securely in the Fundamental Rights section of the Constitution, but we'll see that an unfortunate drafting ambiguity gave recalcitrant judges a loophole through which they might escape. Moreover, two other decisions of his, comprehensible at the time, have over time made women's lives worse: the decision to allow the four major religions to continue to control property and family law; and the decision to eschew substantive due process, without giving separate recognition to a privacy right (secured in the United States through substantive due process), or to the related idea of human dignity. Creative judges have fixed the second and partly fixed the first.

I know of no statements ever made by Ambedkar on the question of sexual orientation and gender identity, so this is an equality/inclusion issue not faced by him. Nonetheless, his ideas are pertinently invoked in litigation on these issues. Here, because the primary obstacle for these minorities is law, the power of law to change things is great. Productive change – decriminalizing sodomy – was first accomplished in 2009, then undone in 2013; and then in a related area, the status of transgender people, progress was made again in 2014, with annoyed implicit reference to the 2013 judgment. All this shows, I will argue, a kind of instability and vulnerability to political whim that would have been anathema to Ambedkar but that are the direct outgrowth of certain aspects of the conception of the Supreme Court that himself favored.

Finally, I turn from substance to form. Here we reach, I believe, the deepest failure of Ambedkar's constitutional vision. Ambedkar favored a type of "constitutional morality" that put procedure ahead of substantive outcomes, fostering a respectful polity in which the sheer adherence to structure was intended to promote civility rather than a fractious winner-take-all mentality (see Mehta 2010). This noble ideal, which marks Ambedkar's vision as profoundly liberal and anti-Marxist (as he often said, since the Left parties were his major critics), has to a considerable extent been lost today, in the politics of mistrust and suspicion that now reigns. Perhaps his spirit can be recovered, perhaps not.

II   AMBEDKAR'S CONSTITUTION

The British codified criminal and commercial law for the nation as a whole, basing it on Victorian British law. Civil law, by contrast, they left to the four major religions to control, thereby ceding large parts of law, not just family law but also property, to unelected and unaccountable parties. (Muslim and Parsi law had venerable histories, and the British simply helped them "reform" or redraft certain parts. Hindu law had been plural, decentralized, and mostly oral, so the British codified it for the nation. Christian law remained and remains the preserve of the different religions and national origins: thus Christians in Goa, for example, continue to be governed by the Portuguese Civil Code.)

One choice made at the time of the founding, with broad general support, was not to undo this basic division. Laws would henceforth require the approval of Parliament as a whole, but would be binding only on a particular religious community. The primary reason for leaving things balkanized in this way was (somewhat ironically, in light of subsequent developments) a reason of inclusion and equality. Muslims remaining in India (rather than going to Pakistan) feared that they would be trodden upon in Hindu India, a fear made utterly reasonable by the mutual violence of Partition. Showing respect to them by allowing them to continue a limited degree of legal self-rule seemed appropriate, and I believe, in the historical context, it was appropriate. Ambedkar, who believed in general that parochial identities should eventually drop away, saw the arrangement as temporary.[9] The aspirational but unenforceable part of the document states that the nation "shall endeavour to secure" a Uniform Civil Code in the future, but meanwhile the religions

---

[9]   See Ambedkar (1948): defending the safeguards for minorities in the draft, he says that the best solution is one that would "recognize the existence of minorities to start with. It must also be such that it will enable majorities and minorities to merge someday into one."

were left to run the show (with particular respect to sex equality, see Nussbaum 2000: ch. 3; 2004a; 2012a).

Another fundamental choice, much fought for and emphasized by Ambedkar, was to write the Constitution on the US model, not the British model: that is, with a written Bill of Fundamental Rights that would be bulwark, against majority tyranny and that would be upheld through a process of judicial review. Here Ambedkar encountered some opposition from Nehru, who did not want US-style judicial review, because he feared that it would be used by conservative judges (and in a nation with very low literacy judges were bound to be elites) to block land reform and other economic measures. So these Rights were bulwarks only when the Constitution itself was not amended to remove or alter them; but, as Nehru wished, it could be amended by majority vote. At one later time, during the Emergency, most of the Fundamental Rights were indeed amended away by majority vote. That defect was corrected long after Ambedkar's death,[10] and the Fundamental Rights are no longer amendable insofar as they are found to form part of the Constitution's "basic structure."

These Fundamental Rights were meant to be enforceable against the religions. There seems to be no doubt that this is what Ambedkar intended: they thus would circumscribe the authority of personal laws. Indeed, Article 13 of the Fundamental Rights section clearly states that "All laws in force," and any subsequent laws that might be made are null and void insofar as they are inconsistent with the Fundamental Rights. However, Ambedkar did not write "All laws in force, including the personal laws." He probably thought that he had been clear enough: that "All" meant "All." But wily traditionalists did an end run around him. A Supreme Court case in 1952, shortly after the Constitution was adopted, held that the personal laws were immune from the scrutiny of Article 13.[11] Here we can see that Ambedkar did his best, and perhaps he would have been even more explicit but for the vociferous outcry on the part of religious leaders that is well documented, both then and subsequently, focusing especially on sex equality, a topic very much in play in the personal laws. Indeed Ambedkar resigned his law ministry in 1951 after failing to secure the passage of a broad statute, the Hindu Code Bill, which sought to secure women's equality in property and inheritance. It is very clear from that debate how tied his hands were. With characteristic pungency, he made this parting statement: "To leave untouched the inequality between

---

[10] By *Kesavananda Bharati* (1973) 4 SCC 225, but confirmed and extended by judgments after the assault on civil liberties during the Emergency (1975–1977), when Indira Gandhi attempted to amend away the entire list of rights.

[11] *State of Bombay* v. *Narasu Appa Mali* (AIR 1952 Bom 84).

class and class, between sex and sex, and to go on passing legislation relating to economic problems is to make a farce of our Constitution and so build a palace on a dung-heap."

In two areas, Ambedkar's study of US history and his conversations with US jurists (in particular Felix Frankfurter) led him to make drafting choices that were intended to head off threats to the project of inclusion. First, noting that affirmative action measures could easily be challenged on grounds of non-discrimination, he headed off these problems ex ante: sections 3 and 4 of Article 15 (non-discrimination) reads:

> (3) Nothing in this article shall prevent the State from making any special provision for women and children. (4) Nothing in this article or in clause (2) of article 29 shall prevent the State from making any special provision for the advancement of any socially and educationally backward classes of citizens or for the Scheduled Castes and the Scheduled Tribes.

A similar rider is attached to Article 16 (equality of opportunity in public employment) – although this rider does not explicitly mention women. A theme that Ambedkar harped upon with obsessive insistence during the constitutional debates was that "rights are nothing unless remedies are provided whereby people can seek to obtain redress when rights are invaded."[12] As we'll see in the following section, his strategy was multidimensional, but the permissibility of affirmative action was one linchpin. In notes explaining the constitutional provisions, he writes: "In a country like India where it is possible for discrimination to be practiced on a vast scale and in a relentless manner Fundamental Rights can have no meaning. The remedy follows the lines adopted in the Bill which was recently introduced in the Congress of the U. S. A. the aim of which is to prevent discrimination being practiced against the Negroes" (Thorat 2006: 309).

The history of the Lochner era, urged on Ambedkar by Frankfurter, had shown him the danger of substantive due process as a weapon conservative judges might use to strike down progressive economic legislation. So Ambedkar sedulously avoided it, and Article 21 accordingly states: "No person may be deprived of his life or personal liberty except according to procedure established by law." Procedural, not substantive, due process, then. It did not last. A need for substantive due process was subsequently felt in four areas: (1) protection of citizens from unwarranted police surveillance (the Constitution has no analogue of our Fourth Amendment); (2) protection from arbitrary and cruel punishments (it also has no analogue of our Eighth

---

[12] December 9, 1946, in Thorat (2006: 297). All otherwise unattributed citations from Ambedkar
    derive from this valuable collection (which also has a first-rate introduction).

Amendment); (3) sexual and personal privacy; and (4) the idea of respect for human dignity. In the first two cases, the invented "right to privacy" has done some good work (though the concept of privacy, always elusive, certainly does not direct thought well in case 2). Still, that work might have been avoided by including explicit clauses analogous to our Fourth and Eighth Amendments, without getting entangled in the difficulties of substantive due process. Nor was substantive due process necessary to craft a privacy right or to incorporate human dignity into the understanding of Article 21. It would perhaps have been better to construct a provision protecting what needed protecting, rather than leaving the construction of a privacy right to the creativity of judges working with the ill-defined idea of due process. The guarantee of sexual privacy has proven a slippery one, in some cases advancing the dignity of excluded groups, in others insulating male behavior from legal scrutiny – just as feminist critics of the privacy right had long warned (Nussbaum 2002). Since India has never had any serious controversy about contraception or abortion, the privacy right did not need to do the work that US feminists wanted it to do, and it has ended up shielding such retrograde measures as the forcible restitution of a woman to her conjugal home (Nussbaum 2002). More recently, however, the privacy right has been productively invoked in the struggle against sodomy laws. And it has been productively linked to the idea of dignity, which has also been read into Article 21 through judicial interpretation. (Once again, however, all this might have been achieved without substantive due process: Ambedkar had a good intuition here.)

One more feature of the text remains to be introduced. Article 32 provides access to the Supreme Court by petition for every citizen. This idea that courts would be not remote and elite but people friendly and approachable directly, not only through a long appellate process, was fundamental to Ambedkar's vision of social inclusion, and it was very popular at the time, as it still is today (Robinson 2013a; 2013b; 2016). On "Audition Day," people crowd the Court with their causes, and get at least a little time to present them. There is no doubt that this provision has been a great success in terms of giving people without elite education confidence in the Supreme Court. And it also gives the Supreme Court power to exercise a quasi-legislative role when Parliament is dithering around, as it often does.

Thus, some particularly popular and significant quasi-legislative measures are the result of cases heard by petition. One is the mandatory midday meal to be served in all schools all over the nation. The policy originated in Tamil Nadu and was already in force in Kerala, but the Supreme Court, noting its excellent results in getting children into the schools (the 99 percent both male and female adolescent literacy rate in Kerala is a gold star item in the development literature), made it mandatory for the nation, even specifying that the meal must contain (as of 2014) 450 calories and 12 grams of protein for primary school, 700 calories and 20 grams of protein for upper primary school.[13]

Another landmark was a case involving sexual harassment, *Vishaka* v. *Rajasthan* (1997), brought by petition by an NGO working in the field. Responding to the complaint that the law neglected sexual harassment of working women, the Court, invoking India's treaty obligations under CEDAW, instructed Parliament to draw up suitable legislation, and even specified in great detail what the legislation should look like, including, famously, a creative monitoring role for NGOs.[14] That legislation was eventually passed in 2013, in very much the form specified by the Court.

Looked at in the widest way, then, the right to petition has had and continues to have some excellent and fascinating results. But of course a court open to all comers has to have a way of dealing with the swollen workload, even if it rejects most of the petitions that it hears. The Court has therefore grown over time. It began with eight justices, and now has a maximum number of thirty-one, although the current number is twenty-eight.[15] From the beginning, they did not even attempt to sit *en banc*, but used two- or three-judge panels, rarely up to four or five in very important cases (see Robinson 2013a; 2013b; 2016). And of course this introduces a large element of uncertainty and unevenness into judicial proceedings. Sometimes cases are assigned by a randomized procedure, which has one sort of problem. Sometimes the chief justice exercises discretion and chooses the panel, which has another sort of problems (Robinson 2013b). There is no provision for *en banc* rehearing. Although there is provision for a "curative petition" to be filed in "extraordinary situations, wherein gross misconduct of justice or

---

[13] *People's Union for Civil Liberties v. Union of India and Others* (2001); for an assessment of the program, see Rutledge (2012).

[14] *Vishaka v. Rajasthan* (1997) 6 SCC 241. See Nussbaum (Forthcoming 2016b) and also Nussbaum (2004b) where I commend the approach to the problem by the Supreme Court in *Vishaka* over the problematic attempts of some feminists in the Bajaj case to ground sexual harassment law in notion of female "modesty" in the Criminal Code.

[15] Of the current twenty-eight only one is a woman, Mrs. Justice R. Banumathi. Justice K. G. Balakrishnan (now retired) was the first Justice from the *dalit* community, and also the first *dalit* chief justice (2007). In 2010, a Parsi, S. H. Kapadia, became chief justice, and stated that he saw this appointment as a sign of India's inclusiveness. (Although small, and growing smaller, the Parsi community has, however, typically included numerous wealthy and advantaged people, and has never been particularly stigmatized, so I am not sure I agree with him.) I am unable to discern whether there is currently any *dalit* member of the Supreme Court. There would appear to be one Muslim member, Justice Fakkir Mohamed Ibrahim Kalifulla; and Justice Joseph, from Kerala, may well be a Christian member (going by the combination of name and origin).

immense public injury has been caused, on account of a decision of the Supreme Court,"[16] this remedy (introduced by the Supreme Court itself in 2002) is used but rarely, and, even when such a petition is submitted, the Court rarely agrees to consider it. In Section VI we will see some of the disturbing results of the panel system, which can insulate stigma and oppression from reasoned critique, or, just as capriciously, give surprising dividends to the long-oppressed.

The activist and people-friendly role of the Supreme Court requires that it remain to a degree insulated from the pressures of the majoritarian political process. So far as I know, Ambedkar did not express a view about how the members of the Supreme Court would be chosen. For a long time, the president of India (a mostly honorific office, and one that is supposed to be, but is not always, above the political fray) used to appoint the justices. In 1993, however, the system changed: a collegium consisting of the chief justice and the four most senior justices appoint new members. Recently, however, the system has changed again, in a most ominous development. In August 2014, a National Judicial Appointments Commission was created by amendment of the Constitution (which can be amended by a two-thirds vote of Parliament, and a mere majority vote of those actually present and voting, although ratification by at least half of the states would also have been required). The Commission was to recommend appointments, and the objection of any two members would block an appointment. The Commission was to consist of: the chief justice, two other senior Supreme Court Justices, the cabinet's law minister, and two other "eminent persons" chosen by a committee consisting of the chief justice, the prime minister, and the leader of the opposition in Parliament, provided that one of the two eminent persons chosen would be either from the scheduled castes and tribes, or from the OBCs (Other Backward Castes), or from the religious minorities, or a woman. This change would have greatly diminished the independent power of the Supreme Court, which has in many respects been a thorn in Modi's side, and gives him tremendous power to influence its composition. Obviously it would not be terribly easy to get agreement within the committee, but once the eminent persons were chosen, a person friendly to the government, together with just one other member of the commission, could block any appointment. The likely result would have been that justices would have to be acceptable to the government. Since the government is

---

[16] See the explanation at www.lawyerscollective.org/updates/naz-foundation-files-curative-peti tion-challenging-supreme-court-judgment-section-377.html.

carrying on a related campaign to destroy the autonomy of national universities,[17] one need not be paranoid to read the change in this way.

The change was challenged through petitions, and in April 2015, a three-judge panel referred the case to a larger Constitutional panel. In October 2015, the amendment creating the new Judicial Commission was declared unconstitutional by a five-justice panel of the Supreme Court, on the ground that the Commission violates the ideas of separation of powers and the independence of the judiciary set forth in the Constitution in Article 124 (on the Supreme Court). This judgment (with leading opinions authored by two religious-minority justices, Justice Singh and Justice Joseph), is 1,040 pages long, and immensely detailed in its historical analysis. Ambedkar's name occurs dozens of times in the opinion, and the opinion rests its analysis on a scrutiny of his statements before the Constituent Assembly regarding the role of the judiciary. In arguing for its conclusion that the proposed mode of judicial appointment violates the Constitution, the Court quotes Ambedkar's statement that "the independence of the Judiciary from the Executive should be made as clear and definite as we could make it by law" (83–4, para. 30). They further note that Ambedkar unequivocally stated that "our judiciary must be independent of the executive," and that appointment of Supreme Court justices by the Executive would be "improper" and "dangerous" (145–6, para. 76). Following Ambedkar's reasoning in detail, they argue that the manner of appointment of the justices is part of the independence of the judiciary guaranteed under Article 124 (148, para. 79).[18] Ambedkar's voice still speaks, in this case saving the nation from a disastrous breakdown of judicial independence and hence of the security of fundamental rights.

One more note. Ambedkar, albeit a lawyer, spoke of legal education as a low priority for India. He thought scientific, economic, and technical education were far more important. Nehru shared this view. Whether for that reason or other reasons, legal education in India has lagged behind other areas of scholarship and training, particularly in areas pertinent to Ambedkar's concerns. Thus the curriculum is very private-law focused and certainly lacks the

---

[17] Legislation has been proposed, though it is not yet before Parliament, according to which all students and all faculty in national universities must move to a different university every few years, going round and round the country in a perfectly absurd manner. The clear aim is to break up the unity and solidarity of the intellectual community, and especially of an institution such as JNU (Jawaharlal Nehru University), which has been a source of autonomous critical opinion.

[18] *Supreme Court Advocates-on-Record-Association and Another* v. *Union of India.* I note that on p. 372 of the opinion the Supreme Court cites Tom Ginsburg's article with Nuno Garoupa, "Guarding the Guardians: Judicial Councils and Judicial Independence", which appeared in the *American Journal of Comparative Law* 57: 201–32 (2009).

emphasis on gender, race, and other social-justice issues that one would find in US law schools (along with a lot of other things of course). Nor is law a prime destination for upwardly mobile young people (or for their parents, setting goals for them), as it is in the US; so the talent that flocks to law in the US, even now after the economic crisis, is not parallel to any similar influx of top talent into law in India, particularly not into the social-justice part of law. I would say that things are changing, and in some law schools the changes are already bearing fruit. But we cannot yet say that lawyers are educated so as to be independent social thinkers, responsive to justice concerns.[19] Here Ambedkar made a large error, I believe, in terms of his own goals. Constitutions need constitutional lawyers, and progressive constitutionalism also needs progressive legal NGOs to keep pressure on courts. There is less of this than one might hope, in such a large nation. The Lawyers Collective is a fine legal NGO, but it is virtually alone, and it has almost no money, whereas in the US the ACLU and Lambda Legal, for example, are able to raise a lot of money and therefore to bring a lot of challenges to exclusionary laws.

Now, however, let us turn to the concrete areas.

III   CASTE

Before assessing the Constitution's normative vision of caste, we need to put on the table Ambedkar's radical and as yet utterly unrealized goal: not just an end to caste discrimination, but the total "annihilation of caste." That title was given to a lecture he agreed to deliver to a group of sincere Hindu reformers, but its radicalism upset them, and they canceled the conference, hence his invitation (Ambedkar 2014: Prologue). Ambedkar printed the lecture at his own expense, however, and sold copies (Gandhi thought the fee he charged was too high); it became famous.[20] Ambedkar's attack on caste has two parts, one less upsetting to Hindu reformers, and one more upsetting. The less upsetting part is his insistence on the abolition of all forms of caste discrimination. The more upsetting part, often repeated by him during the constitutional debates, is his utter opposition to caste divisions as sources of restriction on the free choice of occupation, as sources of identity in personal life, and as sources

---

[19] One problem is youth: entering law school at age seventeen, even students in five-year programs in the national law schools are immature, and of course they have no prior liberal education at the university level as do their US counterparts. This problem obtains in many nations.

[20] Ambedkar (2014), including Gandhi's critique. Gandhi thought he should charge 2 annas rather than 8 annas!

of mobilization in political life.[21] "How can people divided into several thousands of castes be a nation?" he asks. Castes "are anti-national," because they foment antipathy and separation (Ambedkar 1949).[22] It was crystal clear that the affirmative action measure pertaining to caste were intended as remedial and temporary, and that the long-term goal was the total annihilation of caste identities in favor of a spirit of fraternity. "Without fraternity equality and liberty will be no deeper than coats of paint" (Ambedkar 1949). For now I address only the Constitution's way of dealing with discrimination.

Ambedkar's approach to the problem of caste discrimination had three parts (Thorat 2006: Introduction). The first was an explicit guarantee of fundamental rights, including a constitutional declaration that untouchability is henceforth illegal. The second was affirmative action in politics, public employment, and education, to be specified as permissible in the Fundamental Rights section and then urged in the constitution's aspirational section. The third was a set of economic measures including state socialism and land reform. Since these were left for statutory implementation and were mentioned only in the aspirational section, I shall not discuss them further here. In any case they also required in many respects the cooperation of the states and were implemented very differently in different states. (Only West Bengal and Kerala had land reform, for example.) Assessing state socialism is well beyond the scope of this chapter, although I note that it had good results in the early years of the republic.

Fundamental rights first. Untouchability is forbidden by Article 17: "Untouchability" is abolished and its practice in any form is forbidden. The enforcement of any disability rising out of "'Untouchability' shall be an offence punishable in accordance with law." Article 15, non-discrimination, additionally prohibits all discrimination along lines of caste. (This is not redundant, since caste-based discrimination affects many who are not in the scheduled castes and scheduled tribes.)

But, as Ambedkar insisted, rights are no good without remedies. We must mention first the fact that untouchability, like domestic violence, is virtually impossible to police, since so much of it takes place in households. And

---

[21] See Ambedkar (1949; 2014). Gandhi, while agreeing with Ambedkar's critique of caste-based discrimination, supported caste along all of these further dimensions in 1936, although his view gradually evolved. One of Ambedkar's novel insights is that caste limits on occupation make a revolution virtually impossible by denying the lower caste the use of weapons and access to education, the two central prerequisites of a successful revolution. For a valuable overview of Ambedkar's views on caste, see Jaffrelot (2005).

[22] In Ambedkar (2014) he has much more to say about Hinduism, denouncing the authority it vests in texts and priests. In effect he is proposing the type of rational reform that the nineteenth-century radical reformers carried out in Judaism, although he is unaware of that precedent. This type of reform has not caught on in Hinduism: instead, rationalists have become non-religious.

untouchability is thriving today, despite its illegality. The India Human Development Survey, conducted by the National Council for Applied Economic Research, reported in 2014 that 30 percent of rural households and 20 percent of Indian households said that they practiced untouchability. (This would involve, for example, restrictions on who could enter the kitchen and use cooking utensils.) When we consider that this represents a yet larger proportion of Hindu households, the results are distressing indeed.[23] As for miscegenation, only 5 percent of Indians say that they have married someone of a different caste. There are hundreds of castes,[24] so this is a pretty amazing result.

What of the situation out in the larger world, where remedies can have more bite? With Ambedkar's urging and with the constitution's permission, quotas ("reservations") were adopted in political offices, public employment, and higher education, for both the scheduled castes and tribes (SC/STs) and the OBCs.[25] The Mandal Commission in 1980 increased the size of these quotas. What has been the outcome of this quota-based approach to the politics of inclusion?

In politics, the quotas have certainly given the lower castes power they would not otherwise have had. The form this power has taken would not have surprised Ambedkar, who kept saying that the lower castes could not have their interests adequately represented by someone else, but would have to elect their own representatives. What has happened is that a range of caste-based parties has emerged around the nation, often local in nature (as are some of the castes), and it is largely through these parties, rather than through

[23] See *The Hindu*, November 13, 2014. www.thehindu.com/data/just-5-per-cent-of-indian-marria ges-are-intercaste/article6591502.ece.

[24] Because caste is to a great extent regional, it would be very difficult to get a precise number. Even when mandatory quotas are concerned, as with the OBCs (Other Backward Castes), state lists often differ from national lists. The national list of "scheduled castes" recognizes 1,108 castes, and the list of "scheduled tribes" recognizes 744 such tribes. As for OBCs, the Central list recognizes ninety-nine in West Bengal alone, and other states are similar.

[25] The scheduled castes are those formerly considered untouchable and now called *dalits*; the list of scheduled castes is given by enumeration. Scheduled tribes are, as the name implies, people belong to an enumerated list of tribes who have typically lived in accordance with their own norms and somewhat isolated socially from the surrounding society. OBCs are castes that are judged to be socially, economically, and/or educationally "backward," meaning suffering from stigma and deprivation, but were not considered untouchable. Individual members of these castes may be quite wealthy and influential. It goes without saying that many members of the upper castes are extremely poor, indeed they may be pavement dwellers and utterly destitute. But the thought of upper-caste birth retains its consolations: thus in Mulk Raj Anand's searing novel *Coolie* (1936), the fifteen-year-old hero Munoo, arriving destitute in Bombay and getting thrown out of a café where he has tried to buy a soda with one of his remaining pennies, consoles himself: "I am not an untouchable. I am a Hindu Kshatriya, a Rajput, a warrior" (Anand 1936: 157).

the national parties, that the lower castes have attained political power. Thus the nation's most powerful *dalit* politician ever, Mayawati of Uttar Pradesh, rose to power through the BSP, a lower-caste party, although she has also made alliances at times with other parties, including the BJP. The influential OBC Laloo Prasad Yadav of Bihar also rose to power through a caste-based party, the RJD, and mobilization through caste has been essential to his unlikely political resilience (as he has been in and out of jail). His persistent nemesis, Nitish Kumar, an individual of impressive talents who seems free from corruption, is also an OBC, from the Kurmi agricultural caste. Unlike Laloo, he has not depended on caste-based mobilization for his success, and let us hope he gets onto the national stage sooner rather than later.[26]

In general, caste-based politics basically cannot be national, both because the menu of castes varies with region and because people without elite education can be contacted only in their regional language. So basing politics on caste means – given the educational deficiencies that prevent most of India's citizens from learning a second language in school – that politics has become highly balkanized, and governments usually must be formed by coalition. This means, in turn, that national politics is often unduly influenced by the whims of leaders of local parties who may be popular and populist, but who are not dedicated to any principled program.[27] This balkanization is probably bad for the economic interests of the lower castes, and for the nation as a whole; and it would surely have horrified Ambedkar, who warned that caste was anti-national and could disable national politics (Ambedkar 2014; Nussbaum 2015). A deeper analysis of the issue, however, lies beyond the scope of this chapter (Rao 2009).

Let us focus instead on reservations in higher education, a tractable slice of the question. We must, however, begin with overall data on literacy, since that is a key part of the picture. As Jayati Ghosh has shown, there are distressing gaps in basic literacy between SC/STs and others, with OBCs on average in the middle, "others" at the top (and note that "other" includes Muslims, which surely pull down the average, so the gap is in fact larger than it appears). When

---

[26] His remarkable development achievements in Bihar are combined with a strong rejection of the politics of religious division, so he quit the BJP over the elevation of Modi, and Congress, far from welcoming him in, as they should have done, immediately ran the corrupt Laloo against him. So he is at present a man without a national party, though he has regained the Bihar chief ministership.

[27] It's worth noting that the other charismatic regional populist leader of long influence, Tamil Nadu's Jayalalitha, is actually a Brahmin. Ditto the longtime leaders of the Communist Party of West Bengal, Jyoti Basu and Buddhadeb Bhattacharjee. So much for the dictatorship of the proletariat. Is Mayawati a good representative of *dalit* interests? Her enormous ego and her dedication to personal luxury do not bode well.

these are put together with gender gaps and rural/urban gaps, we get the astonishing result that the highest category urban males who are "other" are 52.4 percentage points above rural tribal women, the most disadvantaged group. (See Appendix for Figures 9.1 and 9.2 from Ghosh (2012).)

As we ascend through the stages of education, the gaps grow wider. As they grow wider, the quota-based system proves more and more inadequate to produce good outcomes. By the time we arrive at the coveted places in elite institutions of higher education, SC and ST students who fill the allotted reserved spaces are distinctly less well prepared than the Others, with OBCs, again, somewhere in the middle. (But because OBCs do not suffer early educational deprivation nearly as uniformly, those who do get selected may in fact be quite well prepared.)

What ought to be agreed, but isn't: this situation represents an enormous waste of human capital (Patnaik 2012). But of course when people harbor feelings of disgust and contempt toward another group they rarely grant that their human potential is equal to their own. What cannot be denied, however, is that preparation is indeed quite unequal, with reference to fluency in English particularly, but all across the board. The place to address the gap productively is in very early childhood; but when it has not been addressed there, and when students are given places in higher education on an unequal footing, trouble is bound to ensue. The discourse about affirmative action in India is somewhat simplistic, prone to using crude notions of "merit" that need critique, as if entrance exams for IITs and IIMs really showed natural human capital, or fitness for a productive social contribution. So this cultural belief in the inequality in "merit" of the SC and STs, combined with the real fact of their unequal preparation, creates a toxic situation in the IITs and IIMs.

In a deeply disturbing paper, D. Parthasarathy (2012), a professor of Humanities at IIT-Mumbai, describes the culture hostile to SCs and STs at his elite institution. (Note *en passant*: Parthasarathy, as his name reveals, is a southern Brahmin. The problem of caste in higher education shows itself nowhere more clearly than in the menu of scholars doing excellent work on caste in higher education. The Indian contributors (Hasan and Nussbaum 2012) to our collection were all invited by Zoya Hasan, a Muslim by birth[28] and at that time member of the Minorities Commission, so her choices are not likely to show prejudice. Nonetheless, in the entire list there was not one SC or ST, or even OBC – apart from the *dalit* politician Sukhadeo Thorat, by training an

---

[28] An odd conception, since nobody is born a member of a religion really: but in India children are registered as members of a religious group at birth. Hasan does not identify herself as a "Muslim scholar," and I mention the classification for purposes of historical/political understanding only.

economist, and editor of the collection of Ambedkar's papers to which
I frequently refer, but he was at the conference qua politician, as head of the
University Grants Commission, which funded it. Thorat has written movingly
about his own Ambedkar-like encounter with stigma and exclusion.)

The first element in the toxic brew is a total absence of remedial support for
SC and ST students. Faculty just don't want to do it; it isn't the "institutional
culture." Second is a refusal to offer these students exams in their vernacular
language, although this is required by law. Again, faculty don't want to be
bothered. Third is the refusal of upper-caste students (again with the support of
faculty) to form project teams or do reports with SC and ST students.
No doubt they want to get good marks and feel, not without some reason,
that the SC and ST students are less likely to do well. But probably they don't
like them and harbor discriminatory feelings toward them, at least in many
cases – which they can all too easily cloak in rhetoric about "merit."[29] Studies
of unconscious racism in the US have shown that even people who believe
that they are progressive still often harbor stigmatizing stereotypes of African-
Americans. The same is extremely likely to be true in India for attitudes to SCs
and STs.[30]

Were reservations wrong? That would be the natural conclusion in the
United States, and in the next section I shall show sympathy with some reforms
of the system.[31] Nonetheless, given the attitudes that prevailed and still in large
part do prevail, the result for SCs and STs would have been far worse, surely,
without reservations. It is interesting that in politics, where life-experience and
force of thought and personality are more important than academic training,
SCs do pretty well and attain positions of national power. The academy is
a tougher nut to crack, since someone who has had a totally inadequate
primary education is extremely unlikely ever to achieve success.

---

[29] In the role played by joint student projects in success, the critique reminds one of the recent
critique of gender practices in US business schools.

[30] And one must mention the effect of such attitudes on behavior and performance. Even in the
cloistered progressive academic circles I frequent, one hears people say, "Oh one cannot
include X in anything, he is so socially awkward and impossible." X is a *dalit*, and X is indeed
socially awkward. But in a manner that would have been no surprise to Ambedkar, X brightens
up and unbends in the presence of Americans, believing quite correctly that they do not harbor
discriminatory feelings toward him (not because they are morally better, of course, but because
they have different sources of implicit bias). X laughs at no joke made by any Indian. He laughs
delightedly at jokes made by Americans.

[31] In Hasan and Nussbaum (2012), Thomas Weisskopf of the University of Michigan, who has
published a comparative study of the US and Indian systems, offers different suggestions for
reform, more in line with our US experience; but, resting as his proposals do on the discretion
of admissions officers, they seem quite unsuitable for India, where corruption would quickly
swamp any non-mechanical system. See Weisskopf (2012).

One thing, however, is utterly clear: that by now the politics of reservation has taken a form that flies in the face Ambedkar's second, and deeper, critique of caste: for it has made caste far more central in people's lives than it might otherwise have been, creating caste-based parties and a politics of competitive bean-counting that is just the sort of thing he blames on caste, and for the sake of which he wishes to annihilate caste. Could discrimination have been ended without further entrenching caste identities? Possibly. But this is not what has happened.[32]

Ambedkar had the right ideas, and made some progress; but majority tyranny is sticky, and the gross failure of the nation in primary education has taken its toll. One can certainly ask whether the time frame is too short to perform an assessment, but it would seem that, no matter how deplorable the situation of African-Americans in the United States currently is, they have come a lot further in a comparable period of time.

IV RELIGIOUS MINORITIES

India's religious minorities were omitted from the scope of affirmative action at the time of the founding and once again as a result of the Mandal Commission in 1980, which reaffirmed the caste-based system of reservations and increased the quotas (for pertinent history, see Hasan and Nussbaum 2012: Introduction). (From now on I shall omit the Parsis, which are rarely discussed in this context, and the Jews, who are too few today to constitute a separate interest group; I shall focus on Muslims and Christians. The peculiarity of counting Buddhists, Jains, and Sikhs along with Hindus is a curious problem, and one should note that they too would appear to suffer from the caste-based quota system, but are rarely discussed in this connection.[33]) The reason for the omission was the fear that "separate electorates" would be the logical next step, and that was an electoral system that had been vigorously rejected. However, as I've observed, Ambedkar and others, early on, favored separate electorates for scheduled castes, and he himself favored them for Muslims as well (see Thorat 2006: Introduction). Yet people did not use the alleged danger of separate electorates based upon caste as a reason against affirmative action for the scheduled castes and scheduled tribes. So we can only say that it is

---

[32] One might also draw attention to the way in which Hindu religion has been increasingly captured by the Hindu right, who certainly do not favor the rational reform that Ambedkar advocated; the dogmatic atheism of some of the founding generation (often inspired by Marxism), also contributes, making internal reform of Hinduism less likely.

[33] Presumably the reason for not discussing them is that they are originally from some caste or other and can claim reservation under that identity. But the same is true of many Muslims and Christians, most of whom are converts.

a curious outcome, and one that some people probably supported and support out of anti-Muslim bias.

The Constitution does go to great lengths to assure religious minorities of legal protection.[34] The non-discrimination article, Article 15, prohibits discrimination on grounds of religion, as well as race, caste, sex, and place of birth. Article 25 guarantees liberty of conscience and the right to profess, practice, and propagate religion. Article 26 gives religious groups the freedom to manage their own affairs. Article 27 guarantees that no citizen will be forced to pay taxes that go to the support of any religious group, surely a linchpin of religious equality ever since James Madison's Memorial and Remonstrance in 1785. Article 28 prohibits state aid to religious schools and universities, except in the case of certain independent trusts that get state aid; and no pupil in any state institution shall be made to take religious instruction. Article 30 protects the right of minorities to administer educational institutions. Article 29 protects their right to use their own "language or script," a provision extending beyond Muslims and Christians but clearly applying to Urdu specifically. And of course the preservation of the personal laws gave minorities[35] much scope for self-rule – although this has not worked to the advantage of minority women, as we shall see in the following section.

As with caste, there are very many issues we could address. The first and most obvious one is that discrimination against Muslims and Christians is very widespread, in all segments of society: employment, housing (the excuse is often that the smell of beef is revolting), and basic security. The 2002 Gujarat riots, to which I have devoted a book-length study (Nussbaum 2007), showed very clearly that Muslim lives were given scant consideration by the police in the state of Gujarat. In one trial that has reached a conclusion, the Naroda Patiya case, thirty-two defendants, including Maya Kodnani, at the time a minister of the Gujarat state government, have received long prison terms, and a criminal conspiracy has been found.[36] Particularly welcome was the conviction of Babu Bajranji of the Hindu right organization Bajrang Dal, who had boasted on hidden camera of his gruesome murder of a pregnant woman and her child.[37]

---

[34] Ambedkar draws attention to this in Ambedkar (1948), noting that he received a lot of criticism on this point.

[35] Notice that in India the term "minority" means "religious minorities" and does not include caste-based or sexual groups. Thus the Minorities Commission does not consider caste. It would be an awkward term for lower-caste groups anyway, given that put together they constitute a majority of the population.

[36] The defendants were convicted of murder, attempted murder, and conspiracy. Some received life terms.

[37] For the transcript see www.tehelka.com/tag/transcript-babu-bajrangi/. In a now-famous quote, he states: "... there was this pregnant woman, I slit her open, sisterf****r ... Showed them

This is one case in which the activism of the Supreme Court, which appointed a Special Investigative Team, achieved a signal victory for justice (Nussbaum 2012b). It is all too obvious, however, that the vast majority of the crimes committed then will never see justice: because of the refusal of police to take down the complaints of victims, because of witness intimidation and threats against lawyers, and because, in some cases, of likely corruption in the state's court system.

When such crimes can occur with impunity – for it's obvious that the thirty-two who were convicted are a tiny fraction of the criminals of their type around the state, much less the nation – what can we say about religious freedom in India? Christians have also been assailed, both in Orissa frequently and in a string of recent disturbing incidents in Delhi. The prime minister condemned this violence very belatedly, on February 17, 2015, and only after rebuke from President Obama. The future is hard to predict, and ominous.

However, let me focus, as with caste, on the question of affirmative action. Of course, for religious minorities, there is none, and this has led to a situation in which Muslims are doing even worse than lower-caste Hindus. The Sachar Committee Report in 2006 established very clearly with impressively detailed data, that Muslims are India's poorest and most disadvantaged group, below the scheduled castes and the scheduled tribes in economic situation and educational attainment. Furthermore, while Muslims are approximately 14 percent of the population, the overall percentage of Muslims in the civil service is only 2.5 percent.

As for education, the combination of bad primary education and lack of affirmative action means that, unlike the lower castes, Muslims don't even get in the door. One anecdote tells all. On a visit to NALSAR in Hyderabad in 2011, an excellent national law school that is usually ranked number 2 in the nation, I noted that there was not a single Muslim in the entering class, in a region of India in which Muslims comprise 40 percent of the population. The dean's explanation was that the entrance exam is in English and the government schools do not teach English, or not well. When one considers the society's acute need for Muslim lawyers, especially given the fact that some local bar associations refuse legal representation to Muslims charged with terrorism (see Nussbaum 2009) – even when the charges are frivolous and capricious – we can see that there is a social problem here much larger than the injustice done to talented young Muslims whose human capital is being

[Muslims] what's what . . . what kind of revenge we can take if our people are killed . . . I am no feeble rice-eater] . . . didn't spare anyone . . . they shouldn't even be allowed to breed . . . I say that even today . . . Whoever they are, women, children, whoever . . . Nothing to be done with them but cut them down. Thrash them, slash them, burn the bastards . . ."

wasted. And the very fact that a bar association would take such a vote, as quite a few have, shows that the legal profession is in profound need of reform at a very basic ethical level, before it could claim to be an ally of a politics of inclusion rather than its enemy. Ambedkar's lack of attention to the formation of lawyers was very short-sighted.

As for affirmative action as remedy, some have recommended that Muslims and Christians who can document lower-caste origins should get access to affirmative action under the description *dalit*-Muslim or *dalit*-Christian. This remedy, however, would apply only to a relatively small subgroup of those who suffer from exclusion and lack of equal opportunity, since documentation is difficult, and since many Muslims are not converts. Furthermore, many Muslims are disadvantaged qua Muslims rather than qua lower castes, and the proposed remedy would erase this salient fact. In a compelling paper and a related book, political scientist Zoya Hasan (2009; 2012) has recommended that the whole rationale for affirmative action be changed to focus on economic disadvantage, or, at the very least, to weigh this in alongside group membership. Given that this remedy would add to the power of religious minorities, it is not to be expected that it will be adopted any time soon.

In this case, the Constitution itself left a gap, making provision for affirmative action only for some and not for others. But the real problems are deep social and economic problems whose solution lies well beyond the scope of the document and go to the heart of Indian society itself – particularly at the present time, when the idea of full inclusion for religious minorities has apparently been abandoned by many, if they ever had it.

What Ambedkar foresaw has come to pass: in the absence of widespread educational reform, particularly in primary education, the progress of lower castes and religious minorities has stalled. And as recent studies show, the system of primary education, a disaster for many years, is if anything getting worse, producing a more and more stratified society. While the elite institutions have worldwide distinction, they serve a determinedly elite constituency. Sen and Drèze rightly speak of a "remarkable social insensitivity to the unfairness and injustice of such gross disparities, contributing to the persistence of a hugely stratified Indian society" (Drèze and Sen 2013: ch. 5, 129).

How can elites tolerate this waste of human capital, one might ask? Perhaps the answer lies in the changed nature of the economy, which is far less labor-intensive than earlier agricultural and industrial economies; thus a small well-trained elite can produce economic growth, while others die or languish. An IT economy just doesn't need as many bodies as an agricultural economy. When we have witnessed the spectacle of communist cadres shooting Bengali peasants in the back to get them off of land that the government wants to use for a foreign pharmaceutical plant (in which those peasants will never be offered jobs, since schools did not give them the requisite skills) (see Nussbaum 2008), what further evidence of indifference to lower-caste lives could surprise us? It is easy to be reminded of the words of Ebenezer Scrooge: "If they are like to die, then they had better do so, and decrease the surplus population."

V GENDER

The equality of women was an issue close to Ambedkar's heart, and we have seen that he resigned from the government over it. That episode showed that there were strong forces arrayed against the movement for women's equality. Perhaps the fact that the proponent of radical reform in Hindu law was a *dalit* hardened the opposition.[38] Nonetheless, Ambedkar did succeed in getting sex equality mentioned in the Constitution itself, in Article 15, something that the United States has proven unable to do. To what achievements has this commitment led, sixty-five years on?

Let us look first at the overall picture. India's women are doing very badly in world terms, and even by comparison to the women of other South Asian nations. Let's begin with who's alive. Amartya Sen has coined the term "missing women" for the women who would be in a given country, if they had the same sex ratio as (some appropriate baseline representing equal nutrition and health-care), but are not in fact there. He chooses the sex ratio in Sub-Saharan Africa as the baseline and comes up with a figure of around thirty-seven million missing women in India in 1986; others who use a somewhat different baseline arrive at thirty-five million (Drèze and Sen 2002: 230). Female–male ratios vary greatly among states, with the south and east being far more woman-friendly than the north and west. There are no pertinent religious differences, and in general the survey of Muslim women conducted by Zoya Hasan and Ritu Menon (2004) shows that across all pertinent dimensions variations are regional rather than religious. The disappearance of women is due less to outright infanticide than to differential nutrition and health care – and, more recently, to sex-selective abortion. For the natality ratio has been falling, again with the north and west experiencing a greater problem than the east and south (Drèze and Sen 2002: 257).

So one way in which women conspicuously fail to attain non-discrimination is in getting to remain alive. This situation is influenced by many factors, including differential educational and employment opportunities (families

[38] Such is the judgment of Rao (2009: 168–9).

will invest more in sons, who have better prospects), exogamous marriage
(daughters don't stay around to help parents in their old age), dowry (daughters
are very expensive), lack of political influence of women, and still other factors.
Efforts to address these problems by statute (for example, making dowry and
amniocentesis illegal) have not been terribly successful.

In other ways the lot of women is pretty grim. More than 90 percent of
adolescent women in the nation are anemic, a figure worse than that in some
of Africa's poorest nations.[39] This figure is cause and no doubt also effect of
a massive public health shortfall: for example, 43 percent of children under
five in India are malnourished, as compared with 20 percent in Sub-Saharan
Africa, 4 percent in Latin America, and so on. The India figures for female
anemia are worse than those in Bangladesh, Sri Lanka, and even Pakistan.
We could go on and on (see Drèze and Sen 2013: chapter 6). With a recent
20 percent cut in the health budget, we can't expect improvement any time
soon – except in those states that already have high-quality public health
systems, particularly Tamil Nadu.

In education, as my table from Ghosh already shows, women lag
behind, and the double deficit of low caste or Muslim identity with gender
is particularly likely to spell illiteracy (see also Drèze and Sen 2013: chapter 5). Needless to say, all of this is outside of the scope of constitutional law,
or even statutory law (even if there were a statute forbidding sex discrimination, which there isn't). Such matters require large-scale policy
interventions.

What, then, of constitutional law? I shall now mention four problems
created by the document, and then three areas in which constitutional activism has been useful. As we consider these matters, it is useful to remind
oneself that the first female justice of the Supreme Court was appointed in
1990, that there is today but one woman on the 28-judge court, and there has
never been more than one at a time. The autobiography of Leela Seth (2003),
the first female High Court judge, reveals the many obstacles to sex equality in
that still very conservative profession.

1. *The notorious "only."* Article 15 reads: The State shall not discriminate
against any citizen on grounds only of religion, race, caste, sex, place of
birth or any of them." What is the significance of "only"? Evidently it is
meant to show that what is disallowed is arbitrary discrimination on such
grounds, not discrimination that might be taken to be part of a bona fide
occupational qualification, a problematic concept, but one that judges

---

[39] See www.nytimes.com/2015/03/03/world/asia/-pregnant-women-india-dangerously-under
weight-study.html?_r=o. Data are drawn from a study published in the Proceedings of the
National Academy of Sciences.

have worked with for decades. However, judges who have not precisely been woman-friendly decided at one point that if it could be shown that the discrimination is not a matter of biological sex, but results from social norms and prejudices, it does not run afoul of Article 15.[40] Courts have not consistently followed this pattern, but it has made a mess of some non-discrimination claims. Ambedkar should have seen the problem in advance, and did not.

Here's the case I promised, in which a textualist might argue that the Supreme Court interpreted the document correctly. Thus the whole question of whether the Constitution has been implemented or not rests on the interpretive theory one might adopt.

2. *Equality: formal or substantive?* A larger drafting error, though perhaps caused by the limits of what he could get done, was a failure to spell out the concept of equality relevant to Article 14: Is mere formal equality enough? Or is the demand for substantive equality? I have dealt with this at length elsewhere (Nussbaum 2004a) and will not repeat myself, except to say that early courts understood equality in an abstract formalist way, but a more substantive understanding has gradually prevailed. Ambedkar understood this distinction extremely well, but he did not end up articulating it, for whatever reason, leaving courts to play around with idea of relevant and irrelevant distinctions, to women's detriment. The United States has also struggled with this issue, in both race and gender, and courts have had to step in, for example in *Loving* v. *Virginia*, holding that the formal symmetry of the anti-miscegenation laws did not mean that they did not violate the Equal Protection Clause.[41]

3. *Privacy and dignity.* I have already mentioned the decision neither to incorporate substantive due process nor to construct a privacy right in some other way. These twin decisions held up the legal recognition of a privacy right, which has not always promoted women's interests, but has recently been important in analyzing sexual orientation and transgender issues. For related reasons India has been slow to incorporate into constitutional jurisprudence the fertile idea of life with dignity, which is increasingly used by the Court to address issues of inclusion.

4. *Personal laws* (see fuller treatment in Nussbaum 2012a; Nussbaum 2004a). As I've said, Ambedkar did strive to insulate fundamental rights from pressure from traditional religion, but, due to the judiciary, he did not succeed: the personal laws were held to be immune from the scrutiny of the

---

[40] *Air India* v. *Nargesh Meerza*, AIR 1981, 4 SCC 335; *Miss Lena Khan* v. *Union of India and Ors*, AIR 1987, 2 SCC 402.

[41] *Loving* v. *Virginia*, 388 U.S. 1 (1967).

Fundamental Rights. This was a major setback for women, since all the major religions (Parsis perhaps excepted) have striven ever since to display their power by disadvantaging women. Christian women have done particularly badly in the areas of divorce and inheritance. Christian women won the right to divorce on grounds of cruelty only in 2001. And until the landmark case of *Mrs. Mary Roy* v. *State of Kerala*, Christian daughters, under the Travancore Christian Act, inherited only one-fourth of the share given to sons, and a part of their inheritance went to the churches (see Nussbaum 2000: chapter 3)![42] In an end run around the legal obstacle, the Supreme Court, unable to declare this law unconstitutional under Article 15, instead simply ruled that Christians in Kerala would henceforth be under the jurisdiction of the Indian Succession Act of 1925, which gave daughters equal shares and gave nothing to the church. Hindu women often do worse on property issues, since family property is often held in consortia in which women hold unequal shares, and have a hard time extracting their share (Agarwal 2004). The unequal shares in agricultural land have been a focus of feminist action by economist Bina Agarwal and others, and the system was changed by statute in 2005. The situation of Muslim women with regard to maintenance after divorce has been widely discussed, apropos of the famous Shah Bano case,[43] followed by the Muslim Women's (Protection after Divorce) Act, which deprived all and only Muslim women of the remedy that had been found for them under the Criminal Procedure Code (Nussbaum 2000: ch. 3; 2004a; 2012a). As in the case of Kerala's Christians, so here: the Supreme Court did not declare this statute unconstitutional, but in a remarkable exercise of interpretive gymnastics held that it was constitutional only in case it actually meant something very different from what it appears to mean on its face, and actually gave Muslim women ample maintenance.[44] So again the Supreme Court did an end run around the obstacle imposed by precedent and reached a result in Ambedkar's spirit.

The system of personal laws is clearly an impediment to sex equality, but the nation moves past these obstacles in most cases, through statutory or judicial resourcefulness. Nonetheless, the only thing that would really solve the problem, an omnibus non-discrimination statute (whether limited to sex equality or sweeping more broadly),[45] does not yet exist, and is not even on the horizon.

---

[42] AIR 1986, SC 1011.

[43] *Mohammed Ahmed Khan* v. *Shah Bano Begum & Ors.* (AIR 1985 SC 945).

[44] *Danial Latifi & Anr.* v. *Union of India* (2001) 7 SCC 740.

[45] Whether to focus on sex equality or to craft the statue more broadly has been a subject of considerable debate among Indian feminists and is probably moot for the time being anyway,

Now we turn to the brighter side.

5. *Judicial activism: Vishaka.* As I've mentioned, the case of sexual harassment is a real victory for Supreme Court activism in accordance with a petition from an NGO. It took sixteen years for Parliament to draft legislation following the guidelines set down by the Supreme Court in 1997, but in 2013 it happened. We must wait to see whether the legislation will be enforced.

6. *Right to education.* As I've said, Ambedkar understood that education was crucial to the success of all his projects. Nonetheless, he succeeded in getting the right to education into the Constitution only in the unenforceable/aspirational Directive Principles of State Policy, Part IV. In 1992, the Supreme Court held that education actually does have the status of a fundamental right, and thus belongs in Part III, rather than Part IV.[46] The following year, they held that the right to education requires compulsory free education up to the age of fourteen, and after that is in accordance with the economic capacity of the particular state, adding an analysis under Article 21: "The right to education flows directly from the right to life and is related to the dignity of the individual."[47] Following this, the 83rd amendment was added to the Constitution, attached to Article 21 as 21A; it specifies the education right in detail and locates it squarely within the ambit of founding-era constitutional rights. As I've noted, the guarantee of the midday meal was later added by Supreme Court mandate, thus making the education right more secure. The wretched quality of primary education, especially in rural areas, and in most states (Kerala is a striking exception) makes all this legal maneuvering pretty hollow, however. Getting more children into school does not help much if the teachers don't show up.

7. *Women in the panchayats.* In 1992, the 73rd and 74th amendments to the Constitution specified reservations of one-third for women in the local *panchayats.* (A given seat is reserved in one cycle, but then in the next one it is a different seat, so women eventually have to contest their seats.) This move was widely questioned at the time, including by feminist who felt that the women who took the reserved seats would not enact changes benefiting women. But studies since its implementation have shown that the system

since the primary proponent of the statute, Indira Jaising, who was solicitor-general in the previous government, has no role in the current one. Meanwhile, legal theorist Tarunabh Khaitan has been working on a draft antidiscrimination bill for the state of Delhi, still in progress. See Khaitan (2015).

[46] *Mohini Jain* v. *State of Karnataka,* AIR 1992 SC 1858.

[47] *Unnikrishnan J. P.* v. *State of Andhra Pradesh,* AIR 1993 SC 2178.

has had two very significant results: It has increased the demand for the education of girls. And it has led to a larger proportion of expenditure on child health (Buch 2010; Jayal 2000).

These amendments are very much in Ambedkar's spirit, using affirmative action creatively in a way that does seem to be making a difference.

To summarize: Ambedkar did some things quite well. Other things that have been done well are very much in his spirit. He did some other things not so well (or, rather, failed to get what he aimed for), but judges operating in his spirit have to some extent corrected the problems. On the whole, however, the disastrous failings of the nation with respect to health care and primary education swamp his achievements. He was right to focus on education, but he was not in a position to make it work.

VI   SEXUAL ORIENTATION AND GENDER IDENTITY

Here I must and shall be brief, having recently addressed the topic extensively in a recent related paper.[48] In my related paper, I argue that the criminalization of homosexual sodomy under Section 377 of the Criminal Procedure Code is British both in origin (inspired by Macaulay) and in conception (using the very un-Indian idea of a crime "against the order of nature"). (This was also emphasized in the Delhi High Court opinion in *Naz Foundation*.) Indian traditions are, as with every topic, complex, but the most ancient traditions (e.g., the *Kama Sutra*) are tolerant of a wide range of sexual acts and behaviors. Although later developments in Hindu ethics were more restrictive, India remained a place where gay men from Britain (for example, the novelist E. M. Forster) found a greater liberty. The real impetus behind the legal crackdown was Victorian, not Indian. That Victorian critique of Hinduism – epitomized in Winston Churchill's famous statement that Indians are "a beastly people with a beastly religion"[49] – stung deeply, however, influencing the development of Hindu thought in the twentieth and twenty-first centuries, in at least some quarters. Currently we are in the paradoxical situation where books can be banned simply for pointing to real historical features of Hinduism, where sex is concerned.[50]

---

[48]   See Nussbaum (Forthcoming 2016a).

[49]   Churchill was quite friendly to Islam, by contrast, and tried to persuade F. D. R. that Muslims were courageous fighters and Hindus were cowards. Roosevelt's independent examination of the army refuted this proposition.

[50]   I refer to the case of Wendy Doniger's *The Hindus*, which I discuss both in Nussbaum (Forthcoming 2016a) and in Nussbaum (2014).

In such a situation, the existence of Section 377 is no mere relic. Both the government's health ministry and the National AIDS Control Organization, together with The Lawyers Collective, the leading NGO working on that problem,[51] have long held that the existence of the law is a detriment to public health measures, since men who have sex with men (MSM)[52] will not come forward for treatment and testing. Section 377 was thrown out by the Delhi High Court in 2009, citing the constitutional grounds that it violated Article 14 (equality before the law), Article 15 (non-discrimination – after an argument that discrimination on grounds of sexual orientation constitutes sex discrimination), and Article 21 (violating both privacy and dignity).[53] Thus the understanding of Article 21 that incorporates ideas of both privacy and dignity, post-Ambedkar, though very much in his spirit, proved important; even though other grounds for the result were found, Article 21 provided the main line of the court's argument.

Ambedkar was prominently invoked in this eloquent opinion, and his words are quoted in a section where the court is rebutting the claim that majority sentiment can ever provide a compelling state interest.[54] Citing Ambedkar's words as he moved the draft Constitution in 1948, in the Constituent Assembly, they contrast popular morality with "constitutional morality" (a concept for which Ambedkar cites George Grote), and then cite his words of warning: "Constitutional morality is not a natural sentiment. It has to be cultivated. We must realise that our people have yet to learn it. Democracy in India is only a top dressing on an Indian soil which is essentially undemocratic."[55] What the opinion seems to understand by "constitutional morality" is not all that Ambedkar meant, as we'll see in our next section. They mean primarily a spirit of respect for the fundamental rights of all, even when majority sentiment opposes the recognition of those rights. Courts, the opinion continues, are guardians of constitutional morality so understood, hence of all Fundamental Rights, but especially of "the fundamental rights of those who may dissent or deviate from the majoritarian view."[56] The entire reasoning of the opinion emphasizes his cherished aims of ending majority tyranny and stigmatization, and working for social equality and inclusion.

---

[51] Anand Grover, its co-chair, is also UN Special Rapporteur on HIV/AIDS.

[52] The entire debate and the entire set of legal arguments is cast in terms of MSM, and no reference to women is made.

[53] *Naz Foundation* v. *Govt. of NCT of Delhi*, 160 Delhi Law Times 277 (Delhi High Court 2009).

[54] The level of equal protection review had previously been determined to be strict scrutiny.

[55] *Naz*, p. 65.

[56] Ibid., 99.

Indeed, the court makes a direct connection between the situation of sexual minorities and the issue of untouchability through an extensive discussion of the *hijras*,[57] suggesting strongly that their situation as a formerly untouchable "criminal caste" is emblematic of the situation of MSM more generally, since MSM are defined by Section 377 as criminals by nature, and thence excluded and stigmatized. The court summarizes:

> If there is one constitutional tenet that can be said to be underlying theme of the Indian Constitution, it is that of "inclusiveness". This Court believes that Indian Constitution reflects this value deeply ingrained in Indian society, nurtured over several generations. The inclusiveness that Indian society traditionally displayed, literally in every aspect of life, is manifest in recognizing a role in society for everyone. Those perceived by the majority as "deviants" or "different" are not on that score excluded or ostracized.
>
> Where society can display inclusiveness and understanding, such persons can be assured of a life of dignity and non-discrimination. This was the "spirit behind the Resolution"[58] of which Nehru spoke so passionately. In our view, Indian Constitutional law does not permit the statutory criminal law to be held captive by the popular misconceptions of who the LGBTs are. It cannot be forgotten that discrimination is antithesis of equality and that it is the recognition of equality which will foster the dignity of every individual.

Constitutional law struck an important blow here for inclusion and equal dignity. Nonetheless, inclusion ultimately played a double-edged role. The case was heard by a two-judge panel of the Delhi High Court. When it was appealed to the Supreme Court – not by the government, since the government refused to appeal, but by one Souresh Kumar Koushal, a private

---

[57] As I discuss in further detail in Nussbaum (Forthcoming 2016a), these are transgender males who play a receptive role in sexual intercourse; an ancient community, they are mentioned with honor in ancient texts and used to play an auspicious role at weddings and birth ceremonies. Today, however, they are heavily stigmatized, treated as untouchable, subject to arbitrary arrest and police torture, and very poor. For many years they were registered as a "criminal caste," i.e. as criminals by nature. All this is laid out in detail by the court in Naz, and clearly they are using this community as an emblem of the larger situation of MSM, who are excluded from society on account of stigma and disgust. After all, the point is, the sodomy laws do treat MSM as criminals by nature.

[58] Nehru, in December 1946, thus eight months before official independence, was speaking of (and introducing to the Constituent Assembly) the "Objectives Resolution," declaring India an independent nation with the intention to write a Constitution of its own, based on ideas of equality, liberty, and fraternity. He drew special attention to the goal of providing "adequate safeguards . . . for minorities."

individual who runs an astrology center in Delhi – it was again heard by a two-judge panel, in the manner that has resulted from the Court's initial commitment to inclusiveness and hence a large workload. I have been told that this case was one in which the panel was assigned randomly, not one where the chief justice exercised discretion.[59] That panel overruled the Delhi High Court in December 2013, reinstating Section 377. The opinion, as I show in detail in a related paper, is inadequate on matters of both fact and law. First, there is an obvious standing issue. The case is similar to our *Hollingsworth v. Perry*,[60] in which appeal was brought by private individuals since the State of California refused to appeal; it should clearly have had a similar outcome, since the plaintiff had not suffered a legally cognizable harm. And yet, the standing issue was never even mentioned in the Court's opinion. The central legal argument of the Delhi court about majority tyranny is not addressed at all, nor are the other key legal arguments concerning privacy, dignity, and sex discrimination. And the contention that the lower court erred on findings of fact, implausible in the light of the extensive factual record in *Naz*, is not rebutted by any showing of factual error. The opinion, in short, is a mess, but in the absence of any provision for *en banc* rehearing, it stands, and so does Section 377 – unless parliament acts, which it won't. The government filed a review petition, and the Naz Foundation filed a "curative petition" in March, 2014.[61] The Court has agreed to hear the petition, so this is already hopeful; but a year later, nothing has happened yet. People speculate that it will be revisited by a larger panel; typically such a review would include the two original justices but add others. In this case, one of the two original justices has recently retired. But the entire matter is still terribly uncertain. Ambedkar's laudable commitment to judicial accessibility has led, down the road, to a situation in which the luck of the draw can determine matters of immense importance – surely not a result he would have welcomed.

The capriciousness of the system was further revealed in the 2014 case that is the source of my epigraph, a case in which a different two-judge panel of the Supreme Court granted *hijras* and other transgender people the right to be recognized as a third sex, neither male nor female, on passports and other official documents, and also deemed them eligible for affirmative action. Since *hijras* had played a central role in the argument of the Delhi court in *Naz*, and since the case dwells intently on the issue of

---

[59] Conversation with faculty at the National University of Juridical Sciences, Kolkata.
[60] 133 S. Ct. 2652 (2013).
[61] See Nussbaum (Forthcoming 2016a).

inclusion and equal respect, it is pretty obvious that this panel is rebuking the panel who authored the 2013 judgment. But of course they cannot change it. All they can do is talk inclusion, not really achieve it with regard to section 377.

So we are left with the bizarre situation that a group of people whose sex acts are still illegal, who are treated as quasi-untouchable and subjected (as the *Naz* opinion documents) to stigma and police torture, are nonetheless given wide-ranging new rights – by a different panel of judges – that go beyond rights given to transgender people in virtually all modern democracies, in most of which sodomy laws are now a thing of the past.[62] These new rights, coming without the foundation of basic equality, like an exquisite dessert without a main course, seem unlikely to improve their dire situation, in the absence of statutory reform or a good outcome to the curative petition.[63] Of course it is not clear that a different set of procedures would have achieved a better result, since the Supreme Court has never been polled as a whole on the question of Section 377. Still, the swelling size of the Court together with the capriciousness of its procedures has made basic rights quite unstable and jeopardized the very aim of inclusion that the large size of the Court was intended to promote.

VII "CONSTITUTIONAL MORALITY"

This chapter has focused primarily on substance, as is common in the comparative assessment of constitutions. We must not forget, however, that Ambedkar was deeply concerned with form, and from a certain perspective can even be called a formalist (Mehta 2010). In his initial speech introducing the Constitution, he drew attention to the crucial importance of what, following George Grote, he called "constitutional morality."[64] He cited Grote for the proposition that "The diffusion of constitutional morality, not merely among the majority of any community but throughout the whole, is the indispensable condition of a government at once free and peaceable." He went on to describe this morality:

---

[62] Similar rights were recently given to transgender people by Nepal.

[63] Thirty percent of *hijras* are HIV positive, so they more than the MSM community generally badly need the ability to seek treatment and testing without the stigma of illegality.

[64] It is not necessary here to ask whether Ambedkar reads Grote correctly, although I believe that he does.

By constitutional morality Grote meant "a paramount reverence for the forms of the Constitution, enforcing obedience to authority acting under and within these forms yet combined with the habit of open speech, of action subject only to direct legal control, and unrestrained censure of those very authorities as to all their public acts combined too with a perfect confidence in the bosom of every citizen amidst the bitterness of party contest that the forms of the Constitution will not be less sacred in the eyes of his opponents than in his own." (Ambedkar 1948)

One thing Ambedkar clearly means by constitutional morality is what the Delhi High Court took him to mean: a respect for the fundamental (constitutional) rights of all, even in the face of opposing majority sentiment. But we can see from the passage quoted that his idea is broader and more general: he means a spirit of respect for procedure and form, amid the fractious disputes that democratic politics always involves. All parties know that they will sometimes fail to get their way; but they have confidence, nonetheless, not only that their individual rights, including rights of free speech and assembly, will continue to be respected (the point stressed by the Delhi High Court), but, more generally, that the forms and procedures of governance set forth by the Constitution will themselves be observed: losers will abide by the verdict of the law, rather than using subterfuge or force to carry their point.

These liberal ideals have carried India a long way, explaining its utter difference, politically, from Pakistan and even from Bangladesh. The ideals are still alive today, but throughout their career they have been periodically threatened by opponents on both the left and the right. Constitutional morality survived the Emergency: even though Indira Gandhi threw her political opponents in jail and arranged for her party to suspend the Fundamental Rights section of the Constitution, somehow the wisdom of a democratic electorate, together with the authority of the Supreme Court, restored the rule of law in its full force. So "constitutional morality" can potentially survive the threats to free speech and autonomy of thought characteristic of the current era (see Sen 2015 for many examples). But is there still the will to defend and zealously pursue Ambedkar's noble ideal? The transcript of the session marks a response of "hear, hear" at the conclusion of the sentences I quoted. It may be doubted that such sentences would receive many cheers today, whether from the majority or from the opposition.[65] To the extent that "constitutional morality" is losing its

---

[65] That is Mehta's point, in Mehta (2010): the liberal tradition is vanishing, and it is an ominous development.

normative grip, the entirety of Ambedkar's normative vision is in jeopardy. He was an unequivocal opponent of the solidaristic politics of both left (Marxism) and right (Hindu communalism). Who stands for the liberalism of parliamentary proceduralism and individual rights in the politics of India today?

VIII   AMBEDKAR'S UNFINISHED LEGACY

Ambedkar did not draft every word perfectly, from the viewpoint of his aims, but he did remarkably well, especially considering the strong opposition he had from traditionalists, including some in the judiciary itself, and from antidemocratic leftists, who also opposed the liberal spirit of his vision (see Ambedkar 1949). He created a document that continues to inspire. He also created a set of procedures that allow the Supreme Court to hear an extraordinary array of cases and to play an active and often valuable social role. Those very procedures, however, pose new problems, and it is currently difficult to rely on the Supreme Court to be the guardian of Fundamental Rights, in a world of powerful majority sentiment. However, the strong role his unequivocal statements about judicial independence played in the recent defeat of Modi's court-takeover proposal shows that he still lives as a legal mind defending the security of rights from partisan tyranny.

More distressing, however, the economic underpinning for minority inclusion, which Ambedkar understood as well as anyone, does not yet exist and is in some respects receding further from view, with cuts in the health budget and with a growing indifference to the human capital and human rights of those at the "bottom" of the social heap. It would appear that Ambedkar's pessimistic words of 1948 remain true today: "Democracy in India is only a top dressing on an Indian soil which is essentially undemocratic" (Ambedkar 1948). By "democracy" he meant, of course, not tyrannical majoritarianism, which certainly flourishes, but a full commitment to the equality, dignity, and inclusion of each.

The best summary of the current situation was given on November 4, 1948, by Ambedkar himself, at the end of the speech in which he moved the adoption of the new document: "[I]f things go wrong under the new Constitution, the reason will not be that we had a bad Constitution. What we will have to say is, that Man was vile."

APPENDIX

From: *Equalizing Access*, ed. Zoya Hasan and Martha C. Nussbaum. Chapter 9, "Toward a New Paradigm for Ensuring Universal Access to Quality Education," Jayati Ghosh.

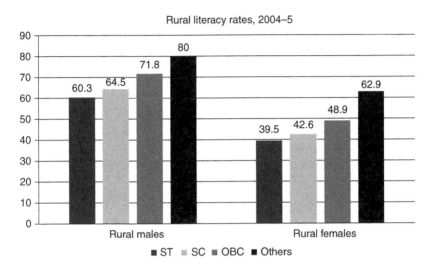

Rural literacy rates, 2004–5

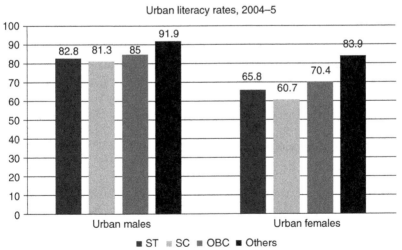

Urban literacy rates, 2004–5

REFERENCES

Agarwal, Bina. 2004. *A Field of One's Own: Gender and Land Rights in South Asia*. Cambridge: Cambridge University Press.

Ambedkar, B. R. 1948. Speech delivered in Constituent Assembly, November 5. http://164.100.47.132/LssNew/constituent/vol7p1.html.

—— 1949. Speech delivered in Constituent Assembly, November 28. http://parliamentofindia.nic.in/ls/debates/vol11p11.htm.

—— 1993. *Dr. Babasaheb Ambedkar: Writings and Speeches*. Vol. 12. Bombay: Education Department, Government of Maharashtra.

—— 2014. *Annihilation of Caste (undelivered speech, 1936)*. With Introduction by Arundhati Roy. Delhi: Navayana Publishing and London and New York: Verso.

Anand, Mulk Raj. 1936. *Coolie*. Delhi: Penguin.

Buch, Nirmala. 2010. *From Oppression to Assertion: Women and Panchayats in India*. Delhi: Routledge India.

Drèze, Jean and Amartya Sen. 2002. *India: Development and Participation*. Oxford: Oxford University Press.

—— 2013. *An Uncertain Glory: India and Its Contradictions*. Princeton and Oxford: Princeton University Press.

Ghosh, Jayati. 2012. Towards a New Paradigm for Ensuring Universal Access to Quality Education. In *Equalizing Access: Affirmative Action in India, United States, and South Africa*, edited by Z. Hasan and M. Nussbaum. Delhi: Oxford University Press: 202–38.

Hasan, Zoya. 2009. *Politics of Inclusion: Castes, Minorities, and Affirmative Action*. Delhi: Oxford University Press.

—— 2012. Trapped in an Invisible Present: Muslims and Disparities in Higher Education. In *Equalizing Access: Affirmative Action in India, United States, and South Africa*, edited by Z. Hasan and M. Nussbaum,. Delhi: Oxford University Press: 239–55.

Hasan, Zoya and Martha Nussbaum, editors. 2012. *Equalizing Access: Affirmative Action in Higher Education in India, United States, and South Africa*. Delhi: Oxford University Press.

Hasan, Zoya and Ritu Menon. 2004. *Unequal Citizens: A Study of Muslim Women in India*. Delhi: Oxford University Press.

Jaffrelot, Christophe. 2005. *Dr. Ambedkar and Untouchability: Analysing and Fighting Caste*. Delhi: Permanent Black.

Jayal, Niraja. 2000. *Gender and Decentralization. Unpublished manuscript*. Jawaharlal Nehru University, Delhi.

Khaitan, Tarunabh. 2015. *A Theory of Discrimination Law*. Oxford: Oxford University Press.

Mehta, Pratap Bhanu. 2010. What Is Constitutional Morality? *Seminar*. www.india-seminar.com/2010/615/615_pratap_bhanu_mehta.htm.

Nussbaum, Martha C. 2000. *Women and Human Development: The Capabilities Approach*. Cambridge and New York: Cambridge University Press.

2002. Sex Equality, Liberty, and Privacy: A Comparative Approach to the Feminist Critique. In *India's Living Constitution: Ideas, Practices, Controversies*, edited by E. Sridharan, Zoya Hasan, and R. Sudarshan. Delhi: Permanent Black: 242–83. A shortened version published as What's Privacy Got to Do with It? A Comparative Approach to the Feminist Critique. In *Women and the United States Constitution: History, Interpretation, Practice*, edited by Sibyl A. Schwarzenbach and Patricia Smith. New York: Columbia University Press, 2003: 153–75.

2004a. India, Sex Equality, and Constitutional Law. In *Constituting Women: The Gender of Constitutional Jurisprudence*, edited by Beverly Baines and Rut Rubio-Marin. Cambridge and New York: Cambridge University Press: 174–204.

2004b. The Modesty of Mrs. Bajaj: India's Problematic Route to Sexual Harassment Law. In *Directions in Sexual Harassment Law*, edited by Catharine A. MacKinnon and Reva B. Siegel. New Haven: Yale University Press: 633–71.

2007. *The Clash Within: Democracy, Religious Violence, and India's Future*. Cambridge, MA: Harvard University Press.

2008. Violence on the Left: Nandigram and the Communists of West Bengal. *Dissent* (Spring): 27–33.

2009. Land of My Dreams: Islamic Liberalism under Fire in India. *The Boston Review* 34: 10–14.

2012a. Personal Laws and Equality: The Case of India. In *Comparative Constitutional Design*, edited by Tom Ginsburg. Cambridge: Cambridge University Press: 266–93.

2012b. When is Forgiveness Right? *The Indian Express*, October 9. www .indianexpress.com/news/when-is-forgiveness-right-/1013768/0/.

2014. Law for Bad Behaviour. *The Indian Express*, February 22. http://india nexpress.com/article/opinion/columns/law-for-bad-behaviour/.

2015. Untouchable. Review of Ambedkar, *Annihilation of Caste: The Annotated Critical Edition*, edited by S. Anand. *The New Rambler Review*, August 19.

Forthcoming 2016a. Disgust or Equality? Sexual Orientation and Indian Law. *Journal of Indian Law and Society* (Kolkata).

2016b. Women's Progress and Women's Human Rights. *Human Rights Quarterly*. Summer issue.

Parthasarathy, D. 2012. After Reservations: Caste, Institutional Isomorphism, and Affirmative Action in the IIT's. In *Equalizing Access: Affirmative Action in India, United States, and South Africa*, edited by Z. Hasan and M. Nussbaum. Delhi: Oxford University Press: 256–71.

Patnaik, Prabhat. 2012. Affirmative Action and the "Efficiency Argument." In *Equalizing Access: Affirmative Action in India, United States, and South Africa*, edited by Z. Hasan and M. Nussbaum. Delhi: Oxford University Press: 89–99.

Rao, Anupama. 2009. *The Caste Question: Dalits and the Politics of Modern India*. Berkeley and Los Angeles: University of California Press.

Rawls, John. 1986. *Political Liberalism, expanded paper edition*. New York: Columbia University Press.

Robinson, Nick. 2013a. The Indian Supreme Court and Its Benches. *Seminar*. http://india-seminar.com/2013/642/642_nick_robinson.htm.

2013b. "Structure Matters: The Impact of Court Structure on the Indian and U.S. Supreme Courts." *American Journal of Comparative Law* 61: 101–36.

2016. India's Judicial Architecture. In *Oxford Handbook on the Indian Constitution*, edited by Sujit Choudry, Madhav Khosla, and Pratap Bhanu Mehta. Delhi: Oxford University Press.

Rutledge, Jennifer Geist. 2012. Courts as Entrepreneurs: The Case of the Indian Mid-Day Meal Programme. *Asian Politics and Policy* 4: 527–47.

Sachar Commission. 2006. www.prsindia.org/administrator/uploads/general/1242304423~~Summary%20of%20Sachar%20Committee%20Report.pdf.

Sen, Amartya. 2015. India: The Stormy Revival of an International University. *The New York Review of Books* 52(13): 69–71.

Seth, Leila. 2003. *On Balance*. Delhi: Penguin.

Thorat, Sukadeo. 2006. *B. R. Ambedkar: Perspectives on Social Exclusion and Inclusive Policies*. Delhi: Oxford University Press.

Weisskopf, Thomas. 2012. Rethinking Affirmative Action in Admissions to Higher Educational Institutions. In *Equalizing Access: Affirmative Action in India, United States, and South Africa*, edited by Z. Hasan and M. Nussbaum. Delhi: Oxford University Press: 44–70.

12

Assessing the Constitution of Kenya 2010 five years later

James Thuo Gathii

In this chapter, I assess the implementation of Kenya's 2010 Constitution, one of the most important efforts in recent years to transform a political culture through constitutional change. Using a case-study approach, I assess the successes, challenges, and failures in meeting the Constitution's ambitious reform agenda.[1] I then offer explanations for these varied outcomes.[2]

The reforms required by the 2010 Constitution have been implemented with varying degrees of success, in fits and starts, as well as with varying speeds. Although the judiciary has transformed to become relatively more independent of the Executive than before the 2010 Constitution, its empowerment has been met with backlash, particularly from Parliament. In addition, corruption in the judiciary has continued.[3] By contrast, the anti-corruption authority, the Ethics and Anti-Corruption Authority (EACC), recognized for the first time as an independent organ in the Constitution, has been hampered by its continued inability to prosecute and instead has had to depend on the Director of

Thanks to Harrison Otieno for his research assistance and comments on earlier drafts.

[1]   I do not, however, examine the vast and complex number of transformational reforms the 2010 Constitution envisages. It has 264 Articles and 49,851 words in the 2010 Constitution. The length of the Constitution was the result of a long period of Constitution making. The Constitution incorporates numerous governance and aspirational goals designed to address the challenges these constitution-making efforts sought to overcome.

[2]   Assessing the implementation and rollout of Kenya's 2010 Constitution using a case-study approach and using quantitative data where it is available. This approach makes it possible to get a bird's-eye view of the state of implementation, its successes, its challenges, and failures. It also makes it possible to assess whether institutional transformation or reform has been achieved by comparison to the pre-2010 political order – particularly the subordination of the judiciary, parliament, and entire bureaucracy of government to an imperial presidency and the disregard of the rights of citizens.

[3]   James Ekwam, "Judiciary Still Reeks of Corruption Admits Rao Team: Vetting Board Admits Some Judges Believed to Be Corrupt Are Still on the Bench," *Daily Nation*, March 2, 2016, *available at* www.nation.co.ke/news/Corruption-is-entrenched-in-courts/-/1056/3099136/-/90w ev/-/index.html.

Public Prosecutions to prosecute suspects. Parliament has since the adoption of the 2010 Constitution been instrumental in the removal of two EACC Chief Executive Officers as well as other senior officials. Thus, the constitutionalization of leadership and integrity principles stands in sharp contrast to continued widespread corruption in all branches of government including in the newly established regional system of governance. A number of factors including new leadership and a swathe of new judges have been critical to the progress made in the judiciary, and the absence of such leadership in the EACC, as well as the lack of a consistent commitment to combat corruption in both the Executive and the Legislature, is a major explanation for the relative difference in outcomes. The resulting picture is one which reminds us of the need for political will to effectuate institutional transformation.

I also attribute the relative success in judicial reform to the highly energized civil society movement, which includes activist lawyers and individuals who have been at the forefront in monitoring the implementation of the Constitution and testing its contours in Court. In addition, donors have provided additional encouragement and funding to assist the very expensive process of implementing these constitutional changes.

There are other successes as well. The Commission for the Implementation of the Constitution has been the major scorekeeper and guardian of the process of implementing the Constitution at all levels and departments of government. Another important point is that the 2010 Constitution contributed toward breaking the cycle of election violence in 2013. The rollout of a devolved government has been undertaken even though major challenges remain.

In short, this chapter finds that the judiciary has undergone significant reforms, and in particular attained institutional autonomy from the Executive, while the establishment of independent commissions has reduced the scope of centralized control. As a result there is a growing capacity and bureaucratic autonomy from political control in parts of the central government. This has contributed to reducing the authoritarian character of the Kenyan state. However, in other parts of the bureaucracy there has only been modest improvement, without transformation.

I proceed as follows. In Part One, a brief overview of the 2010 Constitution is provided. Part Two examines the relative success in the emergence of an independent judiciary, the contribution of the 2010 Constitution to ending election violence, and to setting the embryonic states for bureaucratic capacity and autonomy. Part Three examines the challenges facing implementation of devolved governance, and Part Four looks into the failure of anti-corruption reforms.

PART ONE: A BRIEF OVERVIEW OF THE 2010 CONSTITUTION

The 2010 Constitution was approved by a margin of 66.91% in a referendum on August 4 of that year. It then came into force on August 27, 2010, and in the process inaugurated significant reforms in Kenya's governance system. Like many Constitutions, it establishes governance structures, but it goes beyond that by providing for an enforceable set of leadership values and principles that ought to inform governance processes and decisions. This combination of rules and values runs throughout the constitutional text. The inclusion of leadership and integrity principles reflects the aspirations Kenyans expressed in the almost two-decade constitution-making process to transform authoritarian and unaccountable governance. In terms of governmental structure, it establishes a two-tier structure in which forty-seven regional governments, called Counties, were created and conferred with executive and legislative authority. A second Parliamentary chamber, the Senate, was established with its members directly elected from each County. Although the Constitution adopts a presidential system, presidential powers were significantly weakened relative to the earlier constitution. The Constitution strengthens the power of Parliament by giving it the power to approve presidential appointments to the cabinet members and other senior government officials. Cabinet appointments are limited to twenty-two and must be drawn from outside Parliament. This effectively reduces the ability of the president to leverage appointments to create a system of patronage and, as such, to control Parliament. In addition, the president no longer has power to suspend or dissolve Parliament. Parliament was empowered to conduct hearings to hold the Executive accountable and to have more control over the budgetary process. Parliament may by two-third votes in both chambers override a presidential veto.[4]

Another limitation on presidential authority was the dispersion of presidential powers through the creation of ten independent bodies charged with powers that were previously exercised by the Executive branch. These include the Auditor General; the Controller of Budgets; the National Police Service Commission; the National Land Commission; the Salaries and Remuneration Commission; the Kenya National Human Rights and Equality Commission; the Independent Elections and Boundaries Commission; and the Commission on the Implementation of the Constitution. The heads of these bodies are appointed by the president but are subject to parliamentary approval.

In terms of values, the Constitution provides that Kenya shall be a "multi-party democratic state" that is "founded on the national values and principles

---

[4]   Constitution, art. 115(6) (2010) (Kenya).

of governance."[5] These values and principles include patriotism, national unity, sharing and devolution of power, the rule of law, democracy, and participation of the people; human dignity, equity, social justice, inclusiveness, equality, human rights, non-discrimination, and protection of the marginalized; good governance, integrity, transparency, and accountability; and sustainable development.[6] The judiciary is required to interpret the Constitution in a manner that "promotes its purposes, values and principles," and in a manner that "contributes to good governance."[7] It is particularly instructive that Article 73(1)(b) of the Constitution vests in state officers the "responsibility to serve the people, rather than the power to rule over them."[8] This provision is consistent with the Constitution's goal of replacing a culture of order and corruption with a culture of public service at all levels of government.[9]

The 2010 Constitution also sought to reduce the high-stakes winner-takes-all nature of Kenya's first past-the-post election system. It did so in a number of ways. To win, the president must obtain 25% of the vote in twenty-four of the forty-seven Counties in addition to winning 50% plus one in the national vote. This reduced the probability that a president could be elected on the basis of a narrow ethnic coalition. Given the devolution of power to the Counties, the president's party may win a majority in one house of Kenya's bicameral Parliament, but that may not be the case in the other house. Even if the president's party controlled both houses of Parliament, there are forty-seven County governments and legislatures that give opposition parties a governing opportunity. In fact, the opposition Coalition for Reforms and Democracy, (CORD), was successful in electing eighteen Governors, double the number of the president's party. Thus, given Kenya's heterogeneous ethnic composition, there are more opportunities for communities not represented in the national government to be represented in County governments. In addition, the establishment of the Senate as the second house of the national Parliament was designed as an additional check on executive power, particularly on matters affecting the Counties (Committee of Experts on Constitutional Review 2010).

---

[5] Constitution, art. 4(2) (2010) (Kenya).
[6] Constitution, art. 10 (2010) (Kenya).
[7] Constitution, art. 259(1)(a), 159(1)(d) (2010) (Kenya).
[8] Constitution, art. 73(1)(a) (2010) (Kenya).
[9] The combination of rules with values and principles has been construed by the Kenyan Supreme Court as pointing toward *"an interpretation that contributes to the development of both the prescribed norm and the declared principle or policy; and care should be taken not to substitute one for the other."* In Re The Matter of the Principle of Gender Representation in the National Assembly and the Senate (2012) L.L.R. ¶ 49 (S.C.K.) (Kenya) (emphasis added).

The Bill of Rights is robust and detailed. It includes both civil and political rights, as well as social and economic rights. Some of its unique innovations include rights of marginalized and vulnerable groups including women, children, youth, persons with disabilities, and marginalized communities. It guarantees these groups representation in government. For example, under the two-thirds gender rule, no gender should comprise more than two-thirds representation in any state institution.[10]

To bring into force these transformative changes, the 2010 Constitution mandated Parliament to pass a raft of new laws within a five-year period, established institutions to oversee its implementation, and imposed a possible threat of parliamentary dissolution if Parliament failed to pass these laws.[11] While the set of legislative instructions reflects somewhat of a drafting trend in new constitutions, the Kenyan approach was notable both in the clarity of the mandates – neatly summarized in the Fifth Schedule of the Constitution – together with an enforcement mechanism backed up by the threat of parliamentary dissolution. The Commission on the Implementation of the Constitution was established as an independent commission to monitor progress. In Parliament, a Constitutional Oversight Implementation Committee was established to ensure that the new laws were passed as soon as it was reasonably practicable.[12] Although Parliament has extended the time frame to allow for the passage of laws that were required to be enacted by the end of 2014, it has enacted sixty-eight pieces of legislation in the last five years, which exceeds the approximately forty-nine pieces of legislation required by the 2010 Constitution.[13]

---

[10] Constitution, art. 125 (2010) (Kenya). The Supreme Court decided in an advisory opinion that the realization of this right has to be implemented by the time of the next election.

[11] Parliamentary dissolution is contemplated under Article 261 in the case that Parliament fails to enact the required legislation within the given time line. There is however a rather long procedure for this to occur. First, Parliament can extend the period for one year. They can only exercise this privilege once. If they are still not able to enact the legislation within this period, anyone can petition the high court to make a declaratory order or to transmit an order to Parliament or the attorney general to take steps to ensure that the required legislation is enacted and to report the progress to the chief justice. If Parliament further fails to enact the legislation, the chief justice shall advise the president to dissolve Parliament and the president shall dissolve Parliament. If the new Parliament fails to enact the contemplated legislation, the process begins again from the start. For instance, if Parliament fails to implement the legislation in 2015, they can extend the process up to 2016, whereupon a continued failure can lead to the procedure of going to the high court, then to the chief justice, and finally to the president. As of August 2015, Parliament had not enacted all the pieces of legislation required by the 2010 Constitution.

[12] Constitution, art. 261(4) (2010) (Kenya). The attorney general is also charged with a similar responsibility.

[13] Schedule Five of the Constitution provides a detailed list of the general area in which the laws must be passed. In 2011, Parliament passed twenty-two laws while the Constitution contemplated twenty-two. In 2012, Parliament passed fourteen laws even though the Constitution

PART TWO: RELATIVE CONSTITUTIONAL SUCCESSES

The emergence of an independent judiciary

For decades after independence, Kenyan courts did the bidding of the government of the day. They rarely exercised their power to review abuses of individual rights or the constitutionality of authoritarian executive conduct when invited to do so. The courts overwhelmingly used their authority to defend and protect conservative political and economic interests rather than to defend individual rights from state abuse. The Kenyan judiciary was so subservient to the Executive that its extremely rare exercises of judicial independence were greatly celebrated.[14]

In a remarkable shift that has happened slowly over the last few years and partly by accident, but definitively since the coming into force of the 2010 Constitution, Kenyan courts have attained genuine independence from the Executive. This newly won independence started to become apparent a few years ago before the 2010 Constitution when the judiciary began dismantling, piece-by-piece, its conservative judicial approach. Spurred forward by the reforms of the 2010 Constitution including a new cohort of highly qualified judges recruited in a transparent appointment process, a chief justice committed to transforming the judiciary and a huge increase in financial allocations. The judiciary is no longer a captive of the Executive. Instead, it has vigorously defended individual human rights and has put the values and principles of the 2010 Constitution, rather than the interests of powerful individuals, at the center of its decision-making process. This newly found independence is reflected in a Freedom House report on the Kenyan judiciary titled, "Kenyan Courts Throw Down the Gauntlet" (Lansner 2011).[15]

---

contemplated twenty-two. In 2013, Parliament enacted fifteen new laws although the Constitution contemplated four. In 2014, Parliament enacted nine although the Constitution contemplated eight. Because of the way that Parliament wrote the laws, the nine laws it enacted fell short of meeting the Constitutional requirement by six new laws. Parliament extended the passage of these laws by the end of March 2015. In 2015, Parliament is required to pass at least seven new laws (Ngirachu 2015).

[14] Lack of judicial independence was not unique to independent Kenya. Many African judiciaries were regarded as "subordinate extensions of the bureaucracy," rather than as independent checks on the power of the state (Brietzke 1974: 158). See Paul Brietzke, *Private Law in Ethiopia*, 18 J. AFR. L. 158 (1974). In 1969, President Nyerere of Tanzania argued courts should not "act as a brake upon development and rapid policy formulation," imputing that the role of courts as checks on executive authority was inconsistent with the imperatives of development (Nyerere 1968: 110–113).

[15] Shows the Office of the High Commissioner for Human Rights agreeing with the Government of Kenya and noting that "[t]he judiciary is one of the institutions in Kenya where reforms are clearly on course" (United Nations High Commissioner for Human Rights 2012).

In addition to decisively enforcing the Bill of Rights and reversing both the president and Parliament for unconstitutional conduct, the High Court issued an arrest warrant against the president of Sudan pursuant to Kenya's domesticated Statute of the International Criminal Court, the International Crimes Act.[16] Such assertiveness was unimaginable only a few years ago. The courts' conservative judicial philosophy is in retreat even though elements of the old conservative judicial approach remain in parts of the judiciary. Further, in a remarkable reversal from the past, all election petitions arising from the 2013 Presidential, Parliamentary, and County Elections were decided in a record six months as required by the 2010 Constitution.[17] This demonstrates how a combination of reforms, including administrative and personnel changes in the judiciary, have cumulatively served as engines of moving the pace of judicial decision-making faster than before and away from subservience to the Executive (Judiciary of Kenya 2013; see also Kilonzo 2013; Wainaina 2015).

As noted earlier, the emerging approach to judicial review includes a new trend in reversing presidential and legislative decisions for their unconstitutionality.[18] An assertion of Constitutional supremacy has replaced the doctrine of parliamentary sovereignty. In a sense, therefore, the judiciary has begun reshaping constitutional doctrine that departs from the legal positivism that underlay much of its judicial conservatism.[19] Although this shift is as definitive as it is fundamental,[20] it is uneven and contested (see, e.g., Shamallah 2012).

One of the most important elements underlying the empowerment of the judiciary is the commitment to the judiciary's transformation framework

[16] *Kenya Section of The International Commission of Jurists v Attorney General & another* [2011] eKLR.

[17] In the past, election petitions took so long they were often undecided in the few years before general election.

[18] Examples here include the February 3, 2011, decision of the High Court in Nairobi setting aside presidential nominations of the chief justice, attorney general, director of Public Prosecutions, and controller of the Budget. In the more recent past, the High Court was affirmed by the Court of Appeal for reversing eight clauses of a crucial national security bill for unconstitutionality. The likelihood that this would have happened particularly under President Daniel Arap Moi or under the previous Constitution is extremely low (Ogemba 2015).

[19] For example, in In Re The Matter of the Interim Independent Electoral Commission (2011) L.L.R. 1 (S.C.K.) (Kenya), the Supreme Court noted that "the rules of constitutional interpretation do not favor formalistic or positivistic approaches (Articles 20(4) and 259(1)). The Constitution has incorporated non-legal considerations, which we must take into account, in exercising our jurisdiction. The Constitution has a most modern Bill of Rights, that envisions a *human-rights* based, and *social-justice* oriented State and society."

[20] The reforms in the judiciary have been recognized by Kofi Annan who chaired the Panel of Eminent African Personalities appointed to deal with post-election violence in 2008 (see Kiplang'at 2012). Chief Justice Dr. Willy Mutunga has also been honored by the American Bar Association Center for Human Rights (Mwakilishi 2012).

launched on May 31, 2012 (Task Force on Judicial Reforms 2010). The judicial transformation framework has emphasized four key areas: first, people-focused delivery of justice; second, transformative leadership, organizational culture, and professional staff; third, adequate financial resources and physical infrastructure; and fourth, harnessing technology as an enabler of justice. The framework summarizes the ideas behind its transformation agenda as follows:

> The Constitution of Kenya, 2010, mandates a reconstruction of Kenyan society according to the ideals and values expressed in Articles 4 and 10, and in a host of other provisions. In this respect, the Constitution unmistakably conveys its overriding objective to provide a framework for transforming Kenya into a united, democratic, and prosperous society founded on human dignity, social justice, human rights and the principles of good governance. (Task Force on Judicial Reforms 2010: 12)

Institutional reforms implemented include the establishment of an independent Judicial Service Commission[21] that was not appointed or controlled by the president and that uses judicial appointment criteria such as "high moral character, integrity and impartiality"; the establishment of a Judiciary Fund that gives the judiciary financial autonomy for the first time;[22] and a large cohort of highly qualified new judges and professional administrative staff in the judiciary. These reforms have given significant impetus in the building of a new independent judiciary.

Another element that has given further credibility to the transformation and subsequent empowerment of the Kenyan judiciary is the vetting of all judges and magistrates appointed under the pre-2010 Constitution. Although there had been a more radical proposal to have all judges and magistrates reapply for their positions under the 2010 Constitution, the option adopted instead required the judges and magistrates be vetted for suitability to continue serving (Committee of Experts on Constitutional Review 2010, *supra* note 9: 74–76, 97).

The Vetting Board, which included three prominent foreign judges, has removed several judges and magistrates from the bench for corruption; being more deferential to those in power than is necessary; focusing too much on

---

[21] Judicial Service Committee Members are the chief justice, three other judges and a magistrate, the attorney general, two advocates, two members of the public appointed by the president with the approval of the National Assembly, and a nominee of the Public Service Commission.

[22] In the 2012–2013 financial year, the annual budgetary allocation to the judiciary was 1.18% of the national budget. This was up from 0.36% in the 2009–2010 financial year, but not at the international benchmark level of 2.5% of the national budget. See Judiciary of Kenya, *supra* note 17, at 184, 187. This has been supplemented by donor funding including the largest World Bank grant for judicial building.

technicalities than the justice of the cases before them; engaging in lengthy delays in deciding cases; or being unable or unwilling to deliver justice in "an appropriate manner."[23] A judicial challenge to this vetting resulted in a lengthy legal battle in the courts. The Supreme Court eventually decided that the Constitution did not provide judges with a right of appeal from the Vetting Board's decision.[24]

Another important explanation for the empowerment of the judiciary is the commitment of the chief justice to judicial transformation. Justice Willy Mutunga was appointed in a transparent process that involved televised US style "confirmation" proceedings. His past as detainee without trial and his history in the pro-democracy movement made him an unlikely candidate for the position ("Dr Willy Mutunga" 2013). When he was appointed, Chief Justice Mutunga used the vast public support he had to build the foundation for transforming the judiciary. Unlike prior chief justices he made himself accessible to the public and the staff in the judiciary. He unprecedentedly used his Facebook account to announce that the judges of the Supreme Court would no longer wear their inherited colonial wigs in court; that advocates did not have to wear their robes in Court; and that lawyers could appear in dreadlocks before the Supreme Court. He even unsuccessfully opposed the annual several weeks of leave judges get from their judicial duties. Chief Justice Mutunga brought humility to the judiciary and led the efforts to rebuild public trust and confidence (see Mutunga Forthcoming 2015). When the most senior politicians criticized the judiciary, he defended judicial independence. In the first two years of his tenure he successfully lobbied Parliament and the Executive to ensure that the judiciary was well funded to enable it to perform its role as an independent and impartial arbiter. Public confidence in the judiciary began to wane in 2013 when corruption scandals involving significant amounts of money arose within the judiciary and a big political battle was fought in the media, Parliament and in courtrooms between the chief justice and the Judicial Service Commission, on one hand, and the first holder of the office of Chief Registrar of the Judiciary Gladys Shollei, on the other.

Put together and taking into account the foregoing challenges facing the judiciary, the entirety of judicial reforms have nudged the judiciary to move away from an imperial relationship between judges, one the one hand, and judicial staff and court users on the other – the era of administrative terror in

---

[23] This process was governed by the Vetting of Judges and Magistrates Act of 2011 that Parliament passed pursuant to Article 23 of the Sixth Schedule of the 2010 Constitution.

[24] Judges & Magistrates Vetting Board & 2 others v Centre for Human Rights & Democracy & 11 others [2014] eKLR.

the judiciary is beginning to end. To restore public confidence various mechanisms involving a broad range of stakeholders have been formed and have become operational. For example, the Court Users Committees is a very grassroots initiative in every court station. The National Council on Administration of Justice is the policy organ charged with overseeing policy issues and implementing the administration of justice in the country.

Pursuant to these initiatives, the judiciary has responded with deliberate zeal to address its limited capacity to facilitate access to justice for a large segment of the Kenyan population (Task Force on Judicial Reforms 2010, *supra* note 22: 86–90). The 2010 Constitution guarantees access to justice. To address the uneven distribution of courts in the country more court stations have been added. This has reduced distances that that citizens had to travel to have access to a court. Opening up new courts and infusing meaning to them by naming them after regional heroes who were not given a fair shake in colonial-era judicial systems shows the creativity of the judicial transformation framework – that constitutional implementation is more than merely opening up new courts and finishing structures but infusing local meaning in them ("CJ Apologises for Biased Past Judicial System" 2015b). County governments have given more momentum to the judiciary's access to justice agenda because of their interest in bringing services closer to their populations.

Yet notwithstanding the successes achieved in reforming the judiciary, significant challenges have arisen. Within the ranks of some its judges and magistrates, corruption has continued (Sanga 2015). As noted earlier, a tenacious struggle between the first chief registrar of the judiciary, Gladys Shollei, on the one hand, and the chief justice and the Judicial Service Commission, on the other, surrounding allegations of extremely large sums of embezzled funds from the judiciary greatly undermined public confidence in judicial reforms.[25] Gladys Shollei became the second senior official of the reformed judiciary to be sacked by the Judicial Service Commission for conduct failing to meet the 2010 Constitution's values and principles (Ngirachu 2013).[26] Another source of challenges to the judiciary has come from outside the judiciary. As noted earlier, there have been challenges to the increased assertiveness of the judiciary. State organs have sometimes

---

[25] As evidence of the continuing investigations of corruption in the judiciary, in July 2015, six former judiciary employees were charged on corruption charges arising from the irregular purchase of a Kenya Shillings 310-million (USD 310,000) house for the chief justice (see Makana 2015).

[26] Notably, the Public Accounts Committee of the National Assembly chaired by Ababu Namwaba confirmed the allegations against Gladys Shollei, a factor that added to justifying the Judicial Service Commission's decision to relieve her from the position of chief registrar of the judiciary (see Shiundu 2015a).

disregarded court orders thereby undermining their enforceability. Judges who ruled against the president have been called "activists." Parliament has been very critical of judicial review that impinges on its work and is working on legislation to assert parliamentary sovereignty and "tame the judiciary" from exercising judicial authority over parliamentary decisions (Njagi 2015). A contentious battle over election jurisdiction between the Court of Appeal and the Supreme Court demonstrates that the reforms in the judiciary are unleashing supremacy wars.[27] In addition, signs that the president's party is preparing to influence a successor to Chief Justice Willy Mutunga when he retires in 2017 suggests that the progress made in reforming the judiciary may experience challenges and reversals under a new chief justice (see Menya 2015).[28]

Contribution to ending the cycle of post-election violence

The inauguration of multi-party politics in Kenya in 1991 created a pattern of election violence between ethnic communities. This was the case before the general elections of 1992 and 1997. Violence also followed a failed referendum over a new Constitution in 2005. However, the bloodiest electoral violence that has occurred in Kenya followed the 2007 general elections. The peace agreements struck after the 2007 post-election violence were the catalyst that led to the unexpected enactment of the 2010 Constitution. By contrast, the 2013 General Election – the first election conducted under the 2010 Constitution – was not plagued with violence during the campaigns or immediately after the announcement of the results. This is remarkable particularly because the presidential election was decided by a differential of only 0.7%. The two-horse race between eventual President Uhuru Kenyatta and Raila Odinga could have exploded into violence particularly because the Independent Elections and Boundaries Commission conducted the elections with several hitches, particularly the failure of the biometric technology to confirm voter identity and the widespread failure of electronic delivery of voting tallies from polling stations on voting day. Further, there were long delays in announcing the results following the elections that fueled suspicions that there was foul play.

[27] See *Commission on Admin. Justice* v. *Attorney Gen.* (2013) L.L.R. 1 (C.C.K.) (Kenya). Tom Ginsburg argues that conflicts between supreme courts and constitutional courts are familiar (see, e.g., Hendrianto 2013).

[28] The Judicial Service Commission is also facing off with the executive branch over the appointment of judges after the president refused to appoint about half a slate of over twenty judges already interviewed and recommended for appointment by the Commission (Kadida 2015).

Why was there no explosive violence? The 2010 Constitution provides part of the explanation. Unlike after the 2007 General Election when the Orange Democratic Movement bypassed the judiciary and opted for mass action to challenge electoral irregularities, Raila Odinga opted to challenge the electoral result in the then newly created Supreme Court. In addition, Raila Odinga persuaded his supporters not to resort to violence as they awaited the Supreme Court's decision. The readiness of the police and military services to deal with post-election violence together with widespread calls for restraint from churches, the media, and civil society groups played a role in channeling grievances away from violence. The creation of an independent judiciary led by a chief justice from the civil society movement provided new confidence that electoral disputes could be resolved as contemplated in the 2010 Constitution. Raila Odinga did not prevail in his presidential petition in the Supreme Court, but while he did not agree with the Court, he acquiesced to its authority to conclusively decide whether the election had been conducted in accordance with the law. Again, he urged his supporters to refrain from violence. In effect, the Supreme Court's decision gave the presidential election result a measure of procedural legitimacy while leaving open the option of challenging the substantive outcome in the court of public opinion – peacefully.

The alignment of ethnic alliances in the 2013 election removed one of the critical fault lines of post-election violence after the 2007 election. Unlike in the 2007 election when the Kalenjin and the Kikuyu communities were split into the two major rival parties, in the 2013 election the communities were united in an alliance between two politicians facing charges before the International Criminal Court – Uhuru Kenyatta and William Ruto. This alliance between two previously antagonistic ethnic communities meant that the Rift Valley, which had been the crucible of pre- and post-election violence in prior elections, witnessed a largely peaceful election.[29] Thus, the 2013 election may not necessarily represent a new political equilibrium in the Rift Valley and in the country as a whole. Nonetheless, it is important not to overstate the role of the 2010 Constitution in curbing pre- and post-election violence in 2013. As noted earlier, the judiciary decided all election disputes within a record six months of the 2013 election. With the judiciary establishing its ability to handle electoral disputes expeditiously, it increased its viability as an alternative forum to violence, consistent with the criteria identified in the Introduction to this volume about the importance of peaceful channeling of political conflict.[30]

---

[29] A multi-ethnic alliance between the Kikuyu and Kalenjin is part of the explanation for the absence of violence in the 2002 elections.

[30] One limitation to the effectiveness of expeditious judicial resolution is that the Supreme Court has argued it has jurisdiction to decide election appeals. This practice can prolong the length of

However, the 2013 elections did not necessarily inaugurate a new politics de-centered from ethnicity. Ethnic alliances were a major strategy of the two major alliances that were contending for the presidency. Thus even though election violence did not occur, the challenge of building a more nationa-listic and inclusive politics, particularly in the formation of broad cross-ethnic alliances, continues to bestride Kenyan politics. As a leading Kenyan political analyst has argued, electoral politics is governed by the tyranny of numbers – when two ethnic communities such as the Kikuyu and Kalenjin enter into an electoral alliance, it is almost inevitable that they would shut out any other groups or alliances from winning the presidency (Maina 2013). In addition, appointments to senior government positions have continued to be characterized by ethnicity and nepotism. One study conducted by the National Integration and Cohesion Commission found that seven of the forty-four ethnic communities dominated jobs in the public service – the largest employer in the country. In addition, the overwhelming majority of non-dominant ethnic communities were invisible minorities or completely unrepresented in the public service (National Cohesion and Integration Commission 2011).

It is notable that although Kenya did not experience election violence in 2013, it has experienced a significant increase in terrorist attacks underlined by the siege at Westgate Mall in Nairobi in September 2013 and in the attack at Garissa University in Northeastern Kenya in April 2015. In these and other incidents a large number of deaths have resulted. While these incidents are rather different from those related to election-related violence, they indicate that insecurity even under the 2010 Constitution continues to be a significant political issue – one that the first government elected under this Constitution has been unable to contain (Atta-Asamoah 2015).

Setting the embryonic stages for bureaucratic capacity and autonomy of state organs

In the past, a powerful executive used the Constitution and courts as tools to advance the interests of the president and to ensure bureaucratic compliance with the wishes of the ruling classes. State organs had little capacity or autonomy to limit the exercise of political power and the extensive patronage system upon which an authoritarian state had been built (Widner 2001; see also Ginsburg and Tamir 2008). In addition, the patchwork of legal and

election disputes that end up being appealed twice rather than once as some have argued is the standard established under the Constitution and electoral laws.

constitutional reforms passed in the last decade or so before the 2010 Constitution had left institutions still wedded to their one-party authoritarian and operational character, severely subordinated to an imperial Executive (Kanyinga and Okello 2010).

The enactment of the 2010 Constitution has provided a counterweight against rule by law and as a result given vitality to efforts to constrain the authority of political actors through formal institutions and rules and in the process promised institutional transformation (for an earlier assessment see Aketch 2011). The 2010 Constitution establishes a multi-party democratic state[31] – in which all exercises of power must be justified under the Constitution or under a written law. Government conduct is only justifiable on the cogency of the reasons advanced for pursuing it. Government conduct under the Constitution cannot be based, as in the past, on extra-legal or extra-constitutional grounds.

As already noted, there has been a tremendous growth in the institutional capacity and autonomy in the judiciary and many of the newly independent institutions designed to reduce the power of the Executive. As noted, many new laws have been approved by Parliament pursuant to its constitutional mandate. More often than not, these laws were designed and deliberated by many stakeholders led by government departments, with public participation and assistance and oversight from the Constitution Implementation Commission. This massive raft of new laws and policies reflect the extent to which the 2010 Constitution has become a touchstone for revising and reforming governance structures and policies at all levels as well as in inspiring consequential reform and change in many sectors including in education.

Even though in some sectors such as health, the 2010 Constitution has been a reference point for reform (International Health Partnership 2012), these reforms have not done much to meet the needs of the most vulnerable (Maalim et al. 2014). There is evidence that some of these new laws and policies are taking hold: First, because of the consistent vigilance by civil society actors, the media and the courts, in holding state actors to comply with the requirements of the 2010 Constitution. For example, the Constitution Implementation Commission has brought several suits challenging the constitutionality of new laws that the Commission argued did not meet constitutional muster; issued press statements and advisory opinions on executive conduct, legislation, policies, and procedures of various governmental actors with a view to advocating compliance with the Constitution (Commission for the Implementation of the Constitution 2014a). Second, a broad cross section of actors have repeatedly

---

[31] Constitution, art. 4(2) (2010) (Kenya).

come to the defense of the Constitution – civil society actors; a very engaged group of citizens; the various independent commissions and institutions established under the 2010 Constitution particularly the Kenya National Human Rights and Equality Commission, the Commission on Administrative Justice and the National Cohesion, and Integration Commission. Others state organs that have been monitoring the implementation of the Constitution include the attorney general's office and the Kenya Law Reform Commission. Third, the establishment of forty-seven County governments structured in accordance with the 2010 Constitution has created a broad cross section of actors invested in ensuring functional regional governments and as such with successful constitutional implementation. These widely dispersed set of actors act as monitors of the Executive and Legislative branch when their conduct falls short of faithfully implementing the Constitution.

Yet, the very nature of their dispersion has created many competing centers of power. This has often slowed or stopped forward momentum. The upshot of my claim is that there is a growing bureaucratic autonomy and capacity in state organs particularly at the national level. Thus although the Independent Boundaries and Electoral Commission conducted the 2013 election with some significant challenges, its performance demonstrated more competence than its precursor, the Electoral Commission of Kenya. This is a low but realistic threshold against which to evaluate the Independent Boundaries and Electoral Commission.[32] This is because many of the electoral systems the Commission had to put in place were built from the ground-up in a context of uncertainty not only about the election date but also about the composition of the Commission. Allegations that the Commission was embroiled in corruption in the 2013 elections, exemplifies how the process of implementing the reforms of the 2010 Constitution is far from linear or free of challenges. In 2015, the former Chief Executive Officer of the Independent Boundaries and Electoral Commission faced allegations of corruption thereby reinforcing the opposition's resolve for a major overhaul of the Commission ahead of the 2017 elections (Muraya 2013). The 2017 elections will be a major test of the ability of the framework established by the 2010 Constitution to hold the country together for a second electoral cycle.

There is a final factor that must be mentioned here to fully appreciate the surprising implementation of the 2010 Constitution by the government whose authority it severely limited. The cases against the president and deputy

[32] The December 2007 election was incompetently handled at all stages: voter registration (and the inclusion of about 1.2 million ghosts); distortions in the delineation of constituencies; abuse of polling including bribery, ballot-stuffing; "grossly defective data collection" etc. (Kreigler Report 2008).

president in the International Criminal Court kept Kenya's most senior leadership under an international spotlight in the initial years of the Constitution's implementation. The long-shadow of this spotlight helped to create an atmosphere in which implementing rather than sabotaging the 2010 Constitution was possible. This shadow is most concretized by the role of the Kenya National Dialogue and Reconciliation Monitoring process set up following the post-election violence in early 2008. This process involved international monitors with regular period reports and meetings led by former UN secretary general Kofi Annan. These processes helped to limit the ability of the coalition government, set up after the post-election violence in 2008, from scuttling both the Constitution-making and implementation process. In addition, enacting the Constitution and the establishment of an independent judiciary was one of the arguments made by President Kibaki as a basis for denying the International Criminal Court jurisdiction over Kenyan suspects involved in the post-election violence following the 2007 elections.

PART THREE: WHERE CONSTITUTIONAL REFORM FACES CHALLENGES

Devolution

The 2010 Constitution devolved fiscal, political, and administrative powers to forty-seven Counties. The Counties were established as equal and interdependent organs, rather than as subordinate entities to the national government.[33] National-County relations are required to be conducted through consultation and cooperation. A major goal of devolving governance was to disperse the centralization of political and economic power that had disadvantaged many regions, communities, and individuals. In addition to decentralizing political and legislative authority, the 2010 Constitution guarantees the Counties equitable financial allocations with the national government.[34] Expenditures must be used to promote equitable development.[35] An equalization fund is established with a mandatory allocation to go toward provisioning of basic services to "marginalized areas."[36] In addition, there is a guaranteed 15% of all national

---

[33] Article 189(1)(a) of the 2010 Constitution "requires government at either level to perform its functions, and exercise its powers, in a manner that respects the functional and institutional integrity of government at the other level, and respects the constitutional status and institutions of government at the other level and in the case of county government, within the county level." *See also* constitution, art. 6(2), 189(1)(b), 189(1)(c) (2010) (Kenya).

[34] Constitution, art. 201(b)(ii) (2010) (Kenya).

[35] Constitution, art. 201(b)(iii) (2010) (Kenya).

[36] Constitution, art. 204(1) (2010) (Kenya).

revenues each financial year to be allocated to County governments.[37] There is also a Revenue Fund established specifically for County Governments from which funds cannot be withdrawn pursuant to an Act of Parliament.[38] A new expert commission, the Commission on Revenue Allocation, is charged with making decisions in consultation with county governors and the public how these revenues should be divided amongst them.

Has the implementation of devolution met the constitutional designer's goal of promoting the participation of people in the governance of the country? Has it ensured a framework for equitable access to national resources? Has it promoted respect for diversities, inclusiveness, and community rights? (Committee of Experts on Constitutional Review 2010: paras. 6.3.1(i), (ii), (iii)). In answering these questions it is important to begin by noting that there has been a successful rollout of devolution (Lagat and Wokabi 2015). Just a few short years ago, the country was governed from the center, but all the forty-seven Counties established by the 2010 Constitution are all operational. However, challenges remain.[39]

The Constitution's guarantees of financial security have eased the rolling-out of all forty-seven County governments without exception. Since the County governments began being implemented following the 2013 elections, as contemplated by the 2010 Constitution, it is remarkable that within a little more than a one-year period "key institutional structures and systems in the County Executives and County Assemblies" had been established (Commission for the of the Constitution 2014a). This is particularly so because Counties were designed to take up the functions of overlapping layers of prior administrative structures.[40] Their establishment and their assumption of functions previously controlled from the center as well as efforts to build-up their capacity to deliver on these functions has provided political insulation from easy-reversal.[41] While I provide a brief assessment of the implementation of devolution here, it is a process in its very early stages to draw any definitive conclusions. It is after all going to be a long-term complex process that will invariably come with a variety risks and challenges (The World Bank 2012: xxviii).

These challenges include the fact that so far most County expenditures have been on salaries, fuel and administration costs not development projects.

---

[37] Constitution, art. 203(2) (2010) (Kenya).

[38] Constitution, art. 207, 207(2) (2010) (Kenya).

[39] For example, there is an ongoing process to dissolve Makueni County because the Governor and the Legislature cannot work together (see Mutai 2015).

[40] These were the Provincial, District, and Local Government Administrations that have long served as a fourth arm of the Central government.

[41] The World Bank notes that with the architectural infrastructure of devolution already put in place, it would be "will be impossible to alter the foundations, at least not without knocking it down and starting again" (The World Bank 2012).

By one count, only ten of thirty Counties have met the goal of spending 30% of their budget on development. Instead, most have engaged in wasteful spending on foreign trips, expensive vehicles, office furnishings and iPads (see World Bank Group 2014). County governors have launched a national campaign for more budgetary allocations. The national government has responded with a counter-campaign of its own.

Since many of the newly established County Assemblies have often prioritized spending projects that would most benefit their members, where county governors stood in the way of County Assembly members, they often turned chaotic or used their power to impeach the governors (Commission for the Implementation of the Constitution 2014b: 103). There are a number of pending lawsuits challenging the impeachment of governors. In addition, one County government unsuccessfully petitioned the president for dissolution after it became ungovernable. Several governors are under pressure to resign with the goal of facilitating investigations into corruption allegations. Counties, particularly those in largely rural areas, face the additional challenge of keeping service providers such as doctors and teachers with homes in other parts of the Country on their payrolls. Doctors have gone on strike and demanded a national scheme of service under which they would continue getting paid at the national level, a fact that would re-centralize this County function (Ndii 2013).

PART FOUR: WHERE CONSTITUTIONAL REFORM HAS FAILED TO TAKE ROOT

Corruption

The 2010 Constitution created the Ethics and Anti-Corruption Commission (EACC). The constitutional recognition of an independent commission to implement the new commitments of leadership and integrity as well as to enforce a large body of anti-corruption law was novel. Even though the EACC was not granted prosecutorial authority, it was a victory for civil society and pro-democracy groups that had long regarded constitutional entrenchment of such a body as a necessary precondition of its success. In 2011 when Parliament passed the law establishing the EACC, it discontinued the director and his deputy. Parliament was angry that the Director had declined to stop aggressively pursuing corruption investigations against several members of parliament and the Executive. This removal continued the pre-2010 pattern of lack of a consistent commitment to combat corruption in both the Executive and the Legislature. The first director of the EACC that Parliament sent to the president for appointment had corruption allegations against him.[42] Appointing a person tainted with such allegations set the EACC up to fail. Parliament has also proceeded to weaken institutions established to promote accountability and transparency such as the office of the Auditor General and the Controller of Budgets.

Corruption has thrived in the backwater of a hobbled EACC that is itself embroiled in internal conflict. That conflict boiled over in 2015 when its most senior officials all resigned. But it is not just the EACC, for no state organ has been free of corruption. The president has admitted his office was a den of corruption. The Independent Electoral and Independent Boundaries Commissioners received bribes as confirmed in evidence relied on to convict Directors of the British firm that printed the ballots for the Kenyan 2013 election ("Civil Society Coalition Calls" 2015a). Corruption was at the center of a major crisis in the judiciary that resulted in the dismissal off the chief registrar of the judiciary. Corruption continues to thrive in the largely unreformed Police Service and it is a major problem in the newly established Counties. Even the Committee charged with oversight over corruption matters in the National Assembly was dissolved when its members including its chair were alleged to have received corrupt payments so that the committee could sanitize its reports of corruption investigations (see Shiunu 2015a). The inability to control corruption has perpetuated a rich cohort of Kenyan predatory elites and contributed to its growth (see Kanyinga 2015).[43] Corruption is therefore a major impediment to faithfully implementing the Constitution.

The difficulty with tackling corruption also reveals the insufficient independence and capacity of public financial management institutions and systems. These include the government's procurement systems; parliamentary oversight committees; the judiciary; the auditor and controller general; internal audit systems; as well as both the offices of the Director of Public Prosecution and Attorney General. Leaders of these institutions have often been politicians who had no incentive to build their capacity and independence. In addition, devolution has increased corruption as the number of officials that must be bribed to get things done has increased (Ongiri 2015a).

The recurrence of corruption continues a long legacy inconsistent with the goal of ending impunity as intended by the 2010 Constitution. Although the immediate impetus of enacting the 2010 Constitution was to put an end to

---

[42] The High Court decided that Parliament had violated the Constitution's integrity and leadership values by appointing the new Director without examining the allegations of corruption. That decision is now on appeal in the Supreme Court.

[43] *See* Karuti Kanyinga, "Evolution of Kenya Civil Society." *Daily Nation* (February 28, 2015) *available at* http://mobile.nation.co.ke/news/Evolution-of-Kenya-civil-society/-/1950946/26391 70/-/format/xhtml/-/sh5a9h/-/index.html (showing the continuity in the Uhuru government of Kenya's wealthy political elite).

election violence, its design particularly with regard to the County system of government was to tackle poverty and inequality as well as combat regional development imbalance. The 2010 Constitution inaugurated new laws and institutions to promote transparency, accountability, and to end impunity without changing the underlying social-economic basis of instability – including the uneven distribution of land. In this sense, the Constitution has so far not succeeded in superseding the old order of regional economic imbalances, poverty, and inequality. Allegations of theft of public land by senior government officials including the deputy president and the suspension of the cabinet secretary charged with overseeing the Land Ministry on corruption allegations indicate the continuity of land-grabbing from prior regimes (Mathenge 2015). The 2013–2014 Report of the Auditor General of Kenya revealed that a mere 1% of the monies spent by the Central government had been verified as having been used in accordance with the laid-down law and procedure. Even worse, over 66 billion Kenya Shillings (about USD 650 million), were missing and could not be accounted for (Ongiri 2015b). In this sense, the corrupt, unaccountable, and authoritarian character of the pre-2010 Constitution continues to frame Kenyan politics. Implementing the 2010 Constitution continues to face these structural challenges as major impediments to establishing a political environment in which a more egalitarian distribution of wealth and resources, inter-ethnic political alliances, political moderation, and minority cooperation could emerge.[44] The problems associated with ending corruption also reflect a failure of the values and principles, particularly those related to the integrity of leaders embodied in the 2010 Constitution to take root.[45] At a very basic level, there has been a lack of elite consensus in support of these values and principles particularly as they relate to integrity.

CONCLUSIONS

Assessing the performance of the extremely ambitious 2010 Constitution of Kenya is a difficult task. The relative success in reforming the judiciary and rolling out devolution strongly suggests that this Constitution will not join the proverbial graveyard of great African Constitutions (Ogendo 1993). Indeed, the

[44] Paul Brass (1991) argues that "political accommodation in a multiethnic society is not a system, it is an art."

[45] In his fifth year assessment of the Constitution, the Chairman of the Commission on the Implementation of the Constitution argued that "despite the overarching principles and values in the constitution and a framework that commits governments to transparency, accountability and civic engagement in devolved governance, and while space for citizen interaction in governance has continued to expand, it is still at best inadequate and ineffective and largely viewed as tokenistic" (see Nyachae 2015).

ongoing process of judicial transformation – even with its challenges – is building confidence and credibility that such reform is possible in other governance structures as required by the 2010 Constitution. Given the deliberate speed, the range of judicial actors, and the broad scope of court stations around the country that have implemented reforms, it will be harder to reverse these gains even with the impending retirement of Chief Justice Willy Mutunga in 2017. The chief justice has argued that some of these reforms have "become irreversible, irrevocable, indestructible and permanent" (Mutunga 2015). Yet, as we saw, the judiciary continues to face problems, particularly corruption, which has eroded the public confidence it enjoyed particularly between 2010 and 2013. However, in other institutional contexts where the reform pace has been much slower, the modest gains are likely to be eroded more quickly than in the judiciary, particularly if the current administration is re-elected and there is a crisis surrounding the 2017 election resulting in a weakened opposition that is far less able to keep the incumbent government on its toes. This is likely to be the case where the reforms have constituted small improvements of bureaucratic capacity and autonomy in the government outside of the independent commissions. By contrast, a competitive 2017 election in which there remains a strong opposition is likely to keep the forward momentum on implementing constitutional reform. If the opposition wins the 2017 election, there is a higher likelihood for renewed momentum to continue the process of consolidating constitutional reform.

The differences in the implementation of the 2010 Constitution between the judiciary and other areas show that reform does not take place in the same way in different places. In addition, reforms have been far from linear. Even though the president's power has been de-concentrated, he has begun using workarounds, if not seeking outright reversals of reforms that have curtailed his prerogative to decide without review.[46] The varying success in the implementation of the 2010 Constitution has been accompanied and been limited by continuity of some of the repressive authoritarian practices of the past – including gagging of the media (BBC 2013) and civil society groups (Kaberia 2014).

In addition, there has been little attention paid to the redressing issues of historical disadvantage as required both by the 2010 Constitution and the Agenda 4 items of the 2008 Post-Election Violence Agreement. These issues

---

[46] For example, the president has withheld appointing judges recommended for appointment by the Judicial Service Commission after successful interviewing. The president has objected to having an obligation to appoint every judge recommended for appointment by the Judicial Service Commission. Another example is his decision ordering 10,000 police recruits to report for training after the High Court stopped the recruitment exercise, citing corruption. In this instance, the president argued that a deadly terrorist attack in Northeastern Kenya was in part occasioned by the lack of sufficient numbers of security personnel (see Leftie 2015).

include dealing with unequal access to land; tackling poverty and inequality as well as combating regional development imbalances; tackling unemployment, particularly among the youth; consolidating national cohesion and unity; and addressing transparency, accountability, and impunity. One of the major reasons that accounts for the difficulty with dealing with these issues is that they implicate many political elites in the government and in the opposition. Thus it was not surprising that lustration was primarily directed at the judiciary. Kenya's wealthy and powerful political elites are content that the constitutional order established by the 2010 Constitution has so far not been applied in manner that substantially threatens their wealth and power.

On the positive side, the great success of the Constitution has been in channeling political conflict through constitutional institutions, for which the 2013 election was a major test. However, the Constitution has done less well on the dimension of agency control. Although, there has been some improvement in answerability by state actors, enforceability has not improved to the same extent. Andreas Schedler defines answerability as "the obligation of public officials to inform about and to explain what they are doing" (Schedler 1999). When "informing," leaders must provide reliable facts on a given topic, whereas when "explaining" they must provide reasons for their actions. Enforcement is "the capacity of accounting agencies to impose sanctions on power holders who have violated their public duties" (Schedler 1999). There is a growing recognition that all exercises of power must be justified under the Constitution or under a written law. Sometimes the president has only acted under pressure to demonstrate that governmental conduct is not like in the past based on extra-legal or extra-constitutional grounds. Thus even though President Uhuru Kenyatta did not show a firm resolve or commitment to combating corruption in his first two years in office, he responded to enormous public pressure by ordering several senior government officials alleged to have been involved in corruption to step aside to allow investigations to be conducted (Kenyatta 2015). This is an example of the kind of answerability that is possible because of the governance benchmarks established by the 2010 Constitution.

It is notable that the 2010 Constitution of Kenya sets out an elaborate reform agenda in all spheres of public and private life that has been financially very costly to implement. The Committee of Experts that was responsible for the final draft of the Constitution was fully aware of the enormous cost that the reforms would require. The Committee of Experts concluded that "cost should not override democratic participation and better service delivery, because cost would be borne by the people of Kenya" (Committee of

Experts on Constitutional Review 2010). This argument that Kenyans were willing to pay whatever it cost to ensure democratic participation and better service delivery has turned out to be a costly financial bargain.[47] The implementation of the Constitution is incomplete and so the costs will keep adding up. Thus a growing economy to support its continued implementation seems important.

As a final point, implementing Kenya's 2010 Constitution has so far been a contested and continuing process. Assessing its successes, challenges, and failures is a difficult exercise for many reasons. First, it is a process that will take many more years and that involves many complex challenges and risks. Thus examining its performance after only five years may be too early to say with any level of certainty that the assessments made in this chapter will stick. Second, the Constitution includes goals such as leadership and integrity values that are not readily measurable. Yet, their inclusion in the Constitution was consistent with the overwhelming endorsement of the Kenyan public. The inclusion of these values is a reflection of the recognition that checking and devolving power in Kenya is deeply intertwined with dealing with economic inequality between communities, regions, and individuals. Thus the inclusion of these values in the Constitution is an important recognition that transforming Kenyan politics and economy extends beyond the usual constitutional constraints on exercise of public power to the novel re-distributive goals of the devolution of governance to the goals of economic enfranchisement as well as the recognition and enforcement of a set of leadership and integrity values. This latter set of goals and objectives are not short-term projects. It is in this context that my claim that anti-corruption and related measures have not taken root must be understood. To the extent that the trajectory of these goals and objectives of economic enfranchisement, regional balance in wealth as well as the values and principles underlying the 2010 Constitution is in jeopardy at the moment does not augur well in the long term.

REFERENCES

Aketch, Migai. 2011. "Constraining Government Power in Africa." *Journal of Democracy* 22 (1): 96–106. *Available at* www.academia.edu/2093711/constraining_government_power_in_africa.

Atta-Asamoah, Andrews. 2015. *East Africa Report: Drivers of Insecurity in Kenya, Institute of Security Studies* (2). Institute for Security Studies. *Available at* www.issafrica.org/uploads/East-Africa-Report-2-Kenya.pdf.

---

[47] The International Monetary Fund asserts that extensive institutional reforms are good for the economy but is also calling for more resources (see International Monetary Fund 2014).

BBC. 2013. "Kenya Media: President Signs 'Draconian' Bill." December 17. *Available at* www.bbc.com/news/world-africa-25418234.

Brass, Paul. 1991. *Ethnicity and Nationalism: Theory and Comparison.* Newbury Park, CA: SAGE Publications.

Brietzke, Paul. 1974. "Private Law in Ethiopia." *Journal of African Law* 18 (2): 149–167.

Commission for the Implementation of the Constitution. 2014a. "2013–2014 Annual Report: Counting the Milestones." *Available at* www.cickenya .org/index.php/reports/annual-reports/item/446-2013-2014-annual-report.

———. 2014b. *Assessment of the Implementation of the System of Devolved Government: From Steps to Strides. Available at* www.cickenya.org/index .php/reports/item/440-april-june-2014#.Vv7mTRIrLaY.

Committee of Experts on Constitutional Review. 2010. "Final Report of the Committee of Experts on Constitutional Review." October 11. *Available at* http://mlgi.org.za/resources/local-government-database/by-country/ke nya/commission-reports/CoE_final_report.pdf.

Daily Nation. 2015a. "Civil Society Coalition Calls for Smith & Ouzman Fines to Be Given to the EACC." February 10. *Available at* www.nation .co.ke/news/politics/Smith-Ouzman-EACC-Serious-Fraud-Office-KPTJ /-/1064/2619478/-/ig55mrz/-/index.html.

———. 2015b. "CJ Apologises for Biased Past Judicial System." March 25. *Available at* www.nation.co.ke/news/Chief-Justice-Willy-Mutunga-Western-Kenya -Tour-Judiciary/-/1056/2665738/-/ub3dosz/-/index.html.

Ginsburg, Tom and Tamir Moustafa eds. 2008. *Rule By Law: The Politics of Courts in Authoritarian Regimes.* Cambridge University Press.

Hendrianto, Stefanus. 2013. "The First Ten Years of the Indonesian Constitutional Court: The Unexpected Insurance Role." *I-CONnect,* August 25. *Available at* www.iconnectblog.com/2013/08/the-first-ten-years-of-the-indonesian-constitutional-court-the-unexpected-insurance-role/.

International Health Partnership. 2012. "Joint Assessment of Kenya's Health Sector Strategic Plan." *Available at* www.internationalhealthpartnership .net/fileadmin/uploads/ihp/Documents/Key_Issues/NHP___JANS/Keny a%20JANS%20Report.Nov2012.pdf.

International Monetary Fund. 2014. "Kenya: Article IV Consultation – Staff Report; Press Release and Statement by the Executive Director for Kenya." *IMF Country Report* No. 14/302. *Available at* www.imf.org/exter nal/pubs/ft/scr/2014/cr14302.pdf.

Judiciary of Kenya. 2013. *State of the Judiciary Report, 2012–2013.*

Kaberia, Timothy. 2014. "Uhuru's Threat to Civil Society Groups Is Reminiscent of Moi's Crackdown in 1995." *Standard Media,* October 27. *Available at* www.standardmedia.co.ke/ureport/story/200013 9614/uhuru-s-threat-to-ngos-is-reminiscent-of-moi-s-crackdown-in-1995.

Kadida, Jillo. 2015. "Kenya: Uhuru in Talks to Settle Judges' Appointment." *allAfrica*, March 13. *Available at* http://allafrica.com/stories/201503130563 .html.

Kanyinga, Karuti. 2015. "Evolution of Kenya Civil Society." *Daily Nation*, February 28. *Available at* http://mobile.nation.co.ke/news/Evolution-of-Kenya-civil-society/-/1950946/2639170/-/format/xhtml/-/sh5a9h/-/index.html.

Kanyinga, Karuti and Duncan Okello eds. 2010. *Tensions and Reversals in Democratic Transitions: The Kenya 2007 General Elections*. Nairobi: Society for International Development and Institute for Development Studies.

Kenya Constitution. 2010.

"Kenya: Judiciary Officials Charged with Purchase of Chief Justice Willy Mutunga's House." *Standard*, August 6. *Available at* www .standardmedia.co.ke/article/2000171810/judiciary-officials-charged-over-purchase-of-chief-justice-willy-mutunga-s-house.

Kilonzo, Kethi D. 2013. "The Judiciary Has Done Well, It Could Do Better." *Standard*, October 20. *Available at* www.standardmedia.co.ke/?articleI D=2000095845&story_title=Kenya-the-judiciary-has-done-well-it-can-do -better.

Kiplang'at, Jeremiah. 2012. "Annan's Thumbs Up to Judiciary Reform." *Daily Nation*, October 9. *Available at* www.nation.co.ke/News/politics/ Annans±thumbs±up±to±judiciary±reforms/-/1064/1529430/-/c2e3soz/-/i ndex.html.

Kreigler Report. 2008. *Report of the Independent Review Commission on the General Elections Held in Kenya on 27 December 2007*. *Available at* htt p://fidakenya.org/sites/default/files/kriegler-report.pdf.

Lagat, Copperfield and Charles Wokabi. 2015. "World Bank Lauds Kenya for Devolution." *Daily Nation*, February 3. *Available at* www.nation.co.ke /lifestyle/smartcompany/World-Bank-lauds-Kenya-for-devolution/-/1226/ 2611618/-/4knkydz/-/index.html.

Lansner, Thomas R. 2011. "Kenya's Courts Throw Down the Gauntlet." *Freedom House*, December 15. *Available at* www.freedomhouse.org/blo g/kenya's-courts-throw down-gauntlet.

Leftie, Peter. 2015. "Garissa Attack: Uhuru Orders Training of 2014 Police Recruits." *Daily Nation*, April 2. *Available at* www.nation.co.ke/news/ Uhuru-orders-training-of-2014-police-recruits/-/1056/2674152/-/j66jy3z/-/i ndex.html.

Maalim, Mohamed Isaack et al. 2014. "Kenya's Vision for an Equitable, Rights-Based Health System Fails to Address Specific Health Needs and Barriers to Accessing Health Care of Vulnerable Populations." *Africa Policy Journal*. *Available at* http://apj.fas.harvard.edu/kenyas-vision-for-an-equitable-rights-based-health-system-fails-to-address-specific-health-needs -and-barriers-to-accessing-health-care-of-vulnerable-populations/.

Maina, Wachira. 2013. "What Tyranny of Numbers: Inside Mutahi Ngunyi's Numerology." Africa Centre for Open Governance. Retrieved May 10, 2013. *Available at* www.africog.org/sites/default/files/Tyranny%20of%20 Numbers_final.pdf.

Makana, Fred. 2015. "Former Judiciary Staff Back in Court as Gladys Shollei Denies Breaking the Law." *Standard Digital*, August 25, 2015; accessed April 1, 2016. *Available at* www.standardmedia.co.ke /article/2000174063/former-judiciarystaff-back-in-court-as-gladys-shollei-denies-breaking-the-law.

Mathenge, Oliver. 2015. "Uhuru Suspends Five Ministers." *The Star*, March 27. *Available at* www.the-star.co.ke/news/uhuru-suspends-five-ministers.

Menya, Walter. 2015. "JSC Meets on Monday to Discuss Rev Samuel Kobia's Abrupt Resignation." *Daily Nation*, March 28. *Available at* www.nation .co.ke/news/politics/JSC-Samuel-Kobia-Resignation-Jubilee/-/1064/2669 190/-/5lf6p1/-/index.html.

Muraya, Joseph. 2013. "Oswago, 3 IEBC Officials Freed on Bail in Tender Case." *Capital News*, October 30. *Available at* www.capitalfm.co.ke/ne ws/2013/10/oswago-3-iebc-officials-freed-on-bail-in-tender-case/.

Mutai, Edwin. 2015. "Uhuru Names Commission of Inquiry for Makueni County Row." *Business Daily Africa*, February 10. *Available at* www .businessdailyafrica.com/Uhuru-names-team-to-hear-Makueni-county-dispute/-/539546/2619508/-/147vk8/-/index.html.

Mutunga, Willy. 2015. "2 Human Rights States and Societies: A Reflection from Kenya." *Transnational Human Rights Review* 45.

Mwakilishi. 2012. "Kenya Chief Justice Willy Mutunga to Meet with Kenyans at Kenyan Embassy on Sep 12, 2012." *Mwakilishi*, September 4. *Available at* http://mwakilishi.com/content/articles/2012/09/04/kenya-chief-justice-willy-mutunga-to-meet-with-kenyans-in-the-us.html.

National Cohesion and Integration Commission. 2011. "Towards National Cohesion and Unity in Kenya: Ethnic Diversity and Audit of the Civil Service." *Available at* www.cohesion.or.ke/images/downloads/ethnic%2 0diversity%20of%20the%20civil%20service.pdf.

Ndii, David. 2013. "Why the Doctors Are Fighting Devolution." *Daily Nation*, December 13. *Available at* http://mobile.nation.co.ke/blogs/Why-the-doctors-are-fighting-devolution/-/1949942/2111146/-/format/xhtml/-/plx a90/-/index.html.

Ngirachu, John. 2013. "JSC sends Gladys Shollei Packing Over Sh 2 Billion Scandal." *Daily Nation*, October 18. *Available at* http://mobile.nation.co .ke/news/JSC-sends-Gladys-Shollei-packing/-/1950946/2038778/-/format/ xhtml/-/de2qwpz/-/index.html.

2015. "MPs Approve More Time to Pass Bills." *Daily Nation*, August 25. *Available at* http://mobile.nation.co.ke/news/MPs-approve-more-time-to-pass-Bills/-/1950946/2846384/-/format/xhtml/-/ypmxax/-/index.html.

Njagi, John. 2015. "MPs Back New Bill to Tame Judges." *Daily Nation*, August 19. *Available at* http://allafrica.com/stories/201508201572.html.

Nyachae, Charles. 2015. Speech Made at the Launch of the 2014/2015 Annual Report on the Second Assessment of Devolution at Gusii Stadium, August 25. *Available at* www.cickenya.org/index.php/newsroom/spee ches/item/499-speech-made-by-mr-charles-nyachae-chairperson-cic-at-the-launch-of-the-2014-2015-annual-report-and-the-report-on-the-second-assessment-of-devolution-at-gusii-stadium-kisii-county-on-27th-august-2 015#.Vf8KzyBViko.

Nyerere, Julius K. 1968. *Freedom and Socialism/Uhuru Na Ujamaa: A Selection from Writings and Speeches, 1965–1967.* New York: Oxford University Press.

Ogemba, Paul. 2013. "Judges Reject Appeal in Security Laws Case." *Daily Nation*, January 13. *Available at* www.nation.co.ke/news/politics/Judges-reject-appeal-in-security-laws-case/-/1064/2600358/-/v8no4mz/-/index.html.

Ogendo, Okoth. 1993. "Constitutions without Constitutionalism: An African Political Paradox." In *Constitutionalism and Democracy: Transitions in the Contemporary World*, edited by D. Greenberg, S.N. Kartz, B. Oliviero, and S.C. Wheatley. New York: Oxford University Press.

Ongiri, Isaac. 2015a. "Eyebrows Raised over Massive Spending, Graft in Counties." *Daily Nation*, July 17. *Available at* http://mobile.nation.co .ke/news/Auditor-General-Report-Corruption-Counties/-/1950946/27931 26/-/format/xhtml/-/8kh9y2/-/index.html.

2015b. "Auditor Puts Ministers on the Spot Over Missing Documents for SH66.7 Billion Deals." *Daily Nation*, July 28. *Available at* www.nation .co.ke/news/Use-of-Sh67-billion-queried-by-auditor/-/1056/2812504/-/9tu 04uz/-/index.html.

Sanga, Benard. 2015. "A Third Purge? CJ Willy Mutunga and Lawyers Decry Increasing Corruption in the Judiciary." *Standard*, August 8. *Available at* www.standardmedia.co.ke/article/2000172075/a-third-purge-cj-mutunga-and-lawyers-decry-increase-corruption-in-the-judiciary/?artic leID=2000172075&story_title=a-third-purge-cj-willy-mutunga-and-lawyers-decry-increase-corruption-in-the-judiciary&pageNo=2.

Schedler, Andreas. 1999. "Conceptualizing Accountability." In *The Self-Restraining State: Power and Accountability in New Democracies*, edited by A. Schedler, L. Diamond, and M.F. Plattner. Boulder: Lynne Reinner Publishers.

Shamallah, Jennifer. 2012. "The Intolerance of Liberals Gradually Becoming a Danger to This Our Land." *Daily Nation*, October 25. *Available at* www .nation.co.ke/oped/Opinion/-/440808/1598340/-/l3ic2gz/-/index.html.

Shiundu, Alphonce. 2015a. "National Assembly Approves 27 Public Accounts Committee Members." *Standard*, April 22. *Available at* www.standardmedia.co.ke/article/2000159376/national-assembly-approves-2 7-public-accounts-committee-members.

———. 2015b. "Rarieda MP Nicholas Gumbo Elected Kenya's Public Accounts Committee Chairman." *Standard*, April 28. *Available at* www .standardmedia.co.ke/article/2000160262/rarieda-mp-nicholas-gumbo -elected-kenya-s-public-accounts-committee-chairman.

Standard. 2013. "Dr Willy Mutunga: The Man Kenya Views as a 'Bastion of a Fair and Just Judicial System.'" October 14. *Available at* http://standard media.co.ke/?articleID=2000095585&story_title=the-man-kenya-views-as-a-bastion-of-a-fair-and-just-judicial-system.

Task Force on Judicial Reforms. 2010. *"Final Report of the Task Force on Judicial Reforms." Available at* www.kenyalaw.org/Downloads/Final%20 Report%20of%20the%20Task%20Force%20on%20Judicial%20Reforms .pdf.

Uhuru, President Kenyatta. 2015. "State of the Nation Address." Presented at Parliament Buildings, March 26, Nairobi. *Available at* www.scribd.com /doc/260017548/Speech-by-President-Uhuru-Kenyatta-during-the-State-of-the-Nation-Address-at-Parliament-Buildings-Nairobi).

United Nations High Commissioner for Human Rights. 2012. Kenya. Universal Periodic Review (49).

Wainaina, Ndung'u. 2015. "Only Judiciary Can Save This Country." *The Nairobi Law Monthly*, February 4. *Available at* http://nairobilaw monthly.com/index.php/2015/02/04/only-judiciary-can-save-this-coun try/.

Widner, Jennifer. 2001. *Building the Rule of Law.* New York: W.W. Norton.

The World Bank. 2012. *Devolution without Disruption: Pathways to a Successful New Kenya. Available at* wwwwds.worldbank.org/external/ default/WDSContentServer/WDSP/IB/2012/11/15/000333037_2012111523 0524/Rendered/PDF/NonAsciiFileNameo.pdf.

World Bank Group. 2014. *Decision Time: Spend More or Spend Smart? Kenya Public Expenditure Review 1. Available at* https://openknowledge .worldbank.org/bitstream/handle/10986/21507/940210WP0v10Booorto Vo lo1201400FINAL.pdf?sequence=1.

13

The Arab Spring constitutions
For whose benefit?

Zaid Al-Ali

Who decides what a constitution's purpose should be?

A UNIVERSAL TEST

Scholars and practitioners have long struggled to identify what qualities make a constitution successful. The question is incredibly complex, not least because there is very little consensus on what constitutions should look like, or on the areas that constitutions should deal with. In an effort to resolve this issue, there is a natural tendency amongst many scholars to favor a "universal test," that is, a single set of criteria that can be applied universally to measure the performance of all constitutions. While such an approach is certainly tempting, not least of all because of its simplicity, there are at least two sets of reasons that we should question its applicability in all cases.

The first is related to the fact that any attempt to establish external criteria will necessarily have to remain as general as possible. Constitutions are enacted in countries with widely varying starting points and are also subject to be influenced by a multiplicity of factors. A constitution can be enacted for the purpose of ending violent conflict (e.g. Bosnia), alleviating poverty (e.g. Ecuador) or transforming a previously discriminatory society into a more egalitarian one (e.g. South Africa), while others are designed merely to stream-line government in what is already an effectively administered state (e.g. Switzerland). Some constitutions are well constructed but are applied in states that barely survive in unstable regions and that are subject to overbearing and negative foreign influence (e.g. Yemen), while others still are applied in countries that exist within a broader state of peace and economic development (e.g. Spain).

In that context, the only way to measure constitutional performance through the use of a universal test would be to ignore each country's nuances and idiosyncrasies and to remain focused on general objectives. The alternative would simply be unworkable: If we were to apply a narrow set of criteria to evaluate constitutions, the result would be that many of those individual tests would simply be inapplicable to a large number of contexts. For example, a universal test that measures constitutions' success in promoting racial equality would be inapplicable in Tunisia, which is racially homogeneous. A test that measures a constitution's capacity to end violent conflict would also not be particularly valuable in Switzerland, given the absence of any significant strife in that country to speak of.

As a result, the result is that a universal test could only be practically possible if it included criteria that are broad enough to be applied to all countries. The result of that generality is that (i) however the test is conceived, its relevance will be subject to question in a host of countries, and (ii) the proponents of the test will not be able to establish causation for success or failure in a large number (and possibly even a majority) of cases.

On the issue of relevance, the difficulty is that whoever conceives a universal test will necessarily be doing so based on a particular set of values. To take but one (obvious) example, Western academics and international institutions are very likely to be inspired by liberal democratic values in determining the content of a universal test, and their version of the test would likely revolve around a constitution's ability to bring about two main elements, namely peace and economic development. There is little questioning that these aspirations are shared by most if not all peoples around the world; what is subject to question is whether those aspirations alone constitute the "minimum core" for most countries.

Thus, for example, many states include amongst their list of priorities the desire to promote religious values (e.g. Iran, Afghanistan and El Salvador). Others consider economic development on its own to be unsatisfying, and prioritize the war against inequality (e.g. Columbia, Ecuador). If a universal test based on broad liberal values is applied in either of those cases, the result may be that the relevant constitutions are judged to be successes or failures by outsiders, but national actors may be totally indifferent to the analysis given that the criteria do not reflect their own set of values.

Conversely, in some cases and based on rare circumstances, a people's minimum core of aspirations may be even narrower than those encompassed by standard liberal values. By way of example, the clear priority for Bosnia in the mid-1990s was to end to the conflict, and on that basis the 1996 constitution has been enormously successful. On the other hand, the constitution has clearly not contributed to economic development or national integration. Simply judging the Bosnian constitution to have been a failure on that basis does not adequately convey the challenges that the country was facing at the time when the constitution entered into force. A better summation of Bosnia's position would be to say that the 1996 constitution successful in achieving the overarching goal of ending a violent conflict, but that now the constitution should be either replaced or amended to satisfy a different set of goals. On the issue of causation, broad universal criteria will also be unsatisfying in many causes simply because it will be close to impossible to establish a causal link between the constitution and the very broad criteria that a universal test would include. For example, determining whether a constitution has contributed to peace and stability would not be a particularly interesting exercise in Switzerland, given that its situation depends on factors that extend far beyond the constitution. Also, crediting the 1978 constitution for Spain's relative economic prosperity would not be satisfying, considering that Spain has been a major recipient of financial assistance from the European Union for decades. The same would be true in Qatar, Kuwait and the United Arab Emirates, in which a universal test might find that the constitutions of those three countries to be roaring successes, while it is obviously the incredible abundance of natural resources and the absence of major popular centers that is the main factor there.

On the other hand, where a constitution establishes a very clear and narrow goal for itself, such as to reduce inequality, then the country's success or failure in doing so may be far easier to trace. A genuine attempt to reduce inequality would include specific mechanisms to do so (e.g. the tutela under the Columbian constitution) and it would be possible in many cases to determine whether those specific mechanisms have had any impact in achieving the constitution's objectives.

A final, and perhaps more important, objection to the idea of a universal test is that many constitutions clearly establish a series of context-specific objectives of their own. Many constitutions will often include clear declarations of intent in their preambles or elsewhere in the text, which will also be matched by public statements by drafters, political elites and by members of the general public. The 2014 Tunisian constitution, for example, is clear in its intent to establish "social justice" as a matter of priority, which clearly matches the demands of the popular and spontaneous revolution that commenced in December 2010 (details follow). The Tunisian people and political elites appear to have reached a consensus on what their constitution is supposed to achieve; so it is unclear why anyone would seek to measure that text according to a different standard. It says something about our instincts if we consider that we should be evaluating a constitution's performance according to universal and external criteria if the constitution in question and the people who live in the country in question are already clear on what they are trying to achieve.[1]

THE TEXTS THEMSELVES

In the absence of a universal test, the only alternative is to measure constitutions against criteria that are determined on a case-by-case basis. The challenge is therefore to determine a methodology for deciding how that criteria can be identified, and the obvious place to start is to interpret the text of a constitution itself. The difficulty here is that whatever methodology is adopted will depend on the legal traditions that are in place in the jurisdiction that is under scrutiny. Indeed, it would not make much sense to use US legal interpretative rules to interpret the Egyptian constitution, given that that constitution is heavily imbued in Egypt's own legal traditions, which assume a different set of interpretative rules. As a result, the discussion that follows is based on an application of legal interpretative rules as they are generally applied in the Arab region.

It is a standard rule of legal interpretation that when examining a text, we must first give the words that are used in the constitution their literal meaning. On the question of constitutional purpose, preambles (where they exist) are the natural place to start given that they often seek to encapsulate the text's general objective and describe what type of state is being established. In the Arab region, preambles are often drafted and agreed upon before the rest of the text is completed, and various iterations are normally published in national media, provoking significant discussion.[2]

Standard rules of interpretation also provide that we must move beyond the general and seek to understand the nature of a constitutional text from the remainder of its substantive content. A constitution can expose its objective in the body of the text, either expressly in a statement of purpose or by establishing mechanisms that prioritize the pursuit of certain objectives over others. Importantly, when analyzing a text for this purpose, the reader must adopt a holistic approach, particularly as provisions from opposite parts of

---

[1]   Nevertheless, one might imagine at least two situations in which external criteria may be applied to evaluate a constitution: (i) where a clear objective based on national interests is not easily identifiable; (ii) where a constitution's stated objectives are too narrow and do not respond in any clear manner to the material needs of any segment of the population.

[2]   Tunisia's final constitution was adopted in January 2014, but its preamble was in its final form in June 2012; see "Final Draft of Preamble to 2012 Tunisian Constitution: English Translation by Tunisia Live," Farah Samti, Tunisia Live, published at *Jaddaliya*, 21 June 2012; "The Preamble of Tunisia's Constitution: Agreement and Discord" ("ديباجة الدستور التونسي.. توافق وخلاف"), Ayman Madhab, *Al-Jazeera*, 11 June 2012.

a constitution can work together either to enhance each other or establish a clear priority of objectives. Conversely, provisions may also negate each other's impact in ways that are not obvious upon first reading.

Some preambles are very clear in the objectives that they seek to achieve, others less so. Spain's 1978 constitution is typical of liberal constitutions in that its preamble includes commitments to democracy, the rule of law and a respect for human rights and cultural traditions. The preamble also provides that the "Spanish Nation" seeks a "fair economic and social order," and a "dignified quality of life for all," which places Spain within a socio-democratic tradition of placing emphasis on socioeconomic rights, particularly through the delivery of essential services to the general population (Comella 2013).[3] On its own, however, that specific wording does not clearly indicate the constitution's own order of priorities. For that, a more holistic interpretation of the constitution's substantive provisions is necessary.

The constitution provides that citizens have the right to a number of social and economic rights, including housing (article 47) and health care (article 49). In addition, article 9(2) clearly establishes that it is the government that is ultimately responsible "to promote conditions ensuring that freedom and equality of individuals and of the groups to which they belong are real and effective, to remove the obstacles preventing or hindering their full enjoyment, and to facilitate the participation of all citizens in political, economic, cultural and social life." At the same time, however, the constitution also limits the right of ordinary citizens to directly implement any of the constitution's social and economic rights, in the absence of implementation legislation (article 53(3)), which places the government firmly in control of the state's policy. The constitution's goal of establishing a social order is therefore tempered by its desire to ensure that the government remains unfettered at the summit of the state's pyramid.

The point can be made more clearly through a comparison with the South African text. The preamble to South Africa's 1996 constitution also includes reference to democracy, fundamental human rights and quality of life.[4] Those general principles are given more specific meaning by Chapter 2, which

---

[3] Many other preambles share the same qualities.
[4] Ecuador's 2008 constitution stands apart from both previous examples. It also includes reference to democratic values, to which it adds a commitment to "social liberation struggles against all forms of domination and colonialism." The preamble is followed by a list of the state's prime duties, which includes "planning national development, eliminating poverty, and promoting sustainable development and the equitable redistribution of resources and wealth to enable access to the good way of living" (article 3). The wording here is easily distinct from the liberal values set out in the Spanish and South African texts, and clearly illustrates the constitution's objectives.

provides for a right to housing, health care and education (articles 26, 27 and 29). In contrast to the Spanish text, however, the South African constitution ensures that even in the absence of a law, individuals may petition a court for relief in direct application of the constitution; the courts are specifically told that, when applying a provision of the Bill of Rights (which includes social and economic rights), they "must apply, or if necessary develop, the common law to the extent that legislation does not give effect to that right" (article 8). As a result of this and other provisions, the South African constitution's formal commitment to establishing a social democracy appears significantly stronger than the Spanish case, and can reasonably be considered to constitute one of the constitution's main objectives (Leibenberg 2010).

In the event that different parts of a constitution point in opposite directions, an attempt must be made to reconcile them. On occasion, clear contradictions can be identified in which case the reader must reach her own reasoned view on what the constitution's true objective is, based on an evaluation of the entirety of the circumstances. In that sense, the fact that a constitution establishes a series of political, social and economic rights without saying anything about who enjoys those rights or how they are to be enforced, that it subjects a nominally independent judiciary to legislation while at the same time allowing unelected executives to play a controlling role in the legislative process clearly indicates a clear order of priorities and a sense of the same constitution's objectives.

By way of illustration, Iraq's now-defunct 1970 interim constitution did not have a preamble, but included a general statement of purpose establishing Iraq as a "sovereign people's democratic republic. Its basic objective is the realization of one Arab State and the establishment of a socialist system" (article 1).[5] To underline its supposed commitment to the principle of democracy, the interim constitution also provided that the people are the "source of authority and its legitimacy" (article 2). The constitution's system of government however established a different set of priorities. A "revolutionary command council" was established (article 37) and granted both full legislative and executive functions (article 42). The council was responsible for selecting its own members (who had to be drawn from the Baath party's leadership (article 38)), who were accountable only to the council itself (article 45). The stated objective of establishing a socialist democracy was therefore clearly eclipsed by the desire to perpetuate undemocratic rule by a closed circle of individuals.

---

[5] An unofficial translation of the 1970 interim constitution is available here: www.zaidalali.com /resources/constitution-of-iraq/.

It is important to note that Iraq's 1970 interim constitution not the product of a modern and democratic constitution-building process. The text was essentially drafted by Baath party loyalists who offered few concessions if any to the country's other communities or groups. As the earlier analysis indicates, it is possible to discern what the text's objectives were; but because of the manner in which it was drafted, that analysis says close to nothing about what the general population, or indeed what anyone outside of the Baath party's circle of leaders, were hoping that the constitution might achieve for them. The question therefore is this: In what circumstances should we move beyond an analysis of the text itself and explore the role, statements and behavior of particular national actors when identifying constitutional purpose?

According to another rule of constitutional and legal interpretation, readers should only explore parties' intent through their behavior and writings in specific situations. For example, where a contradiction in the text cannot be resolved through an analysis of the provisions of their own, then we may be justified in determining what the drafter's intent was at the time when the constitution was written. In that situation, a reader may be justified in examining the archives of the constitution drafting committee (if they exist) to determine the drafters' original intent, or even the writings, statements and behavior of the political leaders who influenced the drafting process. This method of interpretation is merely an extension of the type of textual analysis set out earlier: It allows us to determine, through a different means of interpretation, what a constitution's actual objectives might be.

THE PEOPLE

Importantly, there are situations in which a reader seeking to uncover a constitution's objective may be justified in moving beyond the text's wording and even the drafters' intent. This is particularly the case when a constitution does not enjoy any form of internal legitimacy,[6] because it: (i) is clearly undemocratic (as in the case of the Iraqi 1970 interim constitution); (ii) is out of date (because it has not kept up with social norms); or (iii) has been manipulated by specific actors (such that the manner in which the text has been applied does not encapsulate the interests of the general population). In these situations, it is still possible to explore what the constitution's

---

[6] Here, I draw a distinction between internal legitimacy (which can result from a number of factors and circumstances) and international legitimacy (which is achieved through sufficient acceptance of a country's constitutional framework in the international community of nations). International legitimacy does not necessarily depend on the constitutional framework's acceptance by the population that it is designed to govern.

objectives *actually are,* but there is a separate and more important question which is what they *should be.*

Ideally, this new line of inquiry should be answered through an exploration of the needs and desires of the relevant country's general population insofar as their constitutional framework is concerned. But there are a number of challenges that must be met, the first being how to resolve divisions in public opinion. Clearly, there can never be absolute consensus between all the members of the population, so what we are looking for is a sufficient degree of acceptance expressed by community leaders, scholars, protesters as recorded in official statements, negotiated agreements or through actions of public protest. Luckily, there are a number of situations in which that level of consensus is relatively easy to identify. For example, Juan Bautista Alberdi, one of the nineteenth century's leading scholars on Latin American constitutionalism, found that the struggle for independence and against economic backwardness constituted the "great dramas" of the time and that the region's constitutional frameworks should have been geared in favor of resolving those dramas (Alberdi 2015). Today, Roberto Gargarella (Alberdi's successor and a contributor to this volume) identifies "inequality" as the region's modern drama (Gargarella 2013).[7] Since 2011, it has been possible to argue quite convincingly that large majorities of citizens in many Arab countries (although certainly not all) have prioritized social justice and the protection of basic freedoms over other potential objectives (details follow).

Even in those cases, however, significant proportions of the population might disagree with the voice of the majority or of the most vocal elements of the population. In 2011, it would have been reasonable to assume that crushing majorities of Egypt's population supported the calls for greater freedom and social justice, but by 2012[8] and even more so by

---

[7]   For more on the drama of inequality in Latin America and the impact that it has on public acceptance of existing constitutional frameworks, see "The Latinobarómetro Poll: When the Tide Goes Out," *The Economist*, 26 September 2015.

[8]   In Egypt's May–June 2012 presidential elections, 48.27% of voters opted in favor of Ahmed Shafik, losing only narrowly to Mohamed Morsi. Shafik was former dictator Hosni Mubarak's last appointed prime minister, and served as commander in chief of the Air Force from 1996 to 2002. During his election campaign, Shafik referred to Hosni Mubarak as a "role model" ("Egyptians Learn That Democracy Sometimes Produces Tough Choices," *The Post and Courier*, 29 May 2012); Shafik also promised a return to the old order if he was elected, including the reestablishment of a strong security state ("Ahmed Shafik, Mubarak's Last Prime Minister, Is the Surprise Contender in Egypt's Presidential Race," Hannah Allam, *McClatchy Newspaper*, 17 May 2012). For more on Shafik's campaign promises, see "Text of the Candidate Ahmed Shafik's Speech at the End of His Electoral Campaign" ("نص خطاب المرشح أحمد شفيق فى ختام حملته الانتخابية"), *Al-Watan News*, 14 June 2012.

2013,[9] it became obvious that significant proportions of the population prioritized law and order over other considerations. Clearly also, if large segments of Latin America's population prioritizes the struggle against inequality, then so do many seek to maintain their positions of privilege, often on the basis that the economy and the general welfare is better served under the status quo (Frank 1967). Where contradictions of this nature exist, the reader seeking to uncover a population's constitutional objective will have to make her own individual assessment of whether different visions for a country's fundamental text can be reconciled, or even whether one set of objectives should be prioritized over others. In the case of Latin America, one could convincingly argue that failing to priorities the struggle against inequality is inviting a society to breakdown as a whole, which itself would undermine one segment of the population's goal to maintain privilege. Meanwhile, in the Arab region, the result of prioritizing law and order over other considerations has already been made clear through the 2011 uprisings.

Another difficulty arises in distinguishing circumstances in which popular opinion and mobilization is manipulated by specific political actors in order to gain leverage over rivals. The 2013 protests that led to the removal by the military of President Mohamed Morsi were at first assumed to have been the result of a grassroots effort with no political leadership.[10] Since then, it has been widely accepted that the protest leaders enjoyed the support of a large segment of Egypt's security establishment and of its business community.[11] When pursuing my proposed line of inquiry on determining what a constitution's objective should be, if we turn to popular opinion as

[9] By the end of June 2013, a large segment of Egypt's population grew so frustrated by President Mohamed Morsi's performance that millions participated in protests demanding that he resign, and subsequently appeared to support the military's decision to depose him. See "Protesters across Egypt Call for Mohamed Morsi to Go," Patrick Kingsley, *The Guardian*, 30 June 2013.

[10] See "Protesters across Egypt Call for Mohamed Morsi to Go," Patrick Kingsley, *The Guardian*, 30 June 2013 (quoting Michael Hanna, a fellow at the Century Foundation, as saying that the protests were remarkable because they were "a bottom-up, grassroots effort and not directed by political opposition leaders. In a sense, they have latched on to this expanding current. While the organisers were diligent and creative, while lacking organisation and funding, this breadth of mass mobilisation could not have transpired unless the protest movement was tapping into deep and growing frustration and disenchantment with the current course of the country and its leadership").

[11] See, for example, "Sudden Improvements in Egypt Suggest a Campaign to Undermine Morsi," Ben Hubbard and David D. Kirkpatrick, *The New York Times*, 10 July 2013; "Al-Watan Reveals Full Details of the Communications between the Army and Tamarod on 3 July" ("الوطن تكشف التفاصيل الكاملة لاتصال الجيش بـ"تمرد" يوم 3 يوليو"), Mohamed Ali Hasan, *Al-Watan*, 4 July 2015.

a gauge, then we must find a way to distinguish between genuine and unfettered views of the general population and situations where popular opinion may be skewed by special interests. One possible mechanism is to rely on the general population's views only to the extent that those same people have no stake in government and to the extent that no one in government has any specific stake in encouraging the views that are being expressed. Applying that standard to Egypt, we can easily distinguish between the 2011 protesters who faced opposition from most of the state's bureaucracy and security institutions, and their 2013 peers who were encouraged in their actions by the police, the military, the media and others.

Other countries face the opposite problem. In many situations, it is simply not possible to consult the general population (e.g. Bosnia between 1992 and 1995), nor is it possible for ordinary people to disagree with the policies of their governments (e.g. Iraq prior to 2003). In such situations, it would be safe to assume that the general population would prefer to be free from conflict and the yoke of oppression, but it would not be possible to determine where the general population places its priorities. Where there is a lack of basic freedoms to the extent that the general population cannot engage in a discussion on constitutional priorities, the line of inquiry that is being suggested here cannot be approached in the same manner. The only possible solution, inadequate as it may be, would be to carry out an independent inquiry based on whatever data and information may be available on the circumstances of the country in question in order to determine what set of priorities might exist for its constitutional framework. Thus, if such an exercise had been carried out in Bosnia during the 1990s, we would most likely have concluded that ending the conflict was the priority and in that sense the 1996 constitution has been successful. In Iraq prior to 2003, we might have concluded that the protection of fundamental freedoms and national reconciliation (including through the establishment of an inclusive governance framework) should have been prioritized in any post-totalitarian arrangement. If that is the standard, then we can reasonably conclude that the 2005 constitution has been a failure (Al-Ali 2014).

THE PRE-2011 CONSTITUTIONS

The dynamics behind their elaboration

Prior to 2011, genuine political power in the Arab region was concentrated in the hands of small groups of kings, presidents, military officers and other senior executive officers (hereinafter "controlling elites"), none of whom were elected (Salloukh et al. 2015).[12] These individuals were in a prime position to influence each country's constitutional culture, including what each constitution's objective would be. The controlling elites' understanding of constitutional purpose was informed by a number of factors, including their own desire to monopolize power as well as the need to placate other elite circles to guarantee the functioning of a modern bureaucratic state. Aside from the general context in which they operated, the controlling elites' sense of entitlement to exercise authority informed their view of how constitutional frameworks should be constructed. Thus, however a constitution's objectives were to be defined, the controlling elites ensured that there should be no real mechanism for measuring or analyzing their performance and for holding them accountable for their failures (Stilt 2014).

Other groups of elites were influential in their own way. These include other political elites outside of controlling circles, including other political parties (where they were allowed to be active); members of the security establishment, many of whom played a determining role in forming each specific country's educational policy and cultural identity (Simon 2012); members of the legal profession, including lawyers, academics and judges, all of whom self-identified as intellectual leaders who should necessarily be involved in determining their countries' constitutional culture. Religious elites in many countries shared much of the same expectation and, in those situations where they felt that their beliefs were not being properly considered, often formed political parties and movements that they could then use to influence constitutional processes in a more targeted fashion (particularly with a view to ensuring that personal status rights and fundamental rights were not granted in a way that contravened a very traditional understanding of religious values). Finally, broader cultural elites, including prominent journalists and authors, played important roles in channeling and promoting ideas to the national stage. In the Arab region's radical postcolonial environment, these groups of individuals played a key role in defining each country's political priorities, many of which were articulated either directly or indirectly in the constitutions that were drafted over the past 100 years.

Prior to 2011, in the vast majority of constitutional drafting processes, controlling elites would select a small number of individuals from other elite

---

[12] This applied to all countries in the region apart from Lebanon, which has held elections relatively regularly and which has survived on power-sharing arrangements for decades. Even in Lebanon, however, corruption and nepotism quickly took root, to the extent that specific political groups managed to ensure a monopoly of support from each of the country's various communities and the change in political fortunes became more a function of demographics than the relative failure or success of a specific party's policies.

circles to serve as members of drafting committees. In most cases, drafting committees would be mainly populated by jurists, but have also included individuals who did not have a legal background. Although drawn from the elite circles described earlier, constitutional drafters potentially had enormous power to influence the outcome of a constitutional-building process given that they were responsible for translating broad principles into specific constitutional rules. This was particularly true given that controlling elites were generally unfamiliar with their countries' legal traditions and were therefore unlikely to object to legal innovations that fell outside their main scope of interest. In addition, controlling elites would provide only broad direction for what should be included in the constitutional text, leaving the detail to the drafters. In Egypt, then president Anwar Sadat provided the National Assembly, which was tasked with drafting the constitution, with a "short list of specific instructions" (Stilt 2014).

Constitutional drafting processes were generally brief, which reduced opportunities to engage with drafters and influence their work. Even in those cases where the processes nominally lasted months or even years (Iraq in 1925, Tunisia in 1959, etc.), the drafting processes were themselves monopolized by small numbers of individuals (some of whom were not even nationals) who generally worked behind closed doors, further reducing opportunities for outsiders to impact the discussions (Khadduri 1951). Finally, many drafters were selected on the basis of their conservative predisposition and party loyalty and so any attempt to introduce progressive ideas to the process would have met with significant resistance.

Importantly, prior to 2011, the general population played at best a passive role in shaping constitutional discourse. Postcolonial constitutions were grounded in the popular demand for sovereignty and an improved framework for the protection of individual rights. However, controlling political elites constructed drafting processes in a way that ensured that the general population would have no input, which was reflected in the final drafts that were produced. At the time, these procedural and substantive issues attracted very little attention. It took decades for the general population to create enough space for itself to note its discontent with existing constitutional frameworks. Today, the general population has a far better understanding of its rights and has become far more adept at articulating its demands (details follow).

Their objectives

Given all of the aforementioned, I propose to limit the discussion here to determining the objective that the pre-2011 constitutions actually served (as opposed to the objectives that they should have served). In so doing, it is inevitable that we should make reference to Nathan Brown's (remarkably on point) book in which he examines the texts of the pre-2011 Arab constitutions themselves in an attempt to understand what their objectives actually were (Brown 2002). As a starting point, Brown dismisses the proposition that Arab constitutions were deeply cynical documents that were ignored in practice. Arab constitutions have traditionally included long lists of political, social and economic rights. The standard argument that is made is that those rights were designed to placate a demanding population by creating an illusion of liberal constitutionalism. However, the rights provisions were deliberately constructed as non-binding promises that were subservient to the will of the law. Thousands of laws and regulations were passed in conformity with these constitutions, and which restricted all the rights that ordinary people incorrectly thought had been granted to them.

Brown also explores three other possibilities, which were that the constitutions were designed to (i) underscore sovereignty; (ii) signal basic ideological or policy tenets; (iii) organize or augment state authority. Brown finds the first of these possibilities unconvincing mainly because Arab countries had started drafting constitutions well before they had achieved full sovereignty. He also dismisses the second on the basis that many Arab constitutions are entirely silent on ideological issues. He correctly notes that while a growing number of constitutions included historical and political narratives in their preambles, most did not offer any specific ideological grounding. On the other hand, he finds significant evidence to support the proposition that Arab constitutions were principally designed to organize state authority. Indeed, most Arab constitutions were enacted at a time when various groups of elites were jostling against each other in a competition for political power, and so were replete with provisions that regulate the activities of state institutions.

As such, security institutions, members of the legal profession (mainly judges) and a small number of political groups were all given their own spheres of influence. The constitutional texts themselves were principally designed to regulate their behavior in a way that augmented and cemented each institution's sphere of authority, while also cementing them together.

How successful were they?

If we consider, as Brown does in his book, that the pre-2011 constitutions' objective was to organize and augment state authority, then we can consider the constitutions ultimately to have been a failure. In fact, the seeds for constitutional degradation were firmly planted when the constitutions themselves were drafted. Most constitutional texts in the region were drafted by individuals who were handpicked by ruling authorities specifically because of their bias toward authority and control. Libya's 1951 and Iraq's 1925 constitutions were prepared by foreign officials and advisers with only minor input from locals. The king was directly involved in and controlled the drafting of all of Morocco's constitutions and Jordan's 1952 constitution. Syria's 1973 constitution and Iraq's 1970 interim constitution were both drafted under the auspices of harsh authoritarian regimes. Egypt's 1971 constitution was drafted by a committee of eighty individuals, all of whom were members of the National Assembly, which was intensely loyal to the then president (Waterbury 2014). All of these texts included detailed provisions on how parliament should operate, specifically setting out the circumstances in which sessions could not be held, how long sessions should last, how votes should be organized, etc. Meanwhile, the texts were virtually silent on the limits of executive authority.[13] There were no provisions that indicated that governments should always operate in application of the law; states of emergency could be declared and renewed ad infinitum, with no clarity on their impact on rights and freedoms; the role of the executive in the legislative process was left undefined.[14]

The bias in favor of whoever controlled the executive branch of government, whether king, president or prime minister, ultimately created a further incentive for specific individuals or groups of individuals within executive circles to eliminate rivals and purge the halls of power. Therefore, as time progressed, executive power was eventually monopolized by ever-diminishing members of people (sometimes eventually reducing to a single individual, as in the case of Iraq from 1979 until 2003).[15] As the pool of individuals and groups that were involved in designing state policy narrowed, so did the quality of decision-making. As such, although there were few if any genuine

---

[13] Egypt's 1971 constitution included fifty articles (1,942 words in the Arab original) that regulated parliamentary proceedings. It only included seven articles (325 words) on how the government was supposed to function. An unofficial translation of Egypt's 1971 constitution is available here: www.constitutionnet.org/files/Egypt%20Constitution.pdf.

[14] See, for example, "Endless Emergency: The Case of Egypt," Sadiq Reza, 10 New Crim. L. R. 532 (2007); and "Political Participation and Democratic Transition in the Arab World," Lina Khatib, 34 U. Pa. J. Int'l L. 315 (2013).

[15] Behind the scenes purges took place as recently as September 2015 in Algeria, where Mohamed Mediene, who had been the head of Algeria's intelligence service for twenty-five years, was quietly replaced by President Abdelaziz Bouteflika. No reasons were offered. See "Algerian President Fires Intelligence Chief in a Shake-Up of Security Forces," Carlotta Gall, *The New York Times*, 14 September 2015; see also "Bouteflika Puts an End to Head of Intelligence General Mohamed Medien's 'Legend'" ("الاستخبارات بوتفليقة ينهي «أسطورة» الجنرال توفيق قائد"), Atef Qadadara, *Al-Hayat*, 14 September 2015.

challenges to the existing constitutional orders throughout most of the region for a period of decades, poverty, inequality and insecurity increased steadily in practically all countries. Human development indicators and socioeconomic data all reflected an increasingly desperate situation: booming populations, growing unemployment, stubborn levels of poverty and illiteracy, staggering levels of corruption, etc.[16] All of these phenomena led to unprecedented amounts of social unrest starting in Tunisia in December 2010. In the end, state authority was diminished by executive overreach that manifested itself through the desire to monopolize power for as long as possible, without paying any heed to genuine social needs.

Significant hope was placed in specific institutions, including Egypt's judiciary, which had exercised signs of independence in some of its rulings (Moustafa 2007) and the UGTT, Tunisia's largest trade union (Yousfi 2014). Over time, however, governments across the region used the considerable tools that they had at their disposal to control the work of those institutions, notably those that were supposed to be exercising oversight over the government, namely parliamentarians, auditors, prosecutors and judges. Their independence was limited and their senior leadership was offered privileges in exchange for acquiescence (Farouk 2008). In the few instances where state institutions resisted the monopolization of power, the executive amended the constitution and legislation to limit their authority altogether.[17] Even the Egyptian judiciary had been brought under control by the executive (Moustafa 2007).

If, however, we consider that the objective of the pre-2011 constitutions was to preserve power for as long as possible, then they can be considered to have

---

[16] Although Egypt's education section has been in desperate need for reform for decades, the state has been incapable of addressing the basic challenges that it faces. The sector's difficulties have grown significantly worse over time. "Education in Egypt: Key Challenges," Louisa Loveluck, Chatham House Background Paper, March 2012. In 2013, Egypt ranked last out of 148 countries in the ranking of primary education quality; see "Unpacking Egypt's low education score in the Global Competitiveness Report," Egyptian Initiative for Personal Rights, 25 September 2013. The same difficulties are shared by other sectors, including the security sector; see, for example, Roger Owen, *The Rise and Fall of Arab Presidents for Life*, Harvard University Press (2014).

[17] For example, in July 2015, after failing to rein in the Central Auditing Organisation (Egypt's supreme audit institution, which is formally independent in accordance with Article 215 of the 2014 constitution), President Sisi issued a decree granting himself the right to depose its head. See "Sisi Issues Law Granting President Right to Depose Heads of 4 Regulatory Agencies," *Ahram Online*, 11 July 2015; and "Controversy Surrounding the President Granting Himself the Right to Dismiss Board Members from the State's Oversight Institutions" ("جدل حول منح الرئيس نفسه سلطة إعفاء أعضاء الهيئات المستقلة والرقابية من مناصبهم"), *Youm7*, 12 July 2015. President Sisi finally acted upon the decree and dismissed the Auditing Organisation's head in March 2016. See "Egypt's Top Auditor Geneina Removed by Presidential Decree," *Mada Masr*, 28 March 2016.

been partially successful. Ruling elites in a number of countries were forcefully removed via popular revolutions (Tunisia) or palace coups (Egypt), while others were so obstinate in their refusal to reform that they imposed on their countries violent and protracted conflicts (Libya, Syria, Yemen and Iraq).[18] At the same time, ruling elites in other countries have managed to survive in the post-2011 environment. In some cases, ruling authorities offered a number of concessions to restless population, usually in the form of constitutional reform (Morocco, Algeria and Jordan). In many others, mainly Gulf and resource-rich autocracies (Saudi Arabia, Kuwait, Bahrain, the United Arab Emirates, Qatar and Omar), there were no serious threats to the ruling elites' survival and no tangible changes were ever enacted.

THE ARAB SPRING CONSTITUTIONS

The people's objectives

The popular uprising that took place in 2011 from Morocco to Iraq, passing through Tunisia, Libya, Egypt, Yemen, Syria, Jordan and Bahrain, was almost without precedent mainly because it forced controlling elites to take the needs and desires of their own populations seriously.[19] The priority for the revolutionaries who led the protests in many countries (Tunisia, Libya, Egypt, Yemen and Syria) was to cause the downfall of long-standing dictators, but the focus and debate quickly shifted to establishing a reform agenda that included constitutional reform. The exchanges that took place during that early period eventually crystallized around a small number of issues, which were best expressed through popular slogans including

---

[18] Note however that in all cases, the conflicts that are ongoing in these countries were never purely internal affairs. Foreign actors played a significant role in all cases.

[19] The term "Arab Spring constitutions" is designed to refer to those constitutions that were drafted pursuant to the protest movement that commenced in Tunisia in December 2010. These include Morocco (2011), Tunisia (2014), Egypt (2012), Egypt (2014), Syria (2012) and Jordan (2011). As of the time of writing, Algeria, Libya and Yemen's drafting processes are still ongoing. Draft versions of the Libyan and Yemeni constitutions have been published mainly because it forced controlling elites to take the needs and desires of their own populations seriously; Algeria has as of yet not published any drafts of its proposed reform plan. As should be clear from the substance of this chapter, the designation of a constitution as an "Arab Spring constitution" is not designed to reflect any positive or negative connotations, but merely reflects temporal and causal realities. Note also that although Iraq does not qualify as an Arab Spring country (given that its constitution was drafted six years before the Arab Spring started and pursuant to a military invasion and occupation, and not in response to a popular movement), I include some discussion of the 2005 Iraqi constitution here given that the drafting process that led to its adoption matches many of the dynamics that led to the Arab Spring constitutions. Needless to say, I do not include any discussion of the Gulf monarchies' constitutions, given that they were, by and large, unaffected by the Arab Spring.

"عيش، حرية، عدالة إجتماعية" (bread, freedom and social justice), which broadly translated as a desire for the protection of fundamental rights, and the achievement of social justice.

The preambles to the Egyptian (2014),[20] Tunisian (2014), Moroccan (2011) and Syrian (2012) constitutions constitute strong evidence that the drafters sought to address the concerns that were being expressed by the protesters and revolutionaries.[21] All of these preambles offer historical and political narratives, which are designed to encapsulate the state's ideology, and also to divorce the new state from previous generations of ruling authorities or at least to reinforce the importance of certain segments of the existing ruling elite. Although each of these constitutions includes idiosyncrasies that reflect unique national circumstances (e.g. the role of the monarchy in Morocco, or the sense of international isolation in Syria), there are themes and principles that recur in all of the preambles. All four of the texts without exception make reference to the people's or the nation's place in the world community, sometimes through the mention of international institutions and at other times by providing an account of the nation's contributions to world history. More importantly, the texts also strongly emphasize popular sovereignty and social justice, sometimes to the extent that these principles are repeated several times within just a few lines.

The Egyptian preamble states that the purpose of the revolution is to "achieve freedom and social justice together" (an exact reflection of the popular slogan cited earlier), that the Egyptian people believe in "democracy as a path, a future, and a way of life; in political plurality; and in the peaceful transfer of power" and that all people have the right to "[f]reedom, human dignity, and social justice." Tunisia's preamble provides that the constitution has as its objective to establish the "framework of a civil state founded on the law and on the sovereignty of the people," and that the constitution seeks to "build on national unity that is based on citizenship, fraternity, solidarity, and social justice." According to the Moroccan preamble, the state seeks to establish a "democratic State of Law" through "participation, of pluralism and of good governance," and also develop a "society of solidarity where all enjoy security, liberty, equality of opportunities, of respect for their dignity and for social justice." Finally, the Syrian preamble states that the new constitution establishes a number of principles including the "rule of the people based on

[20] Note that since the start of 2011, Egypt has had three separate constitutional texts: an interim constitution that entered into force in March 2011; a constitution that entered into force in 2012; and, after the civil government was deposed by the military in July 2013, a new constitution drafted in 2013, finally entering into force in 2014. The latter two texts, and the processes that led to their elaboration, will both be referred to here.

[21] The Jordanian constitution does not include a preamble. The latest versions of the drafts of Libyan and Yemeni constitutions also do not include preambles.

elections, political and party-based pluralism, [. . .] social justice, equality, equal opportunities, citizenship, and the rule of law."

The wording used in the Arab Spring constitutions can be contrasted against preambles of the previous generation of constitutions. Although the latter made some reference to progressive values that are similar in nature to the desire to achieve "social justice," these were often secondary concerns in comparison with the then ruling authorities' political aims, including the establishment of socialism and the monopolization of power by undemo-cratic forces. The preamble to Morocco's 1996 constitution made quick reference to international organizations and obligations, and to the need to establish peace and security in the world and made no mention of the needs or aspirations of ordinary people. Syria's 1973 constitution essentially con-sisted of a historical narrative from the point of view of the Syrian Baath party. The need for "Arab unity" was emphasized on several occasions, as well as the "establishment of a socialist order." The preamble also stated that "[f]reedom is a sacred right and popular democracy is the ideal formulation" but only after several references were made to the Baath party's special role in guiding state and society. The preamble to Egypt's 1971 constitution was clearly drafted with progressive ideals in mind. Multiple references are made to the "dignity of man," although no clear explanation is offered as to what human dignity consists of. The preamble also committed the state to a broadly progressive agenda that was perfectly suited to the 1970s, including the "integration between science and faith, between political and social freedom, between national independence and social affiliation." Tunisia's 1959 constitution was the only text that would not be out of place amongst Arab Spring constitutions. It made reference to "human dignity, justice and liberty," the "sovereignty of the people," "respect of human rights" and "citizens' right to work, health care and education" (roughly equivalent to the modern conception of social justice in the Arab region). The major difference between the 1959 constitution and its successor was the former's moral conservatism, and specifically stated that the text had as one of its main objections to "protect the family."

The evolution from the earlier generation of Arab constitutions to the Arab Spring texts could not be clearer. Constitutional drafters from 2011 to 2014 were clearly conscious of the need to respond to the demands of the people and adopted the exact same terminology that was used in demonstrations through-out the region (even in Syria). As such, the constitution's stated aims, as expressed in their preambles, overlap to a very large extent with the popular aspirations of the people.

The constitutions' objectives

As noted earlier, however, a constitution's preamble may not accurately reflect the spirit of the remainder of the text, or even the drafters' full intent. Despite the new context and the revolutionaries' early success in imposing themselves on the regional debate, in many of the drafting processes that took place after 2011, the general population was generally unable to apply any significant pressure on drafters, who remained dependent on preexisting elite circles and who have been largely unable to break away from the Arab region's conservative and uncritical legal traditions. In Morocco (2011), Syria (2012), Egypt (2014) and Jordan (2011), drafting committees were directly appointed by presidential or royal decrees, and individual members were almost all selected on the basis of loyalty to the existing power structure.[22] Although some of these drafting committees did organize public outreach efforts, popular opinion did not play an effective role in influencing discussions beyond generalities that were set out in the preambles and in a few other issues. The drafting processes were all completed in either a matter of weeks or a small number of months, effectively preventing civil society from mobilizing and analyzing whatever was being done in the drafting chamber (Madani et al. 2012). In Algeria, the process has been ongoing for four years but is so secretive and centralized within the office of the president that there is no clarity on when it will be completed or even what changes will be made.[23]

Other countries adopted a different approach but often reached the same result. In Tunisia (2011) and Libya (2013), constitutional drafters were directly elected. In Egypt (2012) and in Iraq (2005), drafting bodies were appointed by parliamentary assemblies that were principally elected for that purpose. In addition, in each of those countries, a large number of public meetings were organized to debate key constitutional issues. The largest amount of interaction between drafters and the general public took place in Tunisia, which had the longest of the constitutional drafting processes by far (two years).[24] Uniquely in comparison with other countries in the region, the Tunisian constituent assembly published four drafts and solicited comments from the general public. In Yemen, the actual drafting of the constitution took

---

[22] In addition, although some of the committees included a few progressive members, they were generally in a minority in comparison to the more conservative members.

[23] "Algerie: la nouvelle constitution, l'Arlésienne de Bouteflika," Farid Alilat, *Jeune Afrique*, 24 April 2015.

[24] Libya's constitution drafting assembly was directly elected in February 2014, and had not completed its work by April 2016. However, as a result of the conflict and general state of insecurity that has been ongoing in Libya since 2011, public meetings on constitutional reform issues have been quite rare.

place in 2014, following a full-year national dialogue conference, perhaps the freest and most comprehensive discussion of its kind ever to have taken place in the Arab region (Lackner 2016).

However, in a region with weak democratic traditions and undemocratic political parties, the difference in practice between this seemingly democratic approach and the old manner of proceeding was not particularly marked, for a variety of reasons. First, controlling elites and political party leaders play an important role in selecting the candidates who can run for election, and tend to favor loyalty and reliability over an innovative and reforming spirit. Second, political elites, many of whom are unelected, often take strategic decisions that bind elected officials, thereby undermining electoral results. Finally, controlling elites play a critical role in determining the outcome of constitutional drafting processes even before they begin through their long-term influence over the legal profession. State law schools, which should be dynamic environments for the free exchange of ideas, were instead transformed into static environments that specialize in rewarding an uncritical commitment to applying the law, regardless of its content or its provenance. The absence of a critical element to legal education and judicial training imbued the entire legal profession with a heavily conservative and authoritarian outlook that played a key role in constitutional drafting processes throughout the region. Elected officials are often bound by established traditions that are presented as being beyond questioning, including but not limited to a country's legal traditions. That impression is reinforced by, amongst others, each country's legal professionals and especially judges who typically present their methods and traditions as being above reproach (Shalakany 2012).

The effect of these factors is that the distinction between the constitutions that were produced with more public input and those that were produced with less is not particularly marked. Instead, most of the Arab Spring constitutions largely reflect the drafters' and the controlling elites' prioritization of continuity and incremental change over the desire to establish social justice and protect fundamental freedoms. A quick comparison between Egypt's 2012 and 2014 constitutions will illustrate that point.

The 2012 constitution, which was drafted by a constitutional committee that was appointed by an elected parliament, is supposed to mark a new beginning in Egyptian constitutional history.[25] Instead, the new text was heavily inspired by the 1971 constitution, despite the latter's many flaws. By way of illustration, the drafters claimed that they were intent on establishing a semi-presidential

---

[25] For a full analysis of the 2012 constitution, see "The New Egyptian Constitution: An Initial Assessment of Its Merits and Flaws," Zaid Al-Ali, *openDemocracy*, 26 December 2012.

system of government that could not be dominated by any particular political party in the future (Choudhry and Stacey 2014). However, the drafters were unable to break away from the traditions that had been established by the 1971 constitution. For example, the president's power to appoint members of the upper chamber of parliament was maintained (article 128), giving the president an unjust and undeserved amount of leverage over the legislative process. Given that the upper chamber was responsible for approving all of the president's appointments to the country's independent institutions (including the audit institution and the central bank), that process was skewed in the president's favor in a way that was impossible to justify.

In another example, the drafters decided not to negotiate a new arrangement on decentralization. Despite huge disparities in service delivery and standards of living between the country's major urban centers and much of the rest of the country,[26] the 2012 constitution deferred to the preexisting legal framework on decentralization, which essentially provides that all decision-making should be maintained in the capital.[27] Worse still were the provisions on civil/military relations. The 2012 constitution explicitly recognized (for the first time) that civilians could be tried by military courts for crimes that "harm the armed forces" (article 198). The term was left to be defined by subsequent legislation. Also surprising is the fact that the National Defense Council (which has eight military members and seven civilians) was made responsible for discussing the military's budget (article 197). Unsurprisingly given the context, almost nothing was done to improve the framework for the improvement of rights: Although the list of socioeconomic rights was prolonged, the judiciary was not given any additional authority to ensure their proper

---

[26] Egypt Human Development Report 2004: Choosing Decentralisation for Good Governance, United Nations Development Programme, 2004, p. 22 ("By examining the tables that address urban-rural gaps in human development, one can easily identify human development disparities among the major four groups of governorates and among individual governorates; this is in spite of multiple rural development programs and efforts. Available data are not yet sufficient for estimating urban/rural indices of human development neither at national nor at governorate level, but a number of available sub-HDI indicators are revealing as regards the urban/rural human development imbalance in Egypt, even though urban/rural gaps have been narrowing during the period 1990–2002. In 2001, the average urban/rural gap at the national level was 32.3% in adult literacy rate (15+), compared to 45% in 1992").

[27] Article 188 provided that local councils should be elected but article 190 allowed for any of their decisions to be overturned by the central government in order to prevent "damage to the public interest." Worse still, article 187 did not clearly indicate how governors were to be chosen (whether elected or selected) and made no attempt to define their powers, leaving all of these crucial matters to be decided by subsequent legislation, as has been the case for the past few decades. Finally, earlier drafts called for a financial redistribution mechanism between provinces to remedy the gross disparities that exist in the country. That provision was deleted from the final version.

application, no effort was made to improve the performance of the (woefully underperforming) judicial sector, and litigants were not given any additional rights to bring claims to court. In short, the 2012 constitution departed from its predecessor in ways that changed the balance of power within the state, but not in a way that would directly impact the rights of ordinary Egyptians.

Although Egypt's 2014 constitution was drafted by a committee of fifty individuals who were appointed by presidential decree, it also does not depart from the 1971 constitution's framework to a significant extent (Al-Ali 2015). In fact, the text maintains, and on occasion worsens, many of the negative characteristics that have plagued Egypt's constitutional practice for decades. The tribe-like mentality through which state institutions are granted impressive amounts of independence and privileges despite the fact that they do not deliver adequate services to the people has been reinforced, diminishing the potential for democratic accountability and pressure for improvement.[28] In addition, although the list of socioeconomic rights is more detailed than in the past, they remain generally non-justiciable. Meanwhile, basic civil and political rights such as speech and association are hardly improved. The constitution also does not offer any convincing mechanism for the enforcement of rights: Apart from even more independence than before, the judicial sector remains unreformed and no additional mechanisms have been created, meaning that those additional rights that are provided for will almost certainly remain unprotected. Just as worryingly, the new constitution tilts the balance of power firmly back in the president's favor, which is not particularly reassuring given the circumstances.[29]

On the issue of rights, the 2014 constitution includes a small number of provisions that are designed to impose the obligation on any future government to adopt a more progressive set of investment priorities. By way of example, article 18 provides that "The state commits to allocate a percentage of government expenditure that is no less than 3% of Gross Domestic Product (GDP) to health. The percentage will gradually increase to reach global rates." Article 19 also provides that "The state commits to allocating a percentage of government spending that is no less than 4% of Gross Domestic Product (GDP) for education. It will gradually increase this until it reaches global

---

[28] See, for example, article 203, which provides that the armed forces' budget should appear as a "single figure" in the state budget, and that it is the National Defense Council (a majority of whose members are drawn from the security institutions) that is responsible for debating it, as opposed to the parliament; and article 185, which also provides that the judiciary's own budget should appear as a single figure in the state budget, with no quid pro quo on accountability and transparency measures offered in return.

[29] For example, although the government is formed by the prime minister, the president has the right to appoint the ministers of justice, interior and defense (article 146).

rates." Although these provisions are designed to show that some importance was given to the improvement of living standards of the poorest segment of society, there is significant doubt as to whether they will make any difference in practice, given the innate difficulties that exist in implementing provisions of this nature.

Many of the other Arab Spring constitutions follow the same pattern of improving some of the details while maintaining the same overall structure of government. By way of example, Moroccan opposition parties were granted some new standing under the 2011 constitution,[30] but the king still maintains firm control over key state institutions and still has significant influence over the government (on which he can impose his will at any time)[31] and the judiciary.[32] An analysis of the 2011 amendments to the Jordanian constitution leads to the same conclusion (Sufian Obeidat. Unpublished. *The Amended Constitution of Jordan: Analysis and Recommendations Study*. International IDEA). The little information that has been made public about the planned reforms in Algeria also points in the same direction.[33]

Tunisia's 2014 constitution constitutes a partial exception to that trend (Al-Ali 2016). Importantly, many of the controlling elites who had been in power prior to the popular uprisings lost all of their influence in 2011 and so the impetus to prioritize continuity over other concerns disappeared. Instead, debate during the drafting process focused almost entirely on how to bridge the divide between two sides of a deep political chasm. The priority then became to prevent backsliding toward a new authoritarianism, by ensuring that state institutions could never again be captured by a single political force. While this presented an enormous opportunity to progress on many fronts, some of the other factors mentioned earlier, including the deeply conservative

[30] For example, article 10 specifically provides that the parliamentary opposition has the right to freedom of expression, airtime on official media (proportional to its representation), public finance, etc. Article 82 provides that "[o]ne day per month at least is reserved for the examination of the proposals of law of which are [of] the opposition."

[31] Article 48 provides that the king may preside over the government's sessions. Although the constitution is silent on the government's rules of procedure when the king is present, given his status within the Moroccan state and society it is clear that individual ministers would not be in a position to disagree with any of the king's initiatives or decisions issued in that context.

[32] Article 107 provides that the "King is the guarantor of the independence of the judicial power." Article 115 provides that the Superior Council of the Judicial Power is presided over by the King, and that the King has the right to appoint five "notable persons" to the Council. Article 130 provides that six of the Constitutional Court's twelve members, as well as the Court's president, are appointed by the king. Three of the remaining members are to be elected by the Chamber of Representatives, and the other three by the Chamber of Councilors.

[33] See "General Presentation on the Recommendations on Constitutional Reform" ("عرض عام حول اقتراحات تتعلق بالتعديل الدستوري"), Presidency of the Republic's official website (undated).

tendencies of legal professionals,[34] impeded that effort. The result is that the final Tunisian constitution is a mixed bag of what appear to be effective checks and balances, on the one hand,[35] and missed opportunities, on the other.[36] Most importantly, the people's interest of achieving social justice was not particularly well served by the constitution.[37]

How likely are they to succeed?

It is too early to say whether these new constitutions have succeeded or failed, whether in relation to the people's objectives, the constitution's own set of priorities or any other criteria. Despite the revolutionary context, most countries in the region have opted to pursue an incremental approach to reform. So the question will be whether state institutions in countries such as Egypt, Morocco, Jordan, Algeria and Tunisia will maintain a sustainable timeframe for reform that will outpace and address demographic changes, security risks and economic challenges. However, given how existing authorities have

[34] I am in possession of four fully fledged proposals for constitutional reform that were prepared by different groups of leading Tunisian academics. All four proposals were circulated before the end of 2011. All four are so similar to the 1959 constitution that they were hoping to replace that they were practically indistinguishable from it. The four proposals do not appear to have been formally published and are not available online, but I have them in my possession and can make them available upon request.

[35] In an effort to prevent the constitutional court from being dominated by any single branch of government or any particular political force, article 118 of the Tunisian constitution provides: "The President of the Republic, the Assembly of the Representatives of the People, and the Supreme Judicial Council shall each appoint four members, three quarters of whom must be legal specialists." In addition, the constitution provides the courts with significant additional authority through article 49, according to which: "The limitations that can be imposed on the exercise of the rights and freedoms guaranteed in this Constitution will be established by law, without compromising their essence. Any such limitations can only be put in place for reasons necessary to a civil and democratic state and with the aim of protecting the rights of others, or based on the requirements of public order, national defence, public health or public morals, and provided there is proportionality between these restrictions and the objective sought. Judicial authorities ensure that rights and freedoms are protected from all violations."

[36] The Tunisian constitution's provisions relating to the security sector are highly perplexing, particularly for a country that is still emerging from a period of autocratic rule. The constitution merely provides that the president is the commander in chief of the armed forces (article 77); that the president is responsible for appointing and dismissing senior military and security officers (article 78); and states that the president is "responsible for national security" (article 77) without providing any detail at all as to what these powers entail.

[37] It is worth noting that Yemen's draft constitution also proposes to introduce a large number of reforms to the country's constitutional framework. Amongst other things, the draft provides for the establishment of a real federal arrangement and significantly strengthens the framework for the protection of rights. Regrettably, the country lapsed into a new conflict immediately after the draft constitution was published in January 2015. At the time of writing, it is unclear whether the draft constitution will ever be adopted.

performed since 2011, a better question would be whether a timeframe for reform even exists.

To take Egypt as a first example, the country's ability to break out of its cycle of poverty and deep inequality will depend on its capacity for policy formation and accountability, which itself will depend on having an effective parliament in place. The country has been without a parliament since 2012 and the president has been ruling by decree in the absence of any meaningful discussion on policy since 2013. Parliamentary elections were organized in October 2015, and the new parliament is likely to sit shortly thereafter. The political environment in Egypt during 2014 and 2015 was such that the new parliament has been characterized by analysts and others as being totally loyal to the new president, which reduces the likelihood of serious discussion on policy and oversight of government performance for some time.[38] Nevertheless, even the remotest possibility of debate has stirred consternation amongst Egypt's controlling elites, causing them to argue against the application of the 2014 constitution's framework on the powers of parliament, which grants only slightly expanded provision on parliament.[39] In the meantime, the state has been punishing dissent, further reducing the likelihood of a serious discussion on policy to the extent that the president of the republic has threatened anyone who expresses any form of dissent with extreme violence (Human Rights Watch 2015).[40]

In Morocco, the political opposition has been able to point to some small victories in terms of its ability to express its views and to exist within certain institutions, but none of those developments have translated into any tangible improvements in people's lives. Instead, the royal court and the remainder of the political elite have prioritized continuity and stability over all other considerations, considerably slowing the reform effort in the process (Zerhouni 2004).[41] In fact, the pace of reform is so slow that it has caused consternation even within royal circles.[42] By way of illustration, the parliament

---

[38] "Next Parliament Will Be Worst in Egypt's History: ESDP Secretary General," Mahmoud Mostafa, *Daily News Egypt*, 21 September 2015.

[39] "Al-Sissi: The Egyptian Constitution Was Written with Good Intentions, but States Are Not Built on Good Intentions" ("السيسي: الدستور المصري كتب بنوايا حسنة والدول لا تبنى بالنوايا الحسنة")، Mohamed al-Galy, *Youm7*, 13 September 2015.

[40] "Sisi Tells Egyptians: Don't Listen to Anyone but Me," *Aljazeera*, 24 February 2016. For more detail on President Sisi's comments, see: "Full Text of President Sisi's Speech on 'Egypt's 2030 Strategy'" ("النص الكامل لكلمة للرئيس السيسي بـ «استراتيجية مصر 2030»")، Hany Mohamed, *'Akhbar El-Yom*, 24 February 2016.

[41] The same attitude and strategy has been in place for many decades.

[42] On 9 October 2015, in a speech to the Moroccan parliament, the king repeatedly questioned the pace of legislation reform, stating: "The question is: Why are the laws relating to a number of institutions still waiting to be updated, four years after the adoption of the Constitution? Why

needed years to change a single provision in the criminal code that allowed for rapists to marry their victims.[43] Even when reform does take place, it has not always led in the direction that many Moroccans and analysts have appreciated. For example, in April 2015, a draft criminal law was published and was immediately criticized, first for being very similar to the previous law (despite the 2011 constitution), and second because of its heavily conservative and paternalistic spirit. The draft includes a series of worrying provisions, including the criminalization of "engaging in activities that weaken citizens' allegiance to the state," "insulting or mocking religion, God or the prophets" and "Muslims breaking the fast in public." Meanwhile the new law de-penalizes "crimes of passion," in that it states that an individual who murders his spouse can claim attenuating circumstances in the event he has caught her in an act of adultery.[44]

In Tunisia, the country's first peaceful transfer of power has taken place, and a reform effort is ongoing. However, significant economic and security problems will continue to serve as serious impediments to stability over the long term. Perhaps most seriously, there is significant evidence that the benefits of the revolution have not been equally shared; the south of the country, which was the source of the initial uprisings that launched the revolution, remains deeply impoverished and considers itself to be completely marginalized from the far wealthier, coastal areas.[45] The constitution's mechanisms are struggling

are we waiting for the new institutions stipulated in the Constitution to be set up?"; "King Mohammed's Speech before Moroccan Parliament," *Morocco World News*, 9 October 2015.

[43] "The Moroccan Parliament Toughens Punishment for Rape After Repeated Tragedies" ("برلمان المغرب يشدد عقوبة الاغتصاب بعد تكرار المآسي"), Khadija Fathi, *Al-Arabiya*, 9 January 2014.

[44] See "Morocco: Facebook Campaign Against the Draft Criminal Law because of 'Honour Crimes' and 'Weakening Citizens' Loyalty to the State'" ("المغرب: حملة «فيسبوكية» على مسودة القانون" «الجنائي» بسبب «جرائم الشرف» و«زعزعة ولاء المواطنين للدولة"), Taher al-Tawil, *Al-Quds al-Arabi*, 7 April 2015; and "Relations sexuelles hors mariage, rupture du jeûne en public … Mustapha Ramid, ministre de la Justice et des libertés individuelles, ne recule pas," *HuffPost Maroc*, 20 April 2015.

[45] The November 2014 presidential election results revealed that Tunisia is deeply polarized, with the north favoring an octogenarian establishment man who campaigned on the basis of a promised return to stability, while the south mainly supported the second post-revolution interim president who was secular but supported by the country's main Islamist party. For more information on how deep the divisions run, see "Présidentielle: Tableau interactif des votes par circonscription, la Tunisie coupée en deux, Siliana et Sidi Bouzid se démarquent," *HuffPost Tunisie*, 26 November 2014. Geographic divisions are manifesting themselves in increasingly worrying ways; see for example, "Tunisian Brothers Text Home: We Are in Libya and Everything's Fine," Eileen Byrne, *The Guardian*, 15 July 2015 (describing an incident in which thirty-three young Tunisians from a poor desert town crossed into war-torn Libya in an attempt to escape their own poverty; the article quotes a Tunisian from the same town as saying "[s]ome are just fed up with the poverty and unemployment here; the arrogance of the north [of Tunisia] towards the south").

to relieve that pressure in the short term, particularly as the political divide between Islamists and non-Islamists continues to distract so much attention. Finally, Algeria's pace of reform was so slow that it took five years to introduce only modest changes to the draft.

Each of the countries that are in discussion here are subject to the whims of deeply entrenched interests (economic, institutional and religious) that impact their respective constitution's chances of succeeding in achieving its aims. The 2011 uprisings represented a revolutionary moment for Arab countries, but the response from most elite circles in the region was merely to tweak with existing constitutional frameworks, without changing any of the fundamentals. There was hope back in 2011 that the uprisings would create a sense of urgency across the region, but that has clearly not happened. The question now is whether rapidly changing demographic and economic circumstances will throttle elites and the constitutional institutions that they have created into action or whether they have already sown the seeds of their own failure. Time will tell.

* * *

REFERENCES

Al-Ali, Zaid. 2014. *The Struggle for Iraq's Future: How Sectarianism, Incompetence and Corruption Have Undermined Corruption.* Yale University Press.

2015. "Egypt's Third Constitution in Three Years – A Critical Analysis." In *Egypt's Revolutions: Politics, Religion and Social Movements,* edited by Bernard Rougier and Stephane Lacroix. Palgrave Macmillan.

Alberdi, Juan Bautista. 2015. *Obras de Juan Bautista Alberdi.* IberiaLiteratura.

Brown, Nathan. 2002. *Constitutions in a Nonconstitutional World: Arab Basic Laws and the Prospects for Accountable Government.* SUNY Press.

Choudhry, Sujit and Richard Stacey. 2014. *Semi-Presidentialism as Power Sharing: Constitutional Reform after the Arab Spring.* Center for Constitutional Transitions at NYU Law and International IDEA.

Comella, Victor Ferreres. 2013. *The Constitution of Spain: A Contextual Analysis.* Hart Publishing.

Farouk, Abdel Khalek. 2008. *The Roots of Administrative Corruption in Egypt* ("جذور الفساد الاداري في مصر"). Dar al-Shourouk.

Frank, Andre Gunder. 1967. *Capitalism and Underdevelopment in Latin America: Historical Studies of Chile and Brazil.* Monthly Review Press.

Gargarella, Roberto. 2013. *Latin American Constitutionalism, 1810–2010: The Engine Room of the Constitution.* Oxford University Press.

Human Rights Watch. 2015. "Egypt: Year of Abuses under al-Sisi."

Khadduri, Majid. 1951. *Independent Iraq*. Oxford University Press, London.

Lackner, Helen. 2016. *The Yemeni Peaceful Transition from Saleh's Autocratic Rule: Could It Have Succeeded?* International IDEA.

Leibenberg, Sandra. 2010. *Socio-Economic Rights: Adjudication under a Transformative Constitution*. Juta Academic.

Madani, Mohamed, Driss Maghraoui and Saloua Zerhouni. 2012. *The 2011 Moroccan Constitution: A Critical Analysis*. International IDEA.

Moustafa, Tamir. 2007. *The Struggle for Constitutional Power: Law, Politics, and Economic Development in Egypt*. Cambridge University Press.

Salloukh, Bassel F., Rabie Barakat, Jinan S. al-Habbal, Lara W. Khattab and Shoghig Mikaelian. 2015. *The Politics of Sectarianism in Postwar Lebanon*. Pluto Press.

Shalakany, Amr. 2012. *The Rise and Fall of Egypt's Legal Elite: 1805–2005* ("ازدهار وانهيار النخبة القانونية المصرية"). Dar Al-Shorouk.

Simon, Reeva Spector. 2012. *Iraq between the Two World Wars: The Militarist Origins of Tyranny*. Columbia University Press.

Stilt, Kirsten. 2014. "The Egyptian Constitution of 1971." In *Constitutions in Authoritarian Regimes*, edited by Tom Ginsburg and Alberto Simpser. Cambridge University Press.

Waterbury, John. 2014. *The Egypt of Nasser and Sadat: The Political Economy of Two Regimes*. Princeton University Press. Reprint edition.

Yousfi, Hèla. 2014. *L'UGTT Une Passion Tunisienne: Enquete sur les syndicalistes en Revolution 2011–2014*. Edition Med aLi.

Zerhouni, Saloua. 2004. "Morocco: Reconciling Continuity and Change." In *Arab Elites: Negotiating the Politics of Change*, edited by Volker Perthes. Lynne Rienner Publishers.

14

Stability in flexibility
A British lens on constitutional success

Erin F. Delaney

INTRODUCTION

On many of the external metrics outlined in the Introduction to this volume, the United Kingdom ranks among the most successful nation states: It is a functioning democracy with robust rights protection;[1] its public sector is one of the least corrupt;[2] and its citizens benefit from an array of public goods, including health care,[3] education,[4] and a variety of other social welfare programs.[5] From an internal perspective, the flexible British constitution appears well matched to the wants of its citizenry – as J.A.G. Griffith wrote more than thirty-five years ago, "the constitution is no more and no less than what happens. Everything that happens is constitutional. And if nothing

---

[1] Eisgruber (2001: 22) describes Britain as "one of the world's most successful democracies".

[2] In 2014, the United Kingdom received a score of 78 out of 100 in the corruption perceptions index, making it the fourteenth least corrupt country out of 175 other countries and territories. The United States was ranked seventeenth, with a score of 74, and Denmark ranked first with a score of 91. www.transparency.org/cpi2014.results.

[3] *See* Organization for Economic Co-operation and Development, *OECD Health Statistics,* www.oecd.org/unitedkingdom/Country-Note-UNITED%20KINGDOM-OECD-Health-Statistics-2015.pdf. In addition, life expectancy is high and infant mortality low. *ProQuest Statistical Abstract of the United States 2015* 875 (2014).

[4] *See* Organization for Economic Co-operation and Development, *OECD Data: Education, available at* https://data.oedc.org/eduresource/public-spending-on-education.htm#indicator-chart. For UK student mean scores in reading, science, and mathematics proficiency, see *ProQuest Statistical Abstract of the United States 2015* 892 (2014).

[5] The United Kingdom provides unemployment, family, and social benefits. *See* Organization for Economic Co-operation and Development, *OECD Data: Public Unemployment Spending, available at* https://data.oecd.org/socialexp/public-unemployment-spending.htm#indicator-chart; Organization for Economic Co-operation and Development, *OECD Data: Family Benefits Public Spending, available at* https://data.oecd.org/socialexp/family-benefits-public-spending.htm#indicator-chart; *see* Organization for Economic Co-operation and Development, *OECD Data: Social Benefits to Households, available at* https://data.oecd.org/socialexp/social-benefits-to-households.htm#indicator-chart.

happened that would be constitutional also" (Griffith 1979: 19). In short, there is no obvious gap between the aspirational and the actual.

This exceptional performance suggests we should look to the United Kingdom as a model for constitutional design. But, of course, the British constitution sits uneasily in contemporary constitutional studies. As an uncodified set of written laws and political practices with ancient roots (e.g., Magna Carta 2015) and modern fruit (e.g., The Fixed-Term Parliaments Act 2011), the constitution is difficult to pin down with precision and certainty.[6] Even senior judges and politicians struggle: Lord Scarman described the constitution as "hidden, and difficult to find" (1993: 319), and Lord Callaghan suggested it has a certain "back of an envelope" quality to it (Hennessy 1995: 6). Academics agree that the specific substantive elements that make up the constitution are subject to debate (Hennessy 2007: 346) as well as that different understandings of the constitution – in Scotland and England, in particular – have coexisted for centuries (Feldman 2005: 347).

Yet, even if it were possible to extrapolate a modern model from this historically contingent and idiosyncratic system, an antecedent question niggles: How confident should we be in this positive assessment of the United Kingdom's constitutional success? A closer look at life in the British state uncovers roiling constitutional politics. Complaints abound of constitutional uncertainty, constitutional malaise, constitutional anomie – even constitutional crisis (Bogdanor 2015; Webber 2014). This discourse reveals a higher level of dissatisfaction than might be expected in a country that otherwise seems a paragon of constitutional success.[7] This paradox – the coexistence of

---

[6]   Only two of the world's democracies share a similar constitutional approach – Israel and New Zealand. House of Commons Political and Constitutional Reform Committee, *A New Magna Carta?* Second Report of Session 2014–2015 (10 July 2014). *See also* Hockman and Bogdanor (2010: 74).

[7]   The 2014 Scottish referendum both reflected and heightened the constitutional tension. In 2011, the Scottish National Party (SNP) won an absolute majority in the Scottish parliamentary elections, with an election manifesto commitment to an independence referendum. SCOTTISH NAT'L PARTY, MANIFESTO 2011, at 28 (2011), *available at* http://votesnp.com/cam paigns/SNP_Manifesto_2011_lowRes.pdf. After eight months of "intense negotiations" between First Minister of Scotland Alex Salmond and UK prime minister David Cameron, the Edinburgh Agreement authorizing the referendum was signed on October 15, 2012. *See* Severin Carrell and Nicholas Watt, "Alex Salmond Hails Historic Day for Scotland after Referendum Deal", *GUARDIAN* (15 October 2012, 3:03 PM), www.guardian.co.uk/politics/2012/ oct/14/alex-salmond-scotland-referendum-deal. Just under two years later, on September 18 2014, the Scottish people rejected independence, by a margin of 55% to 45%, with turnout of 85%. The result did little to quiet the constitutional waters, however. Roughly ten days before the vote, a "shock" poll suggesting the Scottish would vote *for* independence galvanized party leaders in the United Kingdom to action with promises for further devolution. *See* Clifford and Morphet (2015: 57). The text of "the vow" is *available at* www.dailyrecord.co.uk/news/politics/

success and crisis – suggests that Ginsburg and Huq's categories have failed to capture some additional dimension of success.

The United Kingdom is experiencing a period of dramatic constitutional change (Bogdanor 2009; King 2001). Unprecedented and fast-moving constitutional developments challenge conventional constitutional wisdom at every turn: Does the United Kingdom need a bill of rights? Is a system of parliamentary sovereignty compatible with a strong judiciary? How should judges be appointed? Can the United Kingdom exist as a federal state? What should a parliamentary upper chamber look like, and what is its role? Much vigorous debate surrounds the substance of these reforms. New parliamentary committees in the House of Lords and the House of Commons, tasked with constitutional reform, have held inquiries on topics ranging from the power of the prime minister to waging war.[8] But the larger source of distress may well be the

david-cameron-ed-miliband-nick-4265992. In the wake of the referendum, therefore, constitutional flux has only increased as politicians struggle to structure a new concept of union.

[8] Since its creation in 2001, the House of Lords Select Committee on the Constitution has conducted the following inquiries: *Reviewing the Constitution: Terms of Reference and Method of Working* (2001); *Changing the Constitution: The Process of Constitutional Change* (2001); *Devolution: Inter-Institutional Relations in the United Kingdom* (2002); *The Regulatory State: Ensuring Its Accountability* (2004); *Parliament and the Legislative Process* (2004); *Waging War: Parliament's Role and Responsibility* (2006); *Waging War: Parliament's Role and Responsibility: Follow Up* (2007); *Relations between the Executive, the Judiciary and Parliament* (2007); *Relations between the Executive, the Judiciary and Parliament: Follow Up* (2008); *The Role of the Attorney General* (2008); *The Constitutional Implications of the Collection and Use of Surveillance and Other Personal Data* (2009); *Fast-Track Legislation: Constitutional Implications and Safeguards* (2009); *The Role of Referendums in the UK's Constitutional Experience* (2010); *The Contemporary Workings of the Cabinet Office and the Centre of Government* (2010); *Fixed-Term Parliaments* (2010); *The Process of Constitutional Change* (2011); *Draft Cabinet Manual* (2011); *Accountability of Civil Servants* (2012); *Judicial Appointments Process* (2012); *Pre-Emption of Parliament* (2013); *The Constitutional Arrangements for the Use of Armed Force* (2013); *Office of the Lord Chancellor* (2014); *Scottish Independence: Constitutional Implications for the Rest of the UK* (2014); *The Constitutional Implications of Coalition Government* (2014); *Inter-Governmental Relations in the UK* (2015). For pre-2010 inquiries, see Caird, Hazell, and Oliver (2014) Appendix. For post-2010 inquiries, see www.parliament.uk/business/committees/committees-a-z/lords-select/constitution-committee/inquiries/. The House of Commons Political and Constitutional Reform Committee was established in 2010 and has addressed: *Government Proposals for Voting and Parliamentary Reform: Fixed-Term Parliaments Bill and Parliamentary Voting System and Constituencies Bill* (2010); *Constitutional Implications of the Cabinet Manual* (2011); *Individual Electoral Registration and Electoral Administration* (2011); *Lessons from the Process of Government Formation after the 2010 General Election* (2011); *Parliament's Role in Conflict Decisions* (2011); *UK Bill of Rights Commission* (2011); *Rules of Royal Succession* (2011); *Introducing a Statutory Register of Lobbyists* (2012); *Recall of MPs* (2012); *Do We Need a Constitutional Convention for the UK?* (2013); *Ensuring Standards in the Quality of Legislation* (2013); *House of Lords Reform: What's Next?* (2013); *The Prospects for Codifying the Relationship between Central and Local Government* (2013); *Revisiting Rebuilding the*

process of change itself. Ad hoc constitutional change without consideration of downstream or interactive effects has led to uncertainty, confusion, and crisis.

The effective management of constitutional change impacts both the external and internal criteria of constitutional success. The ability to modify fundamental arrangements when they are no longer working avoids the danger of whole-scale constitutional replacement and concomitant political instability (Dixon 2011a: 97; Fusaro and Oliver 2011: 424).[9] And change may allow for governance or institutional structures better tailored to new challenges of dispute resolution, assuming that the nature of societal tensions will shift over time. Furthermore, an ability to alter principles and goals may better align the constitution with the capacities of its leaders and the desires of its people – improving its implementation on internal metrics. This need for change does not, in itself, provide an answer to the balance between stability and flexibility in constitutional arrangements. But the British paradox suggests some contextualized assessment of that balance is a necessary element for establishing constitutional success from a functional perspective.

How effectively is Britain managing its constitutional change? The political and academic commentary suggests that Britain is no longer able to manage change in a way that generates broad public acceptance. Why? And what light does this shed on the question of balance between flexibility and stability in constitutional design? This chapter assesses the changing British constitution in context and function and, in so doing, aims to complicate the assessment of constitutional success and to engage broader debates over calibrating constitutional flexibility.

After briefly reviewing the literature on flexibility and constitutional success – a literature that accepts the need for flexibility but identifies critical dangers, including the threat of political self-dealing – the chapter turns to

---

House: *The Impact of the Wright Reforms* (2013); *The Government's Lobbying Bill* (2013); *The Impact and Effectiveness of Ministerial Reshuffles* (2013); *Fixed-Term Parliaments: The Final Year of a Parliament* (2014); *Parliament's Role in Conflict Decisions: An Update* (2014); *Role and Powers of the Prime Minister* (2014); *The Constitutional Role of the Judiciary if There Were a Codified Constitution* (2014); *The Government's Lobbying Bill: Follow-Up* (2014); *The Impact of Queen's and Prince's Consent on the Legislative Process* (2014); *Voter Engagement in the UK* (2014); *What Next on the Redrawing of Parliamentary Constituency Boundaries?* (2015); *The Future of Devolution after the Referendum* (2015); *Committee Consultation on a New Magna Carta* (2015); *Constitutional Implications of Draft Scotland Clauses* (2015); *Government Formation Post-Election* (2015); *Individual Electoral Registration* (2015); *Voter Engagement in the UK: Follow Up* (2015); *Revisiting the Cabinet Manual* (2015). See www.parliament.uk /business/committees/committees-a-z/commons-select/political-and-constitutional-reform-co mmittee/inquiries/.

9   As Edmund Burke said, "a state without the means of some change is without the means of its own conservation." As cited in Murphy (1995: 168).

the United Kingdom. Although its flexibility has long been a point of pride, the British constitution is now being criticized as *too* flexible, a worry that is contributing to discussions of constitutional codification and entrenchment.[10] Some of the dissatisfaction appears to stem from a growing fear of political self-dealing and expedient behavior – a threat that is exacerbated by the increasing amount of constitutional change itself. The heart of the chapter discusses the breakdown in the institutional and social norms that once served to mitigate the dangers of flexibility. In the absence of social stabilization, how can flexibility be contained without constitutional entrenchment? Is it possible to have an entrenched amendment rule without entrenched substantive content? The chapter concludes with a discussion of the challenges in seeking stability in flexibility.

FLEXIBILITY AND CONSTITUTIONAL SUCCESS

A rich literature in constitutional design debates the trade-off between stability and flexibility: A written constitution must provide the stability, predictability, and limitations to permit functional governance, but it cannot be so rigid that it will crack in the winds of social change. Flexibility, therefore, is a necessary component of constitutional success – a "safety valve" allowing for constitutional continuation (Contiades and Fotiadou 2013: 422). But flexibility must operate in conjunction with constitutional provisions that constrain, such as super-majoritarian entrenchment or textual specificity. These strategies for constructing a well-calibrated regime are, in part, based on the dangers that flexibility is thought to pose.

Flexibility can lead to disruption and dissension. For example, if amendment procedures are too easy, groups "disappointed with the outcome of the ordinary political process will have the incentive to campaign for institutional reform" (Eisgruber 2001: 13), and political instability may result from this over-constitutionalization of ordinary politics.[11] Constitutional rigidity, in contrast, creates a content-based distinction between constitutional politics and regular

---

[10] As federal structures are thought by most to require constitutionalization through a written document (e.g. Dicey 1908: 141), these debates for a written constitution are also being driven by the push for increased devolution. For example, in the aftermath of the Scottish referendum, Nick Clegg, leader of the Liberal Democrats, called for a constitutional convention to create a written constitution to codify the division of powers between and among the various levels of government within the United Kingdom. *See* Nick Clegg, *This Opportunity Cannot be Hijacked* (21 September 2014), www.libdems.org.uk/nick_clegg_this_opportunity_cannot_be_hijacked.

[11] Of course, there are many more nuances to these institutional design questions. For example, there are also questions of scope that complicate the flexibility/rigidity balance (Eisgruber 2001).

politics (Rasch and Congelton 2006: 539) and prevents disruptive cycling and short-term fluctuations in how a society's politics are constructed.[12] Melkinsburg see another set of dangers in unalloyed flexibility: the failure to properly reflect the interests of society. An overly flexible system may fail to provide "enduring rules that bind the polity together," and thus flexibility must be paired with specificity and inclusion for effective constitutionalism (Elkins, Ginsburg, and Melton 2009: 82).

Of course, these negative results are not caused by flexibility itself but by how flexibility is used: Flexibility can serve as an invitation to political actors for self-dealing or to circumvent consensus-based politics.[13] Formal amendment rules are designed to get to the heart of this danger. First, they can raise the stakes of a political confrontation and serve an information-forcing function (Dixon 2011b: 649), allowing participants and observers to root out efforts at constitutionalization that are driven by narrow political self-interest. (To the extent informal change occurs outside of these rules, the formal amendment rules also serve as a useful backdrop for assessing the normative and positive justifiability of extra-constitutional change.) Second, the connection between formal amendment rules and constitutional entrenchment usually results in super-majoritarian mechanisms of change (Fusaro and Oliver 2011: 426), promoting consensus-based decision-making and decreasing the possibility for political self-dealing (cf. Sager 1990). And Melkinsburg's concern about reflecting the interests of society taps into this quest for consensus-based amendment, linking consensus and constitutional stability (Contiades and Fotiadou 2013: 435).

But solving for self-dealing, or political expediency, in the absence of formal entrenchment is difficult. Without established rules for constitutional amendment, "an unscrupulous executive [can] make changes to the constitution for reasons of party self-interest and political advantage over its opponents" (Blackburn 2013: 374). And although Versteeg and Zackin suggest that specificity may serve to counter flexibility's dangers, they see a fine line "between people adjusting their government's marching orders and officeholders enshrining their own interests" (2014: 1704). Systems without super-majoritarian entrenchment are forced to rely on social norms, "soft" veto players, procedural requirements, or party-system particularities to constrain

---

[12] On the other hand, the more groups that can be engaged in constitutional politics through flexible amendment procedures, the broader the society's stake will be in the survival of the constitution itself (Elkins, Ginsburg, and Melton 2009: 89).

[13] Cf. Issacharoff who notes that constitutionalism is not only marked by the setting of the rules but by an added assurance that these rules "will not be 'gamed' by momentary majorities attempting to lock themselves in power" (2003: 1997).

self-dealing and foster mechanisms of broader consensus and, thus, constitutional stability.

THE "TOO-FLEXIBLE" BRITISH CONSTITUTION?

The United Kingdom is often used as an example of "complete" flexibility (Elkins, Ginsburg, and Melton 2009: 82) and as such is rarely included in analyses of constitutional amendability (see, e.g., Levinson 1995: 9). Operating under the doctrine of parliamentary sovereignty, the Parliament at Westminster has the "right to make or unmake any law whatever; and ... no person or body is recognized ... as having a right to override or set aside [its] legislation" (Dicey 1908: 38). Furthermore, there is no formal mechanism distinguishing statutes of constitutional importance: "[F]undamental laws are ... changed by the same body and in the same manner as other laws, namely, by Parliament acting in its ordinary legislative character" (84). It is the ability to elect a new parliament, unconstrained by its former instantiation, that serves as the "regulating wheel" of the constitution (Bagehot 1872: 204–205). Of course, as the House of Commons Political and Constitution Reform Committee noted, parliamentary sovereignty "taken literally[,] would infer the UK was an oligarchic state run by politicians at Westminster, rather than the political democracy we aspire to be today."[14] And the formal doctrinal construct does obscure a more complex functional governance system,[15] as British constitutional scholars and political scientists explain.[16]

If constitutionalism means anything, it means limited government. But rather than a written constitution of skepticism and entrenched limitations (see Redish and Heins 2015), the British constitution "presumes more boldly than any other the good sense and the good faith of those who work it"

---

[14] House of Commons Political and Constitutional Reform Committee, *A New Magna Carta?* Second Report of Session 2014–2015, at 381 ¶ 80.

[15] The focus on Parliament, for example, ignores that much informal change happens outside the statutory arena. *See* House of Lords Select Committee on the Constitution, *Changing the Constitution: The Process of Constitutional Change* (2002) ("Constitutional change is not simply a matter of legislation ... the Government may generate policy on constitutional issues which does not require primary legislation in order to carry it into effect."). In fact, "there is no general presumption in favour of statutory regulation" (McHarg 2008: 863). Although there may be reasons of transparency to prefer parliamentary action, either legislative- or executive-led change is "essentially a form of self-regulation" and thus it "does not make much difference in principle whether constitutional rules are statutory or non-statutory" (866).

[16] Lijphart has classified the United Kingdom as one of the most flexible of systems (1999: 220), but Robert Hazell contends that "it is a weakness of Lijphart's classification that it focuses narrowly on the formal powers granted to institutions, and can miss the significance of culture and behavior" (2008: 229).

(Gladstone 1879: 245; see also Bendor and Segal 2002: 686, discussing trust as animating feature). At the heart of British constitutionalism is the belief that "over time . . . 'a people, in acting autonomously, will learn how to act rightly'" (Goldsworthy 2010: 10).[17] This trust is not naiveté but is borne of a belief in self-restraint "imbedded through tradition" (Goldsworthy 2010: 10) and what Contiades and Fotiadou describe as "culture and practice-driven rigidity" (2013: 442, 459). Constitutional change enacted by Parliament may be majoritarian, but it should not be partisan (Fusaro and Oliver 2011: 421). Of course, whether the "values and principles which are deeply embedded in society" (410) have limited British constitutional change is an empirical question – and one that has not yet been satisfactorily answered.[18] But the quantum of constitutional change during the second half of the twentieth century was very low indeed.[19]

At one level, critiquing the constitution has elements of a national pastime; substantive reform always engenders complaint, and reports of the constitution's demise are plentiful.[20] But the constitution's flexibility was historically applauded as a mark of its efficiency and proof of its "capability to meet the challenges of rapidly changing circumstances" (Contiades and Fotiadou 2013: 463). In contrast, today critics charge that the constitution is "overly flexible" (Blackburn 2013: 359).[21] Many are discussing the heretofore largely unthinkable notion of codifying and possibly entrenching the constitution.[22] And the

---

[17] Goldsworthy's internal citation is to Robert Dahl, *Democracy and Its Critics* (New Haven: Yale University Press, 1989) at 192.

[18] Party politics may have as much to do with the lack of constitutional change as underlying values. For example, "for most of the past hundred years Labour barely concerned itself with the constitution, in the belief that it was largely a super-structural irrelevancy to securing social justice and the implementation of the party's economic and nationalization programme." House of Commons Political and Constitutional Reform Committee, *A New Magna Carta?* Second Report of Session 2014–2015. And as Professor Dawn Oliver noted, "until about 1979, very little really changed, except in relation to local government, so I think that, politically, the system was a bit inflexible. No one was interested enough in constitutional change to effect it." *Oral Evidence*, House of Commons Political and Constitutional Reform Committee, 7 July 2011, at Q86.

[19] The Constitutional Society, *Written Evidence*, House of Commons Political and Constitutional Reform Committee, 19 November 2012, at ¶ 5.

[20] For example, see Patrick Dunleavy and Stuart Weir, "It's All Over for the Old Constitution," *The Independent*, 30 May 1995.

[21] *See also* House of Commons Political and Constitutional Reform Committee, *A New Magna Carta?* Second Report of Session 2014–2015, at 390 ¶ 112 ("Many, if not most, today believe that in the new era of rolling constitutional change since 1997, the UK constitution has become overly flexible, with its being too easy for alternating parties in government to make fundamental changes without going through a proper process of consultation and approval.").

[22] Codification has been a topic of discussion for about forty years but has not been able to gain traction among the public. Even at the party level, focus was often from backbenchers, and only the Liberal Democrats embraced codification as official party policy. *See* House of Commons

current constitutional debates seem to be driven, in part,[23] by a heightened sense that the traditional limits on expediency are no longer functioning as they ought to.[24] The litany of complaints all point in this direction: from the weakening of a political consensus on constitutional change itself to the increased ability for governments in power to push through measures of constitutional import without processes of consultation and scrutiny (Baker 2009).[25]

In the past ten years, there have been several examples of poor processes leading to the perception of excessive partisanship (at best) or self-dealing (at worst).[26] The extensive reforms ushered in by the Blair Government began the trend. As Aileen McHarg has argued, "different reforms were pursued for different reasons, with electoral calculations playing a significant role both in the adoption of the initial raft of measures which followed the 1997 election and in the subsequent loss of enthusiasm for further reform in areas such as the voting system for the Westminster Parliament" (2008: 875). Perhaps the most

Political and Constitutional Reform Committee, *A New Magna Carta?* Second Report of Session 2014–2015, at 364–365. *See Codifying – or not Codifying – the UK's Constitution: A Literature Review*, Centre for Political & Constitutional Studies, King's College London, Series Paper 1 (2011) at 12–14 (past proposals and texts).

[23] There are also criticisms that the recent changes are "lacking internal coherence" (Bogdanor 2009: 271) and fail to achieve useful settlement, *see* Erin F. Delaney, "Searching for Constitutional Meaning in Institutional Design: The Debate over Judicial Appointments in the United Kingdom," 14 *International Journal of Constitutional Law*, Forthcoming 2016.

[24] A favorite quotation by those skeptical of the flexible constitution is Alexis de Tocqueville's pithy summary: "In England the constitution can change constantly, or rather it does not exist at all" (Tocqueville 2000: 95). And although scholars and lawyers often refer to the need to entrench rights to protect minorities, the counter-majoritarian function of a written constitution does not seem to garner much support from the people. Polling shows "a low public salience of constitutional issues." House of Commons Political and Constitutional Reform Committee, *A New Magna Carta?* Second Report of Session 2014–2015, at 365 ¶ 20, 406 ¶ 176. *See also* Hansard Society, *Audit of Political Engagement* (2008).

[25] British history is, of course, threaded through with moments of *political* crisis and dissension – but these only rarely have resulted in *constitutional* crisis. *See* House of Commons Political and Constitutional Reform Committee, *A New Magna Carta?* Second Report of Session 2014–2015. In a recent article, Martin Loughlin suggests "the British no longer grasp the nature and functions of their inherited political institutions," a fact which undermines their efforts to reform and modernize. Referencing Tacitus, Loughlin notes that "the secret of establishing a new state is to maintain the forms of the old." The adage loses its force where there is little understanding of the conditions and limits of the state and even less tacit observance (2015: 29–30).

[26] Some of these examples have engendered hyperbolic analogies to Hitler's rise to power and the slide into totalitarianism in Germany, a devastating example of the failure of flexible constitutionalism. *See* Baker (2009: 105) (comparing the Legislative and Regulatory Reform Bill of 2006 to the Enabling Law of 1933). The dramatic rhetorical approach is a mainstay of British commentary – in 1976, Lord Chancellor Lord Halisham, arguing for a written constitution, entitled his Richard Dimbleby Lecture "Elective Dictatorship."

egregious example of political expediency and a lack of forethought was Blair's surprise announcement, in a press release concerning a cabinet reshuffle, of his intention to abolish the ancient office of Lord Chancellor and to create a Supreme Court of the United Kingdom (Baker 2009; Banner and Deane 2003; Le Seuer 2009). The eventual Constitutional Reform Bill was proposed without any legislative process – no Green or White Papers, no draft Bill (Oliver 2011: 340). As the House of Commons Political and Constitutional Reform Committee subsequently concluded, "the failures in consultation and process created a major public controversy and disquiet at the high-handed methods of the executive."[27]

More recently, the Conservative-Liberal Democratic Coalition Government has also engaged in constitutional reform, "much of it arguably intended mainly to cement the political bargain between the coalition partners."[28] For example, the 2011 Fixed-Term Parliaments Bill proposed setting parliamentary elections at regular five year intervals, thus "chang[ing] the constitutional rules of the political game" (Rawlings 2015: 196). This major constitutional initiative was presented with no prior consultation and an extremely truncated timeline for parliamentary debate, garnering criticism from both the House of Commons Political and Constitutional Reform Committee and from the House of Lords Select Committee on the Constitution.[29] The cynical view highlighted the "political motivation behind the Bill," which, as "everyone realized, was to cement the life of the government, both as a coalition between two parties who were not natural bed-fellows, and in order to allow the chancellor of the exchequer as long as possible to preside over a recovery of the dire state of the national economy before having to face the electorate again" (Blackburn 2013: 375). The process was described as a "telling cocktail of formal statute and opaque and fraught workings of a famously termed 'political constitution'" (Rawlings 2015: 197).

In their extensive inquiry on constitutional reform, *Codifying – or not Codifying – the UK's Constitution*, the House of Commons Political and Constitutional Reform Committee canvassed the public, politicians, lawyers,

---

[27] House of Commons Political and Constitutional Reform Committee, *A New Magna Carta?* Second Report of Session 2014–2015, at 366–367 ¶ 24.

[28] The Constitution Society, *Written Evidence*, House of Commons Political and Constitutional Reform Committee, 19 November 2012, at ¶ 5.

[29] "It is acutely disappointing to us that we have needed to criticize the Government for the process it has chosen to adopt in the passage of its first two constitutional Bills." House of Commons Political and Constitutional Reform Committee, *Fixed-Term Parliaments Bill*, 2010–2012, HC 436. "We take the view that the origins and content of this Bill owe more to short-term considerations than to a mature assessment of enduring constitutional principles or sustained public demand." House of Lords Select Committee on the Constitution, *Fixed-Term Parliaments Bill*, 2010–2012, HL 69, at 43.

and scholars on questions of flexibility and rigidity in constitutional design. The arguments against codification often relied on the historical constitution, those "very considerable pressures on ministers making the implementation of controversial measures or policies very difficult."[30] But those advocating for a codified constitution raised the issue of political expediency – claiming it had "become too easy for governments to implement political and constitutional reforms to suit their own political convenience."[31] Has the flexible constitution really become *too* flexible?

THE THREAT TO SUCCESS: INCREASING EXPEDIENCY

As outlined earlier, a danger of excessive flexibility lies in expanded opportunities for political self-dealing and the concomitant risk to the broader constitutional consensus. In the United Kingdom, the threat to constitutional stability is from expediency in two senses: first, in the perception of increasing *self-interested political manipulation* on the part of politicians, and second, in the mounting *haste* of ad hoc and frequent constitutional change. The net effect of the interaction is greater than either problem on its own, and is "destablising and erod[ing] ... public confidence in the political system."[32]

On one level, the parliamentary process of constitutional change clearly invites trouble. Any constitutional initiative "virtually always" comes from the government, meaning the prime minister and cabinet. And "the government controls the legislative timetable of the House of Commons, will have a special interest in changes to the rules by which it operates, and has a working majority in the House to support its proposals and block those which lack its endorsement."[33] Thus there exists an inherent threat of political expediency or "ad hoc, opportunistic changes" (Oliver 2011: 354). Electoral accountability provides some check, but it is an ex post corrective and, as such, a blunt tool for monitoring change. Nevertheless, constitutional change has been mediated by a variety of soft veto points that have served to delay and force information sharing in ways similar to those of formal amendment rules.

These informal aspects of political culture and the institutional constructs that worked to prevent expediency appear to be breaking down, partly as a result of constitutional change itself. (An irony is that many of the micro-constitutional

---

[30] House of Commons Political and Constitutional Reform Committee, *A New Magna Carta?* Second Report of Session 2014–2015, at 26 ¶ 11.

[31] Ibid., at 19.

[32] The Constitution Society, *Written Evidence*, House of Commons Political and Constitutional Reform Committee, 19 November 2012, at ¶ 6.

[33] House of Commons Political and Constitutional Reform Committee, *A New Magna Carta?* Second Report of Session 2014–2015, at 363 ¶ 9.

changes are normatively desirable in themselves, but the ad hoc and piecemeal nature of their passage and implementation has failed to account for possible unintended consequences to the broader constitutional balance.) As the "[b]asic ingredients of any constitutional stability recipe are the divergences and convergences between institutional and partisan actors" (Contiades and Fotiadou 2013: 426), constructing the relationship between partisanship and constitutional change will shed light onto questions of expediency.

This section is not intended to prove that politicians have acted in bad faith or to provide a comprehensive list of areas of constitutional change, but its goal is to highlight the increased opportunities for self-interested political manipulation. Beginning with weakened institutional constraints on partisanship, the section first looks at institutional change in the House of Lords, the Civil Service, and the electoral system. It then addresses the changing conventional constraints on the operation of politics. Finally, the section notes the increasing pace of constitutional change and demonstrates how the two senses of expediency interact to threaten constitutional stability in the United Kingdom.

Weakened institutional constraints

The House of Lords
In the current political landscape, the "Government" and "Parliament" are easily conflated – "parliament is widely seen as merely applying its rubber stamp to government bills" (Baker 2009: 100). And given the lack of judicial review of legislation, "there need to be effective *intra*-parliamentary legislative procedures in place to minimize the risk that 'unconstitutional', unwise or imprudent legislation will be passed" (Oliver 2013: 248). Is there any meaningful legislative procedure or power to constrain the executive? The House of Lords (the upper legislative house and a natural option for a limiting role) has few tools for constraint.[34] In the Parliament Acts of 1911 and 1949, the House of Lords lost its veto on most subjects, with the exception of laws seeking to prolong the life of a Parliament, and now has only a one-year delaying power. Even amendments serve only as recommendations to the Commons, and under the Salisbury Convention, the Lords "will not vote against legislative proposals derived from the government's manifesto" (Whitaker 2006: 538).[35]

---

[34] Flinders suggests the House of Lords is one of only three mechanisms "through which a degree of constitutional rigidity ... is generally imposed," in addition to "special procedures in the lower house ... and the use of referendums as a societal validation device" (2010: 218).

[35] Whitaker notes that this convention may be under pressure, as "the Liberal Democrats argued early in the current session that their peers may disregard it" (2006: 538).

This weakening of the Lords reflects the primacy of the House of Commons, a welcome reflection of democratic values, but as Lord Scarman has noted, "the democratization of a part has threatened the constitutional settlement as a whole; indeed the concentration of power in the Commons has capsized the old system of checks and balances."[36] Hard veto power largely rests in the willingness of backbenchers in the Commons to revolt.[37] The Lords are limited to mechanisms of delay and publicity, which can certainly serve to restrain (if not constrain) (Tsebelis and Money 1997). For example, the House of Lords has been able to pressure the government by proposing amendments, leading to extensive legislative ping-pong on certain bills.[38] And Oliver, for one, suggests that the Lords have done well in promoting non-partisan debate and reviewing bills on their merits (2013: 250). But their effectiveness is largely contingent on other political realities outside of their control – the size of the legislative majority in the Commons, party discipline, and governmental impatience (tied to timing and the extent of the legislative agenda) (Whitaker 2006).[39] At bottom, therefore, "the Commons are in control of the legislative programme of Parliament" (Scarman 1993: 320), and the Lords have only moral authority to limit it.[40]

The Civil Service

The Civil Service developed slowly over the nineteenth century (Parris 1969) and only recently was given a statutory basis in the Constitutional Reform and

[36] *Codifying – Or Not Codifying – The UK's Constitution: The Existing Constitution*, Centre for Political & Constitutional Studies, King's College London, Series Paper 2 (2012) at 19.

[37] Measures of party loyalty over time suggest that there is a "decreased cohesiveness of government backbenchers" (Blau 2008: 234). *See also* Crowley and Stuart (2012).

[38] Certainly, the Lords do fulfill scrutiny functions: "More amendments are usually secured to bills in the Lords than they are in the Commons" (Norton 2015: 188).

[39] The Fixed-Term Parliaments Act 2011 has also complicated issues of party discipline. Motions of no confidence, which by convention result in resignation or dissolution of Parliament, can be called by the government or by the opposition. In the latter instance, such motions are threats to the continued governance by the party in power. But when the government itself initiates a motion of no confidence, it might be seeking to ensure party discipline – threatening dissolution of Parliament to force through a legislative agenda item. *See* Huber (1996) (discussing the no-confidence vote called by the Major Government in 1993). The Fixed-Term Parliaments Act removed the power to "ensure the outcome of a particular vote by making it one of confidence; a prime minister could still announce a vote was one of confidence, but it would have no effect in terms of triggering an election if the vote was lost" (Norton 2015: 181).

[40] The issue of House of Lords reform has percolated since 1911 (Oliver 2013: 248) but with little finality: the twentieth century was described as a "century of non-reform" (Ballinger 2012). And any efforts to increase the Lords' role as a check on constitutional excess are complicated by the fact that "that House's own composition and powers are themselves a significant constitutional issue." The Constitution Society, *Written Evidence*, House of Commons Political and Constitutional Reform Committee, 19 November 2012, at ¶ 15.

Governance Act 2010. As an institution, it rests on four fundamental constitutional principles, all of which reflect a goal of independence: "non-partisanship, ministerial accountability to Parliament, admission by open competition and promotion by ability" (Bogdanor 2003: 271). Civil servants must carry out their duties "with integrity and honesty . . . and with objectivity and impartiality."[41] Given its principled role, a functioning and robust civil service could serve as a constitutional check. It "provides an assured conduit for good advice, while civil servants also have some capacity to stand up to ministers without paying a price" (Greer 2008: 123). Indeed, as the House of Lords Select Committee on the Constitution concluded in its inquiry on *The Accountability of Civil Servants* (2002), "it is essential that civil servants provide ministers with candid and fearless advice, including on the constitutionality of proposed actions,"[42] and as Lord Wilson argued, if a minister is behaving in an unconstitutional manner, "it is [the civil servant's] job to go to the head of the civil service, who would take it up with the Prime Minister if necessary."[43]

But the ability of the civil service to serve as a soft veto on governmental power is changing. Demands for efficiency and transparency – normatively desirable aims on their own – have warped the traditional model. The Freedom of Information Act "clearly changed much in the day-to-day working assumptions" of civil servants (Rawlings 2015: 207), and devolution within the civil service has complicated the chain of command. But the biggest threat is the desire for *effectiveness*. A civil service that aids the government in implementing its policy choices seems hardly objectionable, and in fact, in many other systems the civil service incorporates political appointments.[44] But these developments suggest a politicization that threatens the principle of impartiality. Not surprisingly, "[p]oliticians of both parties over decades have wanted the civil service to be their tool more than their guardian, and are reshaping it accordingly" (Greer 2008: 123). Most recently, Coalition Government ministers "sought a greater say in senior appointments in order to reflect their own accountability to parliament for a department's performance," but commentators saw in that claim a desire to undermine the Civil Service's political independence "in favour of (still greater) responsiveness to the government of the day" (Rawlings 2015: 210).

---

[41] Constitutional Reform and Governance Act 2010, s. 7.

[42] House of Lords Select Committee on the Constitution, *The Accountability of Civil Servants*, HL Paper 61 (2012), at 4.

[43] Ibid., at 18 (quoting Lord Wilson of Dinton 2004).

[44] "As from late 2014, the prime minister is allowed to interview and choose the top-most civil servants in Whitehall, those heading the main departments and directly accountable to a Cabinet Minister" (Rawlings 2015: 211).

While ministerial control serves as an argument for greater politicization of the civil service, there has been a simultaneous growth in executive agencies, special advisers and policy units – "rivals for ministerial ears" (Greer 2008: 128) – operating without any assumption of ministerial responsibility. These entities are thought "not to advise impartially, but to deliver at all costs" (Baker 2009: 94) and are not held to the principled expectations of the civil service, actually undermining ministerial control (Bogdanor 2003: 268). There is a danger that these effects will have spillover – weakened ministerial responsibility threatens the anonymity of the civil servant and his or her ability to be impartial (Parris 1969: 294).

The electoral system

The rhetoric of constitutional change is one of bipartisanism: "[I]t can hardly be justifiable to operate on the basis that each alternative majority may customize the constitution to implement its strategies of the moment" (Fusaro and Oliver 2011: 420). And the traditional British model supported this rhetoric by hard power politics: Given two principal parties of relatively equal strength, the chance that there will be a swing sufficient to oust the ruling party at the next election serves to moderate naked grabs for power. As Jennings once wrote, "Not only do opinions fluctuate, but they fluctuate sometimes violently, and the swing of the pendulum is a familiar feature of British politics . . . Majorities are unstable, and the Opposition of to-day is the Government of tomorrow" (1954: 32). The British system may be "the perfect embodiment of the principle of majority rule" (Lijphart 1984: 6), but it also prioritizes policy wins over constitutional change.

The electoral system has been criticized as "'the key to the lock' of the British constitution," largely in light of its effect on outsiders; the Conservative and Labour parties have been able to maintain "their duopoly of power" (Blau 2008: 233). But this balance of power is also what has forced some element of consensus or bipartisanship in relation to constitutional change. Demographic and political change is altering this landscape: Note the first peacetime coalition government since the 1930s, the rise of minor parties (both regional and single-issue), the expanded role of the Scottish National Party and the struggle for Labour voters in the South of England, and the increasing dissatisfaction with the first-past-the-post electoral system.[45] Electoral reform in response to these changes may lead to rationalization of the party system, improved democratic accountability, and better substantive

---

[45] Of course, there have always been smaller parties and groups vying for power. Yet there has been "a 'natural' tendency for Great Britain to follow the two-party system" (Jennings 1954: 56).

representation of the electorate's views. But it also upsets the political calculations that have made consensus and bipartisanship more than rhetoric in advocating constitutional change.[46]

A simple example is the decreasing import of election manifesto commitments. The practice of making political commitments clear in party manifestos had served as an advantage to future governments: The Salisbury Convention (mentioned earlier) insulates the government's legislative proposals from opposition in the House of Lords, and developing manifesto commitments also makes "it more difficult for opposition parties to oppose such changes on principle" (Oliver 2011: 338). The political benefits cut in the same direction as the limitation on possible expedient action: Even if certain topics fail to receive a full airing in the electoral fight, the ex ante statement of proposed changes, expressing the intentions of the party when in government, should nevertheless serve as a limiting factor on that government. But "one of the most significant constitutional changes under the 1997 Labour Government ... was the establishment of the independence of the Bank of England. There was no manifesto commitment; they just said on the first day, 'This is what we are going to do.' There was no indication in advance of that major constitutional change."[47]

In addition, the formal inter-party processes used in earlier times to flesh out competing views and areas of agreement are no longer favored. Royal Commissions and Speakers Conferences have addressed the civil service, local government, devolution, and election law. But (whether true or a self-fulfilling prophesy), these mechanisms are considered to be "less well adapted to modern conditions, particularly the more tribal nature of party politics today."[48] For constitutional reform, the social norm of bipartisanship is a substitute for some element of super-majoritarian consensus. But bipartisanship in a contentious multi-party world is a difficult value to foster.

Changing conventional constraints

In addition to statutory law and the use of the royal prerogative, the British constitution contains conventions – non-legal rules derived from precedent and a form of *opinio juris* (Jennings 1954). Constitutional conventions serve to

---

[46] As Rawlings points out, these changes "command[] attention precisely because many conventions and elements of constitutional practice relating to the Westminster model of parliamentary government developed under single party (commonly majority) rule" (2015: 195).

[47] Professor Sir Jeffrey Jowell, *Oral Evidence*, House of Commons Political and Constitutional Reform Committee, 14 July 2011, at Q101.

[48] House of Commons Political and Constitutional Reform Committee, *A New Magna Carta?* Second Report of Session 2014–2015, at 404 ¶ 167.

constrain political actors, not as a matter of law, but as a matter of practice. The concepts of constitutionality and of legality are not commensurate: an action may be legal (within the power of the actor to perform), but nevertheless unconstitutional.[49] Determining whether a constitutional convention exists and what its scope may be is a challenging task. Even more difficult is identifying "precisely when a constitutional amendment by way of a convention has occurred" (Blackburn 2013: 372). When political actors do not feel constrained by a convention is that because of an alteration in the convention itself (perhaps even by "amendment" to the constitutional convention), or because the convention never imparted a sense of obligation to begin with?

In discussing changing "conventional" constraints, I make no claim to definitional certainty or to determined constitutionality; some of these practices are only that – political practices. But debates over the existence of conventions and observable shifts in practice suggest a weakening of the unwritten and socially constructed rules of politics and historic methods of constitutional change. This may be leading to increased partisanship and greater opportunity for expediency and constitutional self-dealing.

Declared conventions

The bite of a constitutional convention lies not in its legal enforceability but in the moral or political pressure to comply with its dictates. In short, a "breach of conventions is liable to bring political trouble in one form or another" (Wilson 2004: 410). Thus the effort in defining and identifying conventions usually rests on past practice and historical precedent. Scholars debate whether conventions can be created explicitly. A "simple declaration of a minister unilaterally" would not be considered sufficient (Blackburn 2013: 372), but even Jennings does not insist on practice in every instance (McHarg 2008).

In recent years, there has been an increase in what McHarg describes as "declared conventions," such as the Sewel Convention (establishing the practice that "Westminster would not normally legislate with regard to devolved matters in Scotland without the consent of the Scottish Parliament").[50] She challenges the use of the term *convention* "because it has not yet been sufficiently tested by events to determine whether it will be obeyed despite the desire of the Westminster parliament to ignore it" (McHarg 2008: 858; but see

---

[49] Cf. *Madzimbamuto* v. *Lardner-Burke* [1969] 1 A.C. 645, 723 (P.C.) (appeal taken from S. Rhodesia).

[50] 592 Parl. Deb. H.L. (5th ser.) (1998) 791 (U.K.). *See also* Scotland Act 1998, c. 46, Explanatory Notes, at 40 (noting that Lord Sewel's statement in the House of Lords "has come to be known as the Sewel Convention").

Barber 2009). Her main argument is that this type of constitutional rule-making does not generate binding norms but is better understood as "an attempt to *influence* constitutional behavior" (McHarg 2008: 856).

Why are these declared conventions problematic? McHarg suggests that declared conventions are an endrun around the enactment of constitutional norms through formal statutory law (2008: 862), but they lack the historical continuity and consensus that imparts a moral or sociological binding force. How quickly can a convention be created? "A degree of stability is essential to establish that convention norms are binding" (867). Building on McHarg's work, Perry and Tucker describe some of these new attempts at constitutional rules as *standards*, and they see them as "intensely suspicious."[51] They argue that true constitutional conventions are unintentional, implicit, unsystematic, and followed by successive actors from different political parties. These elements "blunt the force of the objection from self-regulation and help to explain constitutional lawyers' historical relaxed attitude to the place of self-regulation at the heart of the constitution."[52] In contrast, declared conventions or constitutional standards do not share these protections. Thus an increase in declared conventions, accompanied by a decline in regulation by historic constitutional conventions,[53] raises the threat of political expediency.

The legislative process for identifying constitutional issues

Rather than form or process, it is substance that distinguishes constitutional legislation from ordinary legislation. As commentators have noted, "no standard practice has been as yet established as a convention, or even the proper means to introduce constitutional change, and no differentiation exists between major and minor changes" (Contiades and Fotiadou 2013: 437; see also Oliver 2011: 340). Nevertheless, the government does have some ex ante control over recognizing constitutional change: it can designate a bill as a "measure of first class constitutional importance" thus requiring the bill to be taken up as a matter of the entire House at the committee stage (Oliver 2011: 345).

How the government uses this designation power has yet to be standardized by stable practice. The potential for manipulation is high, and whether a bill is

---

[51] Adam Perry and Adam Tucker, *Conventions, Standards, and Legitimacy*, at 30. Draft manuscript on file with author.

[52] Ibid., at 23.

[53] House of Commons Political and Constitutional Reform Committee, *A New Magna Carta?* Second Report of Session 2014–2015, at 385–386 ¶ 94 ("As a species of constitutional regulation they are also in a state of decline. Particularly in the post-1997 period of rolling constitutional change, any unwritten conventions have become markedly less robust in shaping political behavior.").

of "first class constitutional importance" is often a function of political incentives and pressures (particularly questions of timing) rather than principled substantive analysis (Flinders 2010).[54] For example, although roughly "twenty bills took their committee stage on the floor of the House [between 1997 and 2005] because they were considered to be of 'first-class' constitutional significance," that list did not include other possible candidates including the Freedom of Information Act 1998, Regional Development Agencies Act 1998, or the Bank of England Act 1998 (220–221). Furthermore, governments have not been following their own rules promulgated for guidance; the 2000 *Code of Practice on Consultation* was "frequently not complied with" and was replaced in 2012 with an even "less robust statement" of principles.[55] As the House of Commons Political and Constitutional Reform Committee has noted, "most would agree there should be an established process of public consultation that governmental proposals should normally follow," but such a process has yet to command compliance.

"Constitutional" referendums

Constitutional referendums are becoming a regularized part of a constitutional amendment process that "has lacked any consistency of purpose" (Blackburn 2013: 377). But they suffer from weak legal justification and inconsistent use. The representative function of Parliament permits a sort of "obfuscation," which implies modern popular sovereignty, while the historic origins of Parliament's power – and the doctrine of parliamentary sovereignty – are somewhat more entwined with the divine right of kings (Loughlin 2007). Under the piercing gaze of the legal theorist, this slight-of-hand is exposed. And because the British constitution is not rooted in popular sovereignty, referendums – the coarsest expression of the will of the people – can have no competing external claim to bind Parliament. And indeed, they have only advisory relevance.[56] And

---

54 As Baker notes, "[t]hat time is allocated by the government, whose stranglehold over Commons business is routinely used to stifle proper debate upon the torrent of legislation which it generates. There has also been a worrying increase in the fast-tracking of legislation so as to preclude scrutiny almost completely, and in the introduction of substantive late amendments to ill-prepared bills, which has the same effect" (2009: 95, citing House of Lords Select Committee on the Constitution, *Fast-Track Legislation: Constitutional Implications and Safeguards*, vol. I, 15th Report of Session 2008–2009 (HL 116-I)).
55 House of Commons Political and Constitutional Reform Committee, *A New Magna Carta?* Second Report of Session 2014–2015, at 391 ¶ 114.
56 An exception is found in the recent Parliamentary Voting System and Constituencies Act 2011, which authorized a referendum on a new electoral system for parliamentary elections. If the referendum passed in favor of using an "Alternative Vote" rather than a "First-Past-the-Post" system, the provisions providing for such a system "must" be brought into force. Parliamentary

the rise of an advisory referendum culture creates more opportunity for self-dealing and politicking, in the name of constitutionality (Flinders 2010).

Cloaked under the guise of popular participation and achieving consensus (in other systems, hallmarks of constitutional amendment), the current approach to referendums lacks the predictability that would make it an actual limitation on constitutional change. Although the Blair Government did hold advisory referendums on devolution, key elements of the reform agenda, such as the Human Rights Act 1998 and the Constitutional Reform Act 2005, were not subject to referendum, and the recent Fixed-Term Parliaments Act 2011 was similarly not put to a popular vote.[57] The House of Commons Political and Constitutional Reform Committee recently complained that the referendum is being used "on an ad hoc basis at the convenience of the government."[58] Holding a referendum allows the government to "circumnavigate the veto capacity of other actors," while avoiding a referendum can "bypass potential veto capacity of the public" (Flinders 2010: 234). Far from serving as a means to identify consensus on change,[59] the referendum is used for political expediency.[60]

Constitutional watchdogs

In the past twenty years, there has been an explosion of new institutions that are independent of the legislature and executive and designed to serve as constitutional watchdogs (Gay and Winetrobe 2008: 197–199). Independent oversight may be a normatively desirable value: Dawn Oliver suggests that the increase in "arm's length bodies" portends "a shift from a culture of authority to one of substantive justification ... the fact that a government has a majority in parliament is not considered to be sufficient of itself to legitimize its decisions and policies in the eyes of the electorate – or of the opposition" (Oliver 2015: 326). But outsourcing responsibility for constitutional monitoring

Voting System and Constituencies Act 2011, c.1, §8. The referendum, held on 5 May 2011, did not pass.

[57] *Codifying – Or Not Codifying – The UK's Constitution: The Existing Constitution*, Centre for Political & Constitutional Studies, King's College London, Series Paper 2 (2012) at 10. *See also* Stanley Henig, *Written Evidence*, House of Commons Political and Constitutional Reform Committee, 19 November 2012, at ¶ 11.

[58] House of Commons Political and Constitutional Reform Committee, *A New Magna Carta?* Second Report of Session 2014–2015, at 393 ¶ 122. *See also* Select Committee on the Constitution, House of Lords, *Referendums in the United Kingdom*, 12th Report, Session 2009–2010, H.L. Paper 99.

[59] Cf. Bogdanor (1981: 91) ("a referendum can articulate a submerged consensus, but it cannot create one").

[60] Stanley Henig, *Written Evidence*, House of Commons Political and Constitutional Reform Committee, 19 November 2012, at ¶ 11.

may paradoxically free actors from self-imposed restraint (Gay and Winetrobe 2008: 212). Without formal powers, the success of a watchdog lies in its ability to engage the public through the media – to activate political pressure to change behavior. And as Lord Wilson has pointed out, publicity as regulation can serve to "induce behavior which is in conflict with [restraining] conventions: for instance, the first announcement of major policy decisions to the media rather than to the Houses of Parliament; the briefing of newspapers in breach of collective responsibility; or even the leaking of information by civil servants and their celebration as 'whistleblowers'" (Wilson 2004: 413). And a watchdog that is all bark and no bite, or one that can be outmaneuvered by canny politicking, cannot serve as a meaningful protection against expedient constitutional change.

The pace of constitutional change

The rapid and accelerating pace of constitutional change also raises a fundamental challenge to the British constitutional understanding, rooted in political consensus and history: At the center of the uncodified British constitution is "an overarching mode of change that respects continuity, at least in form, and the reassurance it affords" (Allison 2007: 235). (This is why the British rarely mention constitutional amendment or even constitutional change, and prefer the phrase "constitutional reform" (Blackburn 2013: 361).) It is general popular acceptance over time that provides the true legitimacy of the constitutional system (Oliver 2011), and "continuous, ad hoc constitution-making" has "doubtful political legitimacy" (Kay 2013: 113), as it does not reflect the core concepts of incrementalism and evolution. The problem is perhaps best reflected in the response to the short-lived Department for Constitutional Affairs, created in 2003 and renamed the Ministry of Justice in 2007: "The Government has unilaterally abolished the constitution, by establishing a department for tinkering with it, spontaneously, as a routine exercise of power" (Baker 2004). In short, the British constitution manifests a tension: Formally, it is at once flexible and easy to change and yet functionally must change "only 'very gradually over time.'"[61] Now, "[c]onstitutional tinkering, whether well-intentioned or self-serving, is [] an established part of every government's legislative programme and there is no reason to believe that this will change in the foreseeable future."[62]

[61] *Codifying – Or Not Codifying – The UK's Constitution: The Existing Constitution*, Centre for Political & Constitutional Studies, King's College London, Series Paper 2 (2012) at 8.
[62] The Constitution Society, *Written Evidence*, House of Commons Political and Constitutional Reform Committee, 19 November 2012, at ¶ 6.

Rooted in history and tradition yet moving relentlessly forward, the British constitution is like a car whose driver uses only the rear-view mirror for guidance.[63] At very low speeds – the incrementalism of traditional constitutional change – curves in the road can be navigated and corrections made. Even a collision will cause only minor dents and scrapes. But the pace of change has been increasing and its scope widening. The car is now moving so fast, a dramatic spinout or devastating crash seems inevitable.

* * *

The House of Commons Political and Constitutional Reform Committee concluded in its 2015 report: "In present circumstances the idea that governments might voluntarily apply a rigorous and consistent approach to its constitutional proposals might be seen as unrealistic, for there is too often a political self-interest in such measures to welcome hurdles and procedures that may obstruct or delay their implementation."[64] Whether the governments and parliaments of the past were truly limited by "those conventions which exists in hearts and minds and habits" is a question for the historians (Baker 2009: 106). But those engaged in the current constitutional debate agree: The mortar is loose between the bricks (Wilson 2004: 414).

THE CHALLENGE OF MAINTAINING A STABLE FLEXIBILITY

The British system has not yet found its equilibrium: "Success" on this measure remains elusive. There has been too much change, too quickly, and with too few in support. To date, the debate on how to constrain or channel what is seen as an increasingly partisan process of constitutional change has failed to coalesce around any particular solution. Some talk of codification. But codification is a dramatic change to the British system raising myriad problems of its own: Beyond the thorny fundamentals (what counts as the constitution, and who should decide) are questions of promulgation, legal authority, and entrenchment. And in erasing the flexibility that had been the touchstone of the historically successful British constitution, entrenchment would require a concomitant effort to introduce new mechanisms of flexibility in an uncertain calibration.

Rather than focusing on the content and codification of a constitution, others seek only to regulate change itself.[65] The challenge is how to keep party

---

[63] With thanks to Bram Elias for suggesting this analogy.

[64] Political and Constitutional Reform Committee, House of Commons, *A New Magna Carta?* Second Report of Session 2014–2015, at 392 ¶ 116; *see also* Blackburn (2013: 379).

[65] Select Committee on the Constitution, *The Process of Constitutional Change*, 2010–2012, H.L. 177 (U.K.).

politics out of constitutional reform (Oliver 2013: 240), while promoting a more broad-based consensus.[66] Scholars and politicians have looked to codified amendment processes for inspiration,[67] but there is a distinct challenge in entrenching a process without defining substance. Assume a process similar to the one currently observed in the breach – a designation requirement by the government of "bills of constitutional amendment" – but followed by bipartisan procedural mechanisms for debate and adoption. This definitional approach to constitutional change would require determining what exactly is constitutional: David Feldman provides a litany of possible suggestions, but he recognizes that "we cannot systematically identify constitutional legislation without a notion of the central function or functions of constitutions" (2013: 357). Can agreement be reached ex ante on the content?

Is it possible to separate formal amendment rules from the substantive content of the constitution itself? There seems to be a desire to maintain a certain element of vagueness about the ex ante status of a particular practice, a certain flexibility in constitutional definition. One contribution to the debate in the House of Commons Political and Constitutional Reform Committee suggested the Israeli example as a way to thread the needle: if the Knesset identifies something as a Basic Law, it is a Basic Law, and even the courts will treat it as such (Feldman 2013: 348–349).[68] Presumably, therefore, were the Westminster Parliament to do the same – i.e., title important bills as "constitutional"[69] – it would be obvious that later reforms or amendments to so-titled statutory schemes were amending content that was once thought to be of constitutional importance. This solution may be information-forcing, engendering (in the longer term) robust political debate and guarding against

---

[66] Sebastian Horden, *Written Evidence*, House of Commons Political and Constitutional Reform Committee, 19 November 2012, at ¶ 7 ("The current arrangements are unsatisfactory because they allow a transient majority in Parliament reflecting the support of only a minority of voters to make major changes, without any obligation to achieve consensus.").

[67] See, e.g., The Constitution Society, *Written Evidence*, House of Commons Political and Constitutional Reform Committee, 19 November 2012, at ¶ 4. *See also* Unlock Democracy, *Written Evidence*, House of Commons Political and Constitutional Reform Committee, 19 November 2012, at ¶ 4.

[68] The Constitution Society, *Written Evidence*, House of Commons Political and Constitutional Reform Committee, 19 November 2012, at ¶ 20–21.

[69] In the list of acts that are thought to comprise the uncodified British constitution, the first to be clearly titled as "constitutional" was the Constitutional Reform Act 2005, which *inter alia*, created the Supreme Court of the United Kingdom. The second, and only other one to be so titled, is the Constitutional Reform and Governance Act 2010. *See* Tarun Khaitan, "The Constitution as "Statutory" Term", *UK CONST. L. BLOG* (7 October 2012), *available at* http://ukconstitutionallaw.org/2012/10/08/tarun-khaitan-the-constitution-as-a-statutory-term/.

political expediency. But the role of the court is an important complicating factor: Given the Knesset's competitive dynamic with the Israel Supreme Court, it may be to the legislature's advantage to take ownership of their political actions and identify laws of higher status. Under the formal doctrine of parliamentary sovereignty, the British Parliament would hardly share that incentive.

But contrary to formal doctrine, the Supreme Court of the United Kingdom has been willing to designate certain statutes as having "fundamental constitutional" status (Perry and Ahmed 2014). These statutes cannot be repealed by implication – an otherwise core aspect of the last-in-time rule of statutory interpretation. As constitutional and ordinary legislative acts are not differentiated by process, it is the Court's definition of constitutional that demarcates these key laws. The list of Acts that would require explicit repeal is short and the constitutional importance of these Acts is not in question – devolution, human rights, and membership of the European Union.[70] But the Court's proclivity toward identifying constitutional statutes might encourage Parliament toward an Israeli-type practice. This "quasi-entrenchment" (Perry and Ahmed 2014) may be all that is needed to encourage governments to take ownership of their laws – at minimum to force a future opposition to repeal any act in explicit terms. And an increased willingness to label acts as constitutional might aid in efforts to construct mechanisms for amendment and change.

Finding stability in flexibility is the central challenge of the current constitutional crisis in the United Kingdom. Given British history, a "too flexible" constitution is unlikely to result in violent revolution or authoritarianism. Nevertheless, failure to meet this challenge may lead to results ranging from increased political disaffection to, at the most extreme, the break-up of the Union. Any analysis of constitutional success that cannot anticipate the likelihood of such a dramatic change will be of limited value. In a functional approach to evaluating constitutional success, the British paradox – constitutional success in constitutional crisis – highlights the importance of analyzing how a system manages its constitutional change.

---

[70] The concept of explicit repeal was introduced by Lord Justice Laws in *Thoburn* v. *Sunderland City Council* [2002] EWHC (Admin) 195 [2003] Q.B. 151 [62]–[63], in specific reference to the European Communities Act 1972, and in general reference to the Magna Carta, the Bill of Rights 1689, the Act of Union 1707, the Reform Acts (expanding voting rights), the Human Rights Act 1998, and the Devolution Acts (Scotland and Wales). More recently, at the Supreme Court, in *BH* v. *The Lord Advocate (Scotland)* [2012] UKSC 24, the principle was developed further by Lord Hope in reference to the Scotland Act 1998.

REFERENCES

Allison, J.W.F. 2007. *The English Historical Constitution*. Cambridge: Cambridge University Press.

Bagehot, Walter. 1872. *The English Constitution*, 2nd ed. London: Oxford University Press.

Baker, John. 2009. "Our Unwritten Constitution, Maccabaean Lecture on Jurisprudence." *Proceedings of the British Academy (2010)* 167: 91–117.

Baker, John H. 2004. "The Constitutional Revolution." Lecture, St. Catherine's College, Cambridge, United Kingdom. April 20.

Ballinger, Chris. 2012. *The House of Lords 1911–2011*. Oxford: Hart Publishing.

Banner, Charles and Alexander Deane. 2003. *Off With Their Wigs!* Exeter: Imprint Academic.

Barber, N.W. 2009. "Laws and Constitutional Conventions." *The Law Quarterly Review* 125: 294–309.

Bendor, Ariel L. and Zeev Segal. 2002. "Constitutionalism and Trust in Britain: An Ancient Constitutional Culture, a New Judicial Review Model." *American University International Law Review* 17: 683–722.

Blackburn, Robert. 2013. "Constitutional Amendment in the United Kingdom." In *Engineering Constitutional Change*, edited by Xenophon Contiades, 359–388. New York: Routledge.

Blau, Adrian. 2008. "Majoritarianism under Pressure: The Electoral and Party Systems." In *Constitutional Futures Revisited*, edited by Richard Hazell, 233–248. Houndmills: Palgrave.

Bogdanor, Vernon. 2015. *The Crisis of the Constitution*. London: The Constitution Society.

2009. *The New British Constitution*. Oxford: Hart Publishing.

2003. "The Civil Service." In *The British Constitution in the Twentieth Century*, edited by Vernon Bogdanor, 237–279. Oxford: Oxford University Press.

1981. *The People and the Party System*. Cambridge: Cambridge University Press.

Caird, Jack Simson, Robert Hazell, and Dawn Oliver. 2014. *The Constitutional Standards of the House of Lords Select Committee on the Constitution*. London: University College.

Clifford, Ben and Janice Morphet. 2015. "Afterward: The Scottish Referendum, the English Question and the Changing Constitutional Geography of the United Kingdom." *The Geographical Journal* 181(1): 57–60.

Contiades, Xeonphon and Alkmene Fotiadou. 2013. "Models of Constitutional Change." In *Engineering Constitutional Change*, edited by Xenophon Contiades, 417–468. New York: Routledge.

Crowley, Philip and Mark Stuart. 2012. "Backbench Rebellion in the House of Commons, 1997–2010: Making a Policy Difference or Barking at the Moon?" *Available at* http://webpages.dcu.ie/~leg/Cowley.pdf.

Dicey, A.V. 1908. *Introduction to the Study of the Law of the Constitution*, 7th ed. London: Macmillan.

Dixon, Rosalind. 2011a. "Constitutional Amendment Rules: A Comparative Perspective." In *Comparative Constitutional Law*, edited by Tom Ginsburg and Rosalind Dixon, 96–111. Cheltenham, UK: Edward Elgar Publisher.

2011b. "Partial Constitutional Amendments." *University of Pennsylvania Journal of Constitutional Law* 13: 643–685.

Eisgruber, Christopher L. 2001. *Constitutional Self-Government*. Cambridge: Harvard University Press.

Elkins, Zachary, Tom Ginsburg, and James Melton. 2009. *The Endurance of National Constitutions*. Cambridge: Cambridge University Press.

Feldman, David, ed. 2013. *Law in Politics, Politics in Law*. Oxford: Hart Publishing.

Feldman, David. 2005. "None, One or Several? Perspectives on the UK's Constitution(s)." *Cambridge Law Journal* 64(2): 329–351.

Flinders, Matthew. 2010. *Democratic Drift*. New York: Oxford University Press.

Fusaro, Carlo and Dawn Oliver. 2011. "Towards a Theory of Constitutional Change." In *How Constitutions Change*, edited by Dawn Oliver and Carlo Fusaro, 405–433. Oxford: Hart Publishing.

Gay, Oonagh and Barry K. Winetrobe. 2008. "Watchdogs of the Constitution – The Biters Bit?" In *Constitutional Futures Revisited*, edited by Richard Hazell, 197–214. Houndmills: Palgrave.

Gladstone, W.E. 1879. *Gleanings of Past Years*. London: John Murray.

Goldsworthy, Jeffrey. 2010. *Parliamentary Sovereignty*. Cambridge: Cambridge University Press.

Greer, Scott L. 2008. "Whitehall." In *Constitutional Futures Revisited*, edited by Richard Hazell, 123–138. Houndmills: Palgrave.

Griffith, J.A.G. 1979. "The Political Constitution." *Modern Law Review* 42: 1–21.

Hazell, Richard. 2008. *Constitutional Futures Revisited*. Houndmills: Palgrave.

Hennessy, Peter. 2007. "From Blair to Brown: The Condition of British Government." *The Political Quarterly* 78: 344–352.

1995. *The Hidden Wiring: Unearthing the British Constitution*. London: Victor Gollancz.

Hockman, Stephen Q.C. and Vernon Bogdanor. 2010. "Towards a Codified Constitution." *Justice* 7: 74–87.

Huber, John D. 1996. "The Vote of Confidence in Parliamentary Democracies." *American Political Science Review* 90(2): 269–282.

Issacharoff, Samuel. 2003. "The Enabling Rule of Democratic Constitutionalism: Fixed Rules and Some Implications for Contested Presidential Elections." *Texas Law Review* 91: 1985–2011.

Jennings, Ivor. 1954. *The British Constitution*, 3rd ed. Cambridge: Cambridge University Press.

Kay, Richard S. 2013. "Changing the United Kingdom Constitution: The Blind Sovereign." In *Sovereignty and the Law*, edited by Richard Rawlings, Peter Leyland, and Alison L. Young, 98–119. Oxford: Oxford University Press.

King, Anthony. 2001. *Does the United Kingdom Still Have a Constitution?* London: Sweet & Maxwell.

Le Sueur, Andrew. 2009. "From Appellate Committee to Supreme Court: A Narrative." In *The Judicial House of Lords 1876–2009*, edited by Louis Blom-Cooper et al., 64–94. Oxford: Oxford University Press.

Levinson, Sanford. 1995. "Introduction." In *Responding to Imperfection*, edited by Sanford Levinson, 3–11. Princeton: Princeton University Press.

Lijphart, Arend. 1999. *Patterns of Democracy: Government Forms and Performance in Thirty-Six Countries*. New Haven: Yale University Press.

1984. *Democracies: Patterns of Majoritarian and Consensus Government in Twenty-One Countries*. New Haven: Yale University Press.

Lord Scarman. 1993. "Why Britain Needs a Written Constitution." *Commonwealth Law Bulletin* 19: 317–323.

Lord Wilson of Dinton. 2004. "The Robustness of Conventions in a Time of Modernization and Change." *Public Law* 407–420. www.sweetandmaxwell.co.uk/Catalogue/ProductDetails.aspx?recordid=469.

Loughlin, Martin. 2015. "What's It For?" *London Review of Books* 37(20): 29–30.

2007. "Constituent Power Subverted: From English Constitutional Argument to British Constitutional Practice." In *The Paradox of Constitutionalism*, edited by Martin Loughlin and Neil Walker, 25–48. Oxford: Oxford University Press.

McHarg, Aileen. 2008. "Reforming the United Kingdom Constitution: Law, Convention, Soft Law." *Modern Law Review* 71: 853–877.

Murphy, Walter F. 1995. "Merlin's Memory: The Past and Future Imperfect of the Once and Future Polity." In *Responding to Imperfection*, edited by Sandford Levinson, 163–190. Princeton: Princeton University Press.

Norton, Philip (Lord Norton of Louth). 2015. "Parliament: A New Assertiveness?" In *The Changing Constitution*, 8th ed., edited by Jeffrey Jowell, Dawn Oliver, and Colm O'Cinneide, 171–193. Oxford: Oxford University Press.

Oliver, Dawn. 2015. "Regulating Politics in Government." In *The Changing Constitution*, 8th ed., edited by Jeffrey Jowell, Dawn Oliver, and Colm O'Cinneide, 307–328. Oxford: Oxford University Press.

——. 2013. "Parliament and the Courts: A Pragmatic Defence of Parliamentary Sovereignty." In *Parliament and the Law*, edited by Alexander Horne, Gavin Drewry, and Dawn Oliver, 309–338. Oxford: Hart Publishing.

——. 2011. "The United Kingdom." In *How Constitutions Change*, edited by Dawn Oliver and Carlo Fusaro, 329–355. Oxford: Hart Publishing.

Parris, Henry. 1969. *Constitutional Bureaucracy*. London: George Allen & Unwin Ltd.

Perry, Adam and Farrah Ahmed. 2014. "The Quasi-Entrenchment of Constitutional Statutes." *Cambridge Law Journal* 73(3): 514–535.

Rasch, Bjorn Erik and Roger D. Congelton. 2006. "Amendment Procedures and Constitutional Stability." In *Democratic Constitutional Design and Public Policy: Analysis and Evidence*, edited by Roger Congleton and Birgitta Swedenborg, 372–401. Cambridge: The MIT Press.

Rawlings, Richard. 2015. "A Coalition Government in Westminster." In *The Changing Constitution*, 8th ed., edited by Jeffrey Jowell, Dawn Oliver, and Colm O'Cinneide, 194–221. Oxford: Oxford University Press.

Redish, Martin and Matthew Heins. 2015. "Premodern Constitutionalism." Northwestern Law & Economics Research Paper Series No. 15–13.

Sager, Lawrence. 1990. "The Incorrigible Constitution." *New York University Law Review* 65: 893–961.

Tocqueville, Alexis de. 2000. *Democracy in America*. Translated by Harvey C. Mansfield and Delba Winthrop. Chicago: University of Chicago Press.

Tsebelis, George and Jeannette Money. 1997. *Bicameralism*. New York: Cambridge University Press.

Versteeg, Mila and Emily Zackin. 2014. "American Constitutional Exceptionalism Revisited." *University of Chicago Law Review* 81: 1641–1707.

Webber, Grégoire. 2014. "Eulogy for the Constitution That Was (Reviewing Martin Loughlin, *The British Constitution: A Very Short Introduction* (2013))." *International Journal of Constitutional Law* 12: 468–486.

Whitaker, Richard. 2006. "Ping-Pong and Policy Influence: Relations between the Lords and Commons, 2005–2006." *Parliamentary Affairs* 59: 536–545.

Index

adaptability, 78, 79, 89, 95, 393–399, 414.
   See also amendment; flexibility; *specific
   countries*
Afghanistan, 5, 6, 28–30, 35, 62–63, 356
Africa, 27, 256t, 321, 322, 343n20. *See also
   specific countries*
African National Congress (ANC), 27
African-Americans, 46, 50, 53, 236, 250, 316, 317
agency costs, 5, 15, 20–21, 27
AIDS, 327
Al Shabaab, 221
Al-Ali, Zaid, 12, 32, 33, 365–391
Alberdi, Juan Bautista, 31, 101, 102, 131, 372
Alberdian test, 102–105, 111, 116, 131
Al-Brahimi, Mohammed, 214
Alemparte, Justo Arteaga, 119, 119n18, 120
Alesina, Alberto, 44
Alevi community, 196
Algeria, 212, 378n15, 379, 380, 380n19, 383,
   388, 391
Ambedkar, B. R., 13, 32, 295; affirmative action
   and, 320, 326; caste and, 296, 303, 311, 317;
   constitutional morality, 304, 327, 330; courts
   and, 309, 310, 329; early life, 296; education,
   297, 310, 320, 325; as formalist, 323, 330;
   Gandhi and, 312n21; Grote and, 330;
   Hinduism and, 312n22; importance of, 302,
   332; Marxism and, 304; minorities and,
   304n9; Muslims and, 317–318; Nehru and,
   296; resignation of, 305; women and, 303,
   323, 324; *See also* India
amendment: adaptability and, 78, 89, 95;
   amendment culture, 284n5; endurance and,
   78–79, 284, 285 (*see also* endurance);
   entrenchment and, 398; frequency of, 284n5,
   285, 286; measurement and, 282; minimum
   core and, 284, 286, 289 (*see also* minimum
   core); public attitudes, 284; replacement
   and, 272, 273, 284; super-statutes, 274;
   unconstitutional amendment, 289
Anand, Mulk Raj, 313n25
ANC. *See* African National Congress
Annan, Kofi, 343n20, 352
answerability, 358
Arab region, 33, 212, 368, 373; Arab Spring, 21,
   33, 365–391, 380n19; Arabic language, 155,
   184; conservatism and, 382, 383; controlling
   elites, 374, 375, 384, 389; executive power,
   378; legal tradition, 383; political elites, 384;
   pre-2011 constitutions, 374, 376, 377, 383;
   preambles, drafting of, 368; priorities in, 372,
   373; religious elites, 374, 375 (*see also*
   Muslims); revolutions, 379–380; rights and,
   377, 382; social justice, 382; *See also specific
   countries, topics*
Arboleda, Sergio, 116
Argentina, 31, 101, 107n6, 148, 164
Aristotle, 4, 57n5
Arrow, K., 7
Asia Foundation, 29
aspirations, 14, 32, 55, 57, 65; agency slack and,
   20; conflicting, 9; convergence in, 6;
   democracy and, 19; entrenchment and, 260
   (*see also* entrenchment); external criteria
   and, 10; gap studies, 236–241; internal
   method and, 9; liberalism and, 366 (*see also*
   liberalism); maturation and, 260, 260f;
   minimum core and, 366 (*see also* minimum
   core); performance and, 10; problem of,
   236–241; rights and (*see* rights); transitions and,
   210 (*see also* transition); welfarism and (*see*
   welfarism); *See also specific countries, topics*